CW00644307

Altered States

Bantam Books
New York   Toronto   London
Sydney   Auckland

Altered States

States

The Auto-biography of Ken Russell

Ken Russell

ALTERED STATES
A *Bantam Book* / *November 1991*

PRINTING HISTORY
Great Britain edition published by William Heinemann Ltd 1989

All photos courtesy of Photofest except:
pp. 26 and 66 courtesy of BBC Television
p. 36 courtesy of the Nautical College at Pangbourne
p. 82 and back cover (bottom) from Mr. Russell's collection
p. 319 used with permission of Pathé Entertainment, Inc.

"Mountain Greenery": by Rodgers and Hart © 1926 Harms Inc.
Lyric reproduced by permission of Chappell Music Ltd.
"Something's Coming": music by Leonard Bernstein,
words by Stephen Sondheim Copyright © 1957 (renewed)
Leonard Bernstein & Stephen Sondheim.
Jalni Publications, Inc., USA & Canadian publisher.
G. Schirmer Inc., worldwide print rights
and publisher rest of the world.
Reproduced by permission of Campbell Connelly & Co. Ltd.,
8/9 Frith St, London W1. All rights reserved.
"We'll All Go Riding On A Rainbow": by Harry Woods.
Reproduced by permission of Cinephonic Music Co. Ltd.,
8/9 Frith St, London W1. International Copyright Secured.
All rights reserved.

Library of Congress Cataloging-in-Publication Data
Russell, Ken, 1927–
    Altered states : an autobiography / Ken Russell.
      p.   cm.
    Includes index.
    ISBN 0-553-07831-3
    1. Russell, Ken, 1927– . 2. Motion picture producers and
directors—Great Britain—Biography. I. Title.
PN1998.3.R88A3   1992
791.43'0233'092—dc20   91-18154
                                                        CIP

Published simultaneously in the United States and Canada

Bantam Books are published by Bantam Books, a division of Bantam Double-
day Dell Publishing Group, Inc. Its trademark, consisting of the words
"Bantam Books" and the portrayal of a rooster, is Registered in U.S. Patent
and Trademark Office and in other countries. Marca Registrada. Bantam
Books, 666 Fifth Avenue, New York, New York 10103.

PRINTED IN THE UNITED STATES OF AMERICA
BVG   0 9 8 7 6 5 4 3 2 1

With thanks to

HUW WHELDON

٢

Contents

Chronology of Ken Russell's Films

Feature Films	Released by	Release Date*
French Dressing	ABPC	1964
Billion Dollar Brain	United Artists	1967
Women in Love	United Artists	1969
The Music Lovers	United Artists	1970
The Devils	Warner Bros.	1971
Savage Messiah	EMI-MGM	1971
The Boy Friend	EMI-MGM	1972
Mahler	Goodtimes	1974
Tommy	Columbia	1975
Lisztomania	Goodtimes	1975
Valentino	United Artists	1977
Altered States	Warner Bros.	1980
Crimes of Passion	New World	1984
Gothic	Virgin	1987
Salome's Last Dance	Vestron	1988
The Lair of the White Worm	Vestron	1988
The Rainbow	Vestron	1989
Whore	Trimark	1991

*American release dates listed where applicable

Films Made for Television	Release Date*
Amelia and the Angel	1957
Peepshow	1958
Lourdes	1958
Poet's London	1959
Elgar	1962
Portrait of a Soviet Composer	1963
A House in Bayswater	1964
The Debussy Film	1965
Always on Sunday (Douanier Rousseau)	1965
Isadora Duncan: The Biggest Dancer in the World	1966
Dante's Inferno	1967
Song of Summer	1968
The Dance of the Seven Veils	1970
Clouds of Glory	1978
Portrait of a Composer—Ralph Vaughan Williams	1986
Ken Russell's ABC of British Music	1988
A British Picture	1989
The Strange Affliction of Anton Bruckner	1990
Prisoners of Honor (for HBO)	(Not yet released)

*American release dates listed where applicable

Foreword

How do I write about Ken Russell?

Well, many things have been written about Ken by others. He brings out passions in people, from the good to the bad. One never hears anyone being so-so about him or his work— they either love him or can't abide him. I can only speak from my experience of the man, and say how he affected my life and my career.

There will always be a very soft spot in my heart for Ken Russell. I love him for his belief in me, his loyalty to me, and for guiding me through my first film, opening doors to a whole new career. This was 1970, long before I'd ever thought of doing anything but modeling. Few directors would have fought for me to star in a major film at the time. The studios making *The Boy Friend* were very nervous—understandably—for although I was a famous model, I had never acted, let alone sung or danced. But Ken had a vision and bless him, he stuck out for me, and when Ken fights for something he fights till the death.

Before we worked together I was already a huge fan of his work. His English television programmes, which were dramas mainly based on the lives of famous composers, were superb. He changed the face of TV drama. Then there were his feature films, *Women in Love* being a particular favourite of mine. Yes, he is outrageous, eccentric, and can shock people, but the visual and dramatic concepts of his work are fantastic, and always brave and original.

As for the man, he was always wonderful to me. He is very funny. When we were making *The Boy Friend* he was always encouraging and helpful. He made me believe I could do it. Yes, he is a bit mad, but thank goodness for that. Time spent with Ken is never dull.

I have wonderful memories of him: picking us up from a hotel in the Lake District, the area of England where he still lives, we heard him before we saw him. From out of the lake rose the sound of a Mahler symphony. Eventually, from around the bend of a tiny country lane, appeared Ken, long grey hair blowing in the wind, driving a 1930s Rolls Royce convertible, speakers blaring. We then understood the source of that wonderful music. He got out of the car to let us in—to the amazement of all around, wearing a long caftan. I mean people in the Lake District had never seen anything quite like it!

Then there was the time we were meant to be having a business meeting about *The Boy Friend* project but instead of meeting in an office, Ken bought tickets for *The Brighton Belle*, a wonderful period train now sadly out of service. We conducted our business in the dining car of this beautiful train, watching the English countryside whizz by. We lunched in Brighton before returning home. That's what I call civilized. I also have many memories of the happy times spent with his lovely family. They will always be special to me.

I am often asked why I think certain things happened in my life. I do believe that Ken Russell was such an important factor in mine—specifically, his belief in me and his ability to make me believe in myself. It's also amazing that through doing *The Boy Friend* I met the other person who would later have such an impact on my career. I had seen Tommy Tune on TV in the States just before Ken had started to cast *The Boy Friend*. Knocked out by his superb dancing, I told Ken about him and consequently Tommy was cast in the film. Twelve years later Tommy— who by then had enough Tony Awards to make a necklace—cast me opposite him in the Broadway hit *My One and Only* in a role I played for eighteen months. So yet again Ken's influence was responsible for that.

The other thing Ken introduced me to was a whole, wonderful exotic world of film, from screenings, for his friends, of classic old films by famous directors like Eisenstein, Fritz Lang, and Orson Welles. I thank him for that alone. So I suppose, I really think of Ken Russell as my mentor, and feel a huge debt of gratitude toward him. Whatever his critics may say about this wonderful eccentric human being, I think he's great. Cheers, Ken.

Twiggy Lawson
1991

Ken the Kid

It was 1976. *Valentino* was in post-production. My marriage was on the rocks. The atmosphere in the house was electric. The fuses blew daily. I spent as little time at home as possible, leaving early in the morning for the studio and working there till late at night. And if I could have persuaded my editor to give up his weekends, I'd have worked then, too. But, unlike me, he enjoyed spending them with the wife and kids. I was wondering how I'd survive the next Sunday dinner when a letter arrived from Southampton. One of the regional TV stations wanted to know if their local lad would be interested in making a documentary on childhood memories of his home town. Would he just! I rang the producer and expressed my interest. He suggested I write a treatment and if this was approved we'd go on to develop a script. He wasn't in a rush, but I was. I promised it in a fortnight's time, hung up and rubbed my hands. The fee was small but the benefits enormous. I could squeeze at least one weekend out of the recce, maybe two.

My wife greeted the news that I was "off" for the weekend with characteristic suspicion. She always knew when I was lying. I told her I was going to research an autobiopic in Southampton. She grimaced and believed me. Saturday eventually came. I said goodbye to the kids and drove south. They weren't sorry to see me go; a peaceful weekend lay ahead of them.

Once on the M3 I started thinking about the film. I'd already thought of a title: *Ken the Kid*. People were always chiding me for not making a film on myself; well, here was my answer. The creator of a dozen or more controversial biopics was going to get the treatment himself. I'd considered the idea before, but not on commercial terms. I'd imagined a glorified home movie, but even home movies cost money and here was somebody actually willing to part with hard cash for what many would call an indulgence. Actually no serious filming is indulgent, it's all bloody hard work.

I thought about the "look" of the picture. I have never seen a film set in the Thirties—the decade of my childhood—which captured authentically the look of that era fixed so indelibly in my mind. No, "indelible" is too strong a word for something as subtle as a watercolour. And watercolour is not a medium one associates with the chemistry of Technicolor or any other film stock. My memories of the Thirties have all the immediacy of watercolours and all their freshness.

I decided on a lightning tour of scenes from my childhood in the hope that a burst of visual shock treatment would revitalise my memory. Chats to relatives with photo albums would help to complete the picture. No use looking at my birthplace for inspiration: Nazi bombs had turned it into a car park. Poor town! Barely recognisable from halcyon pre-war days; except for the parks where nature had made a better job of healing scars than the municipality.

I drove straight to Belmont Road. We moved there in 1930 when I was three and that's where I planned to shoot the opening scenes. The place was a backwater and always had been. Little had changed. It was still a road of middle-class Victorian houses that had seen better days. I looked at No. 31 through my car window. I didn't get out. Semi-detached, pale yellow brick, small front garden connected by a narrow driveway to a larger back garden. And right at the back against the wall, still threatening to push it over and even more magnificent, more monumental than ever, was my castle, my galleon, my magic beanstalk. To everyone else it was a horsechestnut tree, but to me as a child it was a place to continue yesterday's adventures in the cinema. One day I'd be Robin Hood, the next Morgan the Pirate. And when it rained I'd stay indoors, cut out my heroes from *Picturegoer* and stick them in a scrapbook.

I peered into the big front window where I used to wield my scissors and Gloy brush. The day was sunny and made the room appear dark; it seemed empty. The whole house seemed empty. I wound down the car window and looked in the gutter. The remains of a recent shower reflected the sky but I was more conscious of the mud below. Could I have actually once believed there was another world down there—a world of blue grass and white hills where you could run and tumble and never get hurt? You could never play in the sky, but if you could put your foot carefully enough through that magic mirror at your feet there was a wonderful land waiting to be explored, even more wonderful than the conker tree.

A breeze dispelled my fancy. Someone upstairs was looking down at me. I must have looked suspicious. Maybe they thought me a burglar, a thief. Maybe I *was* loitering with intent to steal; though it wasn't money I was after but time, and not for the first time. I'd made a habit of it in my films. But I'd never taken a trip into the past to capture a bit of myself.

Probably my most successful effort had been connected with Delius, who in his later years, while living in France, became blind and paralysed and unable to compose. News of his misfortune came to the notice of Eric Fenby, a young music student living in Scarborough. Being a great fan of Delius, he was moved to write to the afflicted composer offering his services. These were duly accepted, and the film followed the stormy years of their relationship (which resulted in several new works which would never have seen the light of day but for the selfless devotion of Fenby). For over five years he was a virtual prisoner in that lonely house in Grez-sur-Loing, sometimes willing, sometimes reluctant, his love of the music overriding his distaste for the man. Even so, he nursed the sick composer through the last months of his illness and was at his bedside when Delius finally died of syphilis in 1934.

I was fortunate in being able to draw upon Fenby's infallible memory, which recalled incredible details of that time ever so many years later. He refused my invitation to attend the shooting of the film, afraid that he might intimidate the young actor impersonating him. We all assured him this would not be the case and he weakened sufficiently to promise to come along one day and join us for lunch at the end of the morning's filming. A week went by and we never saw him. Then came the day when we were shooting Fenby's arrival at the Delius household in France, a meeting which prophesied disaster. The gauche young Fenby had been shy and tonguetied, Delius rude and boorish. It ended with Fenby almost in tears and a deathly silence. Before I could say "cut" there was a sob from a darkened corner. It was Fenby himself. The real Fenby. He told us over lunch that he had slipped in unnoticed and found himself transported back in time to the day of his arrival, the memory forcing from him that cry of anguish which had remained stifled all those years. So much for his memories; my own were not so vivid.

I started the car and took the first left to Portswood. I tried to think of a tune that might help me evoke those long-lost pictures of the Thirties. I thought of "September in the Rain" and the smell of high-octane fuel, sparks from metal boots dragging on cinders, faces black as miners', rasping motors and mass hush as a dashing motorbike ace crooned "September in the Rain" over the PA system between heats—an autumn evening at the Southampton stadium with the "Saints"; Mum and Dad and a bag of crisps in '38.

"Red Sails in the Sunset" . . . Dad and me sleeping in the hold of a paddlesteamer bound for Jersey with a hundred or so male passengers, Mum segregated aft with the other halfs; Martello towers, cabbages on stalks twelve feet high, de Havilland Dragons landing on the beach and Mum and Dad barefoot on the sand, doing a Hawaiian number in seaweed skirts to the portable gramophone.

"The Teddy Bears' Picnic" . . . Henry Hall and his orchestra on the radio and *Children's Hour* with Larry the Lamb in *Toytown* with Mr. Groucher and Ernest the Policeman. Larry was always bleating, Ernest was plain stupid and Groucher forever growling "Disgraceful." *Children's Hour* was dull and respectable and went with milkloaf and weak tea. It was moral and genteel. I much preferred the smoky voice of Hildegard on Radio Luxembourg singing *"Darling, je vous aime beaucoup. Je ne sais pas what to do, vous avez completely stolen my heart."* I think she advertised Du Maurier cigarettes. Mum found her stuck up and "foreign." Mum smoked Craven "A." Still more I preferred the crooning of Hopalong Cassidy on a Saturday afternoon at the Palladium, full of screaming kids and a spearmint chew thrown in for threepence.

I was just passing the Palladium. It was now a bingo hall. Portswood had been our local shopping area. I didn't have to cross the road to get there so knew it from an early age. Apart from the cinema, I used to visit the barber's shop for a short back and sides, and a toyshop for lead soldiers. Every country in the Empire was represented. There were Bengal Lancers from India, mounted police from Canada and camel regiments from the

Sudan. Entire armies from the frozen north to the tropics marching through a world of lead and bright enamel.

That's where my pocket money went. Racked with indecision, I searched the ranks before me as an old lady in a high-necked Edwardian frock waited impatiently for my threepenny piece. A regiment of Gurkhas marched side by side with a pack of polar bears. The Band of the Coldstream Guards played to a pride of lions on one side and a gaggle of geese on the other, all marching along in serried ranks, right foot forward. I'd picture my toys at home. A lead knight in armour with raised mace fighting an Indian with raised tomahawk, a machine-gunner shooting at a pyramid, a Zulu with assegai contemplating a tank, a crocodile about to be run over by the Coronation coach, and cowboys having a shoot-out among the palm trees in my medieval wooden fort. In childhood we inhabit a world of wonderful contrasts that later we often come to see as bizarre and do our best to rearrange, with everything in its "proper" place. Unusual juxtapositions we label surrealistic. Yet what is surrealism but a second childhood with Freudian overtones which we have to be re-educated to enjoy?—part of the tragedy of growing up.

The toyshop had gone, and the British Empire along with it. As I drove along the Broadway, as the main drag is known, I passed another cinema—another bingo hall—also called the Broadway. It was there I saw my first horror film: *The Secret of the Loch*. Until then I had had a good time at the Broadway, where the double bill was always followed by tea with Mum in the baronial foyer beneath artificially faded murals of Arthurian legends. Mum was not with me the day I saw the horror film. When a film with an "A" certificate was being shown which Mum didn't want to see, I'd station myself on the steps outside the swing doors and accost every patron with a hopeful "Will you take me in, please!" Eventually someone would take my threepence, get my ticket and abandon me in the auditorium. *The Secret of the Loch* was a low-budget British film of the worst kind. The women all talked as if they had a plum in their mouths and the men wore trilbys and spoke in tones as clipped as their moustaches. To Mum and her sister, Aunt Moo, who were great film fans, there was no greater stigma than a "British" picture (never "English" picture, though I never heard of a film coming from Ireland, Scotland or Wales). British pictures were to be avoided like the plague. Foreign pictures were not even mentioned. "Pictures" were, by definition, American. Times have changed.

Before *The Thief of Baghdad*, special effects were unheard of in the British film industry and unless you are incredibly lucky or incredibly patient you can't make a film on the Loch Ness monster without special effects. Most of the action in *Secret of the Loch* consisted of divers climbing over the gunwhale of a rowboat and descending into the ominous depths. Invariably their lifelines went slack and were quickly hauled up to reveal nothing on the end but a severed tube accompanied by a few bubbles. It wasn't until the last reel that we finally got to see what was going on beneath the surface. The model of the diver they used was even worse than the one that blew bubbles around my willie in the bath on Friday nights, and the grotto he was heading for looked like a cracked, upturned flowerpot on the bottom of a fishtank. But what of the monster? I knew the monster was going to appear from behind the flowerpot directly the toy diver bounced inside. I prepared to laugh. I'd seen a smudgy picture of "Nessie" in a newspaper and was expecting a model dinosaur. What actually appeared scared me stiff. It was a naked chicken, plucked and very much alive. Every hair on my head raised in horror, I fled from the cinema and along the Broadway towards home. But such was my fright that I couldn't even slow down to turn the corner into Belmont Road and kept on running non-stop till I ran out of breath at Cobden Bridge. I don't remember being so scared in the cinema ever again and that includes the sight of a dead man sitting up in the bath and plucking his eyes out in Clouzot's Les Diaboliques. That was nothing compared to the naked chicken, with beady eyes and sharp beak, pecking its way with clawed feet over the stones towards the unsuspecting diver in the upturned flowerpot. Beat that, Steven Spielberg!

Leaving Portswood behind me, I turned right and drove up through the Common, which, as the song says, was "a very common Common indeed." It was there I saw my first flasher. I was eleven and on my way home from school. My thoughts of tea were dispelled by a gentle cough. I glanced towards it and there, in a bower of gorse bushes, was the flasher. He was wearing a bowler hat, a pin-striped suit and bicycle clips and, as if posing for a Victorian photograph, stood proudly holding his bicycle in one hand and his cock in the other. I walked on, marvelling. I usually went *behind* a bush to pee, but maybe if I could make it point up instead of down I'd want to show off as well. I had a go in the garage at home with my old Hercules bicycle but was unable to achieve the same effect. I blamed the bicycle.

My first sexual experience happened not on the Common but, more appropriately, in a cinema, called the Empire, a short time later. It was during Walt Disney's *Pinocchio*. I had never enjoyed a film more. And as I watched Pinocchio's stiff little pointed nose grow and grow, so my enjoyment grew with it. And so did my willie. Something else was moving around my crotch. It was a man's hand. I couldn't believe it. How had it got there? And why? I became aware of a shadowy presence in the next seat. He gently cleared his throat and I inadvertently looked down for the cycle clips. He was wearing shorts. The light from the screen spilled onto his knees. They were bony. I got up quickly and went out. Did Pinocchio ever get out of trouble and return to old Geppetto? I don't know. I went off the cinema for a while after that.

The Common is bisected by an avenue of stately trees that makes for one of the most impressive approaches to a town in the whole of England. From there on it's all downhill. I was driving uphill to the outskirts of the town where my parents lived in a discreet cul-de-sac. As usual the street was deserted. The house was detached and built of brick the colour of smoked salmon. It looked as new and unlived-in as the day it was built, a quarter of a century ago. The front garden was a crossword puzzle of cement paths and squares of earth sprouting hybrid tea roses. I negotiated my way to the light-oak front door and knocked. There was no response. I looked at the big picture windows on either side of the porch. The curtains were drawn. This was not unusual, being a precaution of my mother's against the sun fading the carpets. There was little chance of this happening in October, especially as the house faced north, but my mother was nothing if not cautious. "You never know" and "Just to be on the safe side" were two of her favourite expressions. I knocked again.

"Who's that?" I caught my breath. Her voice seemed to come through the keyhole. I breathed again.

"It's me, Mum. Ken." There was a cry of surprise, the rattling of a chain and the click of a lock. The door opened and there stood Mum. To my complete surprise she was in her nightdress—in the middle of the afternoon. My first thought was that she was ill, though surely she wouldn't be wearing a hat in bed, even though the house was always uncommonly cold, even in autumn. Her face lit up at the sight of me. It was nearly a year since I'd seen her. Her eyes were larger and bluer than I remembered, shrewd and glittering like a bird's. She had lost weight and looked younger than her seventy-odd years. Incredibly, she still reminded me of Alice Faye.

"'Ello, Ray, fancy seeing you here. My, you 'ave put on weight. Come in."

Ray is my brother. Apart from the fact that we both have white hair, we are totally dissimilar. She'd been getting names mixed up for a couple of years now so I was unperturbed. I couldn't help correcting her all the same.

"It's Ken, Mum. Ken." I laughed and kissed her.

"I've just this minute put the kettle on. Come in, Zave."

Zave is my eldest son. He does *not* have white hair. I entered and closed the door. The house was very cold. I looked at her bare feet on the parquet floor and shivered.

"Mum, where are your slippers?"

Her pale features tightened. " 'E's 'idden 'em." She led the way into her front room and turned on the light. The house boasted two front rooms—his and hers. His was as austere as hers was flamboyant. Part museum, part showroom, Mum's was choc-a-bloc with furniture, garishly upholstered and highly polished. Every available surface was covered with souvenirs of innumerable package tours, mostly European. Continental food did not "agree" with Dad so he generally stayed behind—"Old misery!"

For the price of an extra ticket, Mum always found a travelling companion to share her "oohs" and "ahs" as the coach sped past tulip fields and windmills. And what better memento than a pair of musical clogs and a little Dutch boy and a little Dutch girl? There were dolls of all nations and knick-knacks of every kind, from cuckoo clocks to castanets. But kitsch eighteenth-century figurines were favourite. Porcelain lords and ladies bowed and curtsied on the mantelpiece and danced a minuet on the cocktail cabinet.

"Like a drink, Ray, Ken?" asked Mum, following my glance. "I know how Ken Bruzh loves a drop of sweet white wine." Ken Bruzh! She hadn't called me that for years. It was how she used to address me in conversation with baby brother. She examined the dregs of a bottle of Sauternes I remembered from the Christmas before last.

"Tea will do fine, thanks, Mum. I'll make it." I walked into the kitchen and saw the electric kettle steaming away on the gas stove. Behaving as if this was the most normal thing in the world, I turned off the gas and made the tea. Mum had grown increasingly absentminded over the last few years and had been at odds with my father for as long as I could remember, but this acceleration of her condition was alarming. It made the reason for my visit seem trivial. I sipped my tea and didn't mention it. Mum did all the talking anyway, reciting a litany of wrongs, some real, some imagined, which she'd suffered at the hands of my father. I'd heard it all before: his selfishness, his neglect, his interest in other women, her drudgery, her loneliness, her martyrdom. It all washed over me as I wondered what to do. What a mess.

She went on and on. " 'E's been a terror to me, Ken, three-six-five of the year."

My father's face suddenly appeared at the window and captured my look of dejection before I managed a smile. He smiled back. His smile was spontaneous. He was a couple of years younger than Mum and in his smart yachting cap looked as debonair as Robert Taylor. He'd been indulging in his favourite pastime, sailing, and was ready for tea. His eyes went to the kitchen table. His five half-slices of brown bread and butter were not there. Neither were his apple and slice of seedcake. I felt guilty.

I was drinking from his special cup. I put it down quickly. As he came in the back door Mum made for her front room.

"I'm fed up being your skivvy," she said, slamming the door behind her. Dad just kept on smiling. He was really pleased to see me and, as he washed his hands at the sink, asked for news of the family and what I was up to. I didn't tell him that life at home was hell or that I was researching a documentary that would involve him. Instead I talked about *Valentino* and said that I'd soon be taking the "fine cut" over to America for the producer's approval. He dried his hands on the tea towel, opened the bread bin and reached for the Hovis loaf. Mum's slippers had taken its place. I suppressed a laugh. I don't know how long it would have taken us to get around to Mum's odd behaviour but there it was staring us in the face. My father did not laugh but simply shook his head, tut-tutted and removed the slippers.

"She's so unhygienic, Ken, you wouldn't credit it."

"Why didn't you write to me about her?" I asked.

"I was waiting for a reply to my last letter, Ken."

I pushed my mind back. I'd received nothing since his last Christmas card. There'd been a few words on that. Was that what he meant? Or had his letter been destroyed by my wife, perhaps?

Dad looked at the blackened electric kettle. "She's becoming impossible. She wanders the streets in her nightdress telling people I ill-treat her."

I was appalled. "What are you doing about it? What does the doctor say? Why isn't someone looking after her?"

"Nothing can be done. She's going into a nursing home in Archers Road tomorrow."

This was overwhelming. All I could say was, "I'd no idea."

"You've been busy on your film. We didn't want to upset you."

I nodded, searching for a ray of hope. "Well, at least Aunt Moo will be able to keep an eye on her. She's just around the corner, isn't she?" The sisters were devoted to each other.

My father shook his head. "She's got her hands full with Jack. He's laid up with a *very* bad cough."

Uncle Jack had been almost a second father to me. I couldn't take it in. Dad had found an apple. He sat down opposite me at the small Formica table and started to peel it. I could think of nothing to say.

An hour later I was knocking on Aunt Moo's door in Cromwell Road. She had no telephone so my arrival was unexpected. Cousin June, a plump and affable Claudette Colbert of forty-five, a few years my junior, opened the door. Her surprise gave way to happiness as she hugged me in her chubby arms.

"Ken, oh Ken, it's so good to see you." Then, over her shoulder into the twilight, "Mum, guess what? It's Ken."

Moo was even more astonished than June. "Bring him up. Tell him to come up." I followed June up the gloomy stairs and into the bedroom. A candle flickered at the bedside, augmenting the fading day. Aunt Moo, the spitting image of Edith Sitwell, was Mum's kid sister and loved her husband with as much passion as Mum hated hers. Moo was crying and talking continuously through Jack's insistent cough. The wavy-haired Liverpool Irishman, known locally as Bogey because of his resemblance to the film star, was barely recognisable. With every cough he seemed to sink deeper into a maelstrom of twisting sheets, from the vortex of which his eyes peered up in despair. He tried to speak and managed the ghost of a smile, which almost choked him. To smile back would have been a mockery.

"He was a good man, Ken," sobbed Moo. "A wonderful man. Not one cross word in all the years of our marriage, not one!"

She mopped his brow. As the room darkened his face became a smudge and his poor sickly body began to blend into the sodden sheets like a canvas by Francis Bacon. I felt the same revulsion I experience whenever I see one of those obscene paintings and the same fascination. His eyes shut tight in pain as another attack clawed at his chest from within like a wild cat fighting to free itself from a putrid sack. There was blood on the pillow. Moo cradled him in her arms, sobbing endearments. June touched my arm and led me downstairs into the front room. She switched on the light and we sat side by side on the settee we'd romped on as children. All the furnishings were familiar. I'd grown up with them. They were faded and shabby. The Codds were poor; they always had been. But I'd always envied them the riches they found in each other. And they were always generous with what little they had.

June poured me a sweet sherry. Her voice was husky, resigned. She lit a cigarette. She smoked almost as much as her father.

"He's had last rites," she said calmly, comfortingly.

I blinked. I'd forgotten he was a Catholic. I'd never known him go to Mass, and certainly Moo and June weren't Catholic. He must be lapsed, like me. But once a Catholic, always a Catholic. Once you join the club you're a life member even if you don't pay your dues—as long as you pay the last one. "Forgive me, Father, for I have sinned." I guessed Jack had been born a Catholic, unlike myself who'd been talked into it by a fanatic.

"What does the doctor sa . . . ?" I barely finished the sentence before remembering I'd just put the same question to my father. Something must have shown on my face. June noticed.

"Are you all right, Ken?"

"Yes, fine . . ."

She guessed. "Don't worry about your mum, Ken. Uncle can't cope with her on his own. That nursing home's not a bad place. She'll have a private room and a nurse to look after her and Mum and I will pop in every day."

After a little pause I said, "I had no idea about Jack."

"We've had a terrible year," she said.

It was getting chilly. I looked at the empty grate and shivered. Unlike my parents who sat in their fireless house, warm in the knowledge they were saving money, the Codds hadn't the luxury of a choice. We sat listening to the awful coughing from above and the sound of Moo's voice, sometimes soothing, sometimes doleful.

There was a rat-tat at the front door.

"That'll be the doctor." She was right. June answered the door and led him upstairs. I finished my sherry and poured myself another glass.

I thought of June and myself playing at doctors years ago. That was when Jack was on the dole and they were living with Moo's parents in a terraced house down by the gas works. There was a spare room with a black leather bag full of spare parts from an old radio set. With these I felt fully qualified to practise. June had no dolls for me to treat so she was both nurse and patient combined. Simple ailments were treated with lemonade and brandy balls, more serious conditions involving thorough examinations were conducted in the darkness of an empty cupboard. June's body had a delicious fragrance—of fresh milk and babies.

The coughing upstairs triggered off memories of the spare room in my own childhood home. Less pleasant ones. That room was bare and sinister. It too had a cupboard, at the far end by a narrow window. The first time I opened the cupboard door I gasped in horror at what I saw lurking in a corner. It was an octopus with an elephant's trunk. I fully expected it to grab my ankle and drag me into the darkness. I fled. At night the fearsome monster joined the ghostly giant at the end of the bathroom corridor to haunt me in my dreams. I started using the garden lavatory rather than pass the spare room to get to the one upstairs, and it wasn't long before my parents noticed. They got the truth out of me and laughed. Reluctantly I allowed Dad to lead me by the hand back into the room and up to the cupboard. The door opened and there was the monster as terrifying as ever. My father grabbed it. It seemed to writhe like a creature trapped in its lair on the ocean floor, throwing up a cloud of dust as camouflage. Its glassy eyes flashed with malice. The ribbed trunk swung towards me. I shuddered, tore myself away from my father's grasp and ran. He shouted something after me, a meaningless phrase drowned by my yell. The monster turned out to be a primitive gas mask, the sort they used to slip over the head and tie around the waist with ribbons. I don't recall if my father explained its function but I learned of its association with the Great War some time later from my maternal grandad, who'd brought it home from the front in his old kit bag. Even so, the words "mustard gas" were confusing. I could only imagine Sunday roast and Dad mixing the mustard and Mum manipulating gas taps as the vegetables bubbled away on the stove. It was much later that the full horror of it all struck home.

I was assembling a sequence on the Great War for a dramatised documentary on the life of Sir Edward Elgar. One of the shots I used showed a line of soldiers, each with bandaged eyes and outstretched arms, gripping the shoulder of the man in front of him. They had been blinded by mustard gas. Their lungs had also been affected and they coughed violently as they stumbled along through the Flanders mud.

Upstairs Jack continued to cough *his* life away. At the front door June was saying goodbye to the doctor. By the time she rejoined me I had my farewell speech prepared.

"Long journey, night driving, early start tomorrow," etc. etc. I refused her offer to say goodbye upstairs on the grounds of intrusion and kissed her goodnight. She promised to keep me posted about Mum and waved goodbye.

What to do? I'd planned to stay with my parents. That was out of the question now. Yet I wasn't expected back in London for another day, and anyway there was still plenty to research now that I was down here. I thought of all the other relatives I could look up. Perhaps I should drop in on Auntie Vi.

I got in the car and drove off. I shivered and turned on the heater. I was cold and hungry. I thought of my home in London, warm and cosy, and wondered what they'd be up to. Just finishing the evening meal, I guessed. Visions of egg soubise and crème brulée teased my hunger pangs. But only momentarily. There would be no leftovers; the kids were voracious. Those who'd escaped the washing up would be sliding off to the partitioned rooms they called "rabbit hutches" on the top floor. There were five children in all, four boys and a girl, all with different teenage interests. Xavier liked heavy metal, James liked electronic music, Alex liked Mahler, Victoria liked the Beatles and Toby liked Chinese Opera. And my wife would be playing my least favourite composer in the entire world. Even so, I changed direction for London.

Suddenly "Ken the Kid" didn't seem such a good idea any more. "Ken the Cuckold" would be more appropriate. So why was I going home? Simple: because I had nowhere else to go. I hadn't a friend in the world, not a real friend. Well, perhaps I had one friend in America . . . perhaps, but America was a long way off. I needed consoling here and now. A programme of British music was playing on the car radio. It suggested a companion I'd almost forgotten. On an impulse I swung off the London road and took the M27 towards the West Country. I had a strong desire to be with a friend I'd never met, who'd died in 1934 when I was seven years old.

2 ...Spirit of Delight

Like a homing pigeon I flew to my destination by instinct. The only milestones I remember passing were those of Stonehenge where, as a young photographer in pre-hippie days, I waited with a group of Druids for the midsummer sun to rise. Perched on the altar stone, I was well placed to catch the highlights of their ceremony. The first was undoubtedly the moment when the chief Druid, a very stout party in Hush Puppies with a white sheet thrown over a brown serge suit, blew a pagan raspberry into my wide-angle lens through a bent Alpenhorn. The second occurred when he drank holy water from a buffalo horn which was then passed among his disciples. The fact that he filled the sacred vessel from a Tizer bottle in no way detracted from the significance of the moment.

I put my foot down and sped across Salisbury Plain towards Elgar country. As far back as my amateur days I'd wanted to make a film on Elgar. I loved nearly everything he ever wrote, but my special favourite was the *Enigma Variations*. The theme on which they were based was never stated and people have been trying to guess its identity ever since; books have even been written on the subject. Some say it was "Rule Britannia," others favour "The Volga Boatmen," though most agree that the theme could simply be "friendship." The variations—there are fourteen of them—each represent a person, and before those in the know object, yes, I *do* count Bulldog Dan as a person and so did Elgar.

His wife is the first variation and the composer himself is the last. In between we have musical impressions of an amateur pianist, an actor, a country squire, a conversationalist, a pupil, an architect, a neighbour, a music publisher, a pretty girl with a stammer, Bulldog Dan, a cellist and a mystery person identified by * * *: the perfect subject for a mini biopic. What a budding film-maker needs above all else is a scenario that's good and tight. Far too many amateur movies are rambling, woolly affairs. One answer to the problem is to kick off with something already in existence that is both highly organised and imaginative, such as a poem or a piece of programme music. Hence my interest in the *Enigma Variations*.

By 1958, when the idea first hit me, I had three amateur movies to my credit, all made on a shoestring over a period of four years. The first was a Chaplinesque comedy called *Peepshow* with sub-titles and a pianola accompaniment. *Lourdes* was my most ambitious effort. It was a documentary on the famous Catholic shrine and had a score by Benjamin Britten borrowed from his ballet *The Prince of the Pagodas*, and it was in colour. But the most popular was a Cocteau-esque fantasy called *Amelia and the Angel*. It had just won the "Film of the Year Award" in the *Amateur Movie Maker* magazine. So far my audience had been limited to family and friends, some amateur film clubs and a convent of nuns. It was time to turn professional and for that I needed financial support and a showcase. In a word, I needed *Monitor*.

Monitor had been going for about a year before I began to notice it. Others were noticing it too. Every other Sunday evening at 9:30 the TV screen glowed a little brighter. Here was a forty-five-minute programme on the arts which actually dealt with esoteric themes in an accessible and exciting way. Duchamp would throw new light on his "Nude Descending a Staircase" and we'd see an extract from Bernstein's *Candide* and hear the composer attack the killers who sent it to an unjustifiably early grave. But for me the regular documentary film was generally the most satisfying item. I was particularly impressed by John Schlesinger's study of the Oldham Repertory Company as seen through the eyes of a young actress joining them for her first big break. *Monitor* was one of the most prestigious programmes on television. I thought it was the best; I wanted to be part of it. I posted off my three amateur films to the BBC and sat back to wait. A week later I was telephoned and told to report on the following day to the Red Lion pub on Ealing Green just across the road from the BBC's West London Film Studios. There I was to meet the Editor of the programme, Huw Wheldon. He also conducted most of the interviews and he was *formidable*. Now it was to be my turn for the hot seat.

I waved my wife goodbye and walked off into the November mist feeling nervous and insecure. My whole future rested on this meeting. If Wheldon didn't like my style of film-making, who would? It was hopelessly unfashionable, the very antithesis of the "free cinema" championed by the British Film Institute, which glorified teddy boys at the Elephant and Castle. Walking down Norwood Hill to the station I said a prayer. It was sink or swim. We had a child to support and another one on the way. We lived in a haunted Regency house in South London that we couldn't afford to heat. It had a leaky roof, rising damp, a jungle of a garden and a ghost on the staircase. We also had a giant Staffordshire bull terrier called Toby who ate us out of house and home. I was a freelance photojournalist with no prospects. Television was making the weekly picture mags redundant and that was where I got most of my work. I also taught photography at Walthamstow Tech but the fee hardly covered the bus fares. I was seriously thinking of putting up a board at the front gate advertising family portraiture. I'd long since parted with my rusty Morris Minor and had just sold my treasured collection of records for twenty quid. We sat about in overcoats and lived on cod pie, and those were the days when cod was something you gave the cat.

On the train from South Norwood to Victoria I wondered how I'd conduct myself during the interview. By nature I was shy and modest, not the best possible credentials for a career in the tough world of TV. I changed onto the Underground and as the train clanked its way to Ealing Common I wondered what on earth I'd say if Wheldon asked me why I wanted to make films, as I felt sure he would. He'd probably scoff if I said films were my very life. I'd been weaned in the cinema. As soon as I could walk I was seeing Old Mother Riley and Flash Gordon twice a week at the Picture House. My childhood companions were Felix the Cat and Betty Boop. I grew up cranking a Pathescope Ace projector throwing images of Harold Lloyd and Charlie Chaplin onto the dining-room wall. At the age of twelve I got hold of an old 35-mm projector and a trunkful of highly inflammable films and nearly burnt the house down. All further shows took place in the garage where a horn gramophone added lustre to the silent films of Fritz Lang. Silent is the wrong word. Outside all hell was breaking loose. Inside, as the spellbound audience watched the blond Siegfried fight the fire-breathing dragon on my glass-beaded screen, his Aryan sons rained down fire from the sky. The proceeds of these tributes to German Art went to the Spitfire Fund. At thirteen the irony of it all escaped me. A few months later in boarding school I was being caned for breaking bounds to see Dorothy Lamour movies. Greater love hath no man. I had a hunger for films. I gobbled them up. Starved in term-time, I gorged myself on leave, pedalling my Hercules bicycle from cinema to cinema, devouring as many as three double-bills a day. And when I'd tired of a Hollywood diet, I developed a more cosmopolitan palette and sampled the great chefs of Europe and Russia—Cocteau, Renoir, Vigo, Murnau, Pabst and Eisenstein. I lived and breathed films. I even dreamed film and wrote down the scenarios at breakfast. I lived in the dark. I wondered if this sort of gourmandising would satisfy Wheldon. It hadn't done me much good so far.

I dragged my feet across the Common and found a quiet corner in the Red Lion where I supped a pint of beer and kept my eyes peeled for Wheldon. The bar was very smoky and filled with a lot of film types standing around in duffel coats talking shop. One-fifteen and still no sign of Wheldon. With a bit of luck he might have forgotten all about it. Oh my God, there he was, coming through the door. His eyes swept past me and found a small leprechaun of a man with pebble glasses leaning against the bar. Wheldon joined him, ordered drinks and launched into an animated speech. What little I knew of Wheldon I'd picked up from reviews and opinions in the papers. He was about forty-five and an ex–Welsh Guardsman with beetling brows, a charming but penetrating manner and a roguish face that lent itself to caricature. I'd once seen him depicted as Punch lambasting Judy (labelled "The Arts") with a big stick. Now it was my turn. I couldn't face him. I had to get away from those gimlet eyes and probing questions that laid bare the soul. I panicked, got up and knocked over my glass. What a fool! I caught his eye and gave a weak grin.

"Russell?" He interjected my name in mid-sentence.

Guilty, I nodded.

He ordered another beer for me and shouted "Cheese sandwich?" I nodded. "Chutney?" Again I nodded. "Pork pie?" I nodded nervously yet again. "Pickled onions?" I hesitated, twitched. He took it as a nod. "Sausage roll, shepherd's pie, Cornish pasty, Scotch egg, Welsh rarebit, Irish whiskey?" I laughed and gave a big nod to the last one. Smiling, Wheldon carried over the tray of food and drink and settled at my table. The ice had been broken, now all I had to do was fall through.

"Ken Russell, I take it?"

I nodded again.

His manner was genial but brusque. "Huw Wheldon. How do you do. So you want to join *Monitor*?"

"Yes."

"How old are you?"

"Thirty-two."

"Grey hair at thirty-two! Married?"

"Yes."

"Children?"

"One."

"Age?"

"One." Wheldon was playing a game with me. I had no option but to play along, so play I did.

"Girl?"

"Boy."

"Name?"

"Xavier."

"Xavier!" he exploded, smelling a whiff of Rome. "Catholic?"

"Yes. He was born on the third of December, the name day of Blessed Francis Xavier."

"I meant you. Are you Catholic? But you've answered my question. You haven't been married long, I take it?"

"A couple of years."

"And your wife's pregnant again." I nodded. His Welsh Presbyterian brows wrinkled disapprovingly. "What's her name?"

"Shirley."

"Where are you from?"

"Shirley, Southampton."

"Education?"

"The Nautical College, Pangbourne."

"Were you from a seafaring family?"

"Yes."

"What does your father do?"

"Sells boots and shoes, but he used to be a ship's detective."

"And you were following in his footsteps."

"I was a cadet."

"Royal Navy?"

"Merchant."

"You saw active service?"

Nodding, "I was discharged, medically unfit."

"Wounded?"

"Anxiety neurosis."

"And then?"

"The Air Force."

"Flying?"

"Acc Room."

"Acc Room?"

"I was an electrician. I charged accumulators—batteries for aircraft."

"I know what an accumulator is. And after you were demobbed?"

"I tried to get into films."

"As an electrician?"

"As a teaboy."

"Very ambitious. What next?"

"I went to evening classes."

"In film?"

"No, ballet. The school was affiliated to the International Ballet Company."

"You graduated?"

"Yes."

"What ballets did you perform? *Swan Lake? Sylphides?*"

"*Annie Get Your Gun.*"

"And then?"

"I became an actor with the Garrick Players."

"Is that anything to do with the Garrick Club?"

"No, it was a small rep company in Newton Poppleford, South Devon."

"Did you play the classics?"

"Not exactly. I was in a play called *When Knights Were Bold*. I played a ghost in a suit of armour."

"And then . . . ?"

"The company went bankrupt."

"Go on."

"I took up photography . . ." He nodded for me to continue. ". . . and learned how to use a movie camera."

"And you made films, amateur films?"

"Yes."

"And now you want to make films for *Monitor*?"

"Yes."

"Have you any ideas?"

"Yes."

"Let's hear them."

I hesitated and decided to be ambitious. "I'd like to make a film on Albert Schweitzer playing the organ in the jungle and looking after lepers." A mistake. Two of my films had Catholic themes. The last thing Wheldon needed was a papist film-maker. He became cautious.

"I see . . . Anything else, a little nearer home?"

"I've always wanted to make a film on Elgar." Wrong again. Wheldon was now deeply suspicious.

"Catholic, wasn't he?"

"Yes." I could feel my chances slipping away. He threw me a lifeline.

"If the world was your oyster, what film would you like to make above all others?" It was a spin of the wheel.

"A film on John Betjeman's London poems."

He became thoughtful. "A bit lightweight, Betjeman."

"It wouldn't cost much," I added weakly.

He looked at me, wondering whether to put his money on me or not. Click! The ball found a lucky number. Wheldon blinked and called across to the bald man finishing his drink at the bar.

"Alan."

Alan came over. Wheldon introduced us.

"This is our film editor, Alan Tyrer. Alan, this is Kenneth Russell. He's going to make a film for us on Betjeman's London poems."

Alan Tyrer smiled and said a few words. I didn't take them in; my scalp had just shrunk a few sizes and I had a funny pinching feeling behind my ears. Before I knew it I was out in the street in my beer-stained overcoat holding the remains of a cheese and chutney sandwich, with one of the most coveted jobs in television in my pocket, although Wheldon made it clear I was on approval. He invited me to have a look at the *Monitor* cutting room, where I'd soon be editing my film with Alan Tyrer. As we entered the studio gates the uniformed commissionaire came to attention and saluted. I smirked.

Wheldon noticed. "What amuses you?"

"Oh, nothing."

He gave me a searching look but my thoughts were private and I kept them to myself. Thirteen years ago that same commissionaire, or his twin brother, had turned me away from those same studio gates. In those days they were the Ealing Film Studios where all those overrated comedies that give such a bogus view of British life were churned out. I'd also been turned away from Riverside Studios at Hammersmith where upper-class musicals like *Spring in Park Lane* and *Maytime in Mayfair* were artificially inseminated into being. I'd suffered the same treatment at Gainsborough

Studios, where Maggie Lockwood reigned as the Wicked Lady in a string of costume melodramas and passion was measured in depth of cleavage. All the bastions of the "British Picture" had been taken over by the BBC. Before that, you had to have connections just to be a teaboy. Now all you needed was talent. I guess that's why television took over.

We walked past two big sound stages—monuments to the genteel, the quaint and the eccentric: films such as *Passport to Pimlico*, which celebrated a cockney way of life that never was; or *The Blue Lamp*—a cosy look at the British Bobby rewarding delinquent kids with sweets and helping old ladies across the street. P.C. Dixon, who trod his beat in carpet slippers, lingered on for a while in a TV series called *Dixon of Dock Green*, and as I passed the studio lot they were shooting a scene outside a plywood and plaster police station. Old habits die hard but Dixon was being driven off the street by *Z Cars*, a tough new series about the crime squad in Liverpool shot with documentary realism. The British public were beginning to learn that their country existed beyond the bounds of Mayfair and Bow Bells.

In the editing room I watched Huw working on the commentary of John Schlesinger's last *Monitor* film—he was leaving the programme to make his first feature film, *A Kind of Loving*. I was taking his place. We were both climbing another rung up the ladder. As yet we didn't realise that the game also included snakes.

At home, over a bottle of wine and what was to be our last fish pie ever, I wondered aloud how on earth I'd landed such a plum job after such an appalling interview. Shirley had the answer: "He must have liked your films, muggins."

Huw went on liking my films for many years, some more than others, but whatever his personal feelings he always helped polish my rough diamonds till they glittered. And when I disappointed him with a paste job, he worked even harder to make it shine—shaping and reshaping, cutting and chipping away until it was ready for his sparkling commentary. To start with I just used to sit next to him over a moviola simply supplying the facts, but bit by bit he began dragging words, phrases, even sentences out of me which I never thought I possessed. Talk about drawing teeth, getting blood from a stone and all that. It was painful. All the other directors in the programme had university degrees. I knew how to navigate and tie a double sheep's bend, and I knew a bit about the arts and that was all. But my education proper began at the age of thirty-two with Huw Wheldon. And so I stammered and stuttered my way through twenty documentaries with him, ranging from Pop Art to the architecture of Antoni Gaudi and still I hadn't made my film on Elgar. The main reason was Huw's hatred of actors in documentaries. We'd crossed swords over this on my very first film on Betjeman's London. Huw won that duel by cutting out a scene in which I'd used friends with Edwardian wardrobes to impersonate the poet's relatives. Huw pointed out that I'd managed to evoke business women taking baths in Camden Town without showing so much as a naked elbow, so I should certainly be able to do the same for Betjeman's childhood memories without dressing up ham actors in Inverness capes and deerstalker hats. He was right, of course.

I'd tried again a year later in a film on Prokofiev called *Portrait of a Soviet Composer*. There was no film in existence on Prokofiev, so I built up a picture of his life from Soviet propaganda films and old Russian news reels. I also had still photographs of the composer but I wanted him in motion. Huw heard about it and there was a confrontation.

"I gather we're planning to get out the dressing-up basket again," he said.

"This time I've got better actors," I said.

"Assuming you have, how do you propose to integrate them with all this old archive material?"

"By degrading the material I shoot myself so that it looks as grainy and contrasty as the real thing," I said.

"That's immoral," he said. "You are deliberately setting out to deceive the public."

"I'm setting out to tell the story of a child of the Revolution who fell out of favour with Uncle Stalin when he refused to turn out muzak glorifying the USSR. At the same time it's about the responsibility of the artist to his public."

"You would do well to remember that," he said. "I'm going to forbid you to have an actor impersonating Prokofiev and pass him off as the real man."

"How about his hands—playing the piano?"

"I will concede that."

"How about his reflection in a pond?"

"So long as it's a murky pond and the water is rippling," he said.

In the event, I was allowed to show the feet and the back of his head as well. These shots, combined with genuine photographs, convinced many of the audience that they had actually seen the man himself. In reality he was a collection of bits and pieces—a pianist's hands, an actor's back, a friend's feet: Ken Frankenstein had made his first monster. There was a cry of outrage (the first of many) from the Soviet Embassy!

Being called into Huw's office was rather like being summoned to the headmaster's study. The fact that he invariably had his feet on the desk did little to put one at ease, though I suspect that was the intention.

"Your next film will be your twenty-first," he said. "You're coming of age. The programme's getting on a bit too, our hundredth anniversary is coming up soon. I want to mark the event with a special. Have you any ideas?"

A special was an entire forty-five minute programme devoted to a single item—a rare event. I saw my big chance.

"I'm still keen to do Elgar's *Enigma Variations*," I ventured. He looked glum, his hands were touching in an attitude of prayer.

"Tell me about him," he said, without enthusiasm, "though I must remind you as I have before that we are not the drama department and it's probably way outside our budget."

Undeterred, I launched into the details.

"Born in 1857, Elgar grew up with music all around him, both in his father's shop in Worcester and in the nearby Malvern Hills. As a composer he was self-taught and spent years fighting for recognition, with his middle-class background and Catholic upbringing very much against him. He taught, played in a band and wrote long-winded oratorios for amateur choirs. His big breakthrough came at the age of forty with the *Enigma Variations*, first acclaimed by the great German conductor, Hans Richter. After that there was no stopping him: the music poured out, sweeping him to a pinnacle of fame crowned with a knighthood. The provincial nobody was suddenly the friend of kings and princes. But after the Great War his music was labelled vulgar, pompous and jingoistic. Suddenly he was as out of date as Colonel Blimp. With the passing of his wife in 1920 he seemed to fade away. He died in 1934, a forgotten man. He still is. I think he's due for a reappraisal."

"I appreciate your concern, but *Monitor* is not a rehabilitation centre. Your story is a romantic cliché. It's flabby. It has no backbone."

For a moment I was stunned. Then I spoke out. Maybe that was what he wanted. "But it does have a backbone," I argued. "It's five miles long and it's called the Malvern Hills. It's a giant switchback on which Elgar took the joy ride of a lifetime—on foot, horseback, by bike and car. He lived first on one side and then the other and at both ends. He played golf on those hills, ate, drank and slept on them, made love on them and spent the happiest days of his life on them. He was born within sight of them and he died within sight of them. They were his inspiration and his solace and whenever the outside world threatened to crush him, he returned to the hills, from whenceforth cometh his strength."

"Amen," said Wheldon, tapping his fingers together. "Forget the *Enigma Variations* idea. Film it as you told it—exactly as you told it. I suppose you'll need actors?" I nodded. "Then treat them as figures in a landscape—no dialogue and, above all, no acting. The hills are your stars here, the hills and Elgar's music. And not too many bloody crucifixes."

I agreed and almost danced out of the room. Huw's genius lay in his ability to tap the enthusiasm of his directors so that the ideas gushed forth. Later he channelled and refined the raw material, but once you had his blessing you were your own man until the rough cut.

My enthusiasm was shared by the entire crew . . . of three—Higgy the cameraman, Jim his assistant and Annie my production assistant. Because *Monitor* was a documentary programme there was no "effort" available. However, the Heads of Departments did what they could to help us, unofficially. The Chief Wardrobe Supervisor donated a hamper of Victorian clothes and washed her hands of us, a sympathetic make-up girl who was going on holiday lent us her make-up kit, and most of the props were begged, borrowed or scrounged around Malvern. I had had a larger crew and more facilities in my amateur movie days but I wasn't complaining. I was lucky to be getting away with it, and as things worked out the restrictions were a blessing in disguise. For what we lacked in numbers we made up for in mobility.

On our very first day on location in Malvern we were rained out. I was sitting in my hotel room waiting for the bar to open or the rain to stop when a beam of sunlight cut through the gloom like a giant arc lamp. It hit a tree on the hillside and completely burnt it out. In seconds I was hammering on my PA's door.

"Annie, get hold of the camera crews. The sun's out. We'll rendezvous at British Camp. I'll take care of Elgar."

"Don't forget his false nose," she shouted after me as I dashed off to the residents' lounge where Peter had promised to wait patiently all day. He was a friend of mine and he was playing Elgar. Actually, he was one of five actors playing Elgar. He was Elgar between eighteen and forty.

"Leave your tea," I said. "The sun's out. Get your clothes and meet me in the stable yard—and don't forget your false nose."

"What scene are we doing?"

"You've only got one set of clothes, what does it matter?"

We ran out of the room in opposite directions.

By the time I'd got the Edwardian boneshaker out of the stable Peter was ready to help me lift it onto the roof rack of the car. We rendezvoused with Annie and the camera crew as arranged and looked at the sky. The sun was playing hide and seek through tiny holes in the thunderclouds and it was setting. We decided to risk it—to lug the equipment up the hill and snatch a sunset shot. Annie and I grabbed the bike, Higgy grabbed his 35-mm Cameflex, Jim grabbed the tripod and battery and joined the dash for the bracken. Peter followed on, doing his best to impersonate Elgar with loose spats, cravat, flopping waistcoat, and his deerstalker hat all askew, struggling with his false nose, desperately trying to mould the putty into that aquiline shape so characteristic of Elgar. We staggered onto the narrow spine of the hill leading to the summit in various states of collapse. But in moments we had the camera set up and Elgar on his bike. Bugger it, the back tyre was flat and the famous nose looked closer to Shylock's than Elgar's. I gave him the fastest nose job in history, helped him on his bike and gave him a big push towards the summit, shouting "Turn over" to the cameraman at the same time. The sun was still shining but black clouds were fighting to get at it.

"What shall I do?" shouted Elgar.

"Pedal towards the sunset, of course."

He pedalled, the film churned through the camera, the sun played ball. In my head the *Introduction and Allegro* was in perfect synch with the image.

"There's a precipice," shouted Elgar, his back to the camera.

"Get off and gaze at the sunset," I shouted back. He obliged and struck an elegantly casual pose.

"OK?" I asked Higgy.

"OK, Ken."

"OK. Cut and up sticks for a close shot."

We all ran towards Elgar. His nose had turned into a parrot's beak but fortunately the lens couldn't see it. The sky was black as pitch but still the sun squirrelled through. Elgar gazed steadily at the dark mountains of Wales. They reminded me of Wheldon's eyebrows. I felt scrutinised. Elgar was rim-lit, haloed, his glowing silhouette burned a black hole in the thunderclouds—a breathtaking image that was to find its way onto thousands of album covers one day. The sun sank below the horizon, and just as I was about to say "Cut" the film ran out. We all cheered. Elgar's nose fell off. We laughed. It was in the can.

Imagine trying to achieve that with the sort of crew you'd be forced to use nowadays—a unit of sixty with catering vans, actors' caravans, honeywagons, generators, make-up and wardrobe wagons and . . . oh well, forget it. Those days have gone for good—or have they? That night the bar at the Malvern Arms was the happiest place on earth.

After three weeks' shooting and as many in the editing room Huw saw the rough cut and had reservations.

"Too many romantic images, old boy. Elgar as a fifty-year-old in knickerbockers flying a kite on a hilltop is an apt metaphor for success but it's bound to be misinterpreted as sheer self-indulgence on your part. And the idea of Sir Edward sliding down a hill on a tea tray is ludicrous. I grant you it goes well with the music but it's too childish by half. Lose it, the film will be all the better for it."

I blinked and spoke out for a second time. "But Huw, it's true, he *did* slide down the hills on a tea tray. And he used to send telegrams to the Greenwich Observatory for meteorological reports to see if it was good kite-flying weather."

He looked at me in amazement. "Those are facts?" I nodded. "Facts you can corroborate?" I nodded again. "Then we must *tell* the audience, old boy, or they'll never believe it."

And so the film was transmitted covered in commentary stating the obvious. I thought this silly at the time; now I'm not so sure. People are still reluctant to believe that artists are often kids at heart. Elgar knew all about that and so did his brothers and sisters. Feeling their parents were getting old and stodgy, the children got together and produced a play

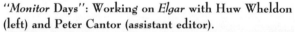

"Monitor Days": Working on *Elgar* with Huw Wheldon (left) and Peter Cantor (assistant editor).

called *The Wand of Youth*. Edward wrote the music and they all played instruments, including a double bass made from a tea chest, and they also acted the parts. The story told of a magic land where one is ever young and how the kids spirited their parents into the rejuvenating territory with the desired results. Elgar reworked it in his old age for a full symphony orchestra and it makes one young just to hear it.

The Elgar film was voted the best single programme of the Sixties by TV viewers. It certainly put me on the map, and it didn't do Elgar any harm either. His renaissance, long overdue, got under way. New recordings of his music trickled and then gushed forth. Today there are forty-one recordings of the *Enigma Variations* alone and not a month goes by without a new addition to the catalogues. Everything he wrote has been recorded. The narrowminded, blinkered, distorted view of the old soldier out of step with the young guard has given way to the true picture of a visionary who captured the spirit of England, past, present and future, more convincingly than any other artist, living or dead. Shooting that film had been a happy experience—one I was hoping to recapture. And as I sped through the moonlight the unforgettable silhouette of the hills seemed to be rolling towards me on waves of sound. Elgar once said, "The hills are singing my music—or I am singing theirs?" That night they were singing the heady *Introduction and Allegro for Strings*. It was coming through the roof like a buzzsaw.

The sleepy, rambling little town of Great Malvern was sleeping soundly as I pulled up before the Horny Old Arms Hotel. My plan was to book into the hotel and spend the following day wallowing. But after a beer and sandwich I couldn't resist the urge to jump back into the car for what I guessed should be a spectacular view of the Vale of Evesham by moonlight. A gravel road winds to the highest point of the highest of the hills, the Beacon, but it's a private access road and closed to the general public. Taking a chance, I turned off my lights and drove up the path where we had filmed the boy on the white horse, the youth on his bicycle and the man in his motor car, racing to the summit, so many years before. There were no ghosts tonight, no courting couples, not even a sheep.

I stopped at the top and popped a cassette of Elgar's greatest hits into the player. "Salut d'Amour," Elgar's wedding present to his wife, seeped through the speakers. It was the most popular piece he ever wrote. It was played in every café and on every bandstand in the land for years and years but he never grew rich on it—his publisher bought it outright for five pounds.

Down in the valley I could see the spot where I'd filmed him one sunny day in 1962, wandering arm in arm with his sweetheart through a field of swaying corn. And there, just below me, we'd shot a terrific backlit sequence of the happy couple tugging reluctant mules up a windswept slope. The courtship dissolved from image to image as the sequence drifted along with the flow of the music. There, where the moonlight shone on the waters of the River Severn, I'd shown them in a skiff with the young Mr. Elgar in bowler hat at the oars, gazing rapturously at Alice in the stern idly twirling a parasol. The music continued, the boat continued, but the figures in the boat changed—the girl in the Edwardian dress was Shirley and the man at the oars was me with a camera around my neck. I stopped rowing and started to photograph my model. Dissolve again as Elgar's courtship gave way to my own: Shirley dancing a ghostly Charleston dressed as a flapper in a ballroom in the ruins of the old Ranelagh Polo Club. Shirley playing panpipes on a fallen pillar in the glades of Arcady as a Fifties nymph in clothes of her own design while my camera went on clicking away. She was an eighteen-year-old fashion student at Walthamstow Tech. I was a twenty-six-year-old student of photography. She wanted to become a fashion designer. I wanted to crash the pages of *Harper's* and *Vogue*. We built up a portfolio of work as we enjoyed our weekend excursions into fantasy.

The images continued, despite my efforts to get into the right memory pattern. Now she was posing in her wedding dress, threatened by dinosaurs in the grounds of Crystal Palace, and now striding the Yorkshire Moors in Victorian clothes on our honeymoon as I try to evoke the world of the Brontës through the lens of my Rolleicord. Well, I never made the pages of *Vogue*, but Shirley did get a job as a designer—pirating Paris fashions for an Oxford Street store. Then Xavier came along, and it was time to drop my student ways and try to earn a living in the overcrowded world of photojournalism.

I turned off the tape. Well, Elgar's marriage had turned out better than mine—or had it? Why is Alice's variation in the *Enigma* the most boring of the lot? Who do the asterisks represent in Variation Twelve? A mysterious lover? Elgar himself was handsome, dashing and a bit of a dreamer. Lady Elgar was plain and dowdy but she didn't lack drive. She coveted the honours more than he did. He buried them with her. During her life she refused to let him have a dog. As soon as she died he got three. And *Minna*, the last piece of music he ever wrote, is far more heartfelt than his portrait of Alice. Minna was a Cairn terrier. In my own case that situation was reversed: Haig Pit, our Staffordshire bull terrier, slept on Shirley's bed.

The windows had misted up. I wiped the windscreen. There was a mist outside, too, or maybe I was in the clouds. I could hardly see beyond the bonnet. I switched on the lights, started the engine, gingerly negotiated a five-point turn and slowly, very slowly, because I didn't want to go over a precipice, drove cautiously down the hill.

The next morning was bright and sunny but the idea of tramping the hills had lost its appeal. I had an early breakfast and drove back to London. I was just in time to carve the traditional Sunday roast. Everyone seemed pleased to see me. I told them about Southampton but made no mention of the Malvern Hills. In the afternoon we all strolled up the Bayswater Road and had a good laugh at all the kitsch artwork manufactured for the tourists: vintage cars and "Big Bens" made out of watch parts, crude pictures of Churchill and the Royal Family copied from newspapers, black ladies painted in luminous paint on black velvet, country cottages, galleons, sunsets unfit for Christmas calendars, and constructions in bent wire masquerading as modern art. A good subject for a *Monitor* essay. But *Monitor* was dead and buried and had been for ten years, ever since Huw had moved on to become Managing Director of BBC TV and earn a knighthood.

After half a mile of trash art we'd had enough; the joke soon wears thin. Then, as we had done a hundred times before, we turned into the park at Lancaster Gate and walked slowly back, admiring the flowers. At the Round Pond we stopped to watch the model yachts. Over the bandstand a splendid box kite was flying, similar to the one I used in *Elgar*. I half expected the band to be playing "Salut d'Amour" but it wasn't. It was playing a selection from *Annie Get Your Gun*. We sat down on the grass with the other spectators. Then, right in front of everyone, two big Alsatians started rutting away, perfectly in time to "There's No Business Like Show Business." We laughed, went home and busied ourselves in our private rooms with our private activities: Alex played Mahler, Xavier played heavy metal, James played electronic music, Victoria played the Beatles, Toby played Chinese opera, Shirley played her favourite composer—I turned up the wick and played "Land of Hope and Glory" and drowned the buggers out!

3 Sailors in Skirts

Monday morning. Seven-thirty in the kitchen. A bite of toast, a sip of tea and two brown eyes staring at me reproachfully.

"There's no need to look at me like that, it's not my fault—altogether." The brown eyes remain unconvinced. "You take her side because she cooks you lamb's liver," I said, throwing him a crust. He snapped like a frog catching flies and swallowed it in a single gulp, barking for more. I "shushed" him and left the room. Footsteps sounded on the stairs but I was out of the door before further confrontation. Jumping into the waiting car, I slammed the door and said "Let's go." We sped off and I relaxed a little. I had escaped again for another day of freedom.

As we crawled through the early morning traffic towards Elstree Studios in North London I sat there, enduring the driver's small talk. I had to. He'd been privy to an ugly family row in the back of the car, with the pot calling the kettle black, and knew more about our marriage bust-up than anyone but the party responsible. Of course, he'd promised to keep his mouth shut but drivers, as I'd recently discovered, are not always to be trusted.

Sounds rather grand, having one's own driver, doesn't it? Well, it's all down to protecting your assets. A director is always insured during working hours by the production company until the film is completed, because if he drove himself, for instance, and happened to be a little tired or a little drunk, he might kill himself and then the delivery of the film would be delayed and the dollars and cents wouldn't be rolling in and the interest on the bank loan would be sky-rocketing and so on. But the day after I delivered the film I'd be back driving my old Crown Custom Toyota and risking life and limb and nobody caring.

After fifty minutes of traffic jams and chitchat we arrived at Elstree Studios where I'd shot my last feature film—and my first, come to that. My God, that takes me back—to 1963 to be exact.

After Elgar I got itchy feet and itchy eyes. I was tired of looking down the wrong end of a telescope at the TV screen. I longed to swing it around and be blown away by the big picture. And right away I was offered a feature film—as quick as that, straight out of the blue, a musical, a British Musical. I mentioned it to Mum and Aunt Moo. Their faces fell.

"Who's in it, Ken?" asked Mum.

"Cliff Richard and the Shadows."

"Mm, nice."

"What's it about?" asked Moo.

"It's about a bunch of kids who buy an old London bus and drive it to Greece."

"Ancient Greece," said Moo with authority. "Seen it, Ken. *Boys from Syracuse.*"

"Eddie Cantor," piped up Mum.

"No, that's *Roman Scandals*," said Moo. "Allan Jones was in *The Boys from Syracuse.*"

"'Keep Young and Beautiful,'" said Mum.

"No, 'Falling in Love with Love,'" said Moo.

"Well, they both wore skirts, I know that," said Mum.

"No, togas, Mum. They were togas," I said, "and they drove chariots We've got a London bus."

"Cliff's going to look silly driving a London bus in a toga," said Mum I blinked.

"They don't write tunes like that anymore," said Moo nostalgically. "Was it Lerner and Loewe?"

"Rodgers and Hart," said Mum. "Who have you got, Ken?"

"Myers and Cass."

They both looked blank. Neither had seen *The Young Ones* starring Cliff Richard and the Shadows and neither attended West End revues. Myers and Cass wrote for both.

I "passed" on *Summer Holiday*, but made the acquaintance of the song-writing team later when the same producer, Kenneth Harper, talked me into directing *French Dressing*. The treatment was promising. A deck-chair attendant has the bright idea of putting his tacky seaside resort on the map by arranging a film festival with Brigitte Bardot as the star attraction. The fun was supposed to start when he went to France to chat her up and bring her back. Harper got financial backing from Elstree Films and a script was commissioned from Myers and Cass.

The very next day we were all packed off to Herne Bay—a miserable resort on the Thames Estuary—to soak up atmosphere and inspiration. We sat in a chilly boarding house looking through yellowing lace curtains and torrential rain at the second longest pier in England. The end was obscured, the script uninspired. I suggested a younger talent to Harper— an actor friend of mine who had played the young Mr. Elgar.

Myers and Cass packed their bags and the young Mr. Elgar, who fancied himself as a writer, joined me in the front parlour. The rain stopped. We saw the end of the pier. The script remained uninspired. We shot it all the same. I learned a lot. The film industry was not yet ready to accept TV directors. Everything was done by the book, impro-visation was frowned upon and there was little team spirit. It was also my first experience with actors. Until then I'd used actors as props, moving them about the landscape like cattle or as set dressing, sitting at tables like tailor's dummies in attitudes of inspiration—hand to head and pen to paper. And as yet they had not been allowed to utter a word. Now they not only spoke, but actually spoke to each other—it was a sort of miracle. I used to watch in open-mouthed wonder and admiration every time it happened, until one day Ken Harper took me aside for a quiet word.

"The actors are very unhappy," he said. "You're not talking to them."

"I don't hang around the bar at night, if that's what you mean," I replied, with dignity.

"I mean when you're shooting a scene," he said. "The most they ever get out of you is 'Action' and 'Cut.'"

"What more do they want?" I asked.

"You could talk to them about their character, motivation and that sort of thing."

"I did, before we started," I said.

"Well, this is supposed to be a comedy. We're not getting many laughs."

"I don't know," I mumbled defensively. "Every time Roy Kinnear falls flat on his face the crew kill themselves."

"A sure sign we've got a dead duck on our hands," he said.

"Well, they're comics, aren't they? That's why we hired them—to get the laughs."

"They need help in delivery, timing. They need encouragement. Tell them they're doing good even if they're doing bad. Buy them a drink in the evening, listen to their troubles, laugh at their jokes."

Marisa Mell poses with Town Counsellors in Ken Russell's first feature film, *French Dressing*.

"You need a psychiatrist, not a film director," I said.

"A film director has to be a psychiatrist," he answered emphatically. From that moment I started to become a psychiatrist. But it was too late as far as *French Dressing* was concerned. The film was a flop. No one offered me a second chance. The big screen, the big time, had been an illusion. Suitably chastened, I returned, like the prodigal nephew, to Auntie BBC where I was able to convince Huw Wheldon that we should drop our traditional documentary form of storytelling with its Ministry-of-Information-type commentary and let our artists speak for themselves. He had misgivings but eventually concurred and I was soon able to put Harper's advice into practice. It was then my drinking days began in earnest.

I was feeling in need of a drink as I stepped out of the car at Elstree and into the cutting room. It had a fridge. Hell, it was empty. I sent the driver to wait outside the off-licence till opening time and sat down at the moviola where my editor had a sequence from *Valentino* all lined up to show me. He pushed the "start" lever and the frosted glass screen came to life with a horn gramophone playing a Twenties tango in a Deco ballroom. The couple on the floor, immaculately dressed for a *thé dansant* of the period, moulded in each other's arms, danced as one—the epitome of stylised sexuality. Valentino, the silent screen's greatest lover, was giving Nijinsky, the greatest dancer in the world, a lesson in the tango. I marvelled as I watched Nureyev and Anthony Dowell move around the dance floor to "*La Cumparsita*," tails twirling, feet flashing. I forgot about the booze, caught up in the intoxication of the dance. To tell the truth, dialogue scenes often bore me. The body is so much more expressive than the tongue—on film anyway. There's a lot of dancing in my work—or perhaps I should say choreography—and if the actors aren't making patterns the camera is usually doing it for them. Watching the artistry of Nureyev, I always regret not making that film on Nijinsky with him—it nearly happened, twice. The script was the problem. For years he had it written and rewritten and by the time he found it to his satisfaction he was too old for the role.

My first chance at choreography came at the Nautical College, Pangbourne. I'm not sure why I went there. Perhaps it was because most of the schools in Southampton were either piles of rubble or evacuated, or because my cousin Roy attended a nautical college. My parents had been impressed by his uniform, I know. It was identical to that of an officer in the Royal Navy and looked very smart. But we had closer nautical ties than that. Two doors up from us lived the captain of the *Queen Mary*. And Dad was a skipper in his own right—in the AFS on a fire-fighting launch three nights a week. We'd also been weekend sailors before the war and Dad had been a ship's detective, as I said before, so to him it

Rudolph Valentino (Rudolf Nureyev) teaches the tango to
Russian ballet star Nijinsky (Anthony Dowell) in *Valentino*.

seemed inevitable. I wasn't mad on the idea of the sea as a career but I
went along with it because of my love for Dorothy Lamour. I saw her
films over and over, wrote to her once a month, and drooled over the
signed photos she sent me. I adored everything she appeared in but especially her South Sea Island features: *Typhoon*, *The Hurricane* and *Aloma
of the South Seas*. Who knows, if I joined the Merchant Navy I might
bump into her one day on a South Sea atoll shooting a movie. Besides,
I was tired of being blitzed all the time. Southampton with its docks and
factories was in the front line with nothing between us and the Luftwaffe
but a few ack-ack guns and a pathetic balloon barrage. The war had not
touched Berkshire and it would be nice to get a good night's sleep for
once, far away from the deadly vibrations that rocked the metal cage,
known as a Morrison shelter, in which I'd tried to sleep for the last couple
of years.

At Pangbourne I escaped the bombs but not the vibrations. Every
night row upon row of metal bunks rattled to the rhythm of mass mas-
turbation. I suppose it was because we missed our mums. After a week I
was ready to brave the bombs again. At thirteen and a half I found life
could be hell. Everything about me was wrong, from my accent to my

uniform. Suddenly I discovered I wasn't talking proper. I didn't talk posh. I said "Mum" instead of "Mater." One of my chief tormenters was Cadet Leader Forbes-Marlborough.

"I say, Russell, you sound like a common dockland matey." He turned to the group who'd found this worm of a junior trespassing in the "Seniors' Wood." "His pater isn't a footwear retailer but a 'Dad wot sells boots and shoes.' He doesn't visit the cinema but 'goes to the flicks.' His uniform isn't of the Gieves of Bond Street superfine variety but common serge from 'Biker's, Sarfampton.' Say 'Bikers,' Russell . . . (silence) . . . the label on that appalling cap falling over your ears reads B A K E R S . . . say 'Bakers,' Russell . . . (silence). Help the poor sod say 'Bakers,' someone." Half a dozen senior idiots grab me and twist my lanyard round my neck so it's nearly choking me. Between my teeth I mutter "Bikers." Screams of laughter as they let me go. But Forbes-Marlborough hasn't finished yet.

"Name and number, Russell."

"Russell, sir, 157."

"You forgot your initials. What are they?"

Silence.

"I'll remind you, they are H.K.A. Say it."

Ken Russell as a cadet at the Nautical College, Pangbourne.

They twist the lanyard again. It cuts into my neck again.

" 'Aitch, kiy, aye," I say, defiantly.

" 'Aitch, kiy, aye," they chorus, falling about.

"What's the 'kiy' for?"

"Ken," I splutter.

"Not Kenneth? 'Ow common, our Ken. How often do you bathe, our Ken?"

"Every Friday."

"You've appalling BO. Our Ken's a dirty nipper, he stinks just like a kipper, let's fill his ass with broken glass and circumcise the skipper."

Whereupon they throw me, fully clothed, into a stinking bog.

This sort of thing went on for weeks, months—it seemed years—until Forbes-Marlborough left for the Navy. After the war he became a District Commissioner in India. I pity the poor natives. No wonder they chucked us out. But he was typical of the majority—a bunch of class-conscious pricks, aged between thirteen and eighteen, living in our glorious past. Sir Philip Devitt, a wall-eyed baronet with a monocle and knee breeches, was the founder of the college. His father, or perhaps it was his grandfather, had once owned a fleet of sailing ships with illustrious names such as *Harbinger, Hesperus* and *Macquarie*. His instructors, who probably served in them, taught knot-tying, club-swinging and semaphore and, if the occasion demanded, knew how to use the rope's end for a good flogging. But generally a simple cane was used for corporal punishment.

A five-pound note vanished from Forbes-Marlborough's pocket one night while he was "tossing off" in the dormitory. Suspicion fell on me. Only someone who was not a gentleman would steal from a gentleman. I was beaten. I broke bounds to see Dorothy Lamour in *Star Spangled Rhythm*. I was beaten. I was discovered reading *Picturegoer* in the chapel. I was beaten. I talked in my sleep. No talking after lights-out. I was dragged out of my bunk, marched into the housemaster's rooms and beaten—in my pyjamas.

The following night as I was about to turn in I was summoned to his rooms again. What was it this time? I passed my only friend, Robin Lee-Smith, on the way. He too was in his pyjamas, blubbing. I guessed what had happened. It looked as if I was in for another beating. Yesterday's cuts were still red and deep. Soon, I thought, they'd be able to play noughts and crosses on my ass. I knocked on the housemaster's door.

"Hum."

I opened the door and hesitated on the threshold.

"Hum in, Russell. Hum in." He was nicknamed "Handy" because

he couldn't keep his hands to himself. He also had big feet and bore more than a passing resemblance to Frankenstein's monster as played by Boris Karloff. He also had a speech impediment.

"Hit down, Russell, hit down."

I sat gingerly on a hard chair. "Hoxo hor Hovaltine?" So this was to be a social visit. My throat went dry.

"Hox . . . Oxo, please, sir," I murmured nervously. He lit the gas ring and put a kettle on.

"Have you seen these b . . . before?" He indicated a sheaf of drawings lying on the table.

"Yes, sir." I knew Robin had spilt the beans and been punished for it. There was nothing to hide. "Lee-Smith and I found them in a ditch on the way to the boathouse. Somebody must have dropped them."

"Someone," he corrected.

"Someone must have dropped them. There's an artist lives in the village, sir." He ignored that and pointed at the drawings with a long, trembling hand.

"Look at them and tell me what you he," he said. I got up, looked at the top drawing and blushed.

"I see a lady with no clothes on, sir."

"Go hon."

"She's lying down, sir, on her back."

"Go hon."

"Her knees are up."

"Go hon."

"Her legs are open."

"What do you see between her legs?"

". . . just a line, sir, a thin line."

"Do you see any hu . . . hu . . . hair?"

"There's hair on her head, sir."

"Lee-Smith admits to self-abuse in regard to that picture."

"D . . . does he, sir?"

"Do you?"

"No, sir."

"Come here." He patted his knee. Reluctantly I sat on it. "You're living in f . . . f . . . fools' paradise, Russell. There's no slit there, it's more . . . more like an open sewer of stinking fish, eels, sea anemones hidden in a bush of sli . . . sli . . . slimy hu . . . hu . . . hair and sometimes there's blu . . . blu . . . blood that smells like . . . sm . . . smell my f . . . fi . . . fingers. Smell tha . . . that?"

I tried to hold my breath but finally gasped in the fumes of the Oxo cube he had crumbled in his fingers a moment ago. It was strong and acrid and I wanted to throw up.

"Get up," he said. "F . . . f . . . fools' paradise. Drop your pyjamas." I froze. "P . . . pu . . . please. I . . . I'm not go . . . go . . . going to h . . . hurt you." I gritted my teeth and obeyed.

"B . . . b . . . bend over."

I closed my eyes and obeyed. There was a pause. I was trembling, then I felt something moist touch my backside. It was his fingers. He was gently smoothing something moist and sticky into my cuts. I wondered if it was Vaseline. One finger was doing the rubbing now. Fearing the worst, I tightened my buttocks. The kettle started whistling. He hesitated for a moment then went over to the gas ring, turned it off, and said, "Pull up your pyjamas." Then, still with his back to me, he said, "When you grow up y . . . y . . . you will realise that life is a f . . . f . . . fools' paradise. Do you under . . . understand me?"

"Yes, sir."

"Now, turn in and d . . . d . . . don't tell any . . . anyone about the f . . . f . . . first aid or they . . . they will all be com . . . coming to mu . . . mu . . . me instead of mu . . . mu . . . matron."

Back in my bunk I was shaking.

"Pack it up, H.K.I., or you'll go blind," said a voice from below.

I tried to stop. My shaking gave way to occasional shudders. If what he said was true it was frightening. No wonder you never saw it at the flicks. But it couldn't be true. He was just trying to frighten me, teach me a lesson. The idea of Dorothy Lamour being like that was unthinkable. I dropped off to sleep imagining myself stroking her hair—the hair on her head—all soft focus with a balmy breeze blowing and everything in slow motion. Slowly she smiled and kissed me.

Reveille sounds. We tumble out of bed, put on our plimsolls, pull up shorts and stumble out of the dormitory and down the stairs. Six-forty-five on the parade ground. There's a cold wind blowing as we shiver in untidy ranks waiting for directions from the Cadet Captain.

"Around the piggeries, through Seniors' Wood, across Big Side and up Bartholomew's Bottom . . . Go!" The Cadet Captain yawns and returns to his bunk, leaving the rest of us to trot off on the first cross-country run of the day.

Twenty minutes later we take a cold shower, dress and march to breakfast ". . . for what we are about to receive may the Lord make us truly thankful . . ." and then it's Matron, dressed as Florence Nightingale, ladling out lumpy porridge.

"H.K.I., don't eat with your mouth open." Cadets flick butter at the

Georgian ceiling. The butter slowly melts and drips onto Pip Devitt's bald head. "Biscuit" Mealing farts. Everyone moans. We bolt down a college sausage. Muddy coffee skins over. "Brush your teeth, brush your shoes, brush your uniform. Fall in. Division 'shun." The staff look down at us from their podium. The Pope (the Padre) whines a prayer. The Commander, a sheep's head with five o'clock shadow, inspects us. There's "scrambled egg" on his uniform and scrambled egg on his chin. He adjusts my lanyard. My name and number are taken.

The S.O.D. (Director of Studies) says ragging in the classrooms must stop and threatens disciplinary action. The Chief Cadet Captain barks, "Cadets 'shun, right tun, quick harch." Under the arch, clatter, clatter, into the study area, a quadrangle of timber buildings resembling a hospital out of the Crimean War. Oral French with Le Capitaine "Crapaud" speaking in a hoarse whisper because of a bayonet in the throat in the Great War, with us shouting back. Desk lids banging, pandemonium as he dodges a fusillade of ink pellets—unsuccessfully and they splatter his face. Everyone sings "The cat's got the measles" in French. In a rising frenzy Crapaud rubs his neck and stamps his shiny patent leather shoes.

History with another old soldier—the Major—swaying and smelling of booze at nine in the morning. The Pope with the confirmation class "... an inward and spiritual sign of an outward and visible grace ... ," Biscuit farts again, march to lunch, march to afternoon studies, march back, recreation—sawing logs—march to supper, march to evening studies, march to ablutions. Stand by your bunks, one bell, kneel and pray. Silence. Biscuit farts, stifled laughter. Two bells, turn in, lights out, toss off.

It had its moments, life at the NCP, and as time dragged on and the ragging subsided I made a few good friends. I remember five or six of us sailing up the sunny Thames in an old whaler bound for a small island on which plump land girls sunbathed in the buff under the willows. The island was out of bounds so the girls were safe from marauding seafarers, though I doubt if we'd have done much more than pinch their bums anyway. In the winter some of us were allowed to march down to the local farm to do our bit for the war effort with the land girls; we in our navy caps, white sweaters and grey bags called it "potato-picking" while they in their floppy hats, green jumpers and corduroy jodhpurs called it "spud-bashing." When it rained we huddled together in a barn, drinking tea from enamel mugs, linking arms and singing "Run, Rabbit, Run."

The prettiest girl was called Elsie and I had quite a crush on her. So it was a very big moment when I bumped into her by chance one summer afternoon on a lonely cross-country run. It was in a silver birch wood and she was taking her ease, seated with her back to a tree enjoying the dappled sun. She saw me, coo-eed and waved. I broke my stride, veered off the path and ran towards her through wild strawberries.

"Hello," I panted, coming to a halt.

"You look hot," she said. "Fancy a strawberry?"

"Yes, please."

She patted the soft green moss. Hesitantly, I sat down beside her. She had a little mound of strawberries in her hand.

"Stick out your tongue," she said.

With a nervous laugh I did so. She placed a strawberry on it. I drew it back inside my mouth and nibbled away, smiling. She smiled too.

"Like another?"

"Thanks. Yes." I was about to stick out my tongue again when she beat me to it and placed a strawberry deftly on the end of her own. For a moment I didn't know what to do and went to pick it off. She frowned and drew it into her mouth for a moment, then slowly extended it again with a wink. I began to get the message and extended my tongue so that it was touching the tip of hers. The strawberry fell off. She laughed.

"You are a noodle! Come on, I'll show you how it's done. Stick it out, then." I obeyed—a willing patient to her doctor. Delicately she placed a lush, ripe strawberry onto the end of my tongue and leaned towards me, opening her mouth. But instead of taking the strawberry she kept on going and sucked my tongue down her throat and wouldn't let go. I felt as if it was coming out by the roots. Then she loosened up a little and relaxed into a long, incredible kiss. Something was moving in my gym shorts. Soon her hand gently closed over my erection and softly massaged it. This was paradise—a fools' paradise.

A crackle of twigs. I froze for a moment, thinking of the housemaster. Guiltily I pulled away, gasped and looked up. Towering above me was a big, big black man in the uniform of the US Air Force. The girl withdrew her hand with a giggle. They both looked at my gym pants which my erection had turned into a fairy's bell tent. She gave a shrill laugh. It deflated fast. The airman guffawed, then with a flick of his wrist loosened his fly and released something that swung down in front of my face like a big black mamba. I ran and ran and ran and never ran through that wood again. One evening a few months later a Cadet Leader was reading aloud extracts from the *News of the World*. It was a murder case in nearby Reading in which a black in the US Air Force was accused of killing a girl with, as the judge delicately put it, twenty-four inches of uncontrollable flesh. He was found not guilty. I think the verdict was death by misadventure. Poor girl. I wondered if she was living in a fools' paradise too.

That was my last term at the college and I never saw the land girls again. Anyway, my mind was on other things. I'd given up hope of mastering navigation, double sheep's bends and semaphore and decided to go all out for showbusiness, on stage and screen. I devoted every off-duty moment to it. The film was called *The Monster and the Maiden* and I wrote, directed and starred in it; all silent, slapstick stuff, including a fight in which the hero and villain batter each other senseless with college sausages while the monster gets the girl. It had everything, including the slowest chase sequence in cinema history for when I told Biscuit Mealing, the cameraman, I wanted it fast he set the speed to sixty-four frames per second—slow motion.

The stage show was called *Thank Your Lucky Tars*. Usually the end-of-term divisional concert started with a curtain-up on two rows of cadets in traditional grey bags, white sweaters and caps singing "The Fishermen of England are working at their nets," followed by a recitation of the "Boy Stood on the Burning Deck" variety, a patriotic tableau such as the Death of Nelson and an act from *HMS Pinafore*. I had plans for a different kind of show and surprisingly enough had no problem finding volunteers; most of the cadets were only too willing to let their hair down.

The Big Night arrived. The house was packed. The Pope, Handy, Pip and Lady Devitt, Capitaine Crapaud, the Major, the Commander, the Sod, and odds and sods of teachers and their wishy-washy wives plus two hundred sex-starved cadets were in for the shock of their lives. *Thank Your Lucky Tars* was a tribute to the American movie musical with the cadets playing all the parts—dames included. It was a grand opportunity to be mildly outrageous. As Dorothy Lamour in a fetching sarong, I had licence to blow the Commander a kiss as I sang "Aloha-oee," for instance. But the hit of the evening was undoubtedly Robin's impersonation of Carmen Miranda in the *South American Way* extravaganza. With the aid of a pineapple, a pair of platforms and a borrowed dress, augmented in the right places by a couple of rolled-up rugger socks, Robin was the Brazilian Bombshell to the life. And when he rolled his hips and his baby blues and sang, "Do you want my heeps to heep-na-tise you?" many hearts in that audience fluttered and many hands crept into many trouser pockets and they weren't counting change. After ninety minutes of song and dance culminating in a daring kiss at the end of a boy-meets-girl number, the curtain came down to tut-tuts and cheers on Pangbourne's first drag show. As the curtain rose again to much applause and stamping of feet, the Commander could be seen helping the dazed Founder to his wheelchair. That night the bunks shook as never before.

The Passing Out Parade—on Big Side with the band playing "Hearts of Oak"—proud parents watching Princess Elizabeth inspect us, mass club-swinging, marching, counter-marching, shaky pyramids of cadets with a little one on top waving a Union Jack and then the "leavers" marching up one by one to get their seamanship certificates and a handshake from the Commander and each getting a cheer. Being the least senior, I was the last. I marched briskly forward, snapped to attention, smartly saluted and barked out, "157, Russell, H.K.A., sir."

Immediately one of the cadets yelled out, "Hip, hip, hooray, for H.K.A." The cry was taken up and no one except me heard the Commander say as he handed me the worthless certificate with a twinkle in his eye, "Aloha-oee, Russell. Aloha-oee."

All I learned from Pangbourne was how to speak proper and the rudiments of direction and choreography. And as I watched Nureyev and Anthony Dowell I recalled partnering Robin in our weekly dancing class back at the college—a whole roomful of cadets doing the tango to *"La Cumparsita."* Everything goes in circles, everything comes in useful. Nothing is wasted. The tango sequence looked good, it just needed a couple of close-ups to emphasise the highlights. As the editor substituted the shots I went outside to see if the booze had arrived. There was no sign of the driver and I was beginning to feel the need of a drink when the studio postman rode up on his bike with the cutting-room mail. He handed it to me without stopping, and pedalled off. Mostly stuff from the labs, then a letter addressed to me in a familiar hand. It was from a young friend in America. She'd been around on *Valentino* for a while making a documentary on me till Shirley became jealous and got her shipped back to the States. Now she was doing some research for me on the composer Charles Ives, who was a Connecticut Yankee like herself. The letter was a progress report—nothing personal. So why was my heart pounding?

4

Saps at Sea

My work on the fine cut of *Valentino* was over. Twelve cans of film had been sent off to New York for the producer's approval. By the time I arrived a week later he'd have viewed it and decided whether it needed more work or was ready for "dubbing" (making the sound track). Normally I'd have flown over with the film myself but I was going through one of my non-flying phases and could not set foot on an aircraft. I felt in need of a sea change, anyway. Between the misery of *Valentino* and my

marriage bust-up, it had been a gruelling year. Jack was dead. Mum was
in a nursing home. Not the one around the corner from Aunt Moo but
a state institution for more serious cases out of town at East End. Dad
took me there one Sunday morning in late November. Mum had changed
greatly. She was thin and gaunt. Her blond hair, usually a frizzy halo,
was now cropped and straight. She sat there in the visitors' room, in her
pale blue smock, as noble and aloof as an aged Joan of Arc—until Dad
produced a bag of toffees and she dissolved into a giggling schoolgirl. And
that's how he addressed her.

"Eth, this is Ken. You saw him not long ago, remember?" She stared
at me with unblinking eyes and no glimmer of recognition. Dad laughed
good-naturedly.

"Come on, Eth. Don't you know your own son? It's Ken."

She offered me the bag of toffees. "Would the gentleman care for a
sweetie?"

I thanked her, took one and made quite a show of enjoying it.

"Can nothing be done?" I asked Dad as we drove away.

"They gave her shock treatment, Ken, but all it did was straighten
her hair. Shall we drop in on Moo and June on the way? They'd love to
see you, I'm sure."

"They're coming down to wish me *bon voyage*," I said. "Didn't they
tell you?"

"No, they didn't mention it," he replied, and lapsed into silence. I
fancied there might be tension between them. Perhaps they disapproved
of Mum being in a public institution, knowing Dad could well afford
private care.

That evening we all stood around my cabin on board the QE_2, clutching our drinks and sandwiches like mourners at a wake.

"He was a lovely man, Ken, a lovely man," sobbed Moo.

"He was the best father a girl ever had," said June.

"He was a good man," said Dad.

"Yes, he was," I said.

The hooter sounded and we kissed goodbye. I unpacked and went up
on deck. We were casting off. Dusk was falling. I looked for the family
on the quayside—no sign. The tugs began towing us down Southampton
Water. I looked towards the lights of the town. They didn't sparkle as they
used to and there were large areas of darkness. The darkest of these was
undoubtedly the black hole which must have swallowed up that mysterious
galaxy known as "the Ditches." To a little boy in leggings and cowboy
hat, armed with a cap gun, it was a place of high adventure.

Even holding Mum's hand, one always entered the main alleyway,
Canal Walk, with trepidation. It was Aladdin's fairytale Baghdad come

to life, a place of magic carpets and wonderful lamps where you might be ambushed by Ali Baba and the Forty Thieves or help Sinbad rescue the captive princesses calling on high from the Sultan's Palace. In reality, Canal Walk was the Kasbah of Southampton where Lascars from the White Star Line and chinks from the P & O rubbed shoulders with housewives from Bassett Close and Shirley Warren. The stalls that crowded the narrow alley were heaped with all the spoils of the Orient: Persian carpets, Moorish pots, Algerian brassware, Indian cotton, African ivory, Japanese toys, sunshades from China, gongs from Hong Kong and flesh, fish and fowl—both living and dead—from here, there and everywhere.

And there was music: Eastern music filtering through beaded curtains, Western music squeezing through open windows packed with laughing whores from Northam and St. Denys, displaying their wares. I also recall a slave girl.

Mum often used Canal Walk as a short cut between Dad's shop and Aunt Moo's but rarely stopped there, preferring the more sedate High Street with its cinemas and cafés. But one hot summer's day found us both struggling through the crowded alleyway, fair dying for a cup of tea. Throwing caution to the winds, Mum dragged me through the beaded curtains of what she took to be a teashop. Inside, the uncertain light from flickering oil lamps revealed a group of Turks squatting cross-legged, sucking on embroidered tubes stuck into curvaceous bottles. What a contrast it was to our favourite Tyrell & Green's with its big jazz band and bright-eyed waitresses in Art Deco uniforms. But Mum was not to be intimidated and ordered as usual.

"A pot of tea for one and one extra cup." Then, as an afterthought, "Oh, and six slices of bread and butter—milkloaf if you have it, please, Miss." The "miss" was a dusky lady with a red dot on her forehead. From her dress I took her to be a slave girl. She bowed and waved us towards a low divan. I sat down but Mum remained standing.

"Come on, Mum," I said, patting the space beside me. "Sit down."

"You don't sit on them, Ken," she replied disdainfully. "You recline. And we don't know *who's* been reclining on *that*, thank you." Here she gave the slave girl a withering look and exclaimed, "Catch me!" The Turks, thinking it might be an invitation, stopped sucking and looked at her appraisingly. I thought she was going to walk out but she was now dying for a cup of tea more than ever and settled for a cushion on the floor with her legs outstretched beneath the coffee table. I sat down beside her, oriental fashion.

"Manners, Ken!" she exclaimed. "You're showing all you've got." At the age of eight it wasn't much. Even so, I stuck my legs under the table too.

"Put up with it for now, Ken, and tomorrow we'll go to Tyrell's for a nice tea dance," she announced. The slave girl smiled, touched the red spot on her forehead and retired. Across the room a Turk sucked noisily on his big bottle. I guessed it was full of fizzy lemonade and was envious.

"Can I have a lemonade, please, Mum?" I asked, pointing. The Turk stopped sucking and exhaled a great cloud of smoke. I gawped in amazement.

"It's all that curry they eat, Ken. Burns up their insides, turns everything to smoke."

From somewhere out back came the sound of a tinny gramophone playing "The Vamp of Baghdad," a popular tune of the day:

> *She's the Vamp of Baghdad,*
> *Mind she don't bag your Dad.*

Mum and I perked up. Then the slave girl came back carrying a tea tray—on her head—whirling like a dervish. I gawped again. So did Mum. It didn't occur to us that this was her answer to Tyrell & Green's tea dance. With a smile of triumph and a provocative bump and grind, she set down the tray on our table without spilling a drop. There was scattered applause.

"Thank you, Miss," said Mum, surveying the tray, "but you've forgotten the milkloaf."

"No, my lady," said the slave girl proudly, "it is there." She pointed to six bowls of milk, in each of which bobbed a soggy piece of white bread and butter. Needless to say, Mum didn't leave her usual threepenny tip.

The Blitz blew all that away. The Ditches was near the docks. As for Canal Walk, well, that just disappeared. One building alone remained in the wasteland: a surgical goods shop, a pathetic memorial to all the ruptured and randy sailors for whom it had been a frequent port of call. A low mist surrounded it as, at the age of twenty-three and a half, I summoned up courage to buy my first condom. I was a dancer by then and very much in love with a baby ballerina. We were both virgins and eager to go to bed together—if it was safe. I was living in London but spending a few days at home nursing a sprained ankle. Twice I limped past the shop without entering, scared off by a lone figure on the horizon.

Could it be Mum on her way to Aunt Moo's or was it Dad on his way to work?—Russell & Sons was just around the corner in St. Mary's Street. On the third pass I slipped breathlessly inside like a fugitive from a Resistance film. A fat man with pudgy hands in a white overall stood priestlike in a veritable shrine of douche bags and trusses. This religious allusion was further enhanced by what seemed at first glance to be banks of candles on either side of him—till I realised with a chill up my spine that they were not candles but condoms stretched over what I guessed to be broom handles, ranging from a foot to eighteen inches in height. Some were white, some yellowish, some cream, some had teats and bumps which resembled dripping wax. A red light glowed in the background. A Catholic would have genuflected.

"Good afternoon, sir. What is your pleasure?"

His mouth was a slit in a bladder of lard. He resembled a condom himself.

"I'd like a con . . . a French letter, please."

"Just one, sir?" He raised a pale eyebrow. "Then you'll want a washable. I've Torpedo, Conger, Neptune and the Winston Churchill—that's the brown job over there."

I looked at something resembling a big cigar. The significance of the colour escaped me at the time but I blushed at the implication when it struck me later.

"You could have a Torpedo and score a hit with the ladies," he said, "or you might prefer to thrill them with a Conger."

Immediately an appropriate verse from "The Good Ship Venus"—an old Pangbournian sea-shanty—came to mind.

> The Captain had a daughter,
> Forever in the water,
> You could hear the squeals of the Conger eels
> Around her sexual quarter.

Seeing my indecision, he whipped out a condom from under the counter and said, "Try a Conger." Deftly unrolling it, he grasped each end with a grip of iron and stretched it out at arm's length as if it were a chest expander. I winced but it didn't snap. Then, laying it down on the counter like a skinned eel, he produced a shaker and dusted it from end to end with talc. "Wash it in lukewarm water with Lifebuoy toilet soap and it'll last a lifetime," he said, folding it up again, popping it into a plain envelope and handing it across the counter. "That'll be two and three, sir."

My night with the baby ballerina was a disaster. I'd been conned. Conger, my foot! I'd been sold a jellyfish.

The docks slipped astern as the tugs pulled us towards the Solent where I had spent many happy days before the war swimming in calm waters off our little ketch while porpoises surfaced all around. And what sport it was in a southerly breeze to sit astride the bowsprit, jutting out from between my legs like a giant willie, plunging beneath the salty billows and rising up dripping wet to give one in the eye to the sun.

Chimes sounded over the Tannoy, the flashing Needles light signalled adieu to the Solent and I went below to dinner. Sitting at a table for two with just a book for company, I congratulated myself on escaping once again. I was half way through a mediocre crab salad when someone I took to be the Entertainments Officer came up and introduced himself. Apologising for the interruption, he went on to say that there was to be a screening of *The Music Lovers* and how honoured they would be if I'd introduce it. Before I could say "no" there was a bottle of vintage champagne on the table. I promised to see what I could do. Sipping my Dom Perignon I tried to conjure up memories of the Tchaikovsky film.

Inevitably, my thoughts turned to the sea and the ship I joined on leaving Pangbourne in the summer of 1945. She was a merchant ship of 11,000 tons called the *Queen of Rataroa* bound for the South Seas. But first we had to cross the Atlantic. Here's an old chestnut that always caught out the new boys at Pangbourne:

Instructor: "What is the speed of a convoy?"

New boy: "Please, sir, I er . . . er . . ."

Instructor and Rest of Class (chanting in unison): "The speed of the slowest ship!"

We were that very ship. In a Force Eight gale our "full speed ahead" was equivalent to "slow astern." We were also light in ballast and consequently about as navigable as an empty bottle and nearly as leaky—the pumps were going full blast day and night. Our cargo, destined for the Land of Oz, consisted almost entirely of bedspreads and tea services. It seemed the Aussies were determined to have breakfast in bed, war or no war. In the event, many of them were disappointed, for what little of the china arrived intact was filched by the Sydney stevedores.

Back to the storm. We were five days out from Liverpool with five more to go before we reached the shelter of Panama. Keeping on your feet was almost impossible, especially on watch at night, slipping and sliding around the bridge in your own vomit, clamped in a pair of headphones attached to a very heavy "portable" radio-receiver with a mind of its own. Small wonder I found it difficult to receive messages from the convoy's flagship. These were navigational orders designed to keep us on a zig-zag course and thus outwit the U-boat packs we knew were shadowing us—and they were in code. And whoever dreamed up that code must have had a really sick sense of humour for in the circumstances they were the most nauseating words imaginable: chocolate cream, Turkish delight, mint cream, fudge sundae, marzipan coffee whirl, cherry malt liqueur. Every time a sickly message crackled into my headphones I threw up, and by the time I managed to stagger across the bridge to the Third Officer, all was confusion, including the words I was spewing up.

"Cherry fudge delight"—retch—"or was it chocolate mint cream?"—retch.

He flicked through his code book with growing alarm. "Cherry fudge delight isn't listed," he shouted above the howling gale. "Neither is chocolate mint cream. There's cherry malt liqueur, mint cream, Turkish delight, chocolate cream or fudge sundae, but no . . ."

"Stop," I said, throwing up again. "Keep your stinking chocolate. I've had it." And I threw the earphones at him and staggered below to my bunk.

My action was court-martial-able. I'd deserted my post. I could be shot, keel-hauled, made to walk the plank. I awoke at dawn with all these thoughts churning through my mind and was horrified. No point in returning to the bridge now. The watch had changed at 0400 anyway. Suddenly the Third Mate was in my doorway bracing his gangling frame against the ceaseless pitch and toss of the vessel. He had the face of a Norsk troll and often wore an impish smile—but not now.

"By rights I should report you to the Old Man," he said. "He'd probably hang you from the yard-arm as a deserter." My worst imaginings were confirmed. "But I wouldn't give him the satisfaction," he continued. "All the same, you put our lives at risk. You could have dropped us all in the shit. It's a miracle there wasn't a collision. You need a good lesson, my boy." I cowered between the bedclothes expecting a good flogging or even worse, but he went away.

By the time we reached Panama a few days later he seemed to have forgotten all about it. He was as placid as the waters on which we rode at anchor waiting our turn to go through the canal. He even ordered a spot of lifeboat drill when I mentioned that it would be nice to take a closer look at the harbour. In no time the boats had been swung out on their davits and were pulling away from the ship. All except mine, that is. The crew of stewards and stokers, huddled in the bows for some reason, were all at sixes and sevens. Standing at the tiller in the stern, smart and white in my brand new tropical kit, I piped out a command in the gruffest Pangbourne tones I could muster. The men smirked and pulled ineptly on their oars, catching crabs. I got drenched. There was laughter from above. The Third Mate was leaning over the rail enjoying my discomfort. The crew were drowning me. I was learning my lesson and as we bumped and banged along the ship's hull, I felt suitably chastised. But the ordeal wasn't over. The Third Mate suddenly barked out, "Lay on your oars." The men stopped rowing and I looked up for an explanation.

"Now!" he shouted. There was a brown woosh and I was hit full in the face by a waterfall of piss and shit and soaked from head to foot. I'd been manoeuvred underneath the main sewer pipe. The derisive laughter of the crew added to my humiliation but did not complete it. That came next when the Third Mate ordered me on the trip around the harbour as planned. When we were hauled on board an hour later the sun had baked me dry. I had turned into a shit artefact and smelt like one too. No matter how much I showered, I stank for days and days. I never deserted my post again, though I was sorely tempted.

It was the captain who drove me to it. Bligh of the *Bounty* was kindness itself in comparison to the Master of the *Queen of Rataroa*. Everything about him was red and raw. His face was red, his hair was red, his voice was raw, raw Scots, and raw was his temper, raw as the north wind. He was short and squat and would rush up to me with a bow-legged scamper as if he was about to toss the caber. Instead he'd bark out, "Rah, rah, re, rah!" whereupon I'd jump to attention, salute and say, "Aye, aye, sir! Could I trouble you to repeat that?"

Then he'd clench his great red fists till all the blood drained from them and rushed to his quivering, beetroot head, and in a voice that would have shamed a foghorn repeated the order.

"Aye, aye, sir!" I snapped, committing the phrase to memory, and doubled off to find the Third Mate who was one of the very few who understood the code.

"Rah, re, rah, rah," I gasped, saluting.

"That means lower the boats," he said with a smile.

"But we're going full speed ahead, that's madness," I said.

"Lucky for you I heard him myself. He said, 'Rah, rah, re, rah,' which means 'Get me a cup of tea.'" Another disaster had been averted. I breathed again and phoned the galley.

Once through the canal, we and the convoy parted company. They steamed off to a secret destination in the East with men and munitions while we set course across the Pacific for Sydney with our cargo of creature comforts which did not warrant an armed escort.

Alone, alone, all, all alone
Alone on a wide, wide sea,
And never a saint took pity on
My soul in agony.

The agony stemmed from the Old Man's fear that the entire Japanese fleet was out to get us. Everyone was on the lookout from the ship's cat to the Old Man himself—who spent most of his time looking out of his porthole at me. For eight hours a day I could feel his beady eyes boring into me, for I had to keep watch on the port side of the bridge right outside his cabin. Not a ripple on the water, not a cloud in the sky, no shelter from the sun, no walking up and down, no moving, no turning your back on the enemy, no activity of any kind but to search the horizon with your heavy-duty binoculars for a sign of the enemy. But where was the horizon? Everything beyond the bows of the vessel was lost in a white heat-haze, as if one were experiencing a blizzard in the centre of Neb-uchadnezzar's fiery furnace. And where was the enemy? Suddenly the world was celebrating VJ Day, but not on the *Queen of Rataroa*. The Old Man doubled the lookout, fearing attack from fanatical commanders in one-man submarines who would never surrender but hunt down lonely merchantmen and send them to the bottom of the sea.

It was about this time that the Old Man began to take an interest in my legs. My long and slender legs, which in middle age turned me into Humpty Dumpty, seemed more attractive in my youth when I had a body to match. And to a randy Scotsman three thousand miles from a skirt, and a grass skirt at that, they must have seemed unbelievably attractive. Dorothy Lamour had nothing on me when it came to legs, I promise you, and the sight of me standing there with my back to him in my short white shorts and my short white ankle socks and those gorgeous bronzed legs, shifting languorously from one foot to the other, day after day in the tropical heat, must have got too much for him. I began to hear heavy breathing coming from his porthole, increasing in speed and volume and terminating in a groan as from a ruptured bagpipe. I think he must have held me responsible for driving him to self-abuse because he started giving me fatigues when I was officially off duty. One of the worst was chipping away rust a foot above my head with a six-pound hammer in a confined bulkhead that was as hot as an oven. Then it was eight bells and up to the bridge on watch again—to watch nothing!

As in a hot and copper sky,
The bloody sun at noon

Right up above the mast did stand,
No bigger than the moon.

And the moon at midnight rose bigger than the sun, turning Portuguese men o' war into periscopes and sharks into submarines. And all
through the watch they shadowed us until the rushing of the hull through
the water was a whispered invitation to join them in oblivion. But I didn't
jump over the side. I didn't have the energy. Instead I planned to jump
ship when we got to Oz.

Our first stop was Brisbane. It was hot and dusty with wooden sidewalks
and saloons that put me in mind of a hick town in the Wild West. Westerns
left me cold. The prospect of a shoot-out between a local John Wayne
and Gary Cooper had little appeal. Neither did the drunks in Sydney,
stacked six deep in the gutter waiting for the bars to open. Melbourne
was my last chance. But it rained there all the time and reminded me of
Manchester—with koala bears. Oz was not for me. Feeling very depressed,
I bought two pairs of long white trousers, climbed the gangway of the
Queen of Rataroa for the last time, gritted my teeth and sailed for Blighty—
with a cargo of boomerangs, presumably meant for the Home Guard.

We crept across the Pacific as vulnerable as a slug on a mirror. And
every day the Old Man expected the Nips to put the boot in. Wedded to
my heavy-duty binoculars, I became the Ancient Mariner with the Albatross around my neck. I longed to tear it off and throw it into the sea—
but the Old Man still had his beady eye on me. And the white trousers
acted as a red rag to a bull. He guessed I'd tumbled to his little game and
his anger and frustration turned to revenge. I was sentenced to spend my
off-duty hours in the steamy confines of the Gyro Compass Locker Room,
mopping condensation from the walls. And as the dripping never ceased,
it was somewhat akin to the Chinese water torture. But that was nothing.
The chief instrument of torture was the Gyro Compass itself. The appearance of this infernal machine escapes me now, but the noise it produced still haunts me. It was in the nature of a howling scream, more
human than mechanical, as if the Old Man's repressed hysteria had found
a voice, a voice that I could never shake off by night or by day. It stayed
with me even when the machine was shut down and so did the Old Man's
beady eyes when I finally walked off the ship at Southampton. Like two
angry bees buzzing with malice they followed me wherever I went. I went
home.

My two big cabin trunks dominated the tiny sitting room of 309
Winchester Road, Southampton. There was barely room to give Mum
and Dad their presents—a tea set and a bedspread. While they thanked
me I started to unpack.

"Couldn't you 'ave left some of that on the ship?" asked Mum.

"I'm not going back to the ship."

"Not going back to the ship?" said Mum incredulously.

"I hate the sea."

"Hate the sea?" said Dad incredulously.

One end of the settee was stacked high with navy blue uniforms. I started piling tropical whites on the other.

"The captain of the *Queen Mary will* be disappointed," said Mum, who could never remember his name.

"What a pity about all those uniforms," said Dad as I sat down between the two piles of useless clothing.

"There's a thousand pounds odd there," said Mum. "All down the pan."

They stared at the clothes mournfully as if they belonged to a dead child. Then Mum started putting them away upstairs while Dad put the trunks in the shed. I stayed on the settee, staring at the empty fireplace with the bees buzzing around my head. I stayed there day after day. Apart from bed and ablutions I never left the settee. I had breakfast, lunch, tea and supper on the settee, and elevenses as well. Sometimes I sat bolt upright, sometimes I lay down.

Nothing would budge me. Not even Olive, the maid, with her faulty Hoover, which drove the bees to a frenzy. Not even Mum, hoovering behind Olive half an hour later because "she wasn't thorough," stirring the bees up again. Neither would the constant whine of her nagging nor the eternal hum of the radio. Nothing would move me. For weeks I was as still as a beehive until one sunny morning something began to penetrate my mind and cause it to stir. I became conscious of an incredible kind of beauty, the existence of which I had never dreamed. Even the bees stopped to listen and became as entranced as I. Mum too fell silent and switched off the Hoover. I wished the music would never end. When it did I was weeping. The announcer gave particulars of the recording. I got up. Mum's mouth fell open. I pumped up the tyres of my old Hercules, cycled to the nearest record shop and bought Tchaikovsky's Piano Concerto in B Flat Minor played by Solomon and the Hallé Orchestra. From that moment on I was imbued with magical powers. Many years later they enabled me to pay tribute to the composer in *The Music Lovers*.

As I lay tucked up in a deckchair on the heaving QE_2 sipping bouillon, I wondered if that was the sort of anecdote the Entertainments Officer had in mind for my introductory chat about the movie. I suspected not. Perhaps the story of Glenda Jackson lying naked on the floor of a studio railway carriage being rocked on rubber tyres by six lusty prop men as the cameraman swung inches above her body in a breeches buoy would cause

less offence. On the other hand, it did have a rather suggestive dénoue-
ment.

Perhaps the audience would like to learn how it came to be made.
How Harry Saltzman of *James Bond* fame called me into his office and
said how much he admired my television biogs and dreamed of producing
one as a feature film. Knowing my feature credits began and ended with
French Dressing, he suggested I cut my teeth on something commercial.
I fell for it and made *Billion Dollar Brain* for him. Nine months later I
reminded him of his promise regarding Tchaikovsky.

"We're too late," he said, almost gloating, "Dmitri Tiomkin's beaten
us to it. He's even started writing the music." He had indeed, and how
awful Tchaikovsky's delectable *Serenade for Strings* sounded re-scored for
brass and percussion. About the only thing our films had in common was
the humble silver birch. Tiomkin's version with its brash Hollywood score
and Sovexport scenario was as phoney as an official tour of the Tchaikovsky
Museum at Klin.

I once visited this Soviet shrine with an Intourist guide as I was curious

Ken Russell rehearsing Karl Malden and Michael Caine in
Billion Dollar Brain.

to see the house in which Peter Ilyich spent the last unhappy years of his life. My guide, who knew all the Metropolitan bus routes of London and had studied Charles Dickens, the greatest modern authority on the London scene, in anticipation of a visit one day, talked in hushed tones as we viewed the relics. We saw Tchaikovsky's samovar, his antimacassars and pictures of his mum and dad. We heard about his happy marriage and the medals he'd won but never as much as a breath of scandal which might tarnish such a highly polished ikon of the people. In this regard the USSR is far behind the West. There were no pictures of pretty male bottoms to corrupt the young pioneers. How different to the Percy Grainger Museum in Melbourne, I thought, with its drawers of canes and whips.

"When are we going to see a picture of Prince Alexei?" I asked with a certain amount of irritation, as we were shown yet another daguerreotype of his Great Aunt Floradova. My guide stared blankly through his regulation spectacles.

"Who?"

"Prince Alexei, Tchaikovsky's boy friend."

"I know Sandy Wilson's *Boy Friend*. I never heard of this Prince Alexei."

"So you've never heard of the scandal surrounding Tchaikovsky's death?"

He shrugged indifferently. "How can scandal help us appreciate the work of a great artist?"

"*The Music Lovers* turned a lot of people onto Tchaikovsky," I replied. "If I hadn't told United Artists that it was a story about a homosexual who fell in love with a nymphomaniac it might never have been financed."

"And one of our greatest composers would still be resting peacefully in his grave," he said.

"One of your greatest composers quite admired it," I replied.

"Which composer?"

"Shostakovich. He saw it in England after the first performance of his Fourth Symphony. The one you banned for thirty years."

The guide's face darkened. Shostakovich, who had been accused by Stalin of decadent Western tendencies, was only just emerging from a cloud of Soviet disapproval. That he had seen and appreciated a decadent Western movie posed my guide an ideological problem. He dodged it.

"You hate Tchaikovsky," he spat back.

"No, I love him, but my love isn't blind."

"You telescope events and characters," he continued. "You turn his life into a frenzied carnival, all highs and lows, no moments of reflection or tranquillity."

"There's as much tranquillity in my film on Tchaikovsky as there is in his music," I said.

"How can you hope to do justice to a man's life in two hours?" he said dismissively.

"Tchaikovsky condensed his whole life into the *Symphonie Pathétique*, he said so himself, and that runs for less than an hour."

"That's a work of art. Your film is commercial bombast," he said, "devoid of fact."

"You only use the facts that suit you," I said, beginning to get angry.

"Every note of his music is a fact!" he replied heatedly.

"And every bar of his music is open to a different interpretation," I persisted.

"You have denigrated a great Russian hero," he shouted.

"Great heroes are the stuff of myth and legend, not facts. Facts are for computers. I'm a myth-maker," I shouted back. We both shut up simultaneously. People were staring. And anyway, what was the use? He would never change his blinkered position of restraint and I would never abandon my passionate flights of imagination.

And imagination is what you need to see Peter Tchaikovsky played by Dr. Kildare. But that was not my original thought. With the recent success of *Women in Love* in mind, it was only natural that I should try to reassemble some of the same team for my next movie. Glenda agreed right away to play Tchaikovsky's nympho wife, and Alan Bates said he was keen to tackle the role of the homosexual composer, a decision he came to reverse at the last moment. His reason, I believe, was that he thought it might not be good for his image to play two sexually deviant parts in rapid succession. With Moscow being built on the back lot at Bray Studios, within sight of Her Majesty's bedroom window at Windsor Castle, and the cast and crew all set to go, we were suddenly in deep trouble. Naturally U.A. wanted a star, but no one of stature was keen to tackle the role, which was far from sympathetic—until Richard Chamberlain came along. When his name was originally put forward I nearly had a heart attack. I'd only seen him as the bland TV doctor, and until someone showed me a tele-recording of Henry James's *Portrait of a Lady*, I had no idea he could act. Then I knew we had a real contender. When I learned at our first meeting that he could strum through the Grieg Piano Concerto, I knew we had found our man. And with Glenda playing our woman, we had the makings of a great team.

They were both fantasists, Tchaikovsky and Nina Milyukova, whose dreams of a happy marriage turned into a nightmare culminating in the composer's virtual suicide and Nina's death in a lunatic asylum. It was customary in such institutions for the inmates to have their heads shaved,

Richard Chamberlain and Glenda Jackson in *The Music Lovers*.

so as the time approached to shoot the sequence, I talked the situation over with Glenda, who had a lovely head of hair at the time and was all geared up to start work on John Schlesinger's *Sunday, Bloody Sunday* directly we finished. Apparently she had the star role—that of a glamorous woman torn between two men. Hoping against hope, I asked Glenda if the character was bald. She shook her head, her blond ringlets dancing attractively around her shoulders. For a moment I wondered if Schlesinger would consider playing the character as a baldy but thought it best not to ask. Glenda suggested a bald cap. Doubting that it would work, I never-theless agreed to give it a try. As I suspected, the result was grotesque, for no matter how tightly her hair was curled and no matter how hard we pulled the cap down, she still looked hydrocephalic. We both looked at Glenda's reflection in the mirror and laughed. So off it came, both the bald cap and the hair beneath. And how poor Schlesinger hit the roof when, surprise, surprise, Glenda turned up for her first day's rehearsal looking like a shorn lamb. But his loss was our gain, for Glenda gave a perfectly heartrending performance as the pathetic creature who surely contributed to the title of Tchaikovsky's last symphony—the *Pathétique*.

Richard Chamberlain *is* Tchaikovsky in *The Music Lovers*.

It just wouldn't have been the same in a bald cap—sorry, John; the wig you made her wear wasn't really *that* bad—honest. (Won't you ever forgive me?)

Richard Chamberlain was equally dedicated. When not at work on the set, he remained in his dressing room, and, with the aid of a dummy keyboard and a cassette player, rehearsed Tchaikovsky's First Piano Concerto over and over, hour after hour, day after day. For "strumming through the Grieg" is one thing—being note perfect in one of the most taxing concertos ever written is something else. And I defy anyone, as Richard hammers away in the dazzling finale, to say that he is not perfectly in synch with the music. Actually he's miming to a performance by the great Spanish virtuoso Rafael Orozco, and I doubt if even he could fault the fingering. Grieg Concerto, my foot! I bet Richard had trouble getting through "Chopsticks" when he came to that first interview. Some actors will kill for a part they really want, others will lie, all exaggerate. One actor who promised me he could swim nearly drowned when I had him thrown off a boat in the middle of a lake when he broke the news that he was a non-swimmer. But since it was a drowning scene we were shooting at the time, it didn't really matter. Incidents such as this have earned me the reputation of not being an actor's director. I read an interview Richard gave to a magazine not long ago in which he perpetuated this myth. But if I don't kiss an actor's ass before and after each take, it's because I have other ways of making them talk—as Richard went on to admit in his interview:

". . . But Russell does create a fantastic atmosphere on the set as far as I'm concerned. We'd arrive with all our preconceived ideas as to how the scene should go and run through it a couple of times with Ken moving us about like furniture but making no comment on our interpretations. Instead he'd suddenly shout 'That chair is *ridiculous!*' and the emphasis would suddenly be transferred to an inanimate object that had nothing to do with the acting whatsoever. Then seventy people would be running around in a blind panic because of the offensive chair. And when the confusion was at its height, he'd say 'Right, forget the bloody chair, roll camera, ACTION!'"

Richard got it right. When a chair is suddenly more important than an actor being preened and crimped by the make-up and hair people before every take, then he is no longer the centre of attention and stops acting like a movie star. Suddenly it's all happening, and he's carried along by that sudden burst of collective energy that propels him into a more spontaneous interpretation of the scene. The catalyst is not always a chair. It could be an article of clothing or a faulty lamp—almost anything can be used to generate the energy that has been dissipated during the slow buildup to the take. Actually it's not always as long as all that, but to the director striving to keep up to schedule it invariably seems an age when time in a studio rushes by faster than anywhere else in the world. What Richard forgot to mention was that his interpretation of Tchaikovsky was really mine. It was all done at our introductory meeting, when I hosed away his preconceptions with a concentrated brain-washing based on massive research on the man, and a lifetime's passion for his music. And for once the publicity machine got it right . . . "Richard Chamberlain *is* Tchaikovsky."

"Beg pardon, Mr. Russell . . ." I stopped brooding and looked up from my bowl of cold bouillon. It was the Entertainments Officer. "Sorry to trouble you, but I've bad news . . . When the projectionist told me the film was the one in which Glenda Jackson got a good groping, I naturally thought of *The Music Lovers*," he said, with a burst of laughter, "but of course she gets a good groping in all your films, doesn't she, sir?" I did not laugh. He sobered up. "It's *Women in Love,* of course, Mr. Russell."

I nodded non-committally and he went away hoping I wasn't offended. Actually, I was glad because, apart from a few post-production problems, the Tchaikovsky film had gone remarkably smoothly and there was little to talk about. I cast my mind back to the days of *Women in Love.* I suppose

Gudrun (Glenda Jackson) seductively gestures at the cattle
in *Women in Love*.

United Artists initially considered me for the project because they saw it
as a highbrow art movie and were mindful of my work on *Monitor*. And
when they asked me if I'd be interested in looking at a script based on
the Lawrence epic, I naturally said "yes," thinking they meant Lawrence
of Arabia. So imagine my surprise when I discovered there was another
Lawrence besides T.E., who in his way, was equally famous. But judging
by the script they sent me, D.H. seemed overrated, and although the
action was set in a northern mining town, the locales seemed closer to
California than Derbyshire. Reluctantly, I passed. U.A. suggested I read
the book. It was a revelation and full of good things, including Gudrun
hypnotising a herd of cattle and, incredibly, the nude wrestling scene. I
saw the possibilities immediately and communicated my enthusiasm to
U.A., who suggested I meet the author of the screenplay. I did.

"I believe in this project very much," he told me. "And just like
Lawrence, we're gonna probe deeper into sex than ever before." Larry
Kramer, now famous for his championship of gay rights and campaign
for AIDS victims, was virtually unknown when we first met. The success
of his play *The Normal Heart* was more than a decade away. To my
knowledge he had only two screenplays to his credit—*Here We Go Round*

the Mulberry Bush, which hadn't made a big impact, and *Women in Love,* presently under discussion.

I agreed to work with Kramer because, although we were as different as Maryland chicken and Borrowdale lamb, we shared a passion for *Women in Love.* Larry had fought for the rights, which had proved to be an extremely complex procedure, for several years, and for me it was a once-in-a-lifetime chance to bring to the screen a unique classic. I saw it as an extension of my work for *Monitor.* The characters in *French Dressing* and *Billion Dollar Brain* were as thin as the celluloid on which they were printed, whereas Lawrence's characters were based on real people. For the first time in my short feature film career, I felt comfortable with the material I had to work on. I praised a couple of fine scenes of Kramer's own invention, but together we agreed that the screenplay should more closely reflect Lawrence's original work. After a month or so Kramer's revised script went off to the printers and we got down to the casting.

Alan Bates was keen to play the role of Birkin—based on Lawrence himself—and actually grew a beard to convince us of his resemblance to the author. To my mind the likeness ended with the whiskers, but Alan was a fine actor and Larry's first choice. United Artists concurred and also went along with my plea for Oliver Reed as Gerald, a wealthy mine owner.

Choosing the females was more problematic, and we sat through many casting sessions without finding either of the "Women" of the title. Some of those we interviewed sprawled in chairs with mini-skirts riding high, flashing their physical credentials, while others sat prim and proper and displayed only their acting diplomas. It seemed that we would never get lucky until I saw a screen test of Jennie Linden. It was shot on grainy black and white 16-mm film on a drizzly day on a park bench, but her performance fairly glowed. The part the unknown was testing for was that of a princess in *The Lion in Winter* starring Peter O'Toole, who was playing the scene with her. Playing is right. In contrast to Miss Linden's period costume and dedicated performance, O'Toole was casually dressed and clowning about. But nothing seemed to faze her, and it was she who stole the scene. When I learned that she failed to get the part I simply couldn't believe it until I heard a rumour that Katharine Hepburn, who was playing the Queen, saw the test and gave the thumbs-down—too much competition, perhaps. But we all thought that Jennie would make the perfect Ursula and lost no time in signing her up.

That left Gudrun. When Glenda Jackson came in at the end of a long casting session, I hardly noticed her face, because I couldn't take my eyes off her legs, which resembled a pair of walking road maps. I'd seen her in the *Marat/Sade* movie and been hugely impressed, but in that she'd

(Top) Jennie Linden as Ursula and Alan Bates as Birkin
share a moment of happiness, while *(Above)* Oliver Reed as
Gerald and Glenda Jackson as Gudrun share a more
troubled moment in *Women in Love*.

worn a long dress and I only had eyes for her face. Sometimes it seemed downright plain and at others incredibly beautiful, and in that ambivalence lay the secret of her allure. Only her varicose veins stood between her and stardom—so out they came. It only remained to dye her mousey hair a subtle shade of red and give her a Louise Brooks haircut and she was ready to go before the cameras, which, after two months of frenzied pre-production, were ready to roll.

I'm glad they did, for it's the film of mine that people regard most highly. Oddly enough I'm not of the same opinion, but why pick my own work to pieces when there are plenty of others around to do it for me?

Apart from making my reputation as a feature film director, I'm very grateful for another benefit that came my way as a result of the movie. I'm referring to my long association with Glenda Jackson—which because of a last-minute hiccup nearly didn't happen. A week prior to the start of principal photography our insurance doctor dropped a bombshell. Glenda was pregnant. We had no alternative but to think seriously of recasting. In addition to a nude bathing scene there were also a few nude wrestling scenes beneath the sheets, and Gudrun was supposed to be a nubile young woman—not an expectant mother.

U.A., when they heard the news, were aghast, but I was determined to have Glenda at any cost and set about convincing them that her condition would not be a problem. Eventually they decided to take a gamble and we started on schedule as planned. And as everyone knows who saw the movie, we got away with it. Only once was our secret revealed, and that was during the last week of shooting in Zermatt, when Glenda rolled off a sledge and her voluminous cape parted to expose an enormous bulge under a tight red sweater. But it was only on the screen for a second, and as there was a lot of activity by the rest of the group in the picture, no one took it in. Yes, the loose-fitting clothes of the period helped us a lot, as did the fact that Glenda played an artist and carried a large portfolio of drawings around in front of her. It was a demanding role, both mentally and physically, and she certainly earned that Oscar for Best Actress of 1970. I may have been nominated myself for Best Director—I don't remember. In my opinion Oliver Reed also should have received an Oscar—for daring to act opposite Glenda, who has eaten lesser men alive.

My association with Oliver goes back to the mid-Sixties and the time I was preparing The Debussy Film for the BBC. I first saw him on Juke Box Jury, a TV pop show in which the jurors passed sentences on the Top Twenty. Two things in particular struck me about the young Mr. Reed. Firstly, he was the life and soul of the party and, secondly, he bore an extraordinary resemblance to the young Claude Debussy. I rang his agent and Oliver came to see me in my office at the Lime Grove Studios, a room I shared with three other *Monitor* directors. He did his best to lounge in an upright chair and said, "I hear you are considering me for Debussy." I nodded. He fixed me with his hooded eyes, looking moody, mean and magnificent. "What about this?" he asked, sticking out his chin. I looked. It was freshly scarred. "Someone with a broken bottle thought I looked too pretty," he volunteered.

"Well, thanks for coming in," I said.

He nodded and got up looking tight-lipped. "That's what they all say when they see the scar," he said bitterly.

"What scar?" I said.

Oliver was good as Debussy, capturing the brooding sensuality and threatening calm that is so characteristic of the man and his music.

For all his macho image, Oliver is a sensitive artist who approaches his craft intuitively, somewhat in the manner of Glenda Jackson. And if Oliver hasn't quite Glenda's range, he is fully aware of it. From the moment in my next biopic when Oliver, playing the Victorian poet, Dante Gabriel Rossetti (to whom he *also* bears an extraordinary resemblance), bounced into the room looking like Debussy in a top hat, I was aware of it too. We quickly evolved a shorthand in our working relationship.

"Moody One, Moody Two or Moody Three?" he would ask before we shot each scene and, depending on the intensity of the smouldering meanness required, I would call the appropriate number and Oliver and the camera, which loves him dearly, would do the rest. And to hell with motivation. Anyway, Oliver is a physical actor and spends more time wrestling naked than in polite conversation at the dinner table. Which brings us to *Women in Love* where he was called upon to do both and acquitted himself with credit. But there were difficulties.

I was eating a quiet candlelit spaghetti bolognese with Shirley in our kitchen one winter's evening in early '67 when there came a thundering on the front door. We looked at each other and sighed. Being disturbed at dinner always gave us the horrors. I blew out the candles. Perhaps they'd go away.

"I know you're in there, Jesus," bellowed a familiar voice. "I saw your pouffy candles through your pouffy lace curtains."

"Sit tight," I said as Shirley went to get up. "I smell trouble."

Oliver's next bellow came through the letterbox. "If you don't open up I'll kick your pouffy purple front door down." The door was newly painted.

"Better let him in. I'll hide the spaghetti," I said, not wanting it over my head. I was relighting the candles when he walked into the room and fixed me with a mean stare.

Ken talks to Jane Lumb during shooting of *The Debussy Film*.

"Draughty old places, these Victorian houses," I said as nonchalantly as I could. "Fancy a drink?" He ignored the offer. This was ominous, indeed.

"She says the wrestling scene is different in the book, Jesus." I looked sharply at my wife, fearing some sort of betrayal, but she looked even more innocent than usual. At that moment an attractive girl stepped from behind Oliver's back into the candlelight. She wore glasses and an evening dress. Oliver was in a dinner jacket. Shirley waved them to the settee.

"Won't you sit down?"

"She's read the book," said Oliver, pulling out a chair tucked beneath the dining table. It had a plate of spaghetti on it. He pulled out another. It too had a plate of spaghetti on it. Oliver ignored the congealing food and remained standing next to the girl. Shirley and I sat down on the settee with our glasses of Valpolicella, trying to appear relaxed.

"In the script," said Oliver, "you've got the two naked men wrestling in the pouffy moonlight on a river bank."

"Then they fall into the river and continue wrestling in the water," I said.

"All in slow motion like a pouffy commercial," he added disparagingly.

"Well, if Birkin and Gerald are going to strip off and wrestle nude at all then it's more plausible if they do it in a natural setting than in Gerald's stately home amongst suits of armour," I said.

"But that's how it is in the book."

"It's one thing to get away with it in a book and quite another to bring it off on the screen," I said.

"You mean it's more of a challenge," he said.

"It's bloody impossible."

"Is it?" he asked, looking around the room. ". . . And she tells me they're both in evening clothes enjoying a drink by the light of a log fire. Make mine a large brandy."

He turned up the gas logs full blast and dragged two chairs up to the hearth while I poured him a drink. Shirley was eyeing the Staffordshire china displayed here and there and had turned white. She too had read the book and was fearing the worst. So was I. Oliver and I settled down with our glasses on either side of the fire.

"Sometimes I have an overwhelming desire to hit something," he said, quoting the script.

"Meaning me," I replied, following his lead.

"Not necessarily," he said, smiling. "Have you ever tried ju-jitsu?"

"No, and I have no desire to," I said.

"Oh, you'd like it . . ." he said, crossing to the door and locking it.

"Unlock the door, please. The servants will be up to clear away directly."

He took the key out of the lock, and waved it tauntingly. ". . . Yes, you'll like it," he repeated, "once you enter into the spirit of it."

"I'm not interested," I said, going to take the key from his extended fingers, "the servants . . ."

Shirley watched with gritted teeth as I sailed through the air close to a priceless statuette of the young Mozart. I landed on the pine floor near the gas stove. Shirley breathed again.

"You see how easy it is?" said Oliver.

I got up. The key was still in his hand. A tap sounded at the door followed by a muffled voice.

"May I clear away, please, sir?"

"Will you unlock the door or shall I?" No response. I walked towards him and as I reached for the key, ducked and swerved. I wasn't going to be caught a second time . . . Shirley's eyes widened in horror. My right hand knocked the young Mozart off the pianola as I flew through the air for a second time. Mozart landed safely in the dog's basket. Shirley relaxed. I hit the pine floor near the gas fire. My shoulder hurt.

"I see what you mean," I managed to say, still in character. But I couldn't keep it up. I winced. "I think this has the makings of a very good scene," I said, rubbing my shoulder. Shirley took the key from Oliver and opened the door.

Oliver smiled, came over and helped me up. "You'll live to thank me for it, Jesus," he said.

"Shall I come back, sir?" said our old housekeeper, May, looking at the cold spaghetti.

"Give it to the dog, May," said Oliver affably. "I'm taking them out to the White Elephant to celebrate." Without a word Shirley and I went to get our coats. Everything is a game to Oliver and must be played by two simple rules. The game must be played in deadly earnest and it must be played through to the end, whatever the outcome. Any infringement of the rules incurs not only Oliver's displeasure but, what is worse, his contempt. That's why I had no alternative in the kitchen but to act out the scene. I had to work with the man for the next three months and without his respect there would have been no performance. It's all part of the business of directing. But I hope I haven't given the impression that Oliver is a bully. In most contests he will put himself at a disadvantage if he thinks the odds merit it.

Such an occasion arose when I drove down to his country seat one day to discuss a script he had written on the killing of St. Thomas à Becket called *The King's Man*. As usual with Oliver, things did not go as expected.

When he threw open his medieval front door dressed as D'Artagnan from *The Three Musketeers* and ushered me into the hall with a flourish of his plumed hat and a "Welcome, Your Eminence," I had grave forebodings. Expecting to be cast as Thomas à Becket, it seemed that Oliver had me down for Cardinal Richelieu. And as we drank brandy before a roaring log fire (real, not gas) I knew I was going to be put to the test once again. Oliver was just about to star in *The Four Musketeers* and pranced around the room demonstrating his prowess with a rapier. He's warming up for a duel with his old arch enemy, Cardinal Richelieu, I thought to myself. It was time to talk about *The King's Man*. I did so and regretted it.

"I'd clean forgotten," said Olly, striking his dripping forehead with a gloved fist. "Look what I found in a junk shop the other day." And tossing his rapier to one side, he bounded over to the chimneypiece and lifted down a massive broadsword. "I'm sure it's authentic," he enthused. "The man in the shop swore it was a thousand years old."

"It's certainly very rusty," I replied.

"Blood," he said. "Dried blood. A sword like this killed Becket. Here, feel the weight of it." He tossed it to me. I nearly dropped it. "Becket was quite a swordsman, priest or no priest," enthused Olly. "He must have put up one hell of a fight before they killed him." I had a funny feeling I had just been recast. "Imagine you are standing on the altar steps, Jesus, and I'm coming for you, coming to spill your guts and rub your sanctimonious nose in them. It's you or me, trying to split each other in two."

"Where's yours?" I said as calmly as I could.

"My what? My sword? You don't think I've got two of those big bastards, do you? I'll make do with the rapier."

"I rather see Becket defending himself with a crozier," I faltered. "I suppose you wouldn't have a . . ."

"Bullshit, Jesus." His eyes narrowed. "Now, get up on the altar steps." He nodded at a wooden chest behind me.

He was deadly serious. I obeyed, dragging the sword behind me. He walked to the corner of the room and swished his rapier through the air, laughing wildly. With a sigh I heaved the five-foot broadsword above my head and stood there shaking—partly through fear and partly with the sheer physical effort.

"Prepare to meet thy maker, heretic," he shouted, throwing off his tunic. I blinked away a drop of sweat from my eye and braced myself.

"Haayaee!" screamed Oliver launching himself towards me like an avenging demon. I gripped the handle of the sword, waited till he was four paces away and brought it down with all my might. For an eternity nothing seemed to happen. Oliver and his glittering blade were flashing towards me with lightning speed. Then he came into my sights. The giant weapon swung towards him as unnervingly as the lethal blade in *The Pit and the Pendulum*—with the same result. It sliced clean through the victim's shirt. Oliver stopped on a sixpence, dropping his rapier in amazement. The thin red line extending from his chest to his navel was rapidly widening as the blood seeped out. We both watched in silence as his white shirt turned crimson. I waited breathlessly to see what he would do. With a sort of choking laugh he pulled the shirt off and wiped his chest with it until the bleeding all but ceased. The wound was superficial, but another quarter of an inch and . . .

Ripping the shirt in two, he went over to the chimneypiece and lifted a glass dome off a display of stuffed parrots. Soon the birds were roasting on the fire and the bloody relic was safely under glass. He handed me the other half of the shirt and said, a little bashfully, "Now we're blood brothers." I dropped my gaze, looked at the shirt and my bloody hands and nodded, wondering what on earth D. H. Lawrence would have made of it all.

Which brings us back to *Women in Love* and the saga of the nude wrestling match, which was by no means over. Having instigated the script change, Oliver became markedly less enthusiastic about the forthcoming scene as the shooting of the film progressed. So did Alan Bates. At first he had welcomed the idea of reverting to Lawrence and had taken up judo quite seriously, but as the day scheduled for the big match approached, he developed a cold. At the same time Oliver hurt his foot and they both had doctor's certificates to prove it. By now the producers had realised the great potential of the scene and were dead scared it might not happen. Two days before the big fight, with Alan blowing his nose every five minutes and Oliver hobbling around like Joseph Goebbels, they were ready to throw in the towel. I ignored these ailments and just went on directing as if both actors were fighting fit, because I noticed that during "takes" Oliver managed not to limp at all and Alan managed not to sniff, though they more than made up for it directly I said "Cut."

Eventually the call sheet for the next day's filming was issued with the wrestling scene down to be shot as scheduled. At the end of the day both men waved their medical certificates threateningly and went away together, sniffing and limping. This in itself was ominous as they were not the best of friends. The producers and I then retired to a corner and made an alternative schedule, top secret, and prayed they would come to their senses. No one could figure out what was wrong. They had both appeared nude individually during the filming, so what was the big deal about appearing together? Naturally we missed the obvious point.

On the way back to the hotel I dropped off at my local hostelry for some light refreshment. I asked for whelks and learned that Mr. Reed had just polished off the last order. At the far end of the bar Oliver raised his glass. I waved goodbye and made for the door. I got into the Toyota Estate—I'd given my driver the evening off—and started the engine. The car was on the move when Oliver dived onto the bonnet and grabbed the windscreen wipers. I drove out of the car park and up the road, my vision restricted by Oliver's distorted face pressed hard against the glass. When we were doing around sixty he bellowed, "Since when do you refuse to take a drink with me?"

"Since you ate up all the whelks," I shouted back.

"You want whelks, I'll give you whelks," he roared. "Turn back!"

I did so at the next roundabout and put my foot down, hoping the Japanese knew how to make windscreen wipers. Back at the pub I pulled up and Oliver slid off the bonnet. The car park adjoined a gravel beach running down to the waters of a muddy estuary. Deliberately and un-flinchingly, Oliver marched, without even the hint of a limp, into the murky sea, fully clothed. As he disappeared beneath the rippling surface I got out of the car. A quarter of a minute went by, then two fists shot out of the water, dripping mud. Then he started walking ashore and his head and shoulders appeared, draped in seaweed, resembling the Creature

Alan Bates (left) and Oliver Reed in the nude wrestling scene from *Women in Love*.

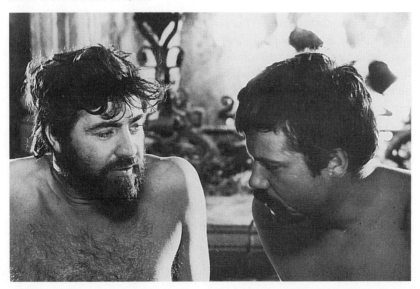

from the Black Lagoon. His fists passed inches from my nose and un-clasped, releasing onto the white bonnet of the Toyota a stream of mud and two shellfish. They weren't whelks but I thought it best not to say so.

"Thank you," I said, picking them up.

"What'll you have?" he asked.

"Half a shandy," I replied, knowing he'd spike it with a double vodka when I wasn't looking.

Back in the bar Oliver caused a few raised eyebrows which were quickly lowered when he tightened his own. I prized open the gritty shellfish and choked them down one by one. It was worse than swallowing two globs of phlegm soaked in sump oil. Oliver noted my discomfort with glowing satisfaction. A few minutes later when Oliver was steaming nicely and deep in his cups I took the opportunity of having a quiet word with his long time stand-in and minder, Reg Prince. From him I learned the truth and kicked myself for being so blind. Fortunately Alan had promised to join Olly later for a drink, so between us we quietly devised a plan which relied on Reg getting the boys to visit the loo for a pee simultaneously. Wishing him luck, I slipped away unnoticed, Oliver having lost interest in our little escapade.

Miraculously, I got back to the hotel without incident, hit the sack and passed out, a victim, yet again, of Oliver's drink-spiking. How he does it I'll never know, unless he bribes the barman. Perhaps Reg was responsible. He'd do anything for Olly, even lay down and die for him. At times it's come pretty close. The last I heard of him he was lying crippled in a hospital bed—himself a victim of his master's high spirits.

The next morning found me on the set at 8:30, bleary-eyed and hung over, waiting for the boys to show. The crew were taking bets. The first assistant whispered that the other actors were all made up and ready for the alternative scene and asked if we should go for it. Reluctantly I was about to give the OK when Reg rushed in breathless with a big grin on his face, closely followed by Oliver and Alan in dressing gowns. With great bravado they threw them off. Tumultuous applause followed as forty pairs of eyes registered the fact that their dongles were *exactly* the same length. Reg and I exchanged winks. That trip to the loo had paid off. Even so, Oliver cheated a bit by disappearing behind a screen before each take for a quick J. Arthur.

Yes, those were the anecdotes I'd trot out for my little chat with the audience prior to the screening. In the event, it was cancelled due to high seas. On top of that, we had a blizzard so the Statue of Liberty finally loomed up through the swirling snow like a spectre of Columbia Pictures' old trademark—an appropriate welcome for all voyagers to the American Dream. Immigration formalities continued long after we had docked in New York at 52nd Street and I was hardly surprised to find no sign of a welcoming committee when I finally got through customs. The baggage hall was beginning to resemble a mausoleum when I asked a policeman where I could find a cab.

Crack! An explosion sounded behind my ear. I thought I'd been shot at. The policeman reached for his gun. A cascade of streamers fell over my face. I spun round in surprise. It was my young American friend.

5 Air Force Blues

The path that led to that happy meeting with my young American friend was long and circuitous and started way back in the late Forties, several years before she was born.

That Tchaikovsky piano concerto which got me out of the armchair and into the record shop was probably the first step of the journey. The second was undoubtedly when Mum booted me out of the house and into the RAF. It was either that or "Go into your father's business." Not being a foot fetishist at the time, I chose to join the Brylcreem Boys, as the Royal Air Force was known at the time.

My service life began in a basic training camp in the Midlands which made the average German Stalag seem like a holiday camp. It was winter and the endless rows of rotting wooden huts were almost afloat on a sea of mud. Our feet were never dry and our billets were never warm, while undernourished stoves, concrete floors, iron beds, threadbare blankets and damp mattresses guaranteed sleepless nights. There was a Mess Hall, aptly named, where they ladled out pig swill, and wash-houses awash with diarrhoea that would have disgraced a cattle stall. I began to wonder who'd won the war. And whenever I pass through the Midlands today I still wonder—it's as grotty as ever.

Yelled at, screamed at, bullied and brutalised—it was Pangbourne turned upside down. Here I was being victimised again, for talking posh and being too good at squarebashing.

"What d'you think you are, Russell, a fucking ballet dancer?"

At the time I didn't know what a fucking ballet dancer looked like but I guessed it was not a pretty sight. I guessed wrong.

After the passing-out parade, at which I was careful to debase my accent ("Free—foive—ite—noine—foive—foive, I.C.2, Aitch—Kai— Aye Russell, sur!"—no cheers), we queued up in a vast aircraft hangar to be allocated a "trade." Six flight sergeants sat at six folding tables and as the line moved forward we peeled off one by one to be interviewed.

Two tables suddenly became vacant at once. I started marching towards the table on the left but when I was almost there veered to the right and came to attention in front of the other one. That decision probably changed the course of my life. A friendly-looking flight sergeant with a handlebar moustache looked up from his papers, gave me a welcoming smile and said, "Stand easy." I relaxed.

"And how would you like to serve your sentence, laddie?" he asked.

"Sentence?"

"Yes. That's how most conscripts see their National Service."

"I volunteered."

He looked at me incredulously. "Volunteered? You must be off your chump."

"That's how I got out of the Merchant Navy," I said brightly, "though I'm all right now."

He looked a little concerned. "Did you tell that to the Medical Officer?"

"I'm fine, really. I just didn't get on with the Captain," I said, reassuringly. "The family doctor kindly certified me mentally unfit for service at sea."

He frowned and a stern note crept into his voice. "That won't wash here, laddie," he said. "You might not be mentally fit to scrub out this fucking hangar, but if anyone from a group captain to a corporal tells you to scrub the fucker out, then you'll get down on your hands and fucking knees and you'll scrub the fucker out, even if it takes you the rest of your fucking time, and you won't get no fucking help from the M.O. neither."

"I knew that when I volunteered," I lied.

He softened, gave me a conciliatory smile.

"Now tell me, why on earth did you volunteer for *this* mob?"

I leaned towards him, confidentially. "Well, for one thing, Mum said I was always under her feet and for another I couldn't stand the sound of the Hoover. Now, I know that sounds strange," I added quickly, "but it had a faulty circuit and used to wail and . . ."

"Then you've come to the wrong place, laddie," he interrupted affably. "There's a new invention called jet propulsion and it works similar to your mum's Hoover; it sucks in air and blows it out—only it's a million times more noisy. What do you want to do when you're demobbed?"

"Anything in show business, really. A film director, preferably, or failing that I might stage musicals."

"Oh! Then something in the entertainment line would suit you," he said enthusiastically, "like organising camp concerts with a lot of pretty WAAFs in short skirts kicking their legs up." He gave me a dirty wink. "Plenty of crotch work, eh, and swinging tits."

I returned the smile and winked back.

"Don't wink at me, laddie," he screamed, showing his true colours, "or I'll stick you on a fizzer. I'll have you on jankers from asshole till breakfast time. I'll have your fucking guts for garters. Name and number!"

"358955, A.C.2., H. K. A. Russell."

"What do you think this is, laddie?" he roared, pointing at the crown and stripes on his sleeve, "Scotch mist?"

"358955, A.C.2., H. K. A. Russell, Flight Sergeant."

"Stand to attention when you speak to me."

I jumped to attention.

"You're a wanker, Russell. What are you?"

"A wanker, Flight Sergeant."

"I had you down for a wanker the minute you mentioned your Mum's Hoover. You're dim, laddie. What are you?"

"Dim, Flight Sergeant."

"You're as dim as a Toc-H lamp. And if you think you can skive your way through your service looking up the skirts of a squad of dancing girls with big knockers, hoping for a flash of pussy, then you're in for a shock, laddie. That's why I'm putting you down as a sparks. Film director! You couldn't direct Sweet Fanny Adams. You're fit for fuck all. What are you fit for?"

"Fuck all, Flight Sergeant."

"I'll tell you something, laddie. By the time we've finished with you, you'll be fit for *one* thing..." He eyed me scornfully. "You'll be fit to mend Mummy's fucking Hoover. Dismiss! Next!"

I saluted and doubled off in a daze, wondering what the hell I was in for.

In the event, learning all about Ohm's Law was no sweat. After six months' instruction the course came to an end, with an oral examination. Once more I was standing in a big hangar before a flight sergeant seated at a folding table. No handlebar moustache this time. He sucked his pipe.

Flight Sergeant: "Name and number."

Me: "358955 A.C.2. H. K. A. Russell, Flight Sergeant."

Flight Sergeant: "State the definition of Ohm's Law."

Me: "Amps times watts equals volts."

Flight Sergeant: "It gives me great pleasure to inform you that you have passed your Trades Examination. You are now a fully fledged electrician and officially promoted to Aircraftsman First Class with a wage increase of two pounds ten a week, bringing your basic pay up to the ten pound mark. You are also entitled to a week's leave after which you will report for duty at Nether Wallop, Hampshire. Congratulations."

He shook my hand. I saluted, beaming. I was no longer a despised "erk." I was now part of the brotherhood of the air.

Mum and Dad were delighted. I'd hardly got through the door before we were all sitting down to a celebratory tea with Moo and June. Mum had done wonders, considering things were still rationed.

"Come on, Ken Bruzh," she said. "All the bread and butter you can eat."

"That fruit salad looks good, Mum. I think I'll try some of that."

"Your favourite, Ken, Libby's."

"Under the counter, I bet," said Moo with a knowing wink. "Trust our Eth."

"Will you have some, Uncle?" said June, passing round the bowl.

"No thank you, June," said Dad, passing it on to me. "Tinned stuff repeats on me." He was spreading a mashed banana onto a thin slice of Hovis bread.

"I haven't seen a real banana for ages," I remarked.

"Now, it's a very funny thing," said Dad, lowering his voice in wonder. "I was trying a pair of slippers on this Turkish sailor in the shop and he said, 'Please take this for winning the war,' and he gave me this banana. Most strange."

We all nodded at the strangeness of it. "I would have offered you half, Ken, but Mother thought it was off."

"It *is* off," sniffed Mum. "And anyway, you don't know where it's been."

"Not with Turks, you don't," sniffed Moo in agreement.

" 'Ave a sticky chocolate finger, Ken," said Mum.

"Pianer fingers," interjected Moo as I reached for a cake.

"Our Dad always said that boys've got pianer fingers."

Everyone looked at my fingers. I was licking chocolate off them.

"Ever thought of taking it up, Ken?" asked June.

"He took lessons from Mr. Tall," answered Dad, seeing my fingers were still in my mouth.

"Money down the pan," muttered Mum.

"Not Tall the Dentist?" asked Moo.

"I really don't know, Muriel," said Dad. "I suppose it's possible. They both tickle the ivories, don't they?" Dad often attempted a weak joke. We all smiled, except Mum.

"We're all tickled to death, I don't think!" she said. "Don't you think our Ken looks smart in his uniform?"

"Very smart," said everyone in unison.

"Like Anton Walbrook, *In Which We Serve*," said Mum.

"That was Noël Coward," laughed Moo.

"Anton Walbrook was in *Dangerous Moonlight*," said June.

"Isn't he a Pole?" said Dad.

"You're up the pole yourself," retorted Mum derisively.

"It had a lovely theme tune, that *Dangerous Moonlight*," said June, trying to keep a straight face. "Who wrote it, Ken?"

Mum got in first. " 'Lovely June'—Grieg's *Walsall Concerto*."

"No, he wrote *The Cornish Rhapsody*," said Moo.

"No, Hubert Bath wrote that one," I said, "for . . . for . . ."

"*Love Story*," said June.

"Margaret Lockwood and Stewart Granger," said Mum and Moo together.

"Snap," said Dad.

We all laughed.

The climate, I noted to myself, was changing. There had been no mention of an American Picture.

A week later, having mended Mum's Hoover—it *was* a loose wire—I reported to Nether Wallop on Salisbury Plain. I'd barely dumped my kit bag in the billet before I was given a dirty great crowbar and pushed into a lorry with half a dozen sparks I recognised from the training camp—each armed with a lethal weapon ranging from sledgehammers to pickaxes.

No one knew why. The corporal in charge sat up front with the driver—effectively keeping us in the dark as to our destination or the purpose of our mission.

We drove south through the New Forest, past landmarks familiar to me since childhood. Nothing had greatly changed, except a few hundred acres of heathland near the Bournemouth Road at Burley which had been bulldozed into an airfield during the war and since abandoned. So this was our destination. We cruised up the runway, where hundreds of vehicles covered in camouflage netting were parked in orderly rows. We stopped, piled out and fell in to await orders from the corporal.

"Right, lads, these here vehicles are mobile radar units, full of top-secret, highly sophisticated systems costing millions of pounds, and it's your duty as highly trained erks to smash the fuckers up. Go to it!"

We stared at him, holding our crude weapons, like a group of Neanderthal cavemen, jaws agape.

"Jump to it when I give an order," he screamed.

We jumped—and smashed and shattered and crushed and splintered everything in sight. It was all very new and exhilarating. As we drove back to Nether Wallop, tired but cheerful at the end of a long day, each and every one of us was brimming over with a great sense of pride and achievement. This spirit is still very much with us in Britain today, as smashed up trains, telephone boxes and housing estates well testify.

Nothing I did subsequently in the RAF ever lived up to that first great liberating experience. For the rest of my time in the service I worked in the acc room, changing batteries, a stagnant existence, far removed from the lively world of show business I had hoped for.

But three nights a week I used to get a little closer, for when the camp projectionist was posted I took over his job. The Music Circle also used the camp cinema for its programmes and I got to spin the records on twin turntables in the projection room while the audience listened in the auditorium. This was in the days of 78s, of course. A plump sparks I remember as Boris, who ran the Music Circle singlehanded before my arrival, was only too glad of a helping hand—his hands were full already, full of "crumpet." My involvement was a godsend; it meant he could have his snogging sessions on the settee in the corner while I sharpened my styluses by a dim blue light and played Debussy.

Boris had been a ballet dancer in Civvy Street and if ever any of his WAAF girl friends were on duty and unable to report for Nookey, he'd treat me to a private recital. On one memorable occasion he danced the Prince's Variation from *Swan Lake*, which completely knocked me out. He even taught me a few steps and soon we were able to do a pas de deux with me as the Swan Queen. In a camp where a peck on a WAAF's cheek spelt jankers, the projection room was a veritable bird sanctuary. And Boris was cock of the roost. He began using it on film nights as well and while Celia Johnson was being frightfully British and frigid in *Brief Encounter* to Rachmaninoff, Boris was choreographing a seduction that would have done justice to the randiest dancer of all time—Roland Petit— more of whom later. But I think Boris's greatest pas de deux on the settee took place while I was playing Scriabin's *Poem of Ecstasy*. While my fibre needle ground through six sides of steamy shellac, two naked bodies made poetry in the shadows, and as a chorus and orchestra of two hundred and fifty reached a mind-blowing climax, the couple of the settee did likewise. The audience in the auditorium didn't know what they were missing. I should have sold tickets. Little did the Education Officer know when he gave me the job what an education it would be.

I suppose some might accuse me of voyeurism, but I guess I've been a voyeur all my life. So is anyone who goes to the cinema or watches TV. There we sit in the dark, eyes glued to the screen, as if it were a two-way mirror, prying into the most intimate moments of others; watching them being tortured in *The Devils*, or going mad in *The Music Lovers*. And if you are watching *Crimes of Passion* on a video in the intimacy of your own bedroom, you will see John Laughlin and Kathleen Turner show you the first six of the sixty-nine positions. So what if I got some of those positions watching Boris and a WAAF on a settee in the dim light of a projection booth in Nether Wallop in the middle of Salisbury Plain in 1947? OK, so you had to wait nearly forty years to share the experience, but share it you did, nevertheless, and paid good money for the privilege.

Good old Boris, he not only turned me into a voyeur but also a "balletomane." I became dance mad and whenever I got leave would drag Mum up to Covent Garden to see *Three Virgins and a Devil* and to the Strand to see the Ballet de Paris in *Les Amours de Jupiter* in which a dishy half-naked French girl was ravished by a swan.

"Oooh, look, Ken, 'e's got 'is pecker stuck up 'er tutu," said Mum during a quiet passage in the music, much to the amusement of the matinée audience. Mum had accepted the fact that I was a balletomane from the day she brought a neighbour back home early for tea and found me leaping naked around the three-piece suite to *The Rite of Spring* played at such a volume on the "Deccola" radiogram as to drown their entrance. I don't know who was more dumbfounded, them or me, but as usual Mum made light of it with, "Ken, could I trouble you to take a look at Mrs. Mann's 'oover when you've got nothing else on." That evening over supper—Ovaltine and digestive biscuits—we talked about my future after demobilisation.

"Your time's nearly up now, laddo," said Mum. "Time you saw sense and went into your father's business."

"We can start you off on twenty pounds a week and your own car," said Dad. "We've got three shops now and in no time you'd be the manager of the St. Mary's Street branch. You could take over from me, and you could live here for as long as it suited you, couldn't he, Eth?"

"Not on what you pay me, 'e couldn't," said Mum hotly. "Still, 'e can't get into films for love nor money, even as an electrician, so what else is 'e fit for?"

"Ballet, perhaps," I said tentatively.

"Ballet?" they echoed incredulously. "In tights with all those homosexuals," said Dad in a hushed voice.

"But there *is* no ballet in Southampton, Ken," said Mum, being practical.

"I shall go to London," I said, "live on my RAF gratuity till I find a job, and join the Shepherd's Bush Ballet Club. My friend Boris teaches there in the evenings. He said I'd pick it up in no time." If I'd told them I was dying of cancer they couldn't have been more horrified.

"I don't know what the captain of the *Queen Mary*'s going to think," said Dad.

"Your father won't be able to lift 'is 'ead down St. Mary's Street," said Mum.

There was no answer to that. They were a rough lot down St. Mary's Street.

Getting a job in London was not easy and the reference I received from the RAF wasn't much help either. On learning that I wanted to get into pictures, the Education Officer had scribbled me out a hurried demob reference: "Would make an excellent picture framer."

Near a doss house I shared with a gang of Irish labourers in Shepherd's Bush was a furniture factory advertising for staff. I thought of trying out my reference there but baulked when I saw the big time-clock at the main gate. That's not for me, I thought, as visions of Fritz Lang's *Metropolis* rose before me with the workers as slaves to the tick of a huge, remorseless clock.

I needed help. Dorothy Lamour came to the rescue. Her likeness caught my eye when I was window-shopping one day in Bond Street. There on display in a swank art gallery was a gaudy South Sea island picture featuring a dusky beauty who bore a distinct resemblance to Dottie.

Ken Russell had this still taken especially
for his acting career.

I went inside to see if there were more. No luck. The walls were covered
in vomit—or so it seemed at first glance. Closer inspection revealed a
collection of paintings, aptly signed "Sickert." I was about to leave in
disgust when I overheard a conversation between a white-haired old fairy
in a powder-blue suit, who I took to be the proprietor, and an irate
customer who had been waiting for attention for some time. The gallery,
it seemed, was short-staffed.

I sidled off and returned next day in my charcoal-gray demob suit and
got into conversation with the blue fairy on the subject of Sickert and his
Camden Town period. After half an hour of art talk he was a little
disappointed to find himself discussing my pay rather than the price of
"Nude in a Brown Study" but he needed another salesman badly and I
really seemed to know my onions. Thank God no other great names came
up, for my knowledge of painting began and ended with Sickert, whom
I'd swatted up in the public library the night before.

I soon realised there was big money in art, but not much of it came
my way; three pounds ten shillings a week, to be exact. By the time I'd
paid thirty bob to my landlady there was very little remaining for food
and drink, let alone my evening classes at the Shepherd's Bush Ballet
Club. Boris was a hard task master.

"*Entrechat, huit, pas de chat, dix pirouettes à la quatrième position, glissade, double cabriole en tournant, brisé volé, triple tour en l'air, ré-vérence!"*

By the time I'd consulted my French dictionary it was all over. But, as it turned out, learning the vocabulary was easier than mastering the steps. I began to notice that Boris closed his eyes when the gawky collection of secretaries and clerks went through their paces. Like me, they were balletomanes who dreamed one day of taking bows at Covent Garden. Dream on, I thought, as I limped off with Boris for a beer one night after a week of frustration.

"They're never going to make it, Boris, are they?" He hesitated, then came out with it.

"It's hard enough when you start as a kid, as I did. You don't think I'd be teaching that shower if it was easy to get work, do you? They're a lot of wankers. The girls are either dikes or doomed to end up as old maids and the boys are all as queer as coots. They can't wait till the end-of-term show when they can perm their hair and put on the slap."

"Slap?"

"Make-up."

"Is that how you see me?" I asked.

"Twenty-one and never been kissed," he said, giving me a sharp glance. I must have looked hurt because he softened. "Well, you never joined in, did you? Even when there were two WAAFs on the settee, you still didn't join in."

"Who would have changed the records?" I said. "Anyway, you seemed more than equal to the situation. It was one of your greatest performances. With me it's got to be love. I'm just waiting for the right girl, that's all."

He shrugged and continued his plain speaking. "You might have quite a wait, and not just for crumpet. You started dancing ten years too late, you know."

"It was you who encouraged me to come up here," I said accusingly.

"You didn't need much encouragement," he replied. "By the way, you know Nancy's crazy about you?"

"Nancy?"

"Yes, that short, squat girl with jockey's legs. She's a librarian, I believe."

"Oh, you mean the one with no bridge to her nose, whose glasses won't stay on," I said.

"Yes, that's Nancy."

Boris took us both to the "Aerated Bread Company" for coffee one night and then quickly bowed out so that we could get better acquainted. Apart from our age and mutual shyness we had quite a lot in common, including our detestation of films, which were going through a really bad period. More positively, we liked Stan Kenton, Heinz Alphabet Soup and Roland Petit's Ballet de Paris. This was a small company of soloists whose work was exemplified by *Les Forains* in which a troupe of strolling players trundle their cart onto the stage, erect a platform, perform their acts, collect their pennies, pack up their bits and pieces and set off to put on another show elsewhere. Apart from the circus, the smell of the music hall was very much in the air with ballets such as *L'Oeuf à la Coque*.

The scores by Kosma, Françaix and Auric had a great sense of the theatre and even survived attempted murder by the boys in the band. These ballets had everything. There was fantasy with *Les Demoiselles de la Nuit*, featuring a group of adorable sex kittens who turned up a quarter of a century later in Andrew Lloyd Webber's *Cats*. There was sophistication in *The Sphinx* starring an acrobatic Leslie Caron with six-inch claws. There was high drama too, with Jean Babilée, the Marlon Brando of ballet, hanging himself in a lonely garret because his girl friend deserted him. Nancy and I held hands in that one. There was classicism with *Treize Danses* to music by Rameau. There was glitter and glitz and a whiff of the Lido with *The Girl Who Ate Diamonds*, and there was sex.

The repertory of the company changed over the years and its fortunes ebbed and flowed, but *Carmen* was always a sell-out. In the title role was the scintillating Zizi Jeanmaire, partnered by the virile Roland Petit, who ran the company and choreographed most of the ballets. I've seen nothing to equal that night of passion shared by Carmen and Don José, on stage or screen, before or since. The pas de deux with the bare-chested Petit in black tights and Zizi, in corselet, white tights and point shoes, used classical ballet technique to create an erotic love duet of breathtaking beauty, unique in the history of *la danse*—and doing so without causing the audience a moment's embarrassment. I saw *Carmen* time and again and always marvelled that, despite all the sexy positions on the bed in the love duet, Roland Petit never got an erection.

When Nancy suggested one evening in her bed-sit that we should try the actions ourselves, as a choreographic exercise, I secretly feared that I might lack Petit's self-control and cause embarrassment, but agreed to have a go nevertheless. So after we had finished our alphabet soup, brewed on Nancy's gas ring, we began setting the stage for the love scene from *Carmen*.

Nancy switched off the lights and turned up the gas fire while I put a record of Bizet on the radiogram. Then she put on her ballet shoes and slipped off her dress. To my surprise, she had nothing on underneath. Following her example, I took off my shoes, shirt and trousers. I was still in my tights from the ballet class so bore a passing resemblance to Don José. We stood in front of the gas fire in fifth position, her spectacles reflecting the glowing flames. I took her gently around the waist. She pirouetted. Her ponytail lashed me in the eyes four times. They started watering. I pretended I was weeping with emotion. I hoisted her on my shoulder. Her head hit the lampshade. The bulb fell out and exploded at my feet. I imagined it was the brigands outside firing their guns. I swung her down gracefully onto the bed. She landed on the edge and slid to the floor, scrambled to her feet and pushed me onto the bed.

We were dropping behind the music. I was on my back with my legs drawn up and my arms bent behind my head. She lay on top of me. I pressed up with all my might. This should have raised me into something between a crab and a coffee table with Nancy sitting on my tummy. But my arms weren't strong enough and only my knees shot up so that she slid down my chest and sat on my face with her thighs over my ears. I could no longer hear the music and consequently forgot what came next. Nancy too seemed to have forgotten the choreography and contented herself with rocking gently back and forth. Breathing was difficult. I opened my mouth. OXO! Thoughts of Handy and the NCP flooded back. I wanted to throw up. I pushed her off and sat up, gasping. The shilling had run out of the meter and the gas fire was going pop-pop-pop. Bizet was stuck in a groove and a neighbour was hammering on the wall. Nancy was crying but strangely enough I was calm and quietly proud. I now shared something in common with that great performer, Roland Petit. I, too, had finished the greatest love scene in the history of ballet without an erection.

Ballet was hard work and progress was painfully slow. Acquiring any sort of technique in art, I began to realise, was a difficult process and to be much applauded. I was even developing a grudging admiration for Sickert. I'd walked through his Camden Town a couple of times and had discovered, much to my surprise, that it was very brown indeed, and when the day came to take down his pictures, most of which had a red dot on their frames indicating they had been sold, I was sorry to see the work of two Scottish painters hung in their place.

When their show had been running for a few weeks and doing rather well, they popped into the gallery to collect a cheque, for they never had a permanent address. They resembled a couple of gypsies, both in their mode of life and their appearance. McBryde, in corduroys, open-neck shirt and a red neckerchief, had a disposition as warm as the sunny fruits he painted and a face as round as a melon. In contrast, Colquhoun dressed more sombrely and was enormously tall and thin, with a long angular face as craggy as the monumental Scottish fisherwomen he celebrated in muted geometric shapes on large canvases. The Powder Blue Fairy talked excitedly of sales to the Tate and the Museum of Modern Art in New York, news they seemed to take without emotion, for neither said a word.

I had grown to admire their work and was pleased at their success. I hoped to be introduced but the Fairy swept them through the swing doors and off to lunch without so much as a nod in my direction.

It was fifteen years before I saw them again but they hadn't changed a bit. Even their clothes looked the same. By then I'd made a few films for *Monitor* and was living in a Regency house with a wife and three kids. My bohemian days were over, but I always looked back on them with nostalgia, so it was inevitable that eventually I would pay them tribute.

My first gesture was a short film for *Monitor* called *Two Scottish Painters*. Filming them turned out to be easier than finding them, but I eventually tracked them down to a low-beamed cottage in the wilds of Suffolk. McBryde was stirring a pot of vegetable stew suspended over the fire when I arrived to talk things over, but of Colquhoun there was no sign. McBryde had received my letter expressing interest in making a programme of their life and work and had been expecting me. With no explanation, he led me out of the cottage, across a field of stubble, around the back of the local pub and into a cobbled yard where Colquhoun was stretched out, dead-drunk. We took an arm each and dragged him home. It wasn't too difficult—he looked half-starved. Negotiating the crooked stairs in the cottage was less easy owing to Colquhoun's enormous length, but at last we managed to roll him onto a mattress on the attic floor to sleep it off. As I caught my breath I became aware of a pungent smell. So did McBryde and dashed downstairs. I followed. The kitchen was full of smoke. McBryde snatched up the smoking saucepan and dropped it into the sink with a yowl and burnt fingers, and quickly turned on the tap, disappearing into a cloud of steam with a shrug and a smile.

Back in the pub and sipping a nightcap, I reflected on all the burnt offerings I'd accidentally sacrificed over the years I'd been down and out in London. Most of those meals weren't worth eating anyway. Poverty becomes a way of life. You get used to baked beans boiled dry on a gas ring, the draughts under the door, the threadbare scrap of carpet in front of the gas fire where the last shilling in the slot ticks away all too quickly, leaving no recourse but to kick off your shoes and trousers, dash over the bare boards and jump into a sagging bed before the glow of the clay elements fades away, whilst you shiver alone in a bed where there are never enough blankets. So you cover it with shirts, towels, trousers, your overcoat and even the tablecloth if you're lucky enough to have one, shiver yourself to sleep, wake up to the clatter of tiny feet, grope for the frying pan, jump out of bed, flick on the bare lightbulb and thwack, bang and boing all over the floor where an army of cockroaches are scuttling for cover, leaving a battlefield strewn with flattened corpses.

That was in Notting Hill Gate. Another place, in Portobello Road, was overrun by mice. It was a poky room under the stairs, six feet long and three feet wide. It didn't even have a gas ring and it was impossible to stand upright. My table was a rickety chair at the side of the bed, on which I used to sit with my back to the wall eating fruit, and vegetable salads. Fortunately it was summer and my tiny open window proved an irresistible target for the spoiled produce aimed by the larky vendors in the street market below. Those were the days when, having failed as a dancer, I was failing as an actor as well. For a while the sport of those stall holders was my salvation.

Then there were the shared loos that never flushed, filled to the brim with shit, the bare stone stairs and the torn lino in the communal bathroom where the water was hot once a week and went to the first in the queue. Sometimes you felt you were never going to get anywhere in life and that, even if you did get lucky, it might not last. McBryde and Colquhoun had known both good times and bad. When I first saw them in Bond Street they were riding on a wave, but in Suffolk they were flotsam and jetsam, washed up by the fickle tide of fashion. But at least they had each other. On your own it's tough. There's no one in bed to cuddle up to at night and reassure you that it's always darkest before the dawn.

The only thing that kept me going in those dark days was the spirit of Gaudier-Brzeska, an unknown artist of genius who met his death on the Somme in 1915. Most of his short creative life was spent in London under conditions of extreme poverty. His story of triumph over adversity was pieced together by an enthusiast called Jim Ede who came across his work in a store room at the Tate Gallery while looking for picture frames. A book resulted from his research called *Savage Messiah* which will ever be an inspiration to anyone down on their luck with a belief in their own talent, despite the hostility of those who should know better. Here was a tale worth telling on film and, although for years it seemed to be nothing but a pipe dream, the time eventually came when it seemed that I might be able to settle my dues with the bohemian way of life.

It was to be the last in the series of tributes that had started with *Two Scottish Painters* and continued at regular intervals with such films as *Pop Goes the Easel*, the adventures of four young pop painters fresh out of art school, *Always on Sunday*, a study of Douanier Rousseau, *The Biggest Dancer in the World*, following the ups and downs of Isadora Duncan, who carried her own Bohemia around with her, *Dante's Inferno*, a peep into the nightmare world of the Pre-Raphaelite brotherhood, and finally the feature film which nearly broke the bank, *Savage Messiah*.

The TV films were ambitious projects but all lacked the important ingredient of colour. Because *Savage Messiah* was about an artist it was labelled an "Art Film" and considered to be a commercial risk. Conse-

Ken Russell rehearsing Dorothy Tutin in *Savage Messiah*.

quently it was difficult to finance. I ended up double-mortgaging my house and finding most of the money myself. There was a chance I'd end up on the street but I felt I owed Gaudier something. It would have been so easy to have gone into my father's business and opted for the easy life, but Gaudier taught me that there was a life outside commerce and that it was worth struggling for. Long live Gaudier!

Alas, his kind seems to have gone for good, just as Colquhoun and McBryde have gone for good, though like Gaudier the two Scotsmen went down fighting, one fighting whisky and the other a London bus. But unlike Gaudier their work seems to have died with them. I went to a retrospective exhibition of Twentieth-Century British Art at the Royal Academy and not one of their canvases was on view. In which cellars of the Tate Gallery are those ripe, succulent fruits rotting? To which vaults in the Museum of Modern Art have those monumental goddesses of the north been condemned? And what has taken their place? Big business! Art packaged and sponsored by the Ad Man—Hype Art. Corduroy trousers and icy garrets are out of fashion. So is passion.

Tailored jeans and the heated pools of Beverly Hills are in. Image has taken the place of Art. It pays to be cool. Maybe that's why *Savage Messiah* was not considered commercial. It was about passion and sweat, it was about a poverty-stricken artist who stole a tombstone from a cemetery, sculpted it into a nude and, when the dealer who had commissioned it refused to pay, threw it through the window of his Bond Street gallery. It was about revolution and fuck the art dealers of Bond Street and Madison Avenue and fuck Pinewood and Hollywood, who have never made a proper film on an artist yet!

We had very little cash to make *Savage Messiah* but plenty of commitment from all those involved, from our production designer, Derek Jarman (probably the last true bohemian), to the Lee boys—a couple of Cockney sparks who put up some money and let me use their studio, a derelict biscuit factory on the banks of a putrid canal in North London.

I was working in my leaky office a week or so before the shoot when my production manager stuck his cherubic face around the door and said, "There's a young American girl here to see you. Seems you met her on *The Devils* and offered her a job."

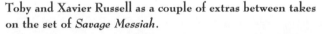

Toby and Xavier Russell as a couple of extras between takes on the set of *Savage Messiah*.

"It must have been after lunch when I'd had a few," I said. "It's news to me. Has she any experience?"

"None at all," he said. "Shall I send her away?"

"We *need* a teaboy, don't we?" I asked.

"Yes," he said. "I'm having trouble finding someone who'll work for nothing."

"If she'll do it for the experience, I'll see her."

He nodded and went out. A minute or two later there was a tap at the door and a freckle-faced blonde around seventeen came in. There was something of the young Ingrid Bergman about her, though her tomboy smile also put me in mind of Huck Finn.

"I understand that I offered you a job back in 1970 while I was filming *The Devils* at Elstree," I said.

"Yes," she said.

"That must have been while I was shooting the cathedral scene out on the back lot."

"Yes."

"And you want a job as a teaboy?"

"Yes."

"And you know there's no pay?"

"Yes."

"Right. You've got it. Can you start tomorrow?"

"Yes."

"Can you find your way out?"

"Yes."

She was about to close the door behind her when I said, "Just for the record, I shot the cathedral scene of *The Devils* on Stage Five at Pinewood in 1971." She smiled and quietly closed the door. And although neither of us presumed it at the time, it was surely the greatest meeting since Stanley and Livingstone.

6 Last Tango in Elstree

Name and ID," growled the cop to my American friend.

"Vivian Jolly," she said, flashing a smile and her driver's licence.

"Your jolly hi-jinks nearly got your head blown off," he said, returning his Colt .45 to its holster. "Watch it!"

"I was just welcoming this gentleman to America," she said, as I brushed away the carnival streamers in which her party poppers had festooned me. The cop scrutinised my grizzly bear coat and white hair.

"Are you John Lee Hooker from Vermont?" he demanded.

"No, I'm Ken Russell from Southampton."

"England!" added Viv.

"Then you might teach this young lady some of that restraint you English are so famous for," he said.

Viv and I were still laughing an hour later as we skipped across Brooklyn Bridge in the snow. Like the Yellow Brick Road, it is a way of enchantment calling you to dance across it to the Emerald City on the other side. The urge is irresistible. Indeed, some people are so eager to get to the other side that they JUMP! I'm sure they die happy. Brooklyn Bridge is not a place for balanced minds. It's a crazy house of delirious sensations. Overhead driving clouds, beneath our feet cars, trains, ships and swirling water; water to the left of us, water to the right of us and radiating in all directions a cat's cradle of flying cables purring in eddies of whirling snowflakes. This must be the place where the Wright brothers learned to fly. As Viv took my hand, I too was borne aloft.

This feeling of weightlessness continued over bubbles of Bloody Marys high above Manhattan in the bar of the hotel where Viv was staying with her father—a big noise in Pratt & Whitney jet engines. We drank to *Valentino*, which had brought us together again three years after we'd said goodbye at the end-of-picture party on *Savage Messiah*. Because of the din from the rock group bouncing off the studio walls our farewells had been brief.

"Thanks for your help," I shouted. "Where are you off to now?"

"The Harvard Film School," she shouted back.

"So you've got the bug," I shouted. "Good. I hope you learned something from us that might come in useful."

"Like babysitting," she yelled. "I don't think that's on the curriculum."

"Or classes in the art of keeping the director's whisky glass topped up in a Force Eight gale on a night shoot," I yelled.

"And thanks for the five pounds a week," she shouted. "You didn't have to."

"I always was a lavish tipper," I shouted.

". . . And for the free eats and accommodation," she shouted.

"We couldn't have you being arrested for vagrancy," I shouted. "It would have looked bad. Anyway, good luck, goodbye and, er, drop me a line now and then."

She did so, once a year on a postcard until her graduation when she phoned my office three weeks into the filming of *Valentino* asking permission to shoot a documentary on the making of the movie. My secretary passed her message on to me one morning as I was being driven to a location a few miles from the asshole of Spain, as the dismal town of Almeria was affectionately known to the crew. Shirley, who was also in the car, immediately burst into tears. I had no idea why. I barely knew the girl and it certainly wasn't because of her that our marriage was in a mess. Viv had always been polite to Shirley and had been a good babysitter. The kids had liked her. Shirley had no cause for complaint whatsoever.

Perhaps it was a premonition. Anyway, I could see no harm in a young film-maker "covering" our movie—we might even get some free publicity out of it—so I gave the OK.

I don't know if what happened next was Shirley's way of showing her disapproval, but I remember the subsequent events vividly. After an hour's drive we arrived at a barren hilltop which, after a little help from the art department, now resembled a war-torn landscape. It was here we were preparing to recreate the big battle scene from *The Four Horsemen of the Apocalypse*, the Hollywood epic which provided Valentino with his first major role.

The reasons we were not shooting in Hollywood were twofold. Firstly, it had changed beyond recognition since the days of the "silents" and, secondly, it was too expensive. For years Almeria and its environs had been a Mecca for those in search of a cut-price California. For the local Spaniards the place had turned into a regular Klondike with prospectors' shacks nestling in the gullies, ranches dotted across the dusty plains and two-dimensional townships straddling the arid hills. We'd already used a tumbledown saloon, veteran of a hundred westerns, for the tango sequence that made Valentino famous and now we were gearing up to shoot the scene in which Valentino's wife-to-be drives onto the battlefield in a Rolls-Royce to look him up during a take—which naturally gets the director, Rex Ingram, hopping mad!

It was a big number but we were well-organised and by the time the Moët et Chandon, cooling in my ice bucket, had reached the desired temperature, we were all ready to go. All except for Rex Ingram, who was still in the wardrobe marquee where he had been getting ready for the past hour. I wondered what was up. As costume designer, Shirley was responsible for every garment in the film, but even allowing for her fastidiousness and the fact that this was Rex Ingram's first appearance, I could see no obvious reason for the delay. The costume itself was classically simple: a pith helmet, bush jacket, jodhpurs and riding boots—the traditional garb of a Twenties director on location in the desert, from D. W. Griffith to Erich von Stroheim.

Not for the first time, I questioned the wisdom of a husband–wife relationship of a professional nature, where the simplest question can often be taken as a criticism. I imagined myself running the gauntlet of the crew's speculation as I crossed no-man's-land to enemy territory and knocked on her tent flap. They wouldn't hear me quietly say, "May I come in, darling? Are we having a problem? Can I help, dearest?" They probably *would* hear her reply, which would be something more in keeping with our present location—the trenches. I still hesitated, knowing that if I delayed much longer the crew would put me down as chicken. The producer, who was going wall-eyed through keeping one eye on me and the other on his watch, was sweating profusely. Spanish peasants, masquerading as *poilus* in heavy overcoats and steel helmets, were suffering from prickly heat. Special-effects men with fingers itching to unleash smoke and flame wiped their hands with grimy rags. Turds from the spectral Steeds of War, Pestilence, Famine and Death steamed in the burning sun. Everything was close to boiling point, including the water in the radiator of the Rolls-Royce. Everyone was waiting for an explosion. I took a sip of my iced champagne and started walking towards the marquee. At that moment the missing actor appeared—dressed in sheepskin chaps, a ten-gallon hat, cowboy boots and a pair of six-shooters.

"Hi, Ken," he said, slapping his guns with an alcoholic burp. "How d'ya like it?"

"Great for Tom Mix," I said. "Not so hot for Rex Ingram. I think you've got the wrong location. They're shooting *Return of the Magnificent Seven* over the hill. Keep walking."

"Awe, come on, Ken. Quit kiddin'. It's great! I love it!" Clearly he and his costume were not to be parted. I looked at the pathetic spectacle and wondered if the public was ready for a gun-totin' director. Von Stroheim had carried a riding crop and I sometimes cracked the whip myself so it was not outside the bounds of possibility.

"Where's the action, Ken?" he asked, slapping me on the back, nearly causing my champagne to spill.

"Up there," I said, lifting my glass towards the top of an eight-foot rostrum from which he was to direct the action.

"It would take danger money to get me up there," he said, looking at the platform with red eyes.

"It's as safe as houses," I said, climbing the wooden ladder and standing on the top without spilling a drop.

"I suffer from vertigo," he slurred.

"I'll cut it down," I said, desperately. "How high *can* you go?"

He swayed towards the ladder and started climbing. "I'm all right at this height," he said, from the second rung.

"That's great," I said, coaxingly. "Take it a step at a time. Try one more."

"I wouldn't do this for everyone, Ken, but for you I'll try." He put his foot gingerly on the third rung.

"Put your weight on it," I said encouragingly.

"They said you were a slave driver," he said, "and by Christ they were right."

"Then put your fucking weight on it," I screamed. Bad psychology. He froze.

"Let's try the dialogue," I said evenly, trying another tack.

"I'm a method actor," he said, "I improvise."

"You've only got to say 'Action' and 'Cut,'" I said, hotting up again.

"Ah, but it's how you say it."

"You shout it."

"What sorta accent d'you want?" he asked. "I've researched the character and it seems he was born in Kentucky but educated at Princeton so . . ." He suddenly threw up and slid down the ladder, totally gone. A couple of ADs dragged him away. The horse turds had stopped steaming and were baked as hard as bricks. Shirley had left the wardrobe tent and was walking towards the catering wagon. I could tell by looking at her ass that she was smiling. The producer was not smiling. Neither were the crew. They were gazing into space with that rapt attention crews always adopt when the director is up shit creek without a paddle. I looked at the producer to see if he had a spare.

"There must be someone here who can play a film director," he said, fixing me with a piercing eye. The eyes of the crew followed his and settled on me like a swarm of flies.

Five minutes later on top of the platform I shouted "Action" twice—once for real and once for make-believe. Luckily the correct costume had fitted me to perfection so with my long white locks pinned up under my pith helmet I reluctantly took over the role of Rex Ingram.

That night, still wearing his cowboy outfit, Tom Mix lurched down Main Street looking for the ornery critter who'd stolen his thunder. Fortunately I was always one bar ahead so he was denied a showdown, though he was still threatening to get me when they carried him on board the plane next day to fly him out. Somehow he got wind that my kids were on board and threw his bile at them. If the crew hadn't poured more booze down him, rendering him paralytic, God knows what might have happened. It was an ugly situation which turned even uglier when we got back to England where filming continued at Elstree Studios.

We'd barely started when the actors' union, Equity, hit us with a bombshell. Because I'd usurped a role which should have been played by one of their members, I was given an ultimatum: either drop the scene from the film or re-shoot it *with* a member of Equity. Both suggestions spelt disaster. The sequence was utterly necessary to the film and the cost of re-shooting it prohibitive. Naturally I told them my side of the story but the union preferred to believe their brother, who denied everything

The reluctant film director, Ken Russell, playing
Rex Ingram in *Valentino*.

and was taking legal advice with a view to suing me for defamation of character.

A week later we were still no closer to a solution when Viv arrived from America with her 8-mm camera. I poured out my sorry story over a "welcome home" drink at the studio bar.

"What's your problem?" she said. "Surely you were an actor yourself once?"

"Sure, once an actor always a horse's ass," I said, quoting Hitchcock.

"Didn't they have unions in your day?" she asked, a little impertinently, I thought.

"Of course! I joined Equity the day I joined the chorus of *Annie Get Your Gun*, but that was some time ago."

"Over a quarter of a century ago, according to your biography," she said. It was then I realised that some members of the general public knew more facts about my life than I did.

"What are you getting at?" I said.

"When did you resign?" she asked.

"How should I know?" I said, rather curtly, having just caught sight of my wife, dressed as a page boy, glaring in through the window. Shirley didn't come in and say hello, though she'd been pleasant enough to Viv in her babysitting days. Instead she beckoned me to come outside.

"This must be important," I said to Viv, by way of an apology. "Please excuse me."

"Sure. I can see she means business," she said with a wave that Shirley ignored.

"Bert Glitz wants us to lunch with him," said Shirley without enthusiasm as I joined her outside. Bert was a big wheel in the company which was financing the film and it would have been undiplomatic to refuse his invitation, so we called a truce and went across the road to the local Italian restaurant.

After kicking around the Equity problem over the antipasto, the conversation turned to meatier stuff with the arrival of the *pollo sorpresa*— Rudolf Nureyev, in fact. Casting Rudy as Valentino had been Shirley's idea and there was good reasoning behind it. Apart from first names, both men had a lot in common: they sprang from humble origins, emigrated and became universal megastars without the need of having to master their adopted language. But who knows what would have happened if Valentino had survived till the talkies? Maybe his premature death was a blessing in disguise, for on the evidence of an old gramophone record he certainly had a very pronounced accent. So did Nureyev, and there was the problem: our émigré was supposed to come from Italy not Russia. They sounded as unalike as a mandolin and a balalaika.

Rudolf Nureyev as screen star and legendary lover Rudolph Valentino in *Valentino*.

However, we hired Rudy because we believed that his prowess as a dancer and mimic would more than compensate for his diction, musical as it was. Unfortunately, Rudy, about to make his screen début as an actor, wanted to prove himself not with actions but words. And the more he stumbled over them, the more stilted his acting became. And the more I encouraged him to cut his dialogue and use the expressive powers of his body, the more he resisted. To him, losing a word was like losing a tooth. He began to imagine I was whittling away his part and if he saw me talking to his co-star he became morosely jealous.

It seemed he must dominate every scene, even when he was playing a subsidiary role such as quietly preparing a meal for a loquacious girl-friend. All Rudy had to do was stir the sauce while she waxed emotional. On Take One Rudy stirred gently as the young actress emoted. On Take Two he stirred more vigorously and began humming *"La Donna è Mobile"* from Verdi's *Rigoletto* as she emoted. By Take Six he was stirring fiercely, adding salt and herbs, shaking pepper and singing the aria with gusto. The poor actress couldn't hear herself speak. It became Rudy's scene—until the dubbing, that is. Then I simply threw away the original soundtrack, re-voiced the actress, who also had a very thick accent, and left Rudy off the new track altogether. The reason I did not re-voice Rudy was that his contract forbade it. The reason I tolerated such behaviour in the first place was simply because he generally complained if his input was ignored or even questioned and it showed in his performance.

"How did the gaol scene go?" asked Bert, knowing that Rudy had had reservations about it.

"With difficulty," I replied. "He seems to be having an identity crisis. Sometimes I wonder who the film is about, Valentino or Nureyev."

"That's what comes of hiring an actor who shares a name with the guy he's playing," said Bert. "So what happened in the gaol scene?"

Not knowing just how familiar he was with the script, I explained fulsomely.

"Valentino and his wife of two hours are arrested crossing the Mexican border and thrown into a tacky gaol on a bigamy charge. She's released right away but no one will stand bail for Rudy who is forced to share a cage with lowlifes of both sexes and endure a night of torment at the hands of a sadistic gaoler, envious of the star's magnetic pull over millions of women. The gaoler spikes Valentino's coffee with 'a little something to make you wanna piss all night' and refuses him toilet privileges. He then sits back to wait, howling along with the other 'animals' for Valentino to 'show us what you're made of.'

"Valentino doesn't give them the satisfaction. He was a modest man and preferred to suffer discomfort rather than gratify the lewd curiosity of the gawpers. However, their screams of mockery and abuse fuel his grow- ing humiliation into a despair that literally drives him up the wall to the top of the cage where the camera zooms in to expose the human suffering of a God in torment."

"That's a neat metaphor, Ken. I think *Rolling Stone* would appreciate that," said Bert. "How did it go?"

"Up until the big moment, fine."

"You mean the moment he pisses his pants?"

"Yes. Hidden by his sweater, a garden hose was inserted in the top of Rudy's knickerbockers and pushed discreetly down to his crotch by the prop master."

"But how were you going to shoot it?" asked Bert.

"Quite simply," I said. "The camera was to register the misery on Rudy's face, tilt down his body, and show him clutching himself in agony, then carry on down his dripping knickerbockers to the spreading puddle on the floor."

"And I had another pair of stockings and knickerbockers standing by ready for Take Two," said Shirley.

"As it happened, we didn't need them," I said. "Anyway, the prop man was all poised to turn on his remote-controlled tap, and I was about to tell the First to roll camera when Rudy characteristically raised an objection.

" 'What do you think I've got there?' he demanded with great hauteur, 'a cunt?' A pregnant silence followed as I wondered what I'd done wrong this time. Then the penny dropped. I was casting doubts on his manhood. Discreetly I asked him which side he dressed and on receiving his curt reply instructed the prop man to pay out more hosepipe. He did so and, kneeling at Rudy's feet, I negotiated it as delicately as possible down the right leg of his knickerbockers—from the outside, of course. Acting the spaniel, I looked up for approval. But the master did not throw me a bone.

" 'More,' he said. I nodded to the prop man. He paid out another inch.

" 'Much more,' he said. The prop man looked at me for guidance. I nodded three times. The hosepipe grew another three inches and appeared to develop a curl. I knelt down to straighten it out and jumped when it gave a wriggle. The hair rose on my neck as I realised I was handling the real thing. We should be making a monster film, I thought, as I coughed and begged pardon—'The Man with Two Dicks.'

" 'More,' he said. I glanced apologetically at the prop man, who grudgingly paid out another inch. The eyes of the crew were out on stalks. It was *Women in Love* all over again.

" 'More,' he said.

" 'Look, Rudy, this is becoming ridiculous,' I said. 'It's going to look as if you've got water on the knee and it's a well-known fact that Rudy was known all over Hollywood as Wee Willie Winkie.'

"He took that as a personal insult and might have left the set but for the fact that he was attached to the hosepipe. Eventually we reached a compromise and the tube was hauled up a couple of inches. We tried a dry run. The crew nearly wet themselves. It looked as if Rudy was wrestling with a snake halfway down his trouser leg. Eventually I persuaded him it would look more convincing if he clutched his bladder, and we got it in the can . . ."

"And you got a few more white hairs," laughed Viv when I repeated the story over supper a few nights later. "I can't wait to get his dongle on film. Do you think he'd feel insulted if I shot it on eight-millimetre?"

"He might," I said. "You can't get smaller than that."

"It is *Super* Eight," she protested.

"Maybe you'll get your big chance tomorrow," I said, filling her glass with champagne. "We're filming the nude love scene."

Michelle Phillips with Rudolf Nureyev in *Valentino*.

"Aren't we celebrating prematurely?" she asked, lifting her glass. "What if he demands a closed set?"

"That's like expecting him to dance *The Sleeping Beauty* with the fire curtain down," I said. "That'll be a pushover. No, we're celebrating VE night—Victory over Equity. I took your advice seriously and asked them to check their records. 'Yes,' they said, I had enrolled in 1950, and 'no,' I had never resigned. I was just a quarter of a century in arrears! Now I'm a fully paid up member with a licence to act."

"Heaven help us," said Viv.

"You've saved the day," I said, ignoring her remark and clinking glasses.

"Cheers," we said. And we meant it. We were both feeling very cheerful. It had been an enjoyable evening but it was nearly midnight and time to go.

"My boy friend will be wondering where I've got to," said Viv.

"Well, Shirley knows where I am so she *won't* be wondering," I replied.

It turned out that Viv was staying close to where I lived so we walked part of the way home together. In no time we were approaching No. 23 Ladbroke Square and sidestepping the wooden stanchion supporting the bulging wall. As with my marriage, the building was being propped up. Before we said goodbye I suggested she give my driver a ring first thing in the morning so that he could pick her up on the way. No point in her struggling out to the studios on public transport when she was living around the corner. She thanked me, gave me a peck on the cheek and was gone.

I looked up at the elegant façade behind which I lived. Its Victorian contours were shrouded in darkness. At a quarter to twelve the family were all abed. In the basement, May, the faithful retainer who had been nanny and housekeeper for nearly twenty years, was probably asleep and dreaming of her daughter who used to share it with her, now grown up with a family of her own in Rhodesia.

On the ground floor, behind discreet lace curtains, Haig Pit, our black pit bull, would be sleeping heavily with one eye open, guarding the Victorian bric-à-brac, the pianola, the pine dresser, the pub table, Shirley's collection of Staffordshire pigs and the Habitat kitchen units, while on the floor above, a Bengal tiger, reduced to a rug, would be staring with glassy eyes at our collection of Art Deco junk surrounded by posters of the Russian Ballet and bits and pieces of Pop Art, including a *Tommy* pinball machine. There was also a modest hi-fi system, lots of records and a large expanse of polished floor where the kids used to dance with me until they grew too big. And what of the glassy eyes on the floor above in the master bedroom? Would they be closed in sleep or staring at the anxious shadows on the ceiling, as Shirley imagined her children tossing restlessly in their sleep, waiting for the roof to fall in?

Idle speculation. I walked up the few steps to the porch, passed between the Corinthian columns and quietly let myself in. I undressed and washed in the bathroom on one of the half-landings, and tiptoed up to the bedroom in the dark. My wife's even breathing came from the seven-foot square bed, along with a whiff of Ma Griffe. Barefoot in the deep pile carpet, I crept past her to the far end of the L-shaped room and slid between the icy sheets of the tiny day bed. Shirley was still breathing evenly—too evenly. We lay, stiff as statues in our separate beds, wide awake, worlds apart.

Next morning, having made my usual surreptitious exit, I was about to step into the car when a woman in a purple headscarf, pink mules and floral dressing gown overtook me and started hammering on the nearside rear window. To my amazement, it was Shirley. Viv, who a moment before had been quietly dozing, had a rude awakening.

"What do you think you're doing sitting in the back there? Get in front with the driver," screamed Shirley.

Viv automatically glanced over her shoulder to see if someone else had got in without her noticing.

"No! It's you! You! Get in the front at once." Acting as if she'd been shot, Viv slid over the top of the passenger seat, ass in the air, exposing a lot of leg and a pair of white knickers peppered with red hearts. This outraged Shirley even more. The air turned blue and froze me into silence.

"And as for you . . ." she shouted, turning on me. Well, you'd have thought I'd committed adultery or something.

"What's wrong?" I said. "I'm only giving her a lift to the studios."

"For the last time!" she said, and stalked back into the house, slamming the door behind her.

Shamefaced, I got into the car and we drove to the studios in silence. That was the first time Viv learned there was something wrong with my marriage. Shirley had never behaved that way on *Savage Messiah* and it must have come as a shock to her. She was in for another one a few hours later. We were between set-ups and Viv was seated in one of the many canvas chairs littering the studio, reloading her camera, when the air turned blue yet again. Shirley, who invariably drove herself to the studio, had just arrived. In her black uniform and jack boots she came on like a storm-trooper.

"What do you think you're doing?" she screamed at Viv. "Get out of that chair at once!" Viv jumped up as if she'd been stung. Indeed, she looked hard at the seat to see if she'd been sitting on a wasp. Shirley immediately took her place and glared at the crew, defying anyone to challenge her proprietorial right. No one did. Stencilled on the back of the chair was the name KEN RUSSELL. I strolled over and with both hands on the arm rests leaned towards Shirley menacingly. Unintimidated, she looked up at me and whispered, "If I see her here tomorrow you can just whistle for your costumes." Not to be outdone, I pursed my lips and blew. Nothing happened. She smiled, knowing she had me by the balls. Feigning indifference, I collected my script from its holder on the side of the chair, and limped away, crushed.

That night Viv and I sat down to our last supper—or so we thought. As we drank more than was good for us I did my best to explain the cause of Shirley's behaviour. We'd been happily married for seven years or so when, in the summer of 1965, Debussy's mistress, Gaby Dupont, came between us at the Grand Hotel, Eastbourne. It was here that Claude Debussy, the Impressionist composer, did some of his best work—watched over by an ever diligent wife. And as Shirley sat by the pool in her maternity smock, placidly knitting something for our fifth child, I was away in the woods with my cast and crew evoking a hazy summer afternoon in the Bois de Boulogne with Gaby as a *fin de siècle* nymph in white lace playing with a balloon and flirting with Debussy, who had fallen under her spell. So had I.

Unfortunately, the make-believe continued after the props had been returned to the shelves and the costumes to their hangers. It was obvious to the actress and myself that we were a great team—rushes never lie. We would conquer the screens of the world together. We would be the Giulietta Masina and Federico Fellini of the BBC, and indeed we were—for one more film, *Always on Sunday*.

This featured another French artist—Henri Rousseau, the humble customs official who became the greatest Primitive painter the world has ever known. And once again I cast my dream girl as a friend of the artist. Not as a *femme fatale* this time but as a *man*—that mad midget of Surrealism, Alfred Jarry. Clothed in a flat hat, shabby jacket and darned knickerbockers with dirty short hair and grubby face, she suddenly seemed a lot less glamorous than Shirley, who was a foot taller and, now that she had given birth to Toby, as slim as Audrey Hepburn (whom she had lately grown to resemble). I seriously began to wonder if she could act. She was also being very understanding about my relationship with "Minnie Mouse" as she called her, owing to her diminutive stature and the fact that she wore shoes as big as boats. I began to see the error of my ways. And as one screen partnership died, so another was born.

After years of trying, Shirley finally got a union card and a relationship that had been fitful and furtive was now recognised officially. In other words, Shirley was allowed to design all the costumes for my films, instead of occasional bits and pieces. Undoubtedly, one of her greatest talents was the ability to sort through mountains of old clothes and unearth a Fortuny dress—the equivalent of coming across a Stradivarius in a junk shop. In fact, some of our happiest moments together were spent in junk shops with me as her willing assistant. And one has only to look at *Savage Messiah*, *The Music Lovers* and *The Boy Friend* to see that it all paid off. Eventually the sources began to dry up but it was fun while it lasted, and when I see the same colourful garments turning up time and again in films by other directors such as Schlesinger's *Yanks*, Beatty's *Reds* and Boorman's *Hope and Glory* it's like meeting old friends.

But the Second Hand Rose, as Shirley is affectionately known by some members of the industry, was equally at home at the drawing board, designing weird and wonderful creations for my more stylised efforts, such as *The Devils*. It was during lunch hours on *The Devils* that Shirley started taking driving instructions from my chauffeur, who was an ex-lorry driver. These lessons often extended well into the afternoon, as I discovered whenever I sent word for her to join us on the set to discuss one of her bizarre costumes and explain, for instance, which way round it should be worn. Shirley was never to be found and, although there was nothing unusual in this because as the director's wife she was a law unto herself, it nevertheless started me wondering if a little back-seat driving might not be involved. There was enough room in the back of our 1947 Rolls Landaulette to sleep six. It also had pull-down blinds! Impossible! After motherhood Shirley was next to sainthood. The very thought was near blasphemy. But hard work dispels morbid fancies as surely as a good whipping purges a nun possessed of devils. And filming exorcism is exhausting.

It was only when Shirley had failed her driving test for the third time that I guessed her halo had slipped. That was four films later, in Madrid. To my question, "Why?" she simply replied, "Tit for tat." I've pondered on the profundity of those three little words ever since. I've also pondered the inevitable question, "Whatever did she see in him?" and concluded that he was nothing more to her than a willing accomplice to her lust for revenge.

"Nonsense!" said Viv. "He's younger than you. She was after his body."

"But he's a yobbo!"

"Then they were obviously made for each other," she said, without a hint of malice.

"And to think I used to invite him for dinners and home-movie shows," I said. "I even gave him records."

"Whatever for?"

"For helping Shirley with her driving lessons, carrying her groceries in the supermarket, and generally providing a service outside of working hours."

"He certainly did that," she said, unable to suppress a smile. "What are you going to do about it?"

"I'm taking fencing lessons," I said.

"I don't get it," she said, looking puzzled.

"I'm going to challenge him to a duel."

She stared at me incredulously for a moment. "You've flipped," she said. "You're off your heads, the both of you. I'm getting out just in time."

"You don't mind going, then?" I said, feeling a bit of a creep. "I'm afraid she might destroy the costumes if you stay."

"Then you'd have an excuse for some more nude scenes," she said with a chuckle which quickly died. "Naturally I'm disappointed. I came over here to make a movie, not to be cast as the 'other woman' in your personal soap opera. It's a bad script."

"I was hoping you'd be the first graduate of the Ken Russell Film School," I ventured.

"My boyfriend might have something to say about that," she countered.

"What does he do?"

"He designs pubs. He's just got a commission for one in Boston. We're flying out together at the weekend. You met him briefly on *Savage Messiah*, remember?"

"No, I'm afraid I don't."

"He remembers you. He gave me hell for getting in late last night."

"You'd better go then . . . and I hope you'll let me pay for your air fare. I'm afraid it's been a wasted journey."

"Not at all," she said, displaying a garnet ring, "I've just had a proposal."

I congratulated her and called for the bill.

"Thanks . . . anything I can do for you in America?" she said, by way of small talk.

"Nothing I can think of just now, thank you." Then, as an afterthought, I said, "Is Boston anywhere near Stockbridge?"

"Not too near," she said, "but I'm often up that way. My folks live in Lakeville, Connecticut. It's just a few miles away."

"Then maybe you'd care to do some research for me?" I said. "Have you heard of Charles Ives?" She shook her head. "He was an American composer, part-time, self-taught; had an insurance business. He celebrated the American way of life in music and composed around the turn of the century; wrote a *New England Holidays Symphony—Washington's Birthday, The Fourth of July*, music full of fireworks and brass bands; oh, and a marvellous piece called *The Housatonic at Stockbridge*. I've always wanted to make a film about him."

"Sounds fun," she said politely.

"I'll send you a treatment and a list of questions. I'm sure your local library will have a few books on him."

"I'm sure it will," she replied, unconvincingly.

We didn't walk home together. I said I had a call to make that would take me in the other direction. She was obviously relieved. We said goodbye, shook hands rather formally and parted. I walked around the block, went back into the restaurant, sat down at the table I'd vacated just minutes before, ordered a bottle of Chianti and got blotto.

And as one innocent bird flew out the window another flew back in. She was waiting for me in the office when I arrived bleary-eyed at the studios next morning. My last personal secretary had taken his designation too literally. Nell was his replacement. Standing there in her tee-shirt and shocking pink mini-skirt I hardly recognised her. I hadn't realised how dishy she was. Nell had been an extra in our crowd scenes and I was used to seeing her dressed as a Twenties flapper in a cloche hat. She'd been really outstanding, throwing herself into the riot scenes with scant regard for life and limb during take after take. Most extras have another string to their bow, so when I learned that she was also a part-time secretary I offered her the job directly the crowd work was over.

Now I wondered if it had been a wise decision; she wasn't the conventional picture of a secretary at all. Wow! Those legs!

"Would you like me to take something down?" she said, a little provocatively for 8:15 in the morning.

"Er, no, thank you," I said, pulling myself together. "I was just admiring your outfit, but they go by appearances around here and you could be mistaken for a groupie. Here, trick yourself out in something a touch more formal." She nodded, took the money I offered and listened intently as I explained her duties. Stage Seven then claimed me till the end of the day, when I returned to the office to be greeted by an alarming sight — Shirley, in her storm-trooper's outfit, doing a war dance. Rhythmically, ruthlessly, remorselessly, she was grinding the contents of an upturned fruit bowl into Nell's clothes.

"That's pretty," I said, looking at the multi-coloured stains. "I hope she's into psychedelia."

Shirley's language was pretty colourful too until she finally marched out of the room, when it became curtly domestic.

"And don't be late for dinner! It's Thursday!" she shouted.

"Mm! Moussaka, yum, yum," I thought, despite myself.

When Nell came back from the post room a few minutes later she found me at the basin in the bathroom up to my elbows in suds, washing her clothes.

"They said you were kinky, but I never expected this," she said, raising an eyebrow.

"Your clothes offended my wife's colour sense," I replied. "I caught her dyeing and pressing them at the same time. Who says I'm kinky?"

"Oh, the extras, the crew, everyone. They say you're evil with it. Surely you've seen the newspapers?"

"Only when I use the toilet," I said. "I wonder you dare share a bathroom with me."

"You look more domestic than demonic," she said, with a smile. "What's all this about, anyway?"

"You gave me a bowl of fruit and left your clothes lying about, that's all," I said.

"That's what comes of going by appearances. Anyway, you haven't said how you like my outfit," she said, doing a pirouette.

"This is getting a little personal, don't you think?" I said.

"I didn't ask you to wash my undies," she said.

"When I asked you to trick yourself out as a secretary I didn't expect you to get a new pair of knickers," I said.

"How do you know I'm wearing any?" she said, cheekily.

"I presume that's why you discarded these," I said, holding up a dripping ball of nylon.

"Well, how *do* you like it?" she said again, putting her hands on her hips.

"You look like a French tart."

"It must be the black beret," she said, whipping off her black wrap-around skirt and revealing black stockings and suspender belt.

"See," she said, "I did buy a new pair of knickers. Are these formal enough for you?" They too were black and frilly, with a cut-away crotch.

"I'm going to have to give you a week's notice," I said. She laughed and bolted the bathroom door. I remembered the moussaka overcooking at home. "Mmm! May as well be hanged for a sheep as a lamb," I thought.

Looking at Viv across the table in that hotel bar in snowy Manhattan, I suddenly felt myself blushing.

"My God, that was less than a month ago," I said, trying to hide my confusion. "It seems a lifetime."

Viv stirred the dregs of her Bloody Mary with a celery stick and looked at me "old-fashioned" (as Mum would say).

"And that was *only* the second time you've been unfaithful to your wife in twenty years of marriage, and you a movie director!" she said with mock incredulity. "Why, you're a disgrace to the breed."

"Third time lucky," I said, with a bashful smile.

"Dream on, old stick," she said. "Dream on!"

7

Just Good
Pen Pals

The following day started with a voyage around the world of Kurt Schwitters. As I was free until noon, Viv suggested we meet at the Guggenheim Museum for a little fast culture. I discovered this cylindrical landmark on Fifth Avenue easily enough and found Viv in the foyer sitting in a wheelchair.

"What's happened?" I asked in alarm.

"Nothing. This is for you," she said under her breath, with one eye on the attendant. "Start limping." I obeyed and, putting my full weight on my see-through plastic walking stick, hobbled around the chair and collapsed into it, gasping. My performance convinced the attendant, if not Viv.

"No need to overdo it," she whispered. "You're not Ironside."

I stopped imitating Raymond Burr and relaxed.

A moment later we were taking an elevator to the top floor. Viv pushed me out onto the landing and across to the guard rail. I looked over and got the picture. A gentle slope spiralled around the inner wall of the building (which was covered with paintings) and finally levelled out back in the entrance hall. About fifty art-lovers were strolling down the hill, taking in Schwitters as they went. We went faster. With Viv on my lap and Schwitters a gentle blur, modern art never looked better.

It was a heady experience that recalled my last day at Pangbourne when a friend and I borrowed Pip Devitt's wheelchair and, with our luggage piled high, sped downhill to the station. That hair-raising journey took place early one winter's morning in the dark. Two headlights coming straight for us up the country lane had our hearts in our mouths. Desperately I jabbed my hockey stick under the wheel to act as a brake but the wheel just continually hopped over it, nearly throwing us out at every bump. Finally, when impact seemed inevitable, I swung the handle hard left and we shot up a grassy bank, the car passed, we came to a halt . . . and gently went into reverse, before regaining the road and continuing on our journey.

This time startled art-lovers were my chief hazard, but with the aid of my plastic stick casualties were avoided and after six delirious revolutions we arrived back in the foyer with a gentle application of the brakes. By the third trip the attendants were suspicious of my disability and after the fourth we were out onto Fifth Avenue.

We needed a tranquilliser after that so popped across the road into the Frick Museum. Here, in a dead millionaire's home, is the most calming picture I've ever seen. Three Gainsborough ladies strolling in Hyde Park. See it and float.

All too soon it was time to come down to earth—for my lunch date with the backers of *Valentino* over on Broadway. Sadly, it was nearly time to say goodbye, but not quite, so I invited Viv to come along with me. Although they must have been millionaires ten times over, lunch with the backers was like eating with a bunch of nice Jewish boys in a small way of business in the rag trade. In other words, you sat around the office eating pastrami sandwiches with lox and bagels balanced on your lap, sipping Tab and lemon tea.

Maybe the informality is supposed to put you at ease and engender a friendly, family atmosphere. Maybe it means that food is secondary to big business. Maybe it's to save money. Anyway, who's complaining? The pastrami was good. It would have been even better washed down with a little Pinot Noir. Whereas it would be unthinkable for the European film community to go without a drink at lunchtime, in the States it helps to be teetotal at this time of day. Most Hollywood commissaries are dry. Once upon a time I was asked to lunch on the Warner Bros. lot in Los Angeles. There would be no alcohol, I was told. Then there will be no me, I retaliated. A pause . . . a solution—in a can. If I ordered Coca-Cola, the contents would be claret. If I asked for 7-Up, I'd get champagne—a typical example of Hollywood hypocrisy. It's OK to get blotto, as long as you do it surreptitiously. All the studios on the West Coast are surrounded by anonymous brown bungalows—*with no windows*—where you can get a lunchtime drink or two without being seen, either from without or within. The flickering night light on the table barely enables you to see the leggy waitress with the sexy smile, even when she sits on your lap to take the order. It's all clandestine and risqué. Perhaps it's a hangover from the days of prohibition, this feeling of guilt you experience when ordering a beer with your hamburger. Other countries, other customs.

Italy, for instance. I remember my first recce. We'd driven around the Umbrian Plain for two hundred hot and dusty miles looking for locations for *Gargantua* and by two o'clock the Italian crew in the car along with me were looking a little glum. It was time and a half for a snack so I suggested pulling up at the next *trattoria* for a quick spaghetti. Immediately the atmosphere lightened. Ten minutes later it was positively festive. Wine appeared on the table automatically and someone ordered as someone poured. Moments later I was tucking into a superb *spaghetti pomodoro*. The others were having salad instead, or so I thought. Actually it was an *antipasto*, which I had forgotten means "before pasta." The pasta followed as I sat with my empty plate before me. At last they finished.

I cleared my throat and was about to say, *"Il conto, per favore,"* when three steaming plates of *escalope milanese* and *zucchini fritti* arrived. I smiled wanly, poured myself another drink, and settled down to watch them eat. I had three more false alarms, one before the cheese, one before the dessert and one before the coffee. As we left the restaurant dusk was falling and so were their eyelids. We drove back to Rome with everyone snoring. Oh well, I thought, if you can't beat 'em, join 'em. We never made *Gargantua* but we had a great time on the way.

Back to the land of the Puritans and the Jewish lunch. Not one of the backers could stomach the gaol scene. It was out of character with the rest of the film, too violent, too disturbing. In vain I argued that it was the keystone of the entire scenario—remove it and the structure would collapse.

"It's as unthinkable as removing the madhouse scene from *The Music Lovers*," piped up Viv.

"We'd have made a lot more money if we had," said a smiling gnome I would have cast as a Jewish tailor. I could see I had a fight on my hands. But you can't fight when you're eating—or can you? They were charming as they plied me with pickles and sauerkraut, persuasive as they poured me more Tab. I nodded and munched and listened. The less receptive I became to their argument, the more they heaped my plate with smoked salmon and sour cream. I felt like throwing up and looked around for a receptacle. Thinking I was still thirsty, they topped me up with Tab—my paper cup brimmethed over.

Basta! I threw the paper plate, the paper cup, the cold food and the calorie-free drink into the trash can. The gaol talk stopped dead.

"'The Twentieth Century' didn't run from Chicago," someone said after a prolonged silence. "That train only ran out of New York Central."

"Thank you," I said, helping them to save face. "Thanks for pointing that out. I'll take care of it directly I get back." Everyone smiled, shook hands and said it was a fine film and that we should give it a sneak preview just as it was, out on the West Coast.

Outside on Broadway, Viv said, "I thought you handled that pretty well."

"I'd have cut anything, even my mother's throat, for a glass of plonk," I replied.

"It'll be a shame if they cut your film just because *they* found it disgusting," she said.

"They could have found it delightful and still wanted to cut it," I said. "As with *The Boy Friend*. They topped and tailed most of the dance routines and dropped the penultimate reel altogether—so bang went two show-stopping numbers and the blossoming of all the back-stage romances. MGM just nipped them in the bud and killed the entire movie. All the relationships in the last reel became completely meaningless."

"Why on earth would they do that?"

"Peanuts!"

"Peanuts?"

"Yes, peanuts. Chopping out fifteen minutes enabled them to get in an extra show a day and sell more peanuts and Tab. I'm getting to hate Tab."

Viv pulled a face. "Couldn't you do anything about it?" she asked.

"I'm not big enough. You have to be as powerful as Spielberg to remain inviolate. Still, I do have the right to my own version in Europe— and, surprise, surprise, that's where my films do best."

"Still, I think that's terrible," said Viv. "No wonder some people say your films are badly edited."

"Butchered is the word. They're handed over to some Hollywood 'cutter' who does a quick hatchet job on something I've slaved long and lovingly over for months. One company who didn't have an editor actually got their lawyer and the projectionist to cut one of my movies. A chimpanzee would have made a better job of it."

"What do you think they'll do with *Valentino?*" said Viv with some concern.

"Come along with me to Tinseltown and find out," I ventured.

For a moment she thought about it, considering the implications.

"I can't," she said finally.

"The boy friend in Boston?"

"And a job there. I work for General Cinema," she said. "They own a string of movie houses right across the States. I've been playing hookey for the last couple of days. It's time to go back."

"What do you do there?"

"Check out the peanut sales," she said, looking me straight in the eye.

My mouth dropped open. "You're joking," I said incredulously.

"Don't knock it," she snapped. "We make a lot more out of peanuts than your movies."

"I see your three years at the Harvard Film School were not wasted," I said, somewhat piqued. "What else did they teach you?"

"Well, I'm also quite an authority on drive-ins," she said.

"Knowledge I guess you picked up on the back seat of an automobile," I said.

"I think you're confusing me with your wife," she said.

Before I could think of an answer she'd disappeared into the crowd.

Twenty-four hours later I was in a record store on Sunset Boulevard drowning my sorrows in shellac. Ever since I started collecting over forty

years ago I've always derived a therapeutic kick from flicking through
record albums. I can do about a hundred a minute. It's not so different
from reading braille; you barely have to look at the sleeves. Like water-
divining, you get a twitch when you're hot and ZAP! You've found a
source of life. And that's what I was in dire need of.

After the brash excitement of New York I could have been on a
different planet. In fact, whenever I approach LA over burning deserts
and red mountains I invariably get the feeling I'm coming in to land
on Mars. But once we touch down the sensation vanishes. This must
be Shangri-la, where the air is full of hummingbirds and the sun-
worshippers eat lotus blossoms and drink at the fount of eternal youth.
Too late! Too late for me, I thought, as I mingled with the golden
boys and girls in the perfumed aisles of Tower Records. Damn it! No
need to rub it in. They were even playing Elgar's *Wand of Youth*.

One youth was breathing impatiently down my neck. He wore a
"Mahler Lives" tee-shirt emblazoned with fake rubies and diamonds he'd
appliquéd with his own fair hands. He had short blond hair, artistically
streaked, and large, brown soulful eyes burning into the back of my skull,
urging me to hurry up. He was aching to dish the dirt with me but knew
this was not the moment. Possessed by a growing religious fervour, I
flicked through the record albums like beads on a rosary. Glory be to the
Father, the Son and the Holy Ghost. Amen! Eureka! I had it. Jubilation!
Out of all the millions of records in the racks, this was the one. I could
hardly believe it. The re-issue of a long-cherished masterpiece, deleted
years ago. I still had my mono copy but it was scratched and worn, and
here it was again, resurrected, in stereo! Martinů's Sixth Symphony performed by Charles Munch and the Boston Symphony. One of the very
first LPs ever issued. It must have been recorded in stereo but never
released in that format because those were the days of mono only. What
excitement! Whatever the outcome of the Viv and *Valentino* situations,
my journey of 10,000 miles had not been in vain. I could return to
England a happy man. Seeing my joy, the youth at my side finally felt
free to speak.

"Hey, what's got into you? I haven't seen you so turned on since
Tommy."

"What turned me on in *Tommy*?" I said, incredulously. "You've got
the wrong opera."

"You know, that time when Ann-Margret in her silver catsuit was
covered in baked beans and soap suds and chocolate and nearly cut her
hand off when you made her dance too close to the smashed TV screen.
We rushed her to the hospital and you carried her into casualty, covered

Ken Russell with Ann-Margret posing on *Tommy* set.
"Loony Tunes" was her comment.

in blood and beans and shitty chocolate, remember? You had a hard-on
then, too."

"OK. So I'm crazy for Martinů and Ann-Margret. What's wrong with
that?"

"I hear your bedhead's covered with Ann-Margret pin-ups."

"Well, you hear wrong," I said. "It's Dorothy Lamour. Now stop
acting the bitchy faggot and let's get out of here."

"Yeah, before you come in your pants."

I gave him the finger, paid for the record and let him buy me a beer
at The Good Earth, a health-food restaurant across the street.

His name was Denny. He was in love with me and always had been—
from the moment he first saw *Women in Love*. Why do people always
equate me with the extreme elements of my work? The men who have
invited me to wrestle nude in front of a log fire are legion. Actually it's

not always a log fire, sometimes it's coal, but more often than not just a two-bar electric. Denny was one of the many I had disillusioned but, unlike the others, he became reconciled to a platonic relationship. He claimed he was my biggest fan, which gave him a right, so he thought, to gross familiarity and all the latest poop.

"So give me the low-down on your big faggot movie," he coaxed, sipping a Budweiser.

"Everyone's a faggot as far as you're concerned," I said, sipping a Coors. "I bet you even think God's a faggot."

"Sure he's a faggot—made man in his own image, didn't he? And Valentino was a faggot for sure. He had it off in his dressing room with John Gilbert and everybody knows it."

"Everybody except me and Nureyev," I said.

"Too bad," said Denny. "It could have been a great scene—another *Women in Love*. I hear he's got a great schlong."

"Yeah! But we'd never get it past the censor," I said.

Denny's eyes widened and, after I'd taken the edge off his voracious appetite for gossip, he drove me to the shrine to show off his latest acquisitions.

The shrine was in the yard behind Denny's Hollywood home—a build-it-yourself bungalow as advertised in the Sears Roebuck mail-order catalogue back in the Twenties. Shipped to the customer ready to assemble, they were similar in principle to those boxes of wooden building blocks with tinted windows and Greek columns kids used to play with before the nursery got buried in plastic. These attractive live-in toys, which owe more to Mexican than classical architecture, were erected all over Hollywood in one form or another between the wars and many still survive, usually set back from the sidewalk and shaded by a tree or two. Next time you see an old Laurel and Hardy short, look beyond the laughs to the back streets of Hollywood and you may see Denny's house or one very similar.

The shrine was an old shack standing in a corner of the yard between a barbecue and a fig tree. On the door was a life-sized painting of Oliver Reed—nude. I leave you to guess the location of the door knob. We entered. Darkness and the smell of burning incense as Denny shut out the big Californian sun.

"Do me a favour, Denny. Give the place an airing once in a while. It stinks worse than a Sixties hippie."

"Yeah, I was wondering what happened to your caftan and beads."

"I put them in storage along with my long hair," I said.

"If you're really through with all that stuff I'd sure appreciate it for the shrine when next you're over," he said, suddenly fawning.

My eyes were growing accustomed to the gloom and the glow of the scented candles lighting the exhibits. What had begun with a signed photograph in response to a fan letter after *Women in Love* had developed into a modern equivalent of *The Picture of Dorian Gray*. For Denny had made it his vocation to beg, borrow and steal bits and pieces from every new feature film of mine that came along. This hadn't been difficult because his selfless devotion to the cause had won him a place in my affections—Shirley's too—to the point of us involving him in a minor way in several of our productions. Denny's part had grown over the years from that of humble acolyte to the more elevated role of Rasputin. Despite this, I had no intention of confessing any sins associated with my marriage for, like his Russian counterpart, Denny was not to be trusted and his sympathies could well rest closer to the Tzarina than the Tzar—though he was quite capable of betraying both.

Fittingly, the shrine was full of ikons of the Russell orthodox church. The sound of a liturgy from *The Music Lovers* sung by a Russian male-voice choir, together with the incense, lent an air of sanctity to a decidedly sinister chapel of unrest, the centrepiece of which was naturally the altar. This was covered in a white lace tablecloth from *Women in Love* and bore the actual plate—according to Denny—on which had rested the fruit that had inspired Alan Bates' Laurentian eulogy to the fig. And where the cutlery should have been were set two hefty syringes used by Cardinal Richelieu's inquisitors to flush out the devils residing in the wombs of possessed Ursuline nuns. These instruments of torture were flanked by two phallic candles similar to those used in *Lisztomania*—my pop version of the life of the greatest stud in musical history. Between the candles, apparently levitating, was a phallus, five feet high, as worn by Roger Daltrey in a Busby Berkeley dream sequence from the same movie. How Denny got that one past customs I'll never know. Resting around the knob like a deadly sex-aid was the yellow lavatory seat, spiked with six-inch nails, from the sadistic Cousin Kevin number in *Tommy*. It reminded me of a Duchamp, and if it had born his signature could have been hanging in the Museum of Modern Art with a million-dollar price tag.

Standing on the floor at either end of the altar, dressed as nuns, were two blow-up sex dolls from my first feature film, *French Dressing*. One wore the habit of a Poor Clare crowned with a Nazi helmet from my last biopic for the BBC, *The Dance of the Seven Veils*. She also suffered the indignity of having her smock pinned up to reveal the black knickers worn by Alma Mahler when she did the can-can on her husband's coffin. And for the very devout, who were not too proud to kneel, there was a worm's-eye view of the crotch decorated with a swastika in gold sequins. The second nun was of the lay variety. She wore a Marilyn Monroe mask and a black and white habit imprinted with pics and headlines featuring the same lady.

Thoughts of *Tommy* and my excursion into the world of "pop" come to mind. When I was a kid, there was no pop music for kids apart from "The Teddy Bears' Picnic." We had to make do with the music of the old folks—as we regarded everyone over twenty-one. Some of it wasn't bad. As a teenager I was a tremendous fan of Stan Kenton—I still am. Next to Tchaikovsky's B Flat Minor Concerto give me Kenton's "Concerto to End All Concertos" with its moody piano intro played by the maestro himself, right through to the syncopated finale of screaming trumpets that were Stan's hallmark. Screaming rock stars never had the same appeal— but by the time they were all the rage I was one of the old folks myself. *Tommy* changed all that.

"Tommy? Tommy who?" I asked when the subject was first mentioned.

"*Tommy* . . . the rock opera," my agent went on.

"I've heard of a soap opera," I said, "but never a rock opera. Who is it by?"

"The Who," he said.

"The what?" I asked.

"No, The Who," he replied patiently, "they're putting on a concert version at the Rainbow. Come along and have a listen."

So I joined him on a pilgrimage to the converted cinema in North London where the event was to be staged—in a symphonic version with a host of guest stars. Just up the road in Harringay Arena I'd once seen a Billy Graham show. *Tommy* and Billy have a lot in common in that they both seem to encourage religious fanaticism verging on hysteria. Both have a pop messiah as a hero, both have their congregation fighting to get up on the stage to touch their respective emissaries. And they both have music. Billy had a choir and *Tommy* had the London Symphony Orchestra. I've never heard it play so badly. The whole show was under-rehearsed, and the P.A. system was a disaster. The only bright spot was Roger Daltrey, who sang the part of Tommy, the deaf, dumb and blind boy who becomes a pop messiah and is exploited and betrayed by his followers. Intrigued by the concept, I got hold of the original album played by The Who, which was much more to my liking.

Even more so was the discovery that certain elements in the plot were very similar to incidents in two scripts of mine I'd been trying to get off the ground for the last couple of years. The first was called *The Angels* and was a sort of Russell 48½—(my age at the time). One of the most memorable sequences in the script dealt with the deification of a pop star called Poppy Day after a report of her death in an air disaster. Poppy's Shrine—a satirical dig at Lourdes—was to feature a giant-size statue of the star herself with cripples praying for a cure as they line up to touch her golden calf. At the end of the script Poppy, in fact one of the few survivors of the crash, is finally discovered wandering in the jungle. She returns to the shrine by helicopter only to be stoned to death by her disillusioned followers, who also destroy her colossal-size pagan image. The resemblance to *Tommy* was uncanny, not only in theme but also in detail. Remember the preacher whose sermon to the faithful was about a woman who could bring "eyesight to the blind"? Well, she turned up in the movie as a gigantic plaster saint in the form of Marilyn Monroe, which Tommy sends crashing to the ground when she fails to answer his prayers for a cure. The other unmade script, *Music, Music, Music*, dealt with a talented young composer who had to abandon work on his rock opera *Jesus on Venus* through lack of finance. To make a living he resorts to writing Muzak for TV commercials, resulting in a crackup with all the products associated with his jingles, including baked beans, detergent and chocolate, all erupting through the TV screen and engulfing him in goo. This sequence also ended up in *Tommy* the movie as his mother, dripping in sables and diamonds, suffers a nervous collapse when she realises to what extent she has been exploiting her handicapped son. Pete Townshend wrote an exciting new number for it called "Champagne," which was very Ann-Margret.

But all this was in the future and far from my mind when I first met Pete, The Who's lead guitarist, who had conceived and composed most of the opera. A producer introduced us at an exploratory lunch in Soho during which Pete spent most of the time predicting that the film would never be made. And the following day when he sent around all the scripts that had already been written on the subject, I began to see why. Some were well written, some were not, but they all had one thing in common— a big negative. They were *not* about a deaf, dumb and blind boy's spiritual journey from darkness to light. I remember one version that had a dedication almost as long as the script itself in which the author thanked everyone from the kitchen cat to the Dalai Lama. Perhaps he hoped to ingratiate himself with Pete, who owned a cat and was deeply into eastern philosophy. I sent them all back to him along with a rough treatment of the piece as I saw it. This in no way deviated from his original, but plugged in the gaps where I found the story obscure, or just plain non-existent. Pete liked most of my suggestions and agreed to write new material. The result was a two-hour vocal and orchestral score without a single word of

(Top) Tommy (Roger Daltrey) surrounded by an adoring mob in *Tommy*. *(Above)* Oliver Reed and Ann-Margret fret over young Tommy (Barry Winch).

(Top) A bearded Ken Russell poses with a group of Marilyn Monroe acolytes during rehearsals for the Preacher sequence in *Tommy*. *(Above)* Elton John revs up for the Pinball Wizard number (Roger Daltrey, right). John Entwistle (far left) plays bass guitar with Keith Moon on drums (rear).

dialogue, which was to take us more than three months to record. When Robert Stigwood finally signalled the green light I chuckled to myself at the irony of it all. The two scripts of mine that had been unceremoniously rejected by the moguls of Hollywood as uncommercial were about to find their way into the most commercial film I've ever made. So what do they know?

Casting and recording went along side by side. As soon as someone was "signed" they came along to The Who's recording studio in South London to play their solo or sing their song or sometimes both. I'd recorded many times with symphony orchestras and knew the form. You simply book them—say, for a four-hour session, from 9 A.M. to 1 P.M., usually in some town hall in the suburbs with good acoustics. And at a minute past nine you have a hundred men and women blowing and scraping away like mad. The pop world plays to a different beat.

"When shall we start, Pete?" I asked as we planned the recording schedule. "Nine A.M.?"

"A little later," he said flatly.

"Ten?" I asked. Pete, whose face is as solemn as an aardvark's, still gave no sign of assent. His nose merely twitched. I could see I was way off the mark.

"How about noon?"

"Afternoon would be better," he said after some consideration.

"Two?" I asked, trying to keep a note of desperation out of my voice. He looked at me sympathetically, knowing as well as I that getting his complex score down on tape with its dubbing and over-dubbing was going to be a monumental task. After a long pause he told me what he felt I was prepared to accept—with bad grace.

"Four, four-thirty," he mumbled, looking at the ground.

I was at the studio at 4:29 P.M. And I was alone, all, all alone with the mice in a rundown building in the middle of nowhere. I noticed a half-empty bottle of Southern Comfort on the piano. By the time the first member of the group arrived, the bottle was empty.

"Wot are you doing 'ere so early, Ken?" asked a surprised Roger Daltrey. "We never do nuffing before nine."

And that, I discovered, was on a good day. After that I went on the night shift and slept in the day, as do most of the rock world. Recording the score was a laborious business that started with a click track, which was built up instrumentally layer by layer using a 24-track recorder until we had the equivalent of a king-size musical sandwich. And Pete would drive himself and those around him for take after take all through the night until he was satisfied with the result, though sometimes, because he is a perfectionist, he had to settle for second-best. I often wondered what he was hearing that I couldn't, for all those takes seemed more or less the same to me. I began to wonder if the tremendous sound levels at which rock musicians work didn't eventually impair their hearing. Frequently I found the noise almost unbearable and took to sitting out in the reception area, where it was still pretty overpowering. Meanwhile, we were making progress with the cast, which had to meet with producer Robert Stigwood's approval. He went along with Ann-Margret and Oliver Reed and Tina Turner, but balked at Pete's suggestion of Tiny Tim as the Pinball Wizard. Stigwood had his heart set on Elton John. We had no quarrel with this choice, but Elton was playing hard to get and we were running out of time.

We were having a similar problem with Eric Clapton. Pete had always wanted him for the preacher, but Clapton had vanished from the scene and was leading the life of a recluse in an isolated country house. Rumour had it that he would never play again, but this did not deter Pete, who eventually managed to gain entry and after several visits succeeded in coaxing Clapton into the recording studio. He was silent and withdrawn and never took part in the sessions, though of course that was our constant hope. Then one day he actually picked up a guitar. We all held our breath. Then he put it down again. A few days later he picked it up again and played a chord. And so it went on until the big night when he was about to join in with the others. Then news came in that Stevie Wonder had flown into town and was recording at a studio in Portobello Road. Clapton was first out of the door. But eventually the miracle happened and Clapton's big comeback was on the move.

There was another member of the group with a problem—Keith Moon. My introduction to Manic Moon happened the night I was invited to The Who's recording studio for the first time, to hear them laying down a track for *Quadrophenia*. Being an innocent, I took a seat a few feet from Moon and his battery of percussion. The explosion when it occurred took me back to the days of the Blitz. It seemed impossible that this slightly built man with the rolling eyes could be capable of such an audio onslaught. Six months later Moon was a wreck. His crazy lifestyle had reduced him to a pathetic shadow not strong enough to knock the skin off a rice pudding. And there were times when Pete had to replace him with an anonymous session man. I began to wonder if he'd be fit enough to play Uncle Ernie, the lecherous old man who debauches Tommy. Arriving several days late for a recording session was one thing, but being a minute late for a unit call at 7:30 A.M. was another. In fact, the producer was worried sick at the prospect of these unreliable rock and rollers playing havoc with our schedule. He'd also heard that they took drugs, destroyed hotels and drove Rolls-Royces into swimming pools. He was particularly worried about Elton John, who had a fleet of R-R's and would probably never miss a couple. Yes, Elton was with us, Stigwood having made him an offer he couldn't refuse. In the event there was no cause for alarm, no one was ever late on the set and there was only one violent act I know of and that was completely justifiable. Moon, who had been hanging on the phone for a word with the hotel porter for some time, suddenly saw him walking across the car park a hundred feet below. Without a moment's hesitation, Moon tore the phone from his bedroom wall, threw it through the open window and while it was still in mid-air, shouted, "You're wanted on the phone!"

But far worse was to come—from an unexpected quarter. We were back in Portsmouth, where we'd shot *The Boy Friend*. We needed an army barracks, we needed sandy beaches, we needed an amusement park, we needed a holiday camp, we needed a theatre, we needed a scrap metal yard full of giant pinballs and we needed an old pier with a dance hall. And they were all to be found in Portsmouth—or Southsea, its next-door neighbour. So we shot the Pinball Wizard in the same derelict theatre where Twiggy had trodden the boards in *The Boy Friend*, and down the road on the Royal pier we shot the dance hall scene where Oliver Reed smooches with Ann-Margret. The pier—an ornate structure of wood and cast iron—was typical of many such structures built in Victoria's reign to grace our seaside resorts. For the price of a few pennies, holiday makers could imagine they were on a cruise, enjoying all the amusements to be found on an ocean liner— and more. Apart from a sprawling penny arcade, there was usually a restaurant, a camera obscura, a theatre and a dance hall. And as often as not, a lifeboat. The pier at Southsea had seen better days. The paint peeling from its fake minarets was as dated as Omar Khayyam and just as unpopular with the general public, who found the local bingo parlours much more to their taste. And if they fancied the idea of water beneath their feet, they could always enjoy the thrill of a short trip by Hovercraft to the Isle of Wight.

No, the pier was nothing but a white elephant and a bit of an embarrassment to the Town Council who owned it. We had no difficulty at all in hiring the dance hall for the day. Those of you who saw the film may remember young Tommy gazing down from the balcony as his mum is swept off her feet by the lecherous Frank, as the saxophones in the band swoon and sway. You may remember the atmosphere being rather smokey—rather too smokey, perhaps. We thought so too and had the place evacuated. A few minutes later the two hundred or so extras were safely on shore while I sat around with the camera crew waiting for someone to find the source of the trouble,

JUST GOOD PEN PALS 125

which we guessed was nothing more than a smouldering electric cable. A sharp splintering sound made us look up. There, in the vast wooden dome above our heads, a crack appeared, followed by a wisp of smoke. A second later there was an almighty explosion as the roof blew apart, revealing an inferno of flame. Everyone jumped to their feet and belted for the exit, grabbing a piece of camera equipment on the way. Moments later the camera was set up on the promenade filming the burning pier—and the press were filming us. And no matter which way I turned, their prying lenses were snapping at me. It was a no-win situation, as was proved next morning when I saw the papers. "Russell turns back on inferno" or "Russell gloats over inferno." Of course, the film unit was held responsible, even though the origin of the blaze was never discovered. The destruction was total. It was all very sad, though I must confess, it made a grand finale for the film. And there it was, frozen for all eternity—a big, coloured blow-up hanging on the wall of Denny's shrine next to a poster of Tommy as the pop Messiah.

As I looked about me I felt a nostalgic pang for the days gone by when I was a devout Catholic.

"It's got everything but a confessional, Denny," I said. "And I've given you plenty of choice, from *Lisztomania* to *Song of Summer*."

". . . in which you played the dirty old priest caught screwing a parishioner in his own church . . ."

". . . as witnessed by Eric Fenby himself when he popped in to say a prayer for Delius."

"That must have rocked his faith some," said Denny. "What made you lose yours? I've often wondered."

"Something larger than human frailty."

"What?"

"Do you really want to know, or is it just morbid curiosity?"

Standing in the candleglow he had the demeanour of a father confessor. "I want to know."

"Skiddaw!"

"Skiddaw?" he repeated incredulously. "You've got to be kidding."

"No, I'm not kidding," I said, wishing I'd kept quiet. "Don't you have any booze in here? No shrine of mine would be complete without some booze. Remember *Tommy*, with the preacher dishing out speed and Scotch to the communicants?"

"How could I forget?" said Denny, going to the tabernacle and taking out a chalice and a bottle of Jack Daniel's. He poured a generous measure and we took it in turns to drink.

"What's happened to all those nice pictures you used to have?" I asked. "You know, the boy on the white horse galloping across the Malvern

Hills, Tchaikovsky and his sister dancing in the silver-birch wood, Mahler and his wife swimming in that wonderful lake in the summer, Strauss picnicking with his family in that alpine meadow, Delius and Jelka on the mountaintop watching the sunset. Where are they?"

"I'm no longer into Julie Andrews stuff," he said. "They're in storage."

"Pity. They'd brighten the place up a bit. It's all darkness and no light. It's turned into a black museum."

"That reminds me!" he said, brushing aside my concern. "There's a new place opened down on Santa Monica Boulevard called 'The Pleasure Chest.' You gotta see it. It's so you!"

"You've got a one-track mind," I said half an hour later as we wandered around a fake dungeon eyeing the exhibits. Everything from dildoes to bondage was on display in what could easily have passed as a medieval torture chamber.

"I thought you'd feel at home here," he said, fingering a spiked whip. "Do you use lubricants? There's a great brand on sale here at a dollar sixty-nine."

"The only lubricant you could sell me right now," I said, "is in a bottle labelled 'Miller Lite.'"

"Naturally," he said. "It's the champagne of beers."

"Let's get out of here."

We walked down the street to a gay bar called "The Palms" where Denny seemed not unknown. Rock music blasted my eardrums. I endured it for the sake of the beer.

"Care to dance?" he asked.

"They'll think me queer," I said.

"They'll think you queer if you don't," he replied.

"OK," I said, "why not? I've danced with my kids, I've danced in an all-male ballet group and I danced with boys at Pangbourne, so why stop now?"

We danced. He did the latest. My steps were a mixture of the twist and modern ballet, both of the European and the American schools—as interpreted by an out-of-practice, overweight forty-nine-year-old. Still, they were a tolerant lot in "The Palms" and no one objected to a little spilt beer and bruised toes—except Denny, who soon discovered he was hungry.

We drove a few blocks north for a bite at Oscar's—an intimate restaurant opposite the Chateau Marmont on Sunset Boulevard. The atmosphere, redolent of a Deco London nightclub in the Thirties *sans* evening dress and dancing, was a cosy retreat for the quiet Englishman nostalgic for public-school dinners. Like everywhere in LA, there is music while you eat but it's all Roy Fox, Carrol Gibbons and Jessie Matthews.

"Did you see her in *Evergreen?*" I asked Denny as Jessie's piping tones helped down a salmon fishcake.

"No, but she's appearing at the Music Hall in Santa Monica if you fancy another look."

"Really? How exciting. *Evergreen* was great: the only British musical of the Thirties to come anywhere near the American variety, and Jessie was every bit as good as Ginger Rogers. You should have seen her in that number, 'Dancing on the Ceiling.' Fantastic! My one regret is that I never saw her in the flesh."

"I hear there's an awful lot of it now," he said. "She'd bring the ceiling down if she started dancing on it today."

"Pity," I said. "None of us fatties are the dancers we once were. Poor Jessie."

"Do you want to drive down and see her?"

"No thanks. I prefer to keep my impressions of her evergreen."

"What do you weigh now?" he asked. "It must be close on two hundred pounds."

"You'll have to convert that into stones," I said. "Anything over fourteen pounds means nothing to me."

"Well, whatever it is, I just can't picture you in tights."

"I didn't always wear tights. Sometimes I wore jeans rolled up to mid-calf. Do you realise I was probably the first Englishman to wear jeans?"

"Oh, when was that?"

"Let me see. I got a scholarship with the International Ballet in forty-eight, left in nineteen-fifty to join the touring company of *Annie Get Your Gun*, joined Lettie Lubin's British Dance Group and London Theatre Ballet in fifty-one and when they went bust joined Bob Riddle's Barefoot Boys, in the same year. He was a Yank. He danced in jeans. All the troupe did likewise. I've never worn them since."

"Trying to block out an unhappy experience?"

"Or enshrining a happy one, Dr. Freud."

"So how was life among the barefoot boys?"

"Oh, we had a gay old time."

"I bet! I always had you down as a latent homosexual."

"You're only saying that because I've slept with men."

Denny's eyes popped. He thought he knew all there was to know about me. This was news and he was hungry for it. Suddenly he lost his appetite for mashed potatoes.

"You may not realise it, but life in the ballet in those days was a rather celibate affair. It's an insular world at the best of times and the sexes seem to segregate quite naturally.

"When I gave up my amateur night at the Shepherd's Bush Ballet and went to a full-time professional school I almost became a monk. Maybe that's because the girls in their black uniforms were treated as novices by the superior mother who ran the school. 'Two gentlemen sharing' became the norm and usually it had more to do with economy than sex. Then occasionally you'd be visiting a pal and miss the last bus home. So the natural thing to do was share a bed. Where's the harm in that?"

"Nowhere! What happened?"

"I remember one chap saying, 'I won't touch you if you don't touch me,' and as I didn't, he didn't either. I guess people were more polite in those days. Even when it came to seduction it was conducted in a very gentlemanly way with a lot of old-world charm."

"For instance . . ." said Denny with controlled impatience, as I took time out to savour a pickled onion.

"I met him in the art gallery. It was empty. I had my back to the door and was practising a few high kicks when a voice from the blue said, 'How much is this Ivon Hitchens?' I spun round and saw a tall, distinguished man in a grey cloak. He had a lean aquiline face and well-groomed silver hair reaching almost to his shoulders."

"How old was he?"

"In his early seventies."

"You sure can pull 'em."

"Anyway, he bought the painting—an abstract woodland scene—and asked if I could deliver it. This was by no means an unusual request, so I took his address and after work ran it over to him in a taxi. He lived on the top floor of a Victorian terraced house in South Kensington in a flat stacked from floor to ceiling with paintings—mostly by Ivon Hitchens."

"Who is this Hitchens?" said Denny. "I've never heard of him."

"And you're never likely to. He belonged to the school of British painters fashionable after the last war. He painted long abstract landscapes in bold autumnal strokes with flurries of colour representing I don't know what—flying leaves or birds perhaps, or just the sheer exuberance of being outdoors on a windy day in the fall—gone now, alas, blown off the scene by pop art . . . Where was I?"

"In the old guy's apartment," prompted Denny. "What happened next?"

"Ah, yes. He invited me to tea. 'Oh, there's a stranger in my cup,'

I said, looking at a solitary leaf floating in the palest liquid I'd ever seen.

" 'Not for long,' he said, with something between a twitch and a wink. 'Now, tell me about your aspirations in *le ballet*.' On a reflex I winked back and told him I was about to start full-time classes at the International School of Ballet just around the corner in Queensberry Mews and would be giving up my job in the art gallery to live on the five-pounds-a-week allowance Dad was providing to launch me on a new career. He laughed, exposing a mouthful of yellowing horse's teeth and said 'Hardly a king's ransom, but even Nijinsky had to endure poverty before he became *le roi de la danse*; long may you follow in his shoes,' and he toasted me with his tea cup and put it to his lips. I hesitated.

" 'Come, what are you waiting for?' he said.

" 'The milk and sugar,' I stammered, turning red. His laughter had a touch of scorn. 'This is Lapsang Souchong,' he said, draining his cup, then 'What is your preference?'

" 'Well, I'm rather partial to Typhoo Tips,' I said, taking a sip. It tasted of tarred hemp and scent. 'Mm, nice.'

" 'Nice!' he snorted. 'It's delectable.'

"Delectable! He's a bit of a queer bloke, I thought, echoing one of Mum's favourite phrases."

"Who exactly was he, this 'queer bloke'?" asked Denny.

"Herbert was a collector and, before he retired, a cellist. He still had beautiful hands, long and delicate, and I could well imagine them tenderly caressing the sensitive instrument between his legs."

"He was a wanker, then?"

"I meant his cello, not his cock, asshole. Anyway, it happened that someone had let him down that evening so he had a spare ticket for the ballet . . ."

"Surprise, surprise!"

". . . and would I care to go along with him?"

"And afterwards he invited you back for another cup of tea?"

"No. For a cup of Instant Postum. He introduced me to quite a few things, actually, and also increased my general awareness in the nicest possible way. There, I've said it: nice! I'm still saying it. I say 'nice' to everything; everything is *nice*. I used to flog that adjective to death. Instant Postum was *nice*, Lapsang Souchong was *nice*, Ivon Hitchens was *nice*, Herbert was *nice*. Must have picked it up from Mum, I suppose. Everything was *nice* and if it wasn't *nice* it was *nasty*. I must have driven him mad with my mini vocabulary. It was nice of him to put up with it. I suppose he wanted something out of me."

"Or something *in* you!"

"Ah, you've guessed: I missed the last train home."

"And he offered to share his sack with you."

"No, he offered me his nice double bed while he slept on a camp bed in the study."

"No comment."

"He even brought me tea in the morning and cooked breakfast and, as he knew I was hard up, offered to put me up at his place for nothing. How incredibly generous, I thought. Not everyone would help a struggling artist, and he seemed genuinely concerned about my career. He encouraged me to bring my tights with me and do a little workout at his place. He even used to sketch me."

"In the nude, I bet."

"Only when I'd exhausted my repertoire of classical ballet positions."

"That couldn't have taken long. Do you have any of those sketches now? I could use them in the shrine."

"Sorry. They're hanging in the Museum of Modern Art."

"You're kidding!"

"I'm kidding. I don't know where they are. He said I was a good model and used to pay me five bob an hour, though I was a bit of a fidget and he often had to discipline me with a few cuts with his paintbrush, which was long and thin and pliant. I remember having to get him to scrub the crimson off my buttocks. Your eyes are widening again, Denny. It was paint not blood, you nerd." Poor Denny was on a switchback of emotions. "Look, what's wrong with a little corporal punishment? After three years at Pangbourne I could take it without flinching."

"Did he get a hard on?"

"I don't know. *I* certainly did, but I think it went stiff with cold more than anything else. Herbert was generous in all things save heating, a general failing with the English, I'm afraid."

"So when did he move back into his own bed?"

"Not for months. First he moved the camp bed back, said the study was draughty. He put up with that for a couple of weeks, until one night, he said, ' . . . it's rather silly making up two beds, don't you think, when there's so much room in yours?'

"And before I could answer he'd slipped in beside me with the usual, 'Don't worry. I won't touch you if you don't touch me.' So I said goodnight, turned my back on him and went to sleep. When I awoke at dawn he was stroking my legs. How he'd got my pyjama bottoms off without disturbing me, I'll never know. 'Are these the legs that will put Nijinsky to shame?' he said silkily. 'No,' I replied truthfully, jumping out of bed, getting dressed and getting out."

"What happened to him?"

"God knows. Bumped into him a few years later hanging around a kids' playground, looking a bit seedy. Died a lonely old, dirty old man, I guess."

"Bit cruel, aren't you? Bit of a tease, bit of a prude."

"I take people at face value. If I get talking to someone in the street, say, and they ask me back to their place for a cup of tea, I expect just that, not for the guy to get me up to his flat and pull his dick out!"

"Did that ever happen to you?"

"Yes, it did, at Earl's Court. Only he invited me up for coffee and doughnuts."

"How long was his dick?"

"Over a foot. Denny, your eyes are widening again."

"What did you do?"

"Stuck a doughnut on it!"

"You're weird. How come none of these stories were in John Baxter's *An Appalling Talent*? That was supposed to be your authorised biography, wasn't it?"

"Yes, like the authorised version of the Bible. Anyway, that's all they are, stories."

"You mean they're not true?"

"Would that worry you? Like most everyone else, you're prepared to think the worst of me. And the worse I'm made out to be, the better you like it." The conversation was heading for deep waters; it was time to get the bill.

As we got up to go, Denny said, "I'm surprised you're not out at MGM watching the preview."

"The preview's tomorrow."

"Yeah, I've got tickets. But there's one tonight as well."

"There can't be. I'd have been told."

"You wanna check? I'll drive you over."

We arrived in time to find the specially invited audience heading for the parking lot. I rushed into the empty foyer and nearly collided with my film editor and his assistant staggering out with a load of cans.

"What the fuck's going on, Steve?" I asked.

"We're taking the cutting copy back to the office, Guv."

"Why didn't you tell me there was a screening tonight?"

"I assumed you knew. Didn't the office tell you?"

I shook my head. "How did it go?"

"Pretty good. They laughed a lot."

"Not at the gaol scene, I hope."

He put his cans down and acted puzzled. "But the whole point of the viewing, Guv, was to see how the film played *without* the gaol scene. I thought it was your idea."

"You know very well it wasn't my fucking idea . . ."

"Well, I take my orders from the guys who hand out my pay packet every Friday, Guv, and if you want my opinion it played pretty well without the gaol scene."

"I don't want your opinion. What else did the pay packet decree?"

He looked shifty. "I don't know," he mumbled. "I'm only the editor, but I know Bob Chartoff thinks Valentino's drunk scene should be cut in half."

"Which half?"

He managed an embarrassed laugh and picked up the cans again. "If you'll excuse us, Guv, they'll be locking up soon. What time shall we expect you in the cutting room tomorrow?"

"Don't expect me. Just cut out that drunk scene and drop it over to my hotel tonight."

He was dumbfounded. "But Ken. That'll take all night!"

"Don't 'Ken' me! It's in the last reel and it's in one shot. It'll take five minutes. Now get cracking."

I turned on my heel and walked out, out of the preview theatre, past Steve, past Denny, past the show case with Judy Garland's emerald slippers, past the cold vats of Mrs. Meyers' chickenshit soup, past the plaster lion, past the empty office blocks of the men who'd butchered *The Boy Friend* and buried *Savage Messiah*, past the crumbling portals of Tara and out through the gates of Munchkin Land to the streets of Culver City where I grabbed a cab to the Beverly Hills Hotel and started packing. Then the phone rang.

Three days later, I was sitting before a roaring log fire at the Red Lion Inn, Stockbridge, sipping hot toddies and nibbling drumsticks with Viv. Outside it was snowing and our faces still glowed from a ski trek along the banks of the Housatonic. I was pouring out the story of my nightmare trip to Hollywood, which had remained bottled up within me until that moment.

"My intention was to go straight home," I explained. "Then you called and I came running."

"And did you bring the drunk scene with you?"

"No. I did as they asked. I took out my nail scissors and cut it in half—right up the middle. So instead of two hundred feet of film there was four hundred feet of film in two useless celluloid ribbons. Then I stuffed it into a hotel laundry bag and next morning, on my way to the airport, dumped it on Bob Chartoff's desk. Unfortunately, he wasn't in so I left a cryptic note asking him to choose the half he wished to keep." As I'd hoped, Viv laughed but I wasn't so happy about her follow-up.

"It doesn't exactly solve the problem, though, does it?"

"It'll solve itself," I said. "By the time I get back to England for the final dub the air will have cleared."

"Even over Ladbroke Square?" asked Viv dubiously. Not being a clairvoyant, I could only shrug and stare into the fire. That was the future. That was the day after tomorrow. For the moment I was content to continue basking in the glow of last night's "country hop" with Viv. Most of the evening we'd been content to sit at one of the trestle tables, sipping clam chowder, chatting and tapping our feet in time to the square dances played on fiddle, banjo and jew's harp so beloved of Charles Ives.

Until the band struck up a polka, that is. Then something inside me went "pow" and I jumped to my feet, grabbed ahold of Viv and polka'd around the floor in dizzy double time. And once again the exhilaration I had shared with her on Brooklyn Bridge and in the Guggenheim flared up and set my blood a-buzzin', just as the jew's harp was a-buzzin'. Around and around the floor we spun at twice the speed of light and in the opposite direction to everyone else. Faces of laughing couples loomed up and sped past us as we yelled with delight. By a miracle there was no collision. Alas, it was over all too soon. The music ended and we collapsed into our chairs, laughing and breathless to scattered applause and good-natured cat calls.

"Wherever did you learn to dance like that?" asked Viv, gasping.

"At the International Ballet School on Wednesday afternoons," I panted.

"Didn't they teach you to go clockwise?" she laughed.

"No, they never did," I said.

"I've never enjoyed a dance more."

"Me neither."

"We must dance some more."

"Sorry. It's the only dance I know. I haven't done it in twenty-five years."

"There seems an awful lot you haven't done in twenty-five years. You've been missing out. Let's hope you don't have to wait another twenty-five years before you do it again. Come on, let's go outside. I need a breath of air."

As we walked out into the New England winter's night I was put in mind of one of the most poignant moments in all music. I never dreamed that one day I'd be living it. It's the moment in the *Holidays* symphony when Charles Ives suddenly grabs the listener by the arm and drags him away from the intoxication of a square dance into the sobering wonder of a moonlit snowscape. There's even a door-slam in the music which immediately changes character into something deep and soulful . . . the ghost of a half-remembered tune played in slow motion on the upper strings. "Goodnight ladies, goodnight ladies, goodnight ladies, it's time to say goodnight." Then, with almost unbearable pathos, the music seems to dissolve into the crisp night air, bringing a greater sense of bliss with every breath one takes. It was in this state of transfiguration that Viv and I said *our* goodnights, the ones that really mattered, that is. We repeated them more formally in the presence of Mrs. Jolly, who had kindly invited me to stay the weekend at her Lakeville home. Next morning Viv dropped me off at Boston Airport on her way to work at General Cinema.

As the 747 dragged me reluctantly away from the delights of New England back to the uncertainty of old England, I raised my glass to the kindred spirit that had brought us together—Charles Ives.

Honeymoon Night in the Elizabeth Taylor Suite

I had been two days AWOL, and although I surrendered voluntarily, a court-martial was inevitable. I pleaded guilty and was placed on probation. But at least the family was back together again. To celebrate we all went out for a slap-up dinner at a fashionable Middle Eastern restaurant in Kensington High Street. Everyone was on their best behaviour but ill at ease. The menu circulated and we all ordered the same main dish—kofta meat balls. While Shirley and I made small talk, the kids, in an effort to be festive, tapped their plates in time to the ethnic muzak until, after an age, the meat balls arrived—all forty-nine of them. What little appetite we had immediately evaporated. The dinner was not a success. There was really nothing to celebrate—except the presence of a ghost in the house.

A few days later came another cause for celebration—twenty years of marriage. Shirley served me breakfast in bed. "Happy Anniversary," she said with heavy irony, swishing out of the bedroom in her mauve kimono. I yawned a late reply, rubbed my eyes and stirred my tea. Mm, what an aroma! I sipped it. Mm, what flavour! The blend of one part Earl Grey, two parts Twinings Nectar worked its usual magic and I was infused with a spirit of peace and wellbeing.

It didn't last. There were some letters on the tray. I ate my peanut-butter toast and opened them one by one with sticky fingers. There was nothing of particular interest except for the single letter which Shirley had thoughtfully opened for me. It was from Viv and looked as if it had been screwed up into a ball and straightened out again. As I smoothed the crumpled pages some passages freshly underlined in red ink caught my eye. I read them first. They referred to me and Viv making love in the snow after the barn dance. That, together with the message I read between the lines, spurred me into action.

I hopped out of bed and started packing. By the time Vince, the driver, was ringing the door bell, my luggage was in the hall, ready to go: two cases of clothes, the modest hi-fi system, a few books and a pile of records. Confusion reigned as the kids poured out of the kitchen on their way to school, chivvied on by Shirley, while Vince came in to help me load up the car. Suddenly the hall was empty. The kids had gone without saying goodbye, the luggage was stowed and Shirley was uncharacteristically clattering away at the sink in the kitchen.

Haig Pit pattered up and looked at me with limpid brown eyes. He knew something the others did not—that I was going for good. Take me with you, he seemed to be saying. Tempted as I was to snatch him up and make a dash for it, I knew that Shirley would resist the attempted kidnap with her life. I might win custody of the children but she would never relinquish custody of the dog. Nevertheless, I patted him gently on the head and said, "Want to come along with father, old Pitbull?"

Shirley was in the hall in a flash. "Get your hands off him," she said, snatching him up, though he weighed a ton. The dog licked his lips. Saliva dripped from his undershot jaw. I retreated to the door.

"Goodbye," I said. "I won't be back."

"Who's going to cook for you?" she scoffed. "You'll be back all right! She might be able to fuck in a snowdrift but I bet she can't cook to save her life."

She's right about the cooking, I thought to myself. The scrambled eggs Viv had prepared for Sunday brunch at Lakeville had been burnt, but she was wrong about the scene in the snow. That was a dream I'd had.

"And don't even think of borrowing the car, will you?" she said, staggering into the kitchen with the dog. I looked at the very off-white Crown Custom Toyota Estate as we drove off and thought, that's no great loss. Aloud I said, "Vince, I'm thinking of getting a new car. Got any ideas?"

"What are you after, Guv, another estate?"

"No, I was thinking of something a bit more sporty."

"I think a Morgan might well suit you. It's British, traditional and not too over the top."

"I don't think that would suit me at all."

"Then why don't I make a slight detour and drive you to the studios by way of Edgware Road? It's full of car showrooms like you wouldn't believe. Then you can take your pick."

And that's what we did, zig-zagging hazardously along one of London's busiest arterial roads—mile after mile with no success, until Vince suddenly applied the brakes, nearly causing a pile-up.

"That's the car for you, Guv," he shouted above the tooting horns. I looked through a showroom window and saw the simplest sports car ever.

Thirty minutes later I was gunning my red Alfa Romeo Spider towards the studios. She was second-hand and with only a thousand miles on the clock was barely "run in." With a thousand pounds knocked off the original cost I had a new image at bargain price. It was a novel and exciting experience to have the wind blowing through one's hair, especially if the hair is white. "Life begins at Forty," sang Sophie Tucker. Well, I was forty-nine and getting younger every minute.

I needed a further two items to start me off properly on my new life and one of them was *Great Dishes of the World* by Robert Carrier. Its gravy-stained pages had taken the place of the family Bible after Shirley and I had become lapsed Catholics, and though I'd never practised what it preached, I'd certainly enjoyed its benefits as dispensed by Shirley. Now I was about to become a novice of the cuisine myself—for just £2.95. Two bargains and not yet ten o'clock. I was doing well.

By the time I arrived at the studio, Vince had unloaded the baggage and set up the hi-fi in my office. Cracking myself a half-bottle of champagne from the fridge, I settled back in an armchair to absorb a dose of Gershwin. I was feeling benign and wished the sensation to continue. I put on *Funny Face* and thought of Viv. The sensation continued. A telex arrived from Hollywood saying, "No cuts. Carry on with the final mix."

I was euphoric and remained so throughout the day while checking things over with the dubbing editor to make sure all his sound effects were in place and the music tracks laid up in synch with the picture. Everything, it seemed, was on schedule and he was confident we'd be ready to go ahead with our dubbing in ten days' time, as planned.

They turned out to be the longest ten days of my life. The office was an office and not a home. It had last been furnished in the early post-war days and the springs of the faded armchairs were squashed and broken. The walls were glaring white and spotted with pictures of flops from the Bryan Forbes period of production when, handed millions of pounds on a plate, he apparently decided to play it safe and turned out a string of B movies—B for Bland, with the accent on Edwardian gentility. Everything was M.O.R.—which can be hazardous even for the most careful driver. The result was R.I.P. and another sad monument in the graveyard of the British film industry. Scenes from *The Raging Moon*, *Dulcima* and *The Man who Haunted Himself* were far from cheerful company to spend the night with curled up under my Canadian wolf coat on a lumpy Ercol settee. The moon shone through the Crittal windows. The curtains didn't meet. I couldn't sleep. I'd had a late supper at the *ristorante* across the road in an effort to prolong the day and the pasta was lying heavily on my stomach despite the flask of Chianti I'd swilled down along with it. Feelings of guilt chased each other around my head.

I turned on the light and flicked through my record collection in the hope of finding something to blow them away. Beethoven's Fifth? No, I needed a breeze, not a whirlwind. Ah, *The Boy Friend*, with Twiggy's elfin face smiling up at me from the album cover. Shirley had produced some of her finest work on that movie—which owes its very existence to a lie I told at a reception organised by Twiggy's boyfriend.

Justin de Villeneuve, the young entrepreneur who lit the fuse for Twiggy's skyrocketing career as an international model, was about to ignite another firework and had hired the Ritz as a launching pad for his latest protégé—a talented young opera singer hoping to soar into the firmament of pop. Justin, knowing I was working nearby, had invited me to drop in for a drink and a display of vocal pyrotechnics he promised would be dazzling. The result was a damp squib; even the cheap champagne had more sparkle. Hoping Justin wouldn't ask my opinion as he circulated among the media, I found myself a plate of food and a quiet corner out of the limelight. Perhaps that's why Twiggy chose to sit in the vacant chair next to mine. It wasn't her affair, and she didn't want to steal the show. And as we chatted about everything but the event itself, I gradually became aware of an inquisitive ear tuning into our conversation. A grinning journalist with champagne in one hand and lobster pâté in the other was starting to rub elbows.

"I didn't know you two were acquainted," he interjected.

"Oh, we've known each other for ages," said Twiggy brightly. Was it really as long as that? I wondered. At the speed Twiggy lived I suppose eighteen months probably seemed a lifetime. One day Justin had rung me up out of the blue, introduced himself and invited me and Shirley to meet Twiggy at their home in a mews flat on the unfashionable side of Bloomsbury. Overflowing garbage cans and a windowless brick wall in no way prepared me for the Arabian Nights interior. What was probably a warehouse had been transformed into a sultan's palace, heavy with exotic drapes. It reminded me of the decor for the ballet *Scheherazade*. The lighting came from star clusters floating in clouds of incense above a pile of voluptuous cushions littering the floor. On the utmost pinnacle of these sprawled Twiggy wearing white silk pyjamas and what appeared to be a pair of giant ear muffs. As Justin introduced us she gave an infectious smile, removed the ear muffs and placed them on my head. I thought I'd entered another dimension. "I Am the Walrus" was happening in my head, which was suddenly as big as the Met. The sound from this 1970 state-of-the-art hi-tech headset was phenomenal. I was transported.

A few hours later I was transported yet again—back home with Shirley—by the state-of-the-art couple in their customised Porsche. It was the closest I ever got to sitting in a space craft with speed to match as we hit Mach 1 in as many seconds. And as my stomach tried desperately to catch up with me, I began to experience life in the fast lane. The purpose of the meeting had been to explore the possibility of us doing a film with Twiggy—a fairy story with music by Paul McCartney. And although nothing came of it, we continued to meet and discuss subjects as diverse as "Sergeant Pepper" and Sandy Wilson. We were actually airing our mutual enthusiasm for *The Boy Friend* when we'd been so rudely interrupted. But you must always be nice to journalists—one day they might write something nice about you.

"So what are you two cooking up?" said the man from the *Daily Bugle*. "Do you want Twiggy to play a naked nun? I've heard what you've been up to down at Pinewood Studios, Ken. I bet Justin might have something to say about that. Eh, Twiggy?" he continued with a leer.

Twiggy just laughed in his face, but I was stung into replying, "Actually you've missed the boat, we finished filming a week ago, but Twiggy *was* in *The Devils*, Justin too. They played two masked courtiers in the retinue of Louis XV."

"This I must see," said the journalist.

Twiggy and Christopher Gable sing "I Could
Be Happy with You," in *The Boy Friend*.

"Yeah, you must," said Twiggy. "I'm dressed as a boy all in gold and
Justin is the one in high heels with a beauty spot and cupid bows. You
can't miss us." And she put her hand over her mouth to stifle another
laugh.

"As a matter of fact, we were discussing a film," I said, piqued by his
persistence.

"I'm going to make *The Boy Friend*, starring Twiggy."

His eyes almost dropped into his champagne.

"Tell me more," he gasped.

"You've got an exclusive," I said. "What more do you want?" He took
the hint and ran off to make his call.

"Well, that got rid of him," I said. Twiggy stared at me open-
mouthed—on her it looked good.

"Cor, Ken," she said in her inimitable Cockney, "you ain't 'alf been
and gone and done it now."

Not for the first time she reminded me of Eliza Doolittle.

"We can dream, can't we?" I said, wishing I'd kept my big mouth
shut. Champagne will be the death of me!

Sure enough, next day at breakfast there it was, splashed all over the
centre pages of the paper. The phone rang, playing havoc with my hang-

over. I answered it and sobered up instantly. It was a lawyer representing MGM.

Had I made that statement? ". . . Er, well, yes . . ."

On whose authority?

"Er, no one's . . ."

Was I aware that MGM owned the screenplay rights?

"Er, no . . ."

Would I kindly make myself available for a meeting in said lawyer's office, tomorrow at nine?

"Er, yes."

Why try and hold the suspense? You've probably guessed the outcome.

When I arrived at Metro's London office dead on nine, the lawyer wasn't there but the president was.

"Do you like *The Boy Friend*?" he asked after a curt greeting.

"I love it," I said. "I've loved it ever since I saw it as a student back in the Fifties."

"Me too," he said. "We've owned the rights for years and never known what to do with it."

"Have you ever thought of filming it straight?" I asked.

"We have a movie of the entire stage production," he said. "As a record of the show it's invaluable, as a film it's a pain in the ass. The Twenties stylisation that works fine on the stage just doesn't translate to the screen. It's mannered and stilted and the cardboard characters never come alive. Do you think you can crack it?"

"I'll have a go," I said, feeling my scalp shrink as it always does when I'm handed the world on a plate.

"Think Twiggy's up to it?" he asked.

"She'll make the perfect Polly," he said.

"They say her voice is even flatter than her chest, if that's possible," he said, "and that she moves with the grace of a young ostrich."

"Give me three months and I'll have her dancing like Ginger Rogers and singing like Judy Garland," I said.

This is beginning to sound like a showbiz success story, and that's how I approached the subject once I got the go-ahead. And as I laboured over the script, Twiggy learned to sing and dance—not quite like those legendary stars, I admit, but with a style all her own.

And as her technique progressed, so her confidence grew. And Justin, who had masterminded her rise to fame in the world of fashion, became a little superfluous. As rehearsals began, I sensed his presence might come to have a deleterious effect on our potential star and suggested Twiggy might be less inhibited if he wasn't around. I was afraid he might criticize or interfere, so I suggested that once we started shooting it might be best for everyone if he kept off the set. At first he was agreeable enough, but as time passed and Twiggy was doing all right without him, he began to brood and grow resentful. Our location probably aggravated his state of mind. Portsmouth, a tacky town on the southern coast, doesn't know whether it's a seaport or a seaside resort and offers little action to a high flyer from the metropolis like Justin. And maybe because he was powerless to interfere on the set, he began to interfere on the contractual side of things, which culminated in a threat to take Twiggy off the movie unless his growing demands were met. Knowing that such an action would ruin Twiggy's career and kill off his golden goose, I took it as an idle threat and let it pass. Even so, I could see that the situation was having a bad effect on Twiggy, who was becoming increasingly isolated.

Except for the big production numbers, all the interiors were actually filmed in a derelict theatre where doves flew in through holes in the roof, rain fell on the stage and Sarah Bernhardt's autograph was preserved under a sheet of murky glass in the star dressing room. I was originally tempted to install Twiggy there, but fearing it might give her a star complex, I put her with all the other girls in a communal dressing room where many of the scenes were shot. I also thought she might absorb a spirit of camaraderie, but all she seemed to soak up was misery. And I began to notice that when she wasn't involved in the filming she'd sit alone in the orchestra stalls shivering in her overcoat. Although she never complained, it was evident that she preferred to freeze in lonely seclusion than endure the bitchery of the warm dressing room. Which was sad, as we had all started out as one big happy family, but petty jealousies soon led to a verbal bloodbath—with Twiggy coming off worst as a result of my giving her two extra numbers. For she had a tenderness and warmth missing from the original heroine that it would have been criminal not to utilise. Accordingly, I introduced two numbers from another MGM musical, *Singing in the Rain*, which expressed her secret love for the handsome juvenile lead, Christopher Gable. They were "You Are My Lucky Star" and "All I Do Is Dream of You," which she performed with great charm and sensitivity. So I finally gave her the star dressing room with my blessing. She'd earned it; she was a real trouper.

So was Max Adrian, who had acquitted himself so well as Delius in *Song of Summer*. He suffered from asthma among other things and had collapsed on the first day of rehearsals—only to insist on carrying on directly he'd regained consciousness. But Metro got to hear about it and wanted to drop him. "He's uninsurable," said an exec. " 'It's Never Too Late to Fall in Love' is a heavy number. What if he drops dead halfway through? We'd be finished."

"Better than having him die of misery if you drop him," I said. "But

Going over the score with Twiggy on the set of *The Boy Friend*.

don't worry, I've already discussed the problem with Max himself and we've come up with a foolproof solution. He can do the number in a wheelchair. He'll be singing to play-back anyway and even if he pegs out halfway through, we'll go on filming in long shot and no one will be any the wiser."

"Russell, you're sick," said the exec, throwing his arms in the air. A day later he came down to earth and gave us the go-ahead with Max, who lived to tell the tale.

But that was the least of our troubles. The backstage bickering eventually spilled over into punch-ups in our hotel, with bedroom doors being kicked down in the middle of the night. And Justin, whose unreasonable demands had been rejected by Metro, was getting really heavy. Finally he delivered an ultimatum: Unless his demands were met by noon the following day, Twiggy's services would be withdrawn from that moment. With potential disaster less than a day away, I dashed back to the hotel directly we wrapped and studied the script. Fortunately, two-thirds of the movie was in the can, including all the dance numbers featuring Twiggy, but we still had a number of dialogue scenes with her that were essential to the plot. Drastic measures were called for, so I wrote an entirely new scene that would still make sense of the story if Justin pulled the plug and Twiggy slipped away at noon.

To allay her suspicions, we started filming next day as scheduled, in a backstage corridor with Twiggy and Tommy Tune in a spontaneous tap routine. Twiggy, who must have been torn between her love of Justin and loyalty to me, was showing the strain, but she pulled out all the stops when I said I was going for the final take, and we got a good one. We were then due to move onto the stage, but before we upped sticks, as the saying goes, I produced the new scene with as few words of explanation as possible. Re-writes were not uncommon, so Twiggy was too busy learning her new lines to smell a rat. And as we rehearsed, the minutes sped by with a rate of knots. Then it was camera, action, cut and print with 20 minutes still in hand to zero hour. Twiggy or no Twiggy, we had a movie. As we broke the setup, I gave our producer the nod and saw him make for the telephone. At noon precisely he appeared in the wings with his face wreathed in smiles and gave *me* the nod. Over lunch he told me how he had rung Metro's office in London, where Justin was explosively holding forth, and with a few deft words, diffused the time bomb.

We heard no more threats from Justin, but come the end of the lunch break Twiggy obviously had. She looked white and shaken. On the one hand she was relieved that the tug-of-war was over, but devastated by the fact that Justin had suffered the ultimate humiliation. I sometimes wonder if she really would have "walked" if Justin had given the order. Either way, she was in a no-win situation, so it's just as well she never had to make the decision. But from where she was standing, it must have looked as if I'd pulled a fast one, and so ended a beautiful friendship—until the night of the première, when we all patched things up and much to the surprise of everyone in the know, stepped out of Justin's Rolls-Royce and walked up the red carpet together, the best of friends.

But after that Twiggy drifted out of my life—and Justin's too, come to that. In fact, she married the leading man in her very next film— an event that seems in danger of becoming a habit. I thought she was marvellous in *The Boy Friend* and was depressed when her talent seemed to go unnoticed. But so did the film, so I guess it's not surprising. Her next movie was an even bigger flop, and it wasn't till she appeared with Tommy Tune on Broadway that America recognised her talent and took her to its heart for doing what she had done every bit as well in *The Boy Friend*.

Ken Russell watching a rehearsal of *The Boy Friend*.

Her face on the album cover continued to stare up at me with a fixed grin. The record held few pleasures for me now and in fact reminded me how insanely jealous Shirley had become on discovering there was something between me and my secretary—the "something" being a little shopping she did for me during a lunch break when I was too busy to do my own. Such a fuss over a tube of toothpaste. I moved on to the next album. Mahler's Sixth: a loving portrait of the composer's wife . . . No! Its heart-on-sleeve romanticism had embarrassed Shirley, especially as she knew that it had likewise once enshrined my feelings for her—why, I'd even put the love theme over her screen credit on *Mahler*. That had embarrassed her even more. Perhaps I should not have turned a deaf ear to the jack-booted destructive element which is also very much part of the symphonic portrait. I flicked on. My fingers touched an old ten-inch 78-rpm shellac disc with a tattered cardboard sleeve. I didn't need to understand braille to read the message in its well-worn grooves.

A lunchtime assembly in the Great Hall at Walthamstow Tech came to mind. The principal had been haranguing the entire college over some misdemeanour or other and we were being played back to our studies by Robert Farnon's *Journey into Melody* on the PA system. It was then I saw her—Audrey Hepburn's double, only more so. The music took wing, the melody soared. She was even more breathtaking in reality than all the portraits of her I'd seen in the portfolios of my fellow students in the photographic course I'd joined the previous week. She was the class pin-up, this local girl from Hollywood Way, and everyone had taken her picture, from the most junior, pimply-faced youth to our bald-headed instructor, Mr. Bell, who used studies of this stunning seventeen-year-old to illustrate his lectures.

As an example of "texture" her gorgeous legs in fishnet tights were crosslit by spotlights; as a representation of "form" she was a provocative silhouette in a one-piece bathing suit against a sunlit wall; while to illustrate "pattern" her lynx-like eyes smiled out through the shadows of a venetian blind. There were photographs of her everywhere, including the darkroom where she first swam before my eyes in a developing dish. At the age of twenty-six I was still painfully shy and had the usual trouble in making overtures, as she must have guessed whenever she caught my eye, hanging around outside her classroom day after day, waiting to pop the question. But how do you address a vision? On your knees, perhaps. I can't remember but I must have managed because eventually Shirley was modelling for me and me alone—much to the annoyance of everyone in the class—bald-headed Mr. Bell most of all.

And as I mentioned before, it was both a working relationship and a romantic one. She posed for me and I photographed her clothes. We fell in love and got married. For many years it had been a fruitful union resulting in a bunch of bright kids and handsome movies. We'd had some great times together.

I took the record out from its cardboard sleeve and put it on the turntable, preparing to wallow. I'd forgotten how much hiss was reproduced from shellac 78s, especially when they were well worn and played on hi-fi equipment. The surface noise was appalling and Robert Farnon's *Journey into Melody*, which had promised to be a journey into nostalgia, refused to take off. The music was grounded in a fog of distortion. I took the record off the turntable, snapped it in two, though the label still held it together, and dumped it in the waste bin.

Disconsolately I flicked through the rest of the pile. Near the bottom was Bernstein's *West Side Story*. Ah! Time to forget the past. Time to look ahead. I dropped the stylus onto Band Two of one of the best musicals ever written and waited for the thrill that never failed.

Could be—who knows?
There's something due any day,
I will know right away,
Soon as it shows.
It may come cannonballing down through the sky,
Gleam in its eye, bright as a rose, who knows?
I got a feeling there's a miracle due,
Coming to me . . .

A few days and a few phone calls later a miracle did come cannon-balling out of the sky—from Boston! I got to Heathrow an hour before the plane was due and knocked back a few at the bar while anxiously counting the minutes till the arrival of flight BA 133. Would it work out? She was half my age, young enough to be my daughter. I was old enough to be her father. Heck, I was almost the same age as her father. I was awash in warm beer and clichés.

"Dear Sob Sister, Young American girl gives up job, family and friends, sells her flat, abandons her possessions, to lead uncertain life with the oldest *enfant terrible* in the film business. Is this wise? P.S. He's married with a large family."

It had all happened so fast. In little over a week she'd given the boyfriend the boot and was on her way to set up home with me in a film studio. Was it love or infatuation? Perhaps it was desperation, who knows? Not me! I hardly knew the girl. But I knew I loved her. I felt I'd always loved her.

The plane was late; it was near midnight when the flight arrival was announced. I rushed to the barrier and stood among a group of grey chauffeurs holding pieces of cardboard with crudely printed names which they offered up apologetically to every likely passenger streaming past. One by one the most unlikely passengers swooped down on them to have their luggage swept away to waiting limos. Businessmen, students, holi-daymakers—but no Viv. The passage leading from the customs hall was long and empty, incredibly long and empty and, for an airport, strangely quiet, as are all places that are normally buzzing with activity. It was a feeling I'd grown accustomed to over the last week or so when I took my nightly constitutional around the deserted studio lot with only the crum-bling plaster remains of Moby Dick for company.

And I was about to return to the studio to do just that when I heard laughter, mingled laughter echoing down the long stone corridor. Desperately I tried to sort out the strands, hoping one would be familiar, but the reverberations made it impossible. Still the corridor remained tantalisingly empty until two women in hats and overcoats lurched into view pushing trolleys piled high with luggage. Their clothing was unfamiliar and I recognised neither of them until the shorter of the two tore off her woolly hat, releasing a mop of golden hair, waved and started running towards me. Her trolley slewed around and crashed into that of her companion, sending the baggage flying. One suitcase sprang open on impact, scattering its contents everywhere. This caused even more hilarity and reduced the girls to helplessness. Naturally I ran to assist them and was quite put out when Viv didn't introduce me.

Getting the clothes back into the suitcase and the right baggage back onto the right trolley sent them into convulsions, so it was left to me to read the labels and sort things out. Finally the girls embraced, swore to meet soon and said reluctant goodbyes. I imagined they were lifelong friends. Barely aware of my presence, Viv permitted me to escort her to the car and help her into the passenger seat. By the time I'd loaded up she'd passed out. Driving back to the studio I began to have misgivings about the welcome I had planned for her.

It had been an exhausting day which had begun at first light with me transferring my bits and pieces from the cheerless office to an exclusive love nest. Fortunately, someone had got wind of my plan to smuggle a little contraband into the studios and kindly placed the Elizabeth Taylor suite at my disposal. The lady herself was no longer in residence and nothing of her aura remained, unless her favourite perfume was Airwick. The suite comprised a luxury bathroom, a simple bedroom devoid of furniture, and a sitting room with deep pile carpet, silk wall-panelling and a mirrored bar.

By mid-afternoon everything was installed, including the hi-fi which seduced me into soaking longer than I should have in Liz Taylor's bath listening to A Place in the Sun, in which she had appeared at her most glamorous. Tearing myself away from her spell, I borrowed a van and paid a visit to the local shopping mall at Brent Cross—for a case of champagne, some perfume and a double bed. That, I reasoned, was all one needed to get by on a studio honeymoon. That, plus soft lights, of course, and sweet music.

I was still pondering on the madness of it all when my headlights picked up the red-and-white striped barrier at the studio entrance. It swung up into the darkness and the guard waved me in, unaware of my smuggled passenger. I pulled up outside Stage Two and gave Viv a prod. She had slid down out of sight and was still fast asleep. She smiled, opened her eyes and said, "Where am I?"

"Elstree," I said.

"Really?" she said, closing her eyes again. I knew all about jet lag, but this was ridiculous. I carried the baggage upstairs, unlocked the suite and dumped it in the bedroom. I then made two similar journeys and on the last one laid out and lit an avenue of night lights along the passage and down the stairs. With some difficulty I lifted Viv out of the car, kicked the door closed and staggered back up the stairs and along the corridor, puffing and panting "Here comes the Bride" as I went.

"How incredibly romantic," Viv whispered drowsily. By the time I reached the bed I was bent double and dropped her down more heavily than I intended. She bounced and continued bouncing of her own volition, giggling as she did so. Then suddenly she stopped—both bouncing and giggling. I went outside and blew out the candles. Damn! Each one was stuck firmly to the carpet with solidified wax. I gathered them like headless mushrooms, collecting a substantial amount of carpet at the same time. And no matter how I peeled and scraped, I couldn't get up all the candle grease. Returning to the suite, I locked the door, got rid of the candles and poured myself a glass of lukewarm champagne, the ice having melted. There wasn't a sound except for the snores coming from the bedroom. I gently closed the door and settled down on the settee, snuggling up in my wolf coat as usual. Some honeymoon night, I thought, and, slightly relieved, fell asleep.

I awoke to voices outside in the corridor. The cleaning ladies were holding a post mortem over their lovely carpet. "How on earth . . . ? Did you ever . . . ? Can that be candle grease? Never! Who in their right mind would burn candles on a carpet?" I kept my mouth shut and looked at my watch. Nine o'clock! Holy Moses! I was due in the dubbing theatre for a run-through of the film with all the sound tracks.

I rushed to the bathroom. Somebody had beaten me to it. There was toothpaste squished all over the bowl and the cap was off the tube. My toothbrush was swimming in soapy water. I washed out the bowl, shaved, gave my mouth a rinse and dressed. I looked in the bedroom. It was empty. God knows where she'd gone. The dubbing theatre was opposite Stage Two—outside my front door, in fact. I went to dash across the narrow road but was pulled up short by the "toot, toot, toot" of an angry lorry driver. The Alfa was blocking his way. Shit! No keys! I pacified the driver and ran upstairs. The door had locked itself automatically. I dashed downstairs, released the handbrake and pushed the car around the corner, arriving in the dubbing theatre fifteen minutes late, angry and flustered.

The first person I saw was Viv, sitting in the front row between the editor and his assistant, looking very calm and collected. She smiled and waved, as did the others. How the hell . . . ? Then I remembered telling her on the phone that dubbing started today. The dubbing crew—three men sitting behind a long desk of faders and coloured lights—wished me a rather frosty good morning. I joined them all, ready to give the chief mixer my comments and suggestions during the viewing. By the time we had run the twelve reels which comprised the 120 minutes of the story and discussed the way the key sequences were to be mixed it was lunch-time. Naturally my mind hadn't been fully on my work all morning and it was infuriating not being able to talk to Viv, with all those technicians around. Outside, when we were alone, she briefly explained that she had awoken bright and early and, not wishing to disturb me, had gone to breakfast in the canteen and thence to the dubbing theatre.

"Why on earth didn't you get me up when you saw I was late?" I asked, rather curtly.

"I was thinking about it when you turned up. Oh, and here's the key. I found it in the door," she said, handing it over. A silly silence ensued during which we seemed unable to look at each other. Playing for time, I suggested lunch at an old Tudor pub about ten miles up the road to St. Albans and dashed upstairs for the car keys. A minute later I was escorting her to the Alfa. When she saw it her eyes lit up.

"Mm. Cute little red car."

"I'm surprised you didn't notice it last night," I said. We got in.

"I was really out of it last night," she said as we drove off.

"Who was your friend?" I asked.

"What friend?" she said, then continued. ". . . Oh, her. I've no idea. Just a girl I met on the plane. She invited me to share a joint in the loo. It was great grass, from Maui, I guess."

We didn't speak again until we arrived at the pub. I think she took my silence for disapproval—which it wasn't. I'd never smoked pot simply because I didn't want to run the risk of becoming hooked. Heaven help me if I'd taken up with a junkie. I elbowed my way to the crowded bar and ordered two pints of beer and a plate of sandwiches. Viv looked pale and jet-lagged and—I had to admit—pretty miserable. I had no idea what to say in the way of anything personal so asked her how she had enjoyed the film.

"Not much," she replied. "I found Nureyev stilted, Leslie Caron a caricature and Michelle Phillips shrill and shrewish. Huntz Hall was a disaster and Seymour Cassel an absolute clown."

I couldn't believe what I was hearing but did my best to remain calm. "What about Ferde Grofé's music?" I asked.

"Pure kitsch!"

"The costumes?"

"Straight out of a Twenties *Vogue.*"

"The photography?"

"Brilliant."

Nurturing this crumb of comfort, I asked my last question. "And what about the direction? What about my contribution?"

She hesitated and then looked me straight in the eye and said, "There's so little joy in you."

I snapped and slapped her across the face—and was instantly appalled. Her only reaction was to take a sip of her pint—and pour it slowly over my head. As laughter echoed around the bar, I realised that life with Viv was going to be . . . fun.

9 Our Mountain Greenery Home

Valentino was a flop, but I was still too close to it to see why. It was only years later when I chanced to catch it again on TV that I finally understood the reason. As a mirror held up to a movie marriage, *Valentino* reflected all of the pain and none of the fun. My next film was to mirror a much happier picture—that of an unmarried couple very much in love in the Lake District. And it was to that part of the world that Viv and I were heading in the red car, having said a fond farewell to the Eliz-

Ken and daughter Victoria waiting for the
sun to go in on location for *Dante's Inferno*.
Victoria played the daughter of artist
William Morris.

abeth Taylor suite forever. We were excited; we were starting a new life,
a new project. Granada Television had commissioned me to make *Clouds
of Glory*, a series of films on the Lake Poets, the first of which was to
feature William Wordsworth.

Coincidentally, it was due to a Victorian poet that I discovered the
Lake District in the first place. Until I chanced upon it while researching
a programme on Dante Gabriel Rossetti, I'd never heard of the place.
How I'd managed to avoid it for thirty-eight years is rather puzzling because
it is one of the most popular beauty spots in the British Isles. One obvious
reason was that we always spent our summer holidays in the south, with
the result that everything north of Regent's Park Zoo was a bit of a mystery
to us and remained so until the day I started working on *Dante's Inferno*,
a TV biopic for *Monitor*.

It appeared that towards the end of his life, when drunk and dissolute,
Rossetti had taken a vacation in the Lake District with his mistress, Fanny
"the Elephant" Cornforth, where they had fought a duel with gin bottles
atop a hill romantically named the Golden Howe. It was my intention
to reconstruct this historic moment and to that end I set off one cold
March morning in my old Morris 8 to find the Golden Howe with as
much excitement as Jason must have felt on setting off to find the Golden
Fleece.

The conception of a film is always so much more thrilling than the pregnancy and even the birth. Driving to Cumberland in the far north-western corner of England took most of the day, and by the time I reached the area it was buried in darkness. My final destination was not marked on the map but from various clues I'd picked up in my research it seemed to be in the vicinity of Keswick on Derwentwater, so it made sense to stop there for the night. But Keswick out of season is a ghost town and the only hotel that appeared to be open looked as inviting as a morgue. I consulted my AA book. Ah! that looked promising: there was a hotel just three miles out of town called the "Lodore Swiss." Another of my subjects, Robert Southey, had written a poem called "The Falls at Lodore" which I intended to feature in *his* programme. All being well, I could take a look at them in the morning.

There was no phone booth in sight so I took a chance on the hotel being open and pressed on into the "Jaws of Borrowdale," as Ruskin christened the valley south of the lake. If the lake was there I didn't see it. I saw only what my headlights revealed—a narrow windy road flanked by seemingly endless dry-stone walls. Then suddenly two fluffy ghosts loomed up and belted off bleating along a drive leading to a turretted Victorian pile of grisly green stone. I followed and pulled up at the front door. I switched off my engine and was greeted by a loud roar. Ah, the first hotel built in England with running water—in the back yard! Two million gallons a day, according to the porter who led me up deserted and ever-narrowing stairways to my room in the turret. He also told me, when I pressed half a crown into his hand, that I was lucky—they had just opened for the season that very day. But on the other hand I was not so lucky—they had just stopped serving supper. I pressed another half-crown into his other hand and was soon sitting down to Guinness and sandwiches in my room by an electric fan heater which the porter had also provided. The wind howled, the heater whirred, the falls roared, my supper went down well and I slept soundly.

Next morning I awoke to sunshine and birdsong. I jumped out of bed, pulled the curtains and froze. My heart pounded, my blood raced, I caught my breath, my eyes widened, my hair stood on end, an unseen orchestra played a tremendous chord. Only clichés can describe what no one has ever been able to portray—a vision of God. Mahler got near it, so did Bruckner, Blake, Turner and perhaps Elgar. So did E. J. Mason, a Victorian photographer who was one of the first to attempt to capture the image of the Almighty while living in his shadow, as did the poet Samuel Coleridge who recognised SKIDDAW as "God made manifest." From my window in the turret, Skiddaw dominated the entire landscape. Before me stretched three miles of Derwentwater, its shores reaching to Keswick. And dominating Keswick like a great pterodactyl with a wingspan of seven miles was Skiddaw. And if the Christian God is three in one, then Skiddaw, the pagan god, is nine in one—Latrigg, Dodd, Longside, Jenkin Hill, Ullock Pike, Lonscale Fell, Carl Side and Little Man—these eight lesser hills forming part of one almighty godhead, SKIDDAW.

Legend has it that after Skiddaw created the world he rested from his labours on a vast throne and covered himself in a shroud which, with the coming of night, turned to stone. Skiddaw still sleeps, but on the last day he will wrench himself from the earth and soar over Keswick on Derwentwater and everything that falls beneath his shadow will be transfigured. Swathed in a veil of mist at dawn or cloaked in the purple robe of evening, Skiddaw was a god when Olympus was a baby. Forget Fujiyama, Etna, the Matterhorn, Kilimanjaro and Everest—Skiddaw the Magnificent dwarfs the lot.

From that day of revelation at the Lodore Swiss Hotel, I contrived to spend as much time as possible in the promised land. Fortunately, the easiest way to do so was through my work. After *Dante's Inferno* came *Song of Summer, Dance of the Seven Veils, The Devils, Mahler* and *Tommy*, all filmed in a magic land that at the sound of a clapper board turned into Iceland, Norway, France or Bavaria, or even itself—as it might have been a century ago.

Up hill and down dale I marched armies of film units in a similar fashion to the Grand Old Duke of York. Film crews became as familiar as ice-cream vans and just as popular with the tourists, many of whom were pressed into service as soldiers of the Wehrmacht or nuns and nymphs, while the locals grew to look upon Victorian costumes as part and parcel of their everyday wardrobe. The hills were alive with the sound of playback. Roger Daltrey sang "Listening to you I hear the music," Delius listened to the "Song of the High Hills" and Richard Strauss played his *Alpensinfonie* at a Nazi-party picnic. The lakes, too, were alive with music: on the shores of Wastwater William Morris declaimed his "Lament for Beowulf" and by the waters of Keswick Mahler composed his First Symphony.

Unfortunately Valentino never went to the Lake District and in no way could the green hills of Cumbria have doubled for the arid hills of Hollywood. There was no such problem with Wordsworth. The famous host of golden daffodils danced on the shores of Grasmere, right outside his front door in the very heart of Lakeland and it was thence I was heading, along with Viv and fifty technicians from Granada Television— forty technicians too many. I'd shot *Dante's Inferno* with a crew of a dozen or so, but that was more than a decade before and things had changed—for the worse.

Granada Television was in the grip of an inflexible union practice geared for studio production but not location filming, which was considered something of a luxury. *William and Dorothy* was to be an intimate film mainly concerned with the simple daily round of the poet and his sister and did not warrant the vast and costly crew that was foisted upon us. For a show that was very light on props we had three prop men: one man to carry Wordsworth's pencil onto the set, another man to place it in the poet's hand and yet another to put it away afterwards. There were also two continuity girls to supervise all this nonsense and write it down in triplicate.

Demarcation lines were firmly drawn, as I was to find out personally when we came to film Wordsworth climbing a storm-swept crag. To enhance the illusion I asked for autumn leaves to be cast into the whirling blades of our wind machine. True to form, the first prop man collected the leaves at his feet and gave them to the second prop man who cast them into the rushing air while the third man stood by to collect them and hand them back to number one for the process to be repeated. But a handful of dry leaves whirling across the scene every minute or so does little to suggest a gale. "If only the crew would join in," I thought, "we'd brew up a storm in no time." Perhaps they needed an example. Having endured the pathetic charade put on by the prop men for a couple of takes I finally threw restraint to the winds along with armful after armful of dry leaves. Fifty mouths dropped open in amazement and fifty brows frowned while a hundred hands stayed firmly in their pockets. To give them credit, I think some of the crew did contemplate lending a hand but were afraid of being reported to the union by their brothers and sisters.

It was hardly surprising that such a costly and unproductive way of working should have repercussions. In the event, the film on the poet Southey was cancelled. Once again the film-maker had become a victim of bureaucracy. His fellow artists just don't know how lucky they are. Imagine David Hockney, for instance, being told that he needed one man to get his brushes, another to hand them to him and a third to take them away, two men to mix his paints and another to prime his canvas. And because he is a multi-media man, there would be someone else to load his camera, another person to focus it and still another to click the shutter after Hockney himself had been grudgingly permitted a peek through the view-finder. It's a wonder there's anything left of the director's vision at all after it's been diluted by fifty technicians. Of course, that's not always the case and there are times when you wish you had more. It's simply that you have very little choice.

I'd often considered the possibility of film-making as a cottage industry, and after the departure of the Granada circus Viv and I talked it over. We had two things going for us—a camera and a cottage. The camera was Viv's Super 8, the cottage was something I'd won in the divorce lottery.

It was a modest dwelling built in local stone a century or so ago. A dry-stone wall enclosed the property and its tiny garden, which seemed to grow nothing but even more stones. The best thing about it was a fantastic view of Skiddaw, which was the main reason I'd picked it some years previously as a handy *pied à terre* for location filming. Now it was to be our home until such time as the British film industry called me back to London. It was a call for which I had to wait eight long years. In the meantime, why not make a film in the place I loved best with the person I loved best to the music we loved best—Mahler's *Song of the Earth*. Eagerly we sketched out a script reflecting the joys and sorrows of life as expressed in one of the most touching song cycles ever written. Our theme was the procession of the seasons in the world about us. It was an idea tailor-made for our situation. Being a film unit of two we could afford to sit and wait for the ideal weather conditions, something that is generally not financially viable, even with the smallest crew the unions will allow. Most films are budgeted on a shooting average of three or four minutes a day, which is why you have to ensure there is always an interior scene standing by as "weather cover" whenever an exterior sequence is planned. Conditional to that is the fact that actors are an expensive item and are invariably hired for the minimum number of days possible, and when time is money you can't afford to hang about waiting for the sun to come out—not for more than a few minutes, anyway, unless you are David Lean. Viv and I couldn't afford actors but we knew a few locals on the end of a phone who for a cut in the profits (if any) would get on their bikes and join us at a moment's notice on the nearest hilltop. It was a dream. The unions, we learned, would have blacked us. Our film would never have been shown. Union projectionists would have been instructed not to screen it. Doing it by the book would have cost millions and no financier in the history of the world has ever invested millions in an "art film."

Philosophically, we turned our attention to a craft where union membership is not, as yet, obligatory—writing. We would write a script based on *The Rainbow* by D. H. Lawrence. His *Women in Love* had been one of my greatest hits, so it seemed reasonable to assume that the earlier novel which featured the "women" of the title as teenagers would prove to be equally successful. Given the circumstances, finding a backer should not be difficult. Having sorted out the copyright situation we set to work, but we only worked when it rained because we were still on the honeymoon that had been interrupted by *Clouds of Glory*.

On fine days we go fell-walking. After a cup of tea, a piece of toast

Ken Russell, Victoria and Sabena Maydelle waiting for the
sun in Hampshire during *The Music Lovers*.

and a snuggle in bed we get up, wash and dress—knee socks, fell pants
and boots, tee-shirts and light sweaters (tied around the waist ascending,
worn descending). Then, as Viv packs a knapsack with sardine sandwiches,
a couple of cans of beer and a few oranges, I'm studying the book of
Wainwright. This old, indefatigable fell-lover has tramped every peak in
the district and compiled a seven-volume study on the easiest, hardest,
most beautiful and most boring ways to conquer them. The instructions
that accompany his mountain sketches are written in longhand and convey
with a dry wit advice on everything from the negotiation of precipitous
paths by the most seasoned fell-walker to the best way up a hill for a
granny in carpet slippers in search of a gentle, grassy slope.

I shuffle through the colourful pack of books covering the seven different regions. Each volume contains information on about twenty different fells (ranging in height from one to three thousand feet or more),
every one of which is honoured with a name.

Despite the barometer, the day seems set fair so we go for Red Pike
towering above the shores of Buttermere, only a short distance from home.
We jump into the red car, throw the roof back and wave to our neighbour,
the blond, bronzed, bare-chested Farmer Weir, herding a flock of sheep
past our front gate. When the last straggler has gone, we set off down the
Borrowdale valley by the banks of the River Derwent as it winds its way

through fields of grazing cattle and on past the tiny village of Grange. On our left is King's Howe, a favourite haunt for rock climbers in search of a sheer face. On the right, rising a thousand feet above Dodd Wood, is a sharp pinnacle of slate known as Castle Crag. A million loose chippings from its abandoned quarries guarantee to make ascent a hair-raising experience. Even so, when we were shooting a scene from *Mahler* on the summit one blustery autumn day a few years ago a succession of fell-runners were to be seen sprinting up those treacherous slopes with canisters of raw film stock and hot ravioli. But they were led by the indomitable Ray McHaffie, a Keswick guide who tackles local climbs that are shunned even by veterans of Everest—and he does them on roller skates!

Now we are passing the Bowder Stone—a giant, diamond-shaped boulder poised on a knife edge, which two centuries of clambering tourists have failed to dislodge. On the other side of the road through silver birches blurring past like a picket fence we glimpse another tourist landmark: Millican Dalton's cave. Hewn out of solid rock above the entrance is his motto: "Don't waste words—jump to conclusions." There is a picture of

Robert Powell as Gustav Mahler and Antonia Ellis as Cosima Wagner in *Mahler*.

grizzled old Millican over our kitchen door. Dressed in a battered straw hat, short-sleeved shirt, bony knees protruding from baggy shorts, gimlet eyes searching the waters for his supper, he sails up Derwentwater on his homemade raft, *The Rogue Herries*, bound for Keswick on a weekly shopping expedition.

Alas, this self-styled Professor of Adventure is no more—empty Coke cans fill the hearth where he used to bake trout caught with his bare hands. His ghost disappears in a roar of exhaust as we swerve around hairpin bends between larches and ancient avalanches of rock immobilised in carpets of moss which glow with that incredible green only seen elsewhere in the Pre-Raphaelite paintings of John Everett Millais, whom I showed eloping here many summers ago with the wife of John Ruskin, his sternest critic.

The whitewashed cottages of Rosthwaite pass in a flash, together with a group of hikers in yellow anoraks tramping up the old pack-horse route to Watendlath and its hidden tarn. Now we're motoring towards Stonethwaite where our future children will attend the village school, and there's the great bastion of Eagle Crag looming up before us—home of the golden eagle circling over Seathwaite, the wettest place in England. Now Glaramara, part witch, part mountain, is bearing down on us, exerting her usual magic. With a twist of the wheel we avoid her spell, remembering that her beguiling ways lead only to treacherous marshland. On we speed, up, up, up Honister Pass, higher and higher—1 in 8, 1 in 7, 1 in 6, 1 in 5—even the goats are hanging on by their fingernails. Hikers and bikers leap aside. It's a one-track road and we're passing everything in sight as pipes drop from the mouths of trilby-hatted tourists in Ford Cortinas.

Left goes the wheel, left, right, left, left, right. We're beating the birds. Viv screams, "I want out! I want out!" A wide-eyed sheep shits itself. The curves get sharper, the road gets steeper—1 in 4, 1 in 3, 1 in 2, 1 in 1. At 1500 feet we're airborne. We fly past the AA box at the top of the pass and plunge down the other side, past a sign reading, "YOU HAVE BEEN WARNED," past motorists climbing slow as snails towards us. And on either side of us, shutting out the light, high screes covered in a network of hardening arteries in the shape of dry-stone walls; then out into the sunlight again, shimmering on the waters of Buttermere. We travel at a more leisurely speed, down the narrow lakeside road on the northern shore, marvelling at the heights of High Stile, rising from the tree-lined shore opposite. At the end of the lake, having driven five miles in as many minutes, we pull into the Bridge Inn and park, promising ourselves a glass or two of Theakston's Old Peculier on the way home. But that pleasure is several hours away. Before us rises the challenge of Red Pike and what promises to be a tough climb of 2,479 feet.

We cross a rustic bridge over a fast-running stream and start climbing up through a rock-strewn pine wood by the gushing waters of Sour Milk Gill. Speech is difficult because of the noise so we save our breath for the slog. The sun climbs with us and soon we are hot and sweating and subject to stinging attacks by swarms of vicious flies. We suffer this for a thousand feet or so before we emerge from the trees onto open ground where a cool breeze achieves what flailing arms failed to do and puts our tormentors to flight, leaving us to enjoy a peaceful stroll up through the heather to Red Tarn—a circular body of water in the crater of an extinct volcano. We stop for a dip, but not for long. It's bloody cold and there's a likelihood of leeches. We hop out and lark about in the bracken to dry off. Dressed and refreshed, we steel ourselves for the final assault. There it stands before us—the ruddy great lump that gives Red Pike its name— as smooth as a piece of sculpture by Barbara Hepworth. We'll need energy to get up there, and stamina. We've already consumed our ration of Kendal mint cake, so start on the sardine sandwiches. This makes us thirsty. We drink our beer. Mistake! Our limbs turn to lead as we drag ourselves up that last agonising thousand feet of compacted red dust in the full glare of the sun.

The last yards seem like miles and our response to greetings from a band of hearty students bounding past us on their way down is limited to breathless grunts. With mouths dry as ovens we collapse back to back on the summit without even the strength to peel an orange. Ten minutes later we're laughing and sucking orange segments and, with the help of Wainwright, naming every major peak in the district: Great Gable to the east, Coniston Old Man in the south, and rising above everything in majesty, Skiddaw to the north where I filmed Coleridge flying a silver kite that dived around the sky, bright as a flaming comet. We fall into silent contemplation of the hills until one by one they gradually fade from view. Minutes later we are enveloped in mist. It is time to go. We pull on our sweaters and set off for the pub—in different directions, each of us certain of the way.

Giant doppelgangers rise before us, causing our steps to falter. Rooted to the spot, we stare up at them in awe and they stare back, inflated egos staring down at us in warning. A gust of wind and they are gone. Viv wonders what the hell it was. I tell her it's a pretty rare optical phenomenon known as Brocken spectres caused by tricks of sun and mist.

But now the sun has gone and the mist is cold and clammy. I suppress a shiver. Holding hands, we start off along what appears from a few droppings to be a sheep track, and narrowly avoid stepping off into space.

"If sheep use this they must be suicidal," says Viv, backing off. I say nothing. I suffer from vertigo. I'm crag-fast, paralysed inches from oblivion. Viv quickly pulls me away and leads me, trembling, back up to the summit. We circle around in search of another path but the ground is hard and yields no secrets and of the guiding cairns marked on Wainwright's map there are no signs. Common sense says we should stay put until such time as the mist lifts or help arrives in the shape of a climber familiar with the terrain. But we are impatient and set off yet again. This time we are lucky—or perhaps I should say luckier. Still no path to raise our hopes, but even if we are going nowhere at least we are going down. The going gets rougher, awkward rocks wrench our ankles and graze our shins. We keep on going. Soon we are wringing wet with sweat and mist. Or are we walking in a rain cloud? Shit! A derelict mine shaft opens up before us. Viv grabs hold of me as we slither to a stop. We skirt it cautiously and—joy of joys—see a footpath. Smiling, we set off with renewed hope and share our last orange.

The mist is still as dense as ever but the going is much easier on the gently undulating grassy track. Ah, signs of life. We'll soon be home now. Look! Fresh orange peel. This must be a public footpath. Fancy that! What a coincidence . . . You guessed it, quicker than we did, I bet! We sit down on a rock, staring in disbelief at our own refuse, not knowing whether to laugh or cry. The wind freshens. Suddenly I feel desperately cold. Something white blows in my face—a wisp of fleece, perhaps. Another white blur in the wind—a feather this time?

"Is this snow?" asks Viv quietly.

"In May?" I reply. "Never!"

Within minutes we are enveloped in a blizzard. Our hair becomes matted into bands of white pain, forever tightening. We crouch down behind the rock, clasping each other tight. I open my mouth to speak and the breath is sucked out of me as if I were in the coils of a freezing boa constrictor. The rock offers scant shelter. The wind lashes us unmercifully from all sides. The world disappears. There is no up, no down, no earth, no sky, nothing but swirling snow. It's a white-out.

We cannot move. We've forgotten how to move. Our limbs are numb, our minds are numb . . . and then . . . a mind-blowing sensation, as if I'm being scalped. Something is digging its claws into my head and ripping open my skull, exposing my brain to a blinding light. The snow, the mist, the clouds are violently torn away revealing a bright blue sky and naked sun.

For a split second we are shown a cruel vision of our surroundings. Cruel because it vanishes before we can assimilate its wonder. But something of the image remains, burnt into the retina. With fresh hope we set off in a new direction. Our confidence seems to quell the elements: the wind drops, the snow dissipates, the mist thins a little. We laugh with relief and rub each other vigorously, restoring the circulation. A pebble bounces by, followed by a stone and then a shower of stones, heralding a sinister black mass hurtling down through the mist like a malignant poltergeist. A distant voice shouts "Fore" as the object materialises into a heavy-duty plastic bag which slurps past us and is lost to sight below.

"A fine time to put out the garbage," says Viv. "We could have been knocked into space."

"What a way to go," I reply. "Killed by a stiff."

"What do you mean?" asks Viv.

"Maybe it's our friendly mountain guide, Ray McHaffie," I reply. Perhaps he'd found another casualty. Heart attacks, wet grass, icy slopes and exposure account for most fatalities up here. I'm told he always carries a few disposal bags in his back pack. And if it's not the most ceremonious way of getting a corpse from 2,000 feet to sea level, it's certainly the fastest. We peer into the mist, waiting for Ray. Maybe he's searching for someone else . . . it could have been us. We listen intently but are only conscious of a distant roar. It must be Sour Milk Gill. Find that and we find the way home.

Once more we set off, once more we are disappointed. The terrain is quite different—no rock-strewn pine wood but dangerous marshland dotted with soggy tufts of coarse grass which we use as stepping stones. Shaking with exhaustion, we scramble down the side of an unfamiliar force, grabbing onto wiry tufts of heather for support. Rushing water cascades through the rotting carcass of a sheep caught in the branches of a dead tree, enhancing the atmosphere of gothic gloom hanging in the spray of the falls. We turn our backs on it and follow the roaring stream, which seems even more eager to reach the shores of Crummock Water than we are.

An hour later, cool refreshing Theakston's bitter cascades from a tap into a pewter tankard and washes away our exhaustion, encouraging us to reminisce. According to Wainwright's map we had very nearly attempted our descent from Red Pike by the correct path, but each step we took magnified our first small error, finally bringing us down to earth two miles to the west at Scale Force, which we agree is a small price to pay in the circumstances.

Under a clear evening sky we drive back to the cottage by an alternative route, winding through the pine forests of the Whinlatter Pass, which eventually reveals Skiddaw from an unfamiliar angle. Reclining languorously at the head of Newlands Valley, she has changed into the great earth mother Henry Moore spent all his life trying to sculpt. We stop for a moment to watch the setting sun clothe her voluptuous curves. Driving on, we bless her for bringing us home safely and share a rejuvenating bath before supper. Then, while Viv catches up on the housework, I bake a shepherd's pie. We leave the washing up for tomorrow to lie on the sheepskin rug before a log fire and play "Monopoly," as we jokingly call our favourite evening game.

A cold flickering light suddenly illuminates Goat Crag, hanging over us through the big skylight. Heavy, reverberant thunderclaps threaten to unseat its boulders and send them to join the others embedded in our back garden. I jump up, pull up my trousers, rush to the record shelves and look under "B." Bax, Beethoven, Brahms . . . ah, Bruckner. Symphonies 3, 2, 5, 1, 6, 7, 4, 9, and . . . good, there it is, No. 8. Switch on the hi-fi, put on the *Scherzo*. Out it thunders—Bruckner's vision of his Christian God of Wrath. Viv chuckles at my improvised *"son et lumière"* as a sonorous brass choir accompanies the peals of light, which seem about to stir Skiddaw into movement. Bruckner is building to a mighty climax. The music of Skiddaw rises to meet him; opposing waves of sound crash against each other in conflict fit to bring the house down. Rolling timpani meets rolling thunder, then a bright flash and a sharp clap as from giant hands above the rooftop—followed by a whimper as Bruckner dies along with the hi-fi. Power cut! We crease up! Rain falls from the skies in waterfalls. We are being pissed on from a great height. We snuggle up before the fire with our wine and sing:

> In our mountain greenery,
> Where God paints the scenery,
> We will laugh at the weather . . .

And we continued to do so, all through the writing of *The Rainbow*, though sometimes our laughter sounded a little hollow. But we did get out for some walks—the highlights of which you've just read about. Well, you don't think they all happened in one single outing, do you? Just as I pack a person's life into ninety minutes of celluloid, so I've just packed the activities of several months into a few minutes. You don't want a second-by-second account of my life, surely? You'd be sitting there for sixty years and, heaven knows, we're all pushed for time.

Back to the *Rainbow* script, with which I was well pleased—mainly due to Viv's contribution. Generally speaking, the moment a director takes up pen to write a script alone he is at a disadvantage. If he's at all worth his salt, he has a picture in his mind of the finished product. In working backwards, in getting his vision down on paper, he consequently takes a lot for granted. But what is crystal clear to him may be pretty murky to everyone but a clairvoyant. Viv is not imbued with psychic powers but at least she could tap my mind and type a script readily comprehensible to a movie exec with limited time and intellect.

With high hopes we posted the script—express—to my Hollywood agent, Bobby Littman, who was, in turn, equally optimistic. *Women in Love* had been a hit. *The Rainbow* was a better script and would therefore be an even bigger hit. *Valentino* would soon be forgiven and forgotten—what film about Hollywood had ever made money, anyhow? With *The Rainbow* I was back on home ground in Lawrence country. There was nude wrestling (a man and a woman this time) and stampeding animals (Shire horses this time), all that lovely scenery and the usual horny miners. Bobby promised to shop the script around to Barry at Paramount, Laddie at Fox, David at Metro and Ted at Warners. No, perhaps not Ted, not after *The Devils*! I wished him luck and tried shopping it around Soho myself. I tried Bernie at EMI. I knew he'd admired *Women in Love* but his memory only went back as far as *The Boy Friend*, when he got his fingers burned. Finally I tried David Puttnam at Goldcrest, who I thought might be more receptive owing to our fruitful association on *Mahler* of which he was justly proud. So was I. Elgar apart, Mahler is my favourite composer and I feel we have a lot in common apart from both being Cancerians and living near a lake surrounded by mighty hills. As is my custom when approaching a film on a composer, I donned my Sherlock Holmes outfit and searched for the soul of the man in his music, while also keeping the facts of his life in mind. And just as I had with Tchaikovsky, I found a lot of bombast on the way—the sound and fury of a tormented artist. I also found music that was brutal, vulgar, grotesque, macabre—and was inevitably pilloried for reflecting these elements in the film. I found joy, poetry and magic too and included them as well. Naturally they were ignored by those suffering from blind prejudice. It's a pity their followers don't trust the evidence of their own eyes (and ears, come to that). But to do that you have to be an individual with a mind of your own.

Such a person is Klaus Tennstedt, arguably the greatest Mahler conductor alive today. I say "arguably" because some of the afflicted mentioned above, who also have cloth ears and nothing in between, call him vulgar. What they really mean is that he has red blood in his veins. They feel safer with rosewater and von Karajan. Tennstedt is a controversial figure with boundless enthusiasm, a vivid imagination and a great love of Mahler. Knowing that you can never get enough of a good thing, be it a symphony, a film or a sunrise, he catches the Mahler film at every possible opportunity. One day he also caught up with me in a Chinese restaurant, and much to my delight virtually conducted his way through the entire film, bar by bar, scene by scene, course by course—chopsticks flying. From the First Symphony, synchronised to Mahler swimming in the lake and the shark-fin soup, to the terrifying funeral march from the

Fifth with Mahler, the Jew, being burned alive by the Gestapo in a Reichs crematorium and crispy fried pork, it was a virtuoso performance.

Pause for intermission and discussion of Mahler's prophetic vision of a nightmarish, jack-booted future which goosesteps through page after page of his music. Mahler eventually rejected Judaism for a safer and more lucrative faith—the form of Aryan Christianity practised by Cosima Wagner, who ruled the musical world of Vienna in his day and despised Jews with a fervour only equalled by her dear father.

I satirised all this in a slapstick sequence cut to the *Rondo Burlesco* from the Ninth Symphony which climaxed with Mahler forging a Nazi sword from the holy star of David—a piece of symbolism not wasted on David Puttnam, who also flirted with Catholicism while remaining a Jew at heart. Without Puttnam's support *Mahler* would never have been made and there would have been no concert with Klaus in that Chinese restaurant.

Flashback to a bierkeller in Munich where our Bavarian backers had sneaked out of the back door leaving Puttnam to pay the bill on the very eve of filming. Curtains? No! Puttnam simply put us all on a train to Keswick, found a new backer and made it possible for us to shoot the film in the Lake District. And although he still can't tell the difference between *der Liebestod* and *die Kindertotenlieder*, he can certainly tell a dollar from a deutschmark and that's all that really matters when it comes to producing a movie.

That was my first film for "Goodtimes Enterprises"—the David Puttnam/Sandford Leiberson production company, and although the latter may well have been a sleeping partner (I never fathomed his function), Puttnam was very much awake.

I signed a contract with his company to write and direct five more musical biopics with one script thrown in gratis. In the event I only wrote two scripts and made one film. I gave Puttnam a choice—*The Gershwin Dream* or *Lisztomania*. He went for Liszt, probably because Roger Daltrey, fresh from his success in my rock movie *Tommy*, was keen to play the randy Hungarian. It was typecasting. Franz Liszt was the first pop star of them all—idolised by the fans and chased all over Europe by mobs of aristocratic groupies. But his womanising was only part of the story. What really intrigued me was his strange relationship with Richard Wagner. However, that had little appeal to Puttnam, who was more at home at a pop concert than in the concert hall. He threw out my first script for being too straight and urged me to write another emphasising the pop element. We had many discussions on the subject, sometimes at his place, sometimes at mine—frequently over dinner. I soon counted him as a friend and although we had little in common but our enthusiasm for movies and music that alone was enough to prevent the conversation flagging. I'd enthuse about Scriabin and Sibelius, he'd rave on about Keith Emerson and Rick Wakeman. I don't know who was the more receptive; I just know that the script became less and less classical—and more and more pop-orientated until it was to Puttnam's satisfaction.

It never dawned on me until it was too late that I was playing Trilby to his Svengali—though Puttnam could have given that master a few tips when it came to hypnotising his victim. In addition to his influence on the script, Puttnam also had a heavy input on casting. Having just worked with Ringo on his pop musical *That'll Be The Day*, he suggested him as the Pope. Rick Wakeman was also cast in a bit part which was to grow imperceptibly into a major role—that of composer of the sound track. The "takeover" was insidious. The casual suggestion that Wakeman should orchestrate one of Lizst's piano pieces was the thin end of the wedge that eventually turned the film into a Panavision pop video. That decision to go anamorphic was another of Puttnam's notions which added ten per cent to a budget which he knew to be unrealistic from the start. However, by friendly persuasion he gradually overcame my misgivings until I came to believe that I could film the five thousand on five pounds. Accordingly, I approved the budget. And when the miracle failed to occur Puttnam got out his collapsible crown of thorns and accused me of crucifying him emotionally and financially—a classic case of role reversal if ever there was one.

If the film had been a financial success Puttnam would undoubtedly have kept quiet and pocketed the profits and the glory. Unfortunately it was a flop—hardly surprising when a film about the music of Liszt starts with an American Square Dance by Rick Wakeman with a "caller" shouting "change your partners" and "dosey-doe"—about as far from the plains of Hungary as you can get, but I guess Puttnam had the American market in mind when he pulled that one off without consulting me. He reminds me of another producer who is fond of grandiose schemes—Bob Guccione. They have a lot in common—apart from accusing me of being unreasonable and going over budget. I wonder how Puttnam explains the fact that when he had no creative input on *Mahler* and I held the reins the total budget was an incredibly low £168,000, but with Puttnam in the driving seat on *Lisztomania* the budget escalated to £1.2 million. Even so, it had far higher production value for money than his film *The Mission*. Seventeen million pounds is just too much to pay for a few Indians and a dummy on a cross going over a waterfall. There's no way that his financiers will ever get their money back on that one, whereas Puttnam himself concedes that *Mahler* made a profit (of which I had a share).

Well, we've had our ups and downs, and as Puttnam has made it universally known that he is a champion of the British cinema I thought he might let bygones be bygones and give me a break. After all, what could be more British than D. H. Lawrence?

I sent him the script of *The Rainbow* and awaited his reaction. He read it quickly and lost no time in calling me. Considering he was meant to be crucified, he was in the best of spirits and very affable. Then, after chatting about the family for a while, he got down to business. "Bit of a downer, isn't it, Ken, and Ursula's a real pain in the arse. Still, nothing that couldn't be fixed by a few re-writes on location—don't need me involved I suppose—you could produce it yourself."

"If that's all right with you," I said.

"Fine," he said. "I'll recommend it to Goldcrest."

I thanked him and, overjoyed, put the phone down and ran to tell Viv. Puttnam was on the Board of Directors and his word was Law. Good old David. We quickly drank his health and sat back to await the call from Goldcrest.

That was some years before Puttnam went to Hollywood to run Columbia Pictures. Well, I'm still waiting to hear from Goldcrest, just as I'm still waiting for my profits on *Mahler*. While I was thinking of who to try next Bobby rang. He waffled on for a long time about this and that but the message was loud and clear: nobody wanted to know. I was UNBANKABLE.

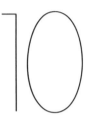

10 Southern Discomfort

Unbankable, and not much left in the piggy bank either—after the divorce settlement was paid up. For nearly twenty years I'd never stopped—one film after another, forty in all, taking the long and the short of it. And now it was all over, with Viv pregnant and wondering where our next crust was coming from. What on earth does an out-of-work film director do? He knows all about editing but can't actually join two pieces of film together. He masterminds his sets and costumes but draws like a child. He supervises the lighting but can't use an exposure meter. He knows how to direct the stars but can't act for toffee himself. Responsible for handling millions of dollars, he can't add up a grocery bill. Jobless, he has no alternative but to queue up at the Job Centre.

But can a film director really go on the dole? I don't know. I've never tried. Maybe he can, but I think not. And he can't retire. Film directors never do. They have to be carried off the set feet first like John Huston in *The Dead*. Some directors make enough money to survive the fallow years, but those of us who are less fortunate have to pray for rehabilitation or, failing that, a "development deal." Hollywood studios are not philanthropic institutions but the "development deal" is the closest they get to a hand-out and it's saved many directors in the dog house from starvation. It's their way of tossing you a bone to gnaw on.

The deal usually starts with the studio commissioning you to either write or supervise the writing of a screenplay. Sometimes the subject is suggested by the studio, sometimes it comes from the director himself (who might have nurtured it for years), or it might originate from a novel owned or optioned by either party. This constitutes the first part of the deal. And so it goes on, through re-writes, polishes and pre-production with the proviso that the studio can terminate the deal at any stage of its development. The whole thing is a nail-biting gamble that pays out nickels and dimes until either the game is over or you hit the jackpot and go into full production—in which case you give up living on peanuts and send out for caviar. And so I hovered by the phone night and day, praying for Bobby to get me a deal on a subject proposed by a studio, which would stand more chance of coming to fruition than anything I might suggest myself.

"Relax," Viv advised. "You've got thousands of records. You can't have played them all. In fact, if you started now and played them non-stop for the rest of your life you'd never get through them all."

"Are you trying to drive me to an early grave?" I said. "There can't be more than three thousand albums on those shelves and if you take the average duration of each disc to be, say, thirty-seven, no, forty-seven minutes, then three thousand times forty-seven . . . no, let's call it fifty for convenience . . . then that makes only . . . let's see, just a mo, I'll get a pencil and paper," but by the time I'd worked it out she'd gone shopping. I made it about sixteen years. So she saw me popping off at sixty-five, did she? Maybe less. After all, she said I'd never get through them. Surely I wouldn't have to wait that long for Bobby to get me a deal. But the winter came before the development deal and it was so bad that most days you couldn't put your head outside the door for fear of it blowing off.

"Take her advice. Relax," I said to myself. "What's the point in worrying? You haven't had a proper holiday for years. Now you've got some free time, why not lay back and enjoy it . . . take it easy . . . play your records. Start at 'A' and keep on going."

"A" is for Adolphe Adam. I put on his *Giselle* and sat down to listen, determined to relax. In a moment my feet were tapping, a minute later I was dancing about the room. Dancing is like riding a bicycle—you never forget how to do it. The steps I'd learned twenty years ago for that ballet in the Floral Hall, Eastbourne, all came back to me. I posed in arabesque, pirouetted, and struck an attitude *en croisé*. During a *pianissimo* I became aware of a sheep bleating. Farmer Weir was standing at the window in torrential rain with a sheep around his neck (they were always getting into the garden from his field next door) and seemed as surprised to see me as I was to see him. I made a *révérence*—and he made off. I was wearing a caftan at the time and he probably thought it was a dress. After five years we were finally on nodding terms and that was considered to be a pretty intimate relationship in those parts, where you are considered to be an "offcomer" if your local roots are less than a century old.

The Weirs had farmed the Borrowdale valley for as long as anyone could remember. I couldn't see us making many friends in that direction and although this didn't bother me personally, being a bit of a recluse, I was concerned that Viv, who'd been Queen of the Campus at Harvard, might start pining for a social life that was gone for good. No theatres, no cinemas, no intimate restaurants, and above all no disco to dance the night away. I had a go at rectifying this one blustery evening in the intimacy of our bedroom, where a flickering orange nightlight and a portable cassette player were poor substitutes for the real thing. Only the music was authentic—a well-worn tape of Isaac Hayes' "Shaft" that Viv carried around as a talisman.

"Don't you think this is sexy?" she said, bopping her hip against my fly in time to the beat. I'm afraid I blushed.

"You mean to say you actually did this sort of thing in a public dance hall?" I asked incredulously.

"That's nothing," said Viv. "Try this for size." And turning around she backed up to me with her ass pressed against my fly and jerked her pelvis from side to side in a syncopated beat to the black man's boogie. If Viv knew a third step I never learned it, for a moment later we were bonking on the bedroom floor. This beats Adolphe Adam any day, I thought, as the music grooved on.

But there was one aspect of life as a swinging single in Boston I felt Viv wouldn't miss quite as much. I refer to her fraternisation with members of the University faculty: intimate dinners with her "old professors," as she called them, in snug corners of candlelit bistros where academic talk over the entrée degenerated to footsie over the port and nuts. I played that game myself in our cosy kitchen over many a meal I'd culled from Robert Carrier's *Great Dishes of the World*. After all, Viv was a pupil of mine, the only pupil of mine destined to graduate with honours from the Ken Russell Film School. But professors, as everyone knows, tend to be sentimental old gentlemen, very much set in their ways, while students have forever been a bolshie, unruly, untidy lot.

Largely due to the ministrations of my one-time housekeeper, May, I'd become accustomed to a comfortably ordered existence over the years. Viv was no May: clothes on the stairs—I nearly broke my neck—baby books on every chair, plastic bottles of beauty lotion on every surface in the bathroom, toothpaste set as hard as cement in the washbowl, cobwebs hanging from the beams, bread and half-eaten food left about at night in the kitchen for mice to feast on. We were overrun with them. They grew more audacious and raided us in the daytime and when I began setting traps Viv got upset at the sight of them, broken-necked and bloody-nosed, in the morning. I also found myself cleaning up after her and beginning to adopt the nagging tones Mum had used on her lackadaisical maids. And you can guess what that unfortunate habit led to.

But Viv didn't walk out—no further than the outside loo, anyway, where I once caught her sneaking a cigarette like a naughty schoolgirl after she'd given them up for my sake. The effort made her edgy, as did the habitual rain and some of my less endearing habits, such as picking my ears with a bent paperclip, snoring all night and leaving soiled hankies around. And all this aggravated by the silent telephone.

Gritting my teeth, I continued playing through my record collection. After Adam came Addinsell, Alfvén, Arnold, Albéniz, Albinoni, Alkan, Alwyn, Arne, Atterberg and Asimov. I gave up dancing and tried con-templation—sitting buddha-wise between the speakers until aching joints and Viv's hoovering around my feet drove me into an armchair. In addition to rather pointed efforts at domesticity, Viv had also embarked on a script of her own and, although the staccato clatter of the typewriter actually enhanced Antheil's *Ballet Mécanique*, it was a poor accompaniment to Arensky's *Egyptian Nights*.

Our life in the sitting room began to take on the nature of a duel until the day when I reached "B" for Bartók and Viv gave up the contest, retiring to the car where she blasted the speakers with "Shaft" and dis-appeared in a cloud of cigarette smoke. Well at least it wasn't "pot"; she'd given that up for good. Nevertheless, things were becoming difficult. A miracle had to happen. It did. The rain stopped . . . and it started snowing. Between blizzards I was able to escape from the house into a world of peace and serenity and I didn't have far to go. A few fields across from the cottage is Catbells, the most popular climb in Lakeland. Its granite peak, polished to a brighter shine than St. Peter's foot in the Vatican by the kiss of a million fell-boots, is hidden on this day by a carpet of snow on which I stand alone looking down on a landscape transformed into the pale memory of a Chinese painting. I have the sensation of being miles above the earth while knowing, courtesy of Wainwright, that my altitude is less than a thousand feet, an illusion created by a shallow cloud of mist covering the entire lake but leaving the tree tops on the islands clearly visible, thus creating an imaginary range of mountain peaks jutting through a high ceiling of cloud. A couple of miles away at the far end of the lake a church spire pierces the mist, turning Keswick into a celestial city watched over by an enormous albatross with outstretched wings fading into the dusk.

Regretfully, I turn my back on Skiddaw and start retracing my steps down into the Borrowdale valley—a curving avenue of stately hills leading to the realm of the Great White Witch, Glaramara, hidden beneath a cloak of snow and ice. And down below, across the frozen meadows, twinkle the lights of Coombe Cottage. Viv will be in the kitchen preparing the supper. She too was learning to cook from a book—of Mid-Eastern recipes. And as most of the ingredients were not available in Keswick, Viv had to improvise. She called these efforts "experiments." I grew to dread the word even as a guinea pig dreads it. But whoever heard of a guinea pig complaining? Of course, I might be lucky. Viv was nearly due to give birth and might have put her feet up for a change. Bread and cheese would suit me fine—if the mice had been kind.

"Mmm . . ." I opened the kitchen door. "That smells nice," I said. "What is it?"

"Felafel," said Viv.

"Makes you *feel awful*," I joked.

"You haven't tasted it yet," she said, putting a plateful of small brown lumps in front of me.

"Looks like sheep shit," I said, with a hearty laugh.

"What do you think of my pictures?" she said, changing the subject. I saw she had taken down some snaps of the kids and replaced them with photos of her family and friends. I was slightly affronted at her presumption. Besides, they were askew and offended my sense of symmetry.

"They're not terribly well hung," I said.

"No comment," she said, walking out of the room.

Oh dear, what had I done now? Why couldn't I keep my mouth shut? I smelt burning, leapt to the oven, and pulled out a blackened chicken with a steaming lemon up its ass. I threw it out of the door for the wild cats to feed on—providing they had any teeth left. The day before I'd chucked out one of my own efforts, a loaf baked to the colour and consistency of a cannonball. I ate the felafel. Accompanied by a glass of retsina, it went down rather well, although I didn't really enjoy it without Viv.

A gust of wind elbowed its way under the door and set the candles dancing. The stuffed pike above the fireplace seemed to give a flicker of life. For the hundredth time I read the legend etched on the curved glass—"Pike, 1 lb. 3 oz. caught by Xavier Russell. Derwentwater, April 1974." It recalled happy days with the family—fishing, boating, climbing, sledging. There were memories everywhere, too many for comfort; fell-boots in the locker under the stove, woolly hats in the dresser drawer and Ma Griffe in the folds of the William Morris curtains in the bedroom where Viv would be sipping carrot juice and reading Dr. Spock . . . time I went in and made the peace.

My eyes popped out of my head at what I saw on pushing open the door. The blankets were all thrown back and there was Viv in the middle of the bed sitting in a puddle with Dr. Spock in one hand and the phone in the other.

"I think my waters have broken," she said to me and the telephone. The telephone was the first to reply.

We both listened intently but all I could hear was the wind whistling around the stone walls. Then Viv said "OK," and hung up.

"They want me to go into hospital right away," she said calmly.

"Are they sending an ambulance?" I asked.

"No, it's too far. The round journey would take too long. They're expecting snowdrifts."

I wondered if Dr. Spock had any advice on that but said nothing and ran out to fetch the car, which as usual was a sod to start. By the time I'd driven through the gusting snow up to the front door, Viv was standing there in the dark with her suitcase. I helped her into the passenger seat and went to get in myself. The snow was up to my ankles.

"I've forgotten the Scrabble," she said. "One of the mothers in my natural childbirth class found it very relaxing."

No point in arguing with a woman about to go into labour. I let myself back into the cottage, found the game under the Monopoly board, took a quick nip of schnapps, locked up again and drove off up the hill. It is the lowest hill in the entire Lake District but the wheels of the Alpha spun ineffectually on the icy surface and back we slid down the hill, engine screaming, into the ditch.

I switched off the ignition. We were unhurt but tilted backwards as if comfortably settled in twin dentist's chairs. I was tempted to say "open wide" but thought better of it.

"Sports cars are hopeless on icy roads," said Viv. "The chassis's too light. I used to put chains on my little Pinto every winter in Connecticut."

"Thanks," I said. "I'll remember that in future. Now what?" Frankly I was scared.

"Better try the farm," said Viv, nodding towards the squat whitewashed building across the road. I gave a grunt and scrambled out, not expecting much help from the neighbours. Farmer Weir himself answered my knock and before I could say a word invited me in. I followed him down the passage and noticed there was blood on his hands. As we entered the kitchen a bizarre sight worthy of a Hammer Horror movie greeted me. Lying on the stone flags in a pool of blood was a skinned creature being carved up by three people. They had bloody hands too. I felt sick. I saw horns; it had been a cow.

"D'you fancy a drop of tea?" said the farmer. I glanced at the pot; there was blood on the handle. A boy was wrapping a chunk of meat in clingfilm. He put it on a shelf piled with similar cuts.

I suddenly remembered the forthcoming birth. There would be blood there too, and complications. I blurted it all out in a rush.

"My wife's sitting in a ditch and she's going to have a breech birth any minute and we've got to get to hospital and there's danger of snow-drifts."

The farmer nodded, went to the sink and turned on the tap. The others, who had paused for my brief speech, went back to work without a word. Watching the farmer methodically scrubbing his hands, I had the uneasy feeling that the baby might be delivered here . . . Then, as he took up a lantern, I remembered that I'd heard calving cows bellowing in the byre and that he might be planning to deliver the baby there instead. Anything seemed possible as time slipped away.

What I wasn't prepared for was the farmer delivering us to the hospital all huddled together in the cab of his tractor. We had only minor snowdrifts to contend with as things turned out, but the giant tyres made for easy going on the treacherous hills and dales we encountered on the way. I don't know if he saw us in his rear-view mirror as we waved goodbye to his broad shoulders disappearing into eddies of snow; he has always re-mained an undemonstrative man, even though we eventually came to share baked potatoes and hot punch on Bonfire nights.

Minutes after checking in, Viv was sitting up in bed holding my hand and gripping it tighter with every spasm. For a moment I let go.

"Where's your hand?" she said, feeling another wave of pain ap-proaching.

"I'm looking in your bag for the Scrabble," I said.

"Fuck the Scrabble," she said, as the pain overwhelmed her, "give me your hand." I did so and nearly had the life squeezed out of it as she yelled and screamed, "Give me a shot!"

Poor Viv, I thought. So much for natural childbirth.

A few moments later she was wheeled away to the delivery room and I followed on till a lady doctor in white apron and wellies said it might be a bit messy and advised me to go to the canteen for a spot of breakfast. The orderly sitting next to me at the table swamped his eggs in ketchup and quite put me off my black pudding. I pushed it aside in favour of a cup of strong sugary tea and looked through the window at the pinky dawn. Would Viv be all right? Would the baby be all right? Would it be a boy or a girl—or both? Shirley had once given birth to mixed twins but only Victoria had survived.

The dawn had turned red, the ketchup was swimming in egg yolk on the next plate, the bloody cow and the farmer's bloodstained hands swam through my weary mind. I said a brief prayer to Skiddaw and then called on the Blessed Virgin for insurance. After all, Viv was born into the faith, though successive schools of uncharitable nuns had beaten it out of her. Even so . . . and then there was the National Health doctor to worry about. She'd looked impossibly young . . . fresh out of medical school . . . was she experienced in breech births? I wondered. We should have consulted a gynaecologist . . . we should have done this, we should have done . . . my God, there was one of the nurses who had been in attendance, tucking into a hearty breakfast. She looked relaxed. No, she looked tense. I sat there, trying to read her features when all I had to do was ask, but somehow I couldn't. I averted my head, not wanting to catch her eye, and backed out of the canteen in the process. I found Viv back in her room sitting up in bed with the Scrabble board on her lap, sipping a cup of tea and looking as fresh as a daisy. I guessed baby was safely tucked up in isolation. We smiled. I kissed her and looked down at the crisscrossed words. They were all names.

"So it came in useful after all," I said.

"Anything there take your fancy?" she asked.

"How about Clarissa?" I ventured. Viv winced.

We baptised our daughter Molly (a diminutive of Mary) in an icy torrent beneath a Maxfield Parrish sky on the snow-clad slopes of Skiddaw—thus giving thanks all round. Molly seemed to change everything. The sun shone, the house became a hive of activity. In between bathing the baby, Viv busied herself on a new script called *Mothers*, based on the individual ways four Keswick mums she'd met at her pre-natal classes were coping with the fresh responsibilities that came along with a new member of the family. I too was busy adapting for the screen a brilliant

stage play sent to me out of the blue by a little-known author called Jo
Anderson. It was a purely speculative venture, but at least it enabled me
to keep my hand in and stopped me brooding over the possibility that I
was all washed up, for there were constant reminders that this might be
so.

Once, for instance, I was invited to a famous publishing house in
London to discuss the possibility of writing a work of non-fiction. After
a dawn start and a six-hour journey by road and rail I entered the busy
foyer of the establishment and gave my name at reception. I was asked
to wait and took a seat in an area that reminded me of an aircraft lounge—
business class. Presently a smart lady executive strode from a lift, swept
the waiting assembly with her eyes and pounced on a handsome trendy
in his mid-thirties. "Ken Russell?" she said with a bright smile. The trendy
shuddered and shook his head, whereupon the lady executive apologised
and went over for a word with the receptionist, who pointed me out. Her
face fell for a moment then she bounced over to me with the bright smile
restored.

"Forgive me for not recognising you, Mr. Russell," she said, eyeing
my white hair. "I was expecting an *enfant terrible.*"

"You're as young as you feel," I said lamely, feeling a hundred and
one.

I followed her into the lift and along corridors on the sixth floor to a
tiny matchbox of an office piled high with books and mountains of ash
and crimson cigarette butts. We squeezed in along with her attractive
secretary and perched on a circle of chairs, knees almost touching. I
declined a cigarette, saying I was a non-smoker.

"We thought you might do something for us on the Swinging Sixties,"
said the lady exec, putting away her cigarette case as her secretary prepared
to take notes. "How it felt to be around at the time of the Beatles, Jimi
Hendrix, the Stones, Andy Warhol, Fellini, David Hockney, the Who,
Hair, flower power, Angela Davis, David Bailey, the Shrimp, Justin de
Villeneuve and Twiggy . . . a personal view of all the celebrities you met,
spiced with anecdotes." I began to feel in urgent need of a large Scotch.

The women craned forward, their faces aglow with anticipation. Our
knees touched but no current flowed, no sparks flew—none of those names
turned me on. The exec was all agog, the secretary's ballpoint was poised.
I tried my best to perform.

"Well," I began diffidently, "I do have a story about Twiggy." Their
eyes lit up. "A party of us went for a day out at Brighton during pre-
production on *The Boy Friend*. We travelled on the Brighton Belle, then
wandered around the Lanes, window-shopping for antiques, ending up

at Wheeler's, the famous fish restaurant, where we enjoyed a leisurely meal. Twiggy had *sole véronique*, I remember." The women seemed to be holding their breath. I hurried on to the punch line.

"After lunch we took a stroll along the pier to have a look at the camera obscura and rounded off the afternoon with a visit to the Royal Pavilion. By the time we got back to the station Twiggy was feeling peckish and dropped a coin into a slot machine for a bar of chocolate. I think it was Aero. Anyway, the drawer jammed halfway and in trying to pull out the bar she got her fingers caught inside. She wasn't hurt, you understand. In fact she was laughing, but no matter how we tugged and pulled we couldn't release her. In the end we had to get a porter to fetch a screwdriver to dismantle the machine . . ." I laughed at the memory.

"What happened then?" said the exec, gasping.

"Well, we got her out in no time, no damage done," I said.

"And then what?" the exec asked with a touch of impatience.

"We missed our train," I said.

"But they run every hour, surely? You couldn't have had long to wait."

"The next train was a slow one," I said. "It stopped at every station."

"Even so, it's a terribly short journey, Brighton to London."

"That's not really the point of the story," I said limply. "It wouldn't do, anyway. It happened in the Seventies." There was a pause while the exec opened her cigarette case and lit up.

"I was hoping for something a little more racy," she said. "You know, the wild parties, the drug scene."

I felt a glimmer of hope and spoke up. "I was an addict myself once . . ."

She brightened. "You had to be," she said. "No one could dream up those images without a little help from something. What were you on? Coke, acid, grass, what?"

"None of those," I said. "My imagery comes from listening to music." Her face showed a moment's disappointment but she quickly rallied.

"Black Sabbath, I bet," she said emphatically.

"No, I don't care for rock music," I said, "and it was snuff that I was addicted to, not the hard stuff. I've never tampered with that." She obviously didn't consider snuff trendy so I dropped it. "As for parties, we usually had an end-of-picture party where we all linked hands and sang 'Auld Lang Syne,' but apart from that the only party I can remember attending in the Sixties was a garden party at Buckingham Palace where I met Princess Margaret."

The exec perked up again. "She was very much into the scene, wasn't she? Did you become one of her set? Did you see her often?"

"No, not often," I said, wishing to be helpful. "Though I saw her once at the theatre and waved—but she didn't wave back . . ."

The exec stared at me uncertainly for a moment and gave a cautious laugh. "You're having me on, aren't you?" she said hopefully.

"I'm afraid not . . ." I murmured apologetically.

She stared at me accusingly and said sharply, "But you were the *enfant terrible* of British films. You were the wild man of the BBC. You gave wild parties and had a terrible reputation. You can't deny it."

"You're right about one thing—I do have a terrible reputation. People get quite upset when they see how mild-mannered I am."

She continued looking at me, still doubting the evidence of her own eyes. "Perhaps you've just mellowed with age," she said, attempting to be kind.

Realising it was all over, the secretary put the cap on her ballpoint pen and closed her notebook. The exec stood up.

"It was a pleasure to meet you," she said, shaking my hand. "You can find our own way out, can't you? Goodbye."

"Goodbye," murmured the secretary with a winsome smile.

"And good luck in the Eighties," the exec called after me down the corridor, as an afterthought.

Whatever happened to the Seventies? I wondered, as I went down in the lift, ageing with every floor.

My journey to the south, to London, had brought me to a state of depression which was destined to increase the further south I travelled. My final destination was Southampton, where I was to appear on a TV chat show. At the same time I was taking the opportunity of dropping in to see Mum, who was now undergoing treatment at Fareham, the local lunatic asylum, where she had often threatened to send me when I mis-behaved as a child. The fact that she was now incarcerated there herself gave me no satisfaction.

I caught an express at Waterloo and two hours later discovered Mum sitting in a long corridor full of senile old women and dutiful visitors. She was wearing a faded pink dressing gown and talking to herself. I noticed with an involuntary shudder that her feet were bare on the cold stone floor. She seemed neither to know nor care and stared straight through me with no sign of recognition. I cornered a passing nurse and demanded an explanation, but Mum wasn't under her care and she was unable to help, though she promised to see what she could do, later.

I took Mum's hand—it was all skin and bone—and tried to catch what she was saying, but her words were drowned in a babble of voices. Someone nearby clapped their hands, awakening in Mum a similar response. She clapped her dry palms together mechanically and continued to do so while her expression remained unchanged. I thought of trying to restrain her but there seemed little point. No one took any notice and out of the corner of my eye I witnessed behaviour even more bizarre. Even so, it was disturbing to see my oldest fan sitting before me, applauding again. It was something I'd come to miss during the years since I heard it last in . . . where was it? . . . In Devon at the Redoubt Gardens, Teignmouth.

It had taken me five years of self-punishment to realise that I was not cut out to be a dancer. Mime, yes. I made a tolerable duke in *Giselle* and a truly formidable Dr. Coppelius, though it's true my interpretation owed more to the sinister Dr. Caligari from Weine's expressionist film than the charming old eccentric conceived by the choreographer, Marius Petipa. But a dancer, no! Whether I was hoofing away as a cowboy, desperately trying to keep time in the back row of a musical in Leeds or limping around a stage in *Swan Lake* at Littlehampton with an overweight cygnet perched on one drooping shoulder, I was a spectacular failure. For, apart from a technique that might, at best, be called eccentric, I had a rather unfashionable shape for a traditional *danseur noble,* and until ladies' legs, pot-bellies and barrel-chests became all the rage, I would never come into my own and by then . . . well, it just doesn't bear thinking about. It was time to move on.

So I bought a copy of *The Stage* to see if the legitimate theatre had something of a less athletic nature to offer. Ah, the "Garrick Players" of Newton Poppleford, South Devon, were holding an audition for a juvenile lead at the Westminster Hall. All applicants were requested to perform a soliloquy from a Shakespearean play of their own choice. I decided on Puck from A *Midsummer Night's Dream.* I had never seen the play staged but was familiar with Max Reinhardt's wonderful film and based my interpretation on that of Mickey Rooney, who had played the role with a heavy Brooklyn accent—"I'll throw a goidle around the oith," etc.

I arrived punctually. Apart from the adjudicator, an elderly man with the sniffles in a voluminous raincoat and trilby to match, the hall was empty. I did my piece, which started with a backbend and finished with the splits, and was asked to wait until the other applicants had taken their turn. I waited a long time and finally got the job—there *were* no other applicants.

My début in the village hall in the stage version of *When Knights Were Bold* found me falling into old habits. My role was that of a forty-year-old doctor spending a civilised weekend at a country house-party. To a young man in his mid-twenties, forty meant old age and doctor meant Dr. Coppelius. Accordingly, I played the character with dragging foot, humped back, flying hair, deep-set rolling eyes, rotting teeth, twisted mouth, sunken cheeks, bushy brows and—this was new—a high-pitched cackle. Although it was only a bit part, I think I stole the show. In the event, I was recast after the first night and stuck in a suit of armour which remained immobile for two acts and only came alive at the end of the third, when it raised a rusty sword.

This was trying enough in the parish halls we toured, but in the Redoubt Gardens on a clifftop at Teignmouth, it was positively traumatic. We were plagued by high winds and summer thunderstorms that week and played to rows of billowing deckchairs as the heavens roared. The draughty armour I could tolerate, but the idea of playing a lightning conductor had little appeal.

I was not sorry when the company went bankrupt. We were given the good news just before the first Saturday night performance of what was to have been a two-week run. All the same, I gave my all to the small audience of malcontents who had failed to get into *Soldiers in Skirts* at the Pier Pavilion and were putting up with second best. There was a particularly fidgety couple in the front row, only partially visible through the slits of my visor. All was soon revealed.

"That's my son," shouted a familiar voice. "'E's playing the title role." The couple were Mum and Dad. I prayed for rain. It never came. The sun shone brightly and, to a chorus of "oohs" and "aahs" from Mum, set interminably. The stars came out.

Finally my big moment came. I raised my sword and thought of Mum and all the third-rate shows she'd sat through on my behalf. Hell! I owed her something. What had I to lose? So, throwing down my broadsword, I broke into Jack Buchanan's soft-shoe routine from the movie version. Considering Jack had the advantage over me in footwear, I didn't do too badly—if Mum's applause was anything to go by. She even vocalised her appreciation by demanding an encore. Being in the open air with rolling thunder, she felt no need of restraint and even shouted instructions across the footlights as to where we should meet up afterwards for a drink.

She was hardly less subdued within the confines of a conventional theatre. At the tiny Salisbury Playhouse Mum had only a Bechstein Grand for competition. That was when I was appearing with the British Dance Group in a barefoot ballet called *Born of Desire*. As Southampton was just down the road, Mum came to all seven performances, including the Saturday matinee to which she invited her next-door neighbour, Mrs. Mann. As usual, Mum had chosen the front row, close to the piano, and under my nose. When the curtain went up I could see that Mrs. Mann, who had poor eyesight, was having trouble reading the programme note, which was almost as long as the ballet itself—a four-minute piece of angst choreographed to Grieg's *The Last Spring*. So Mum read it for her—aloud. It was the nearest thing to *Sprechgesang* Salisbury had ever known, and there were those in the audience, sparse as usual, who could be forgiven for thinking it was an integral part of the performance—which Mum knew by heart. Listening to her anticipate our every movement, I realised that she had missed her vocation—she would have made a wonderful stage prompt:

"'Man born of woman 'as but a short time to live,'" she began. "'Two simple peasants toil from dawn to dusk in the fields.' (Aside) You can tell they're peasants. They can't afford shoes."

"They can't afford tools, by the look of it, either," said Mrs. Mann. "They're doing everything with their hands."

"That's called 'mime,'" said Mum. "You can tell what they're doing by watching their gestures. They're playing rounders now." (Actually we were scything corn.) "'Around them all is ripening. Nature's bosom swells,'" Mum rhapsodised. "'The woman's breasts yearn to suckle the child she is fated not to bear.'"

"A child wouldn't get much nourishment from her!" said Mrs. Mann, eyeing my partner's flat chest.

"'The man wonders why 'is seed will not take root,'" Mum continued, ignoring the interruption. "'Why'er womb will not bear fruit? Their barren loins ache to bring forth the child denied them.'"

As they watched, we alternately rubbed our loins and raised our arms to heaven.

"No one ever got pregnant doing that," said Mrs. Mann.

Mum never took Mrs. Mann to one of my performances ever again. Usually she took a bemused relative, occasionally Dad, who saw the curtain come down on my stage career at Teignmouth (little realising that I was about to ask his assistance to launch me on yet another—photography). Unfortunately, he'd missed my début in *Annie Get Your Gun* at the Sheffield Palace but of course Mum had been there from the moment the doors opened, sitting bang in the middle of the front row. I remember her excitement when, having penetrated my warpaint, she turned to the stranger sitting beside her, masturbating beneath a newspaper, and hissed in a stage whisper, "That's our Ken you've got your eye on." I even heard that above the pit band playing "I'm an Indian, too." And I'll never forget her laughter at the Floral Hall, Eastbourne, when she saw me as a fairytale pussycat in my first classical ballet, *Sleeping Beauty*, dressed in silk tights, high-heeled court shoes, frilly tunic and feathered hat. And my, how the rafters rang when the rest of the audience all joined in, and how I blushed beneath my thick layer of 5 & 9.

Sitting next to her in that chilly asylum corridor, I wondered if even a vestige of memory stirred within her mind? If so it stayed there, locked in. I produced a bar of chocolate from my pocket and Mum stopped applauding, snatched it from my hand, hurriedly undid the wrapper and wolfed it down as if afraid someone might take it from her. A bell sounded. I kissed Mum goodbye. The tide of visitors flowed down the corridor leaving the patients as helpless as jellyfish stranded on a beach. I looked for someone to speak to but the nursing staff seemed to have disappeared. A moment later I was locked out.

I went straight to the nearest footwear shop and bought a pair of comfy slippers. Dad wasn't in when I called at the house, so I left the slippers on the back doorstep with a note. It's just as well he wasn't in, there would have been a row. How could he neglect her so when he owned a bloody shop stocked with hundreds of bloody slippers on every bloody shelf? OK! What if she had driven him nearly mad with her nagging? She didn't deserve that sort of neglect. I glanced at my watch. I wasn't due at the TV station for another hour—ample time for a few drinks to settle my nerves.

I sipped my third scotch in the bar of the Bassett Hotel and wondered what questions my interviewer would ask me. The usual old stuff, I guessed. Am I difficult to work with? Do I hate actors? Am I a misogynist? Do I set out to shock just for the sake of it? Do I distort facts? Does it bother me that many of my films are flops? Is it true that I never go to the cinema? What does it feel like to be the oldest *enfant terrible* in the business? What do I think of the future of the British film industry? Why do I give interviews? That was the question I asked myself as I ordered my fourth scotch. I knew the answer, or thought I did: to promote my work. Time to go.

"Do you still have a bear garden and a moth-eaten old beer?" I asked.

"Beg pardon, squire?" said the barman. "Could you repeat that?"

"Sorry, I meant old bear. You used to have a bit of a zoo in your back garden. There was a monkey, too, or it might have been a chimp or a baboon. There was a branch in her cage with a thick twig filed into the shape of a monkey's cock by a thoughtful keeper."

"That's a new one on me, squire, and I've been landlord here for over twenty years. Sure you've got the right place?"

"Certain," I said, swaying to the door.

I caught a bus to STV and introduced myself at reception. They weren't expecting me. Fortunately I realised my mistake before making an even bigger fool of myself. I'd confused the stations. STV were the people who'd commissioned the autobiographical film script. God knows when they'd get it. I was due at the rival network.

The doorman helped me into a cab and I set off with my head out of the window gulping down air in an effort to sober up. Past half-forgotten landmarks we sped—the gas works, the Six Dials, the Bar Gate, and on and on towards the studios. A production assistant hovering on the pavement paid my fare and led me through reception to the bar where the interviewer and the producer were drinking beer. I joined them for a quick pint and a chat and was dragged off to make-up. A minute later I was in the studio with a stranger putting his hand up the inside of my shirt and clipping on a radio mike. The countdown began. The red light flashed— we were on the air. The interviewer gave me a fulsome introduction and asked his first question.

"Mr. Russell, you have the reputation of being something of a martinet on the studio floor. Is this simply malicious gossip or is there a modicum of truth in it?"

I smiled and gave a mumbled reply. The very next thing I remember was the interviewer saying, "And thanks again, Ken Russell, for joining us on *Viewpoint*. Next week's guest will be Sven Berlin, the New Forest sculptor." The red light went off, the stranger retrieved his microphone and I was whisked off in a daze by the producer and his team to a basement restaurant around the corner where I confessed to my total lapse of memory and ordered bottles of champagne and roast pigeon all round.

The waiter poured, the producer talked, I listened. Apparently, on being asked if I was a martinet in the studio, I'd leaned forward, examined the interviewer's make-up and asked why he'd been made up to resemble a Chinaman, saying that I would have promptly fired the make-up person if they ever produced work as bad as that for me, unless, of course, it was a Chinaman they were making up. I'd also have fired the lighting cameraman for accentuating the bags under the interviewer's eyes, but I'd have fired them both without shouting or fuss. They'd just collect their two weeks' wages and go.

God knows what else I'd said to offend them. I didn't stay to find out. Nausea was sweeping over me in waves. I excused myself and made for the loo, where I arrived just in time to throw up. I felt ghastly and claustrophobic. I needed air. I collected my overnight bag from the cloakroom unobserved and set off on foot for the nearby hotel where I'd been booked in for the night.

The walk did nothing to sober me up and I entered my room at the end of a long corridor in a daze, dropped my clothes on the floor, collapsed onto the bed and passed out. Pressure on the bladder awoke me some time later. It was still dark outside and I couldn't find the light switch. But I could see the light under the bathroom door and lurched towards it, my head still spinning. I threw open the door and stepped inside. It was the largest bathroom I'd ever seen, over two hundred feet long, only there was no bath or loo or bidet. Click! The door closed behind me. I was standing in the hotel corridor—stark bollock naked! I frantically turned the handle of the door back and forth. It didn't open.

Shivering and wretched, I squatted on my haunches, back to the door, waiting for some good Samaritan to pass by and collect my key from reception. Minute after minute ticked by with the pressure on my bladder growing every second, and no means of relieving it without detection. The hotel was new and featureless; twenty dark doors either side of the fitted carpet stretched away to a similar corridor crossing it at the far end. How I longed for the Grand Hotels of the past with potted palms at every corner. I could have relieved myself with ease, but then such a procedure would have been unnecessary in a hotel with doors that were not self-locking.

What to do? I was becoming desperate. Getting up, I crept along the corridor listening at doors. Perhaps I could get help that way. But what would I be able to say before the woman screamed or the man punched me in the face? Of course, there was always the chance that I might get lucky, but I doubted it, not at my age and with my figure. And what if I was arrested? All the same, I listened—and heard nothing, no TV, no snoring, no song of the bedsprings, nothing! I was all alone. I'd never felt more alone, alone, abandoned, unreal, lost in a dream of Jean-Paul Sartre. In dreams the most extraordinary events seem matter of fact and natural. I wanted a pee. It was natural that I should have one. I set off to look for a urinal.

Around the corner was an identical corridor—with one difference— an ice-vending machine, complete with a hole in the top for topping up with water. For a moment I was sorely tempted and a flicker of a smile arose at the thought of all those commercial travellers in frozen foods drinking hard liquor spiced up with ice cubes containing a dash of that nauseous colouring so beloved of the manufacturers of their phoney prod-ucts. Instead I turned the next corner into an elevator hall, complete with a tray of sand for cigarette stubs. At last a non-smoker was about to put it to use. So I took my courage in both hands and, thirty seconds later, feeling much relieved, rang for the elevator. Would it have a passenger or two? No, it was empty. Resolutely I pushed the button marked "G." A few moments later the doors slid open and I peeped out towards reception where the night porter was booking in a shifty-looking couple. I hesitated. The lift doors closed. I leapt back just in time, immediately pushed the "Open Door" button and slipped out into the foyer. The walk to the reception desk seemed endless. Putting my hands in front of me, I shuffled forward and experienced an incredible sense of déjà vu. A grey image came to mind, step-printed, faded and soft-focused, of a pathetic procession of old men, all skin and bone, shuffling along with their hands held pitifully before them with foolish grins on their frightened faces. It was an image that had long haunted and disturbed me, that picture of condemned Jews walking to the gas chamber. I had often wondered why they didn't stride out, heads held high, arms swinging. Now I knew. Hiding behind a pillar, I hissed at the night porter and beckoned him over. Leaving the new arrivals to fill in their forms, he ran to see what was up.

"What the hell do you think you're doing?" he snapped.

"I've locked myself out of my room," I said, inadvertently breaking wind.

"You silly old fart," he sneered. "What's your number?" Fortunately I remembered and followed him silently into the lift and out along the corridor to my door which he unlocked with a pass key.

"What are you hiding there?" he asked, looking at my cupped hands. "The crown jewels?"

I stepped into the room, stone-cold sober, and noticed an envelope on the floor that I must have overlooked before. I opened it. Inside was a telephone message: "Development Deal—*Dracula*." I gave a long sigh and crossed myself.

11

My Hollywood Trip

The publisher's blurb on the dust jacket of Bram Stoker's *Dracula* claimed it was the greatest horror classic of all time and if movie imitations are the sincerest form of flattery they must be right. Film-makers only go for the best—especially when it's out of copyright. Just think what an inspiration the Bible has been to all those in search of truly great box-office receipts. *Dracula* easily outstrips the good book with, at the time of writing, some two hundred and thirty-eight titles owing their very existence to the combined blood-lust of the Transylvanian Count and Joe Public.

So what could I bring to yet another version? A single reading of the novel was enough to tell me. It was a revelation and contained much material unfamiliar to me, including an endearing madman called Renfield with a voracious appetite for flies. But for all its virtues, the book lacks purpose. If you rise from the dead regularly at sunset, you must have a jolly good reason to get hooked on the same dreary nightcap for century after century, even if it is your favourite tipple. So I gave my bloodthirsty Count a purpose in life—the perpetuation of the creative spirit. As every victim knows, once bitten by a vampire you become one of the undead yourself and are cursed with everlasting life which, after a century or two, must become deadly boring, unless perhaps you are blessed with a boundless imagination and the skill to turn it into great art. So my Dracula would be a philanthropist with a taste for the blood of genius. Have you ever considered how much Picasso resembled Turner or Sibelius Beethoven? Think about it.

Mick Fleetwood, the pop star, has something of the look of Sibelius about *him* and it may have been this conceit which endeared him to the project when my American producer showed him the script. A meeting was hastily arranged and in next to no time I was kissing goodbye to Viv and the baby and the Borrowdale rain and Concordeing over to Washington to see if we got on. At the same time I was to attend a concert of his group to evaluate their music in terms of a sound-track album.

I was picked up at the airport in a stretch-limo, driven to their hotel (besieged by fans), installed in a suite and asked to wait. I had barely time to unpack, pour myself a drink and take in the golden palm trees and oversized china dalmatians before Mick Fleetwood arrived, all in black, looking pale and sinister. Of course I'd have to do something about the pigtail, but apart from that he was Dracula to the life. As he locked the door I became conscious of a growing uproar in the corridor. He greeted me briefly and gasped out that the concert was off. One of the band had collapsed and been rushed to hospital. It looked very serious and the fans were going crazy. Catching his breath, he went on to say that he loved the project and during the shooting planned to drain off a pint of blood a day to maintain a deathly pallor. Before I could tell him there were less drastic ways of achieving this he excused himself, saying he had to fly to his friend's bedside. I half-expected him to leap from the window, but he left in the normal way, fighting through a wall of wailing fans. From the sound of lamentation it seemed as if the whole nation was in mourning. As I double-locked the door, the phone rang. It was my producer. The backers had got wind of three more Dracula movies in the air: the project was **DEAD!**

I felt as if a stake had been driven through my heart. How was I going to survive this cruel blow? I called room service and ordered a Bloody Mary. "On the rocks?" inquired the voice at the end of the phone. "You guessed it," I said despondently. No movie, no development deal, no stretch-limo waiting to take me to the airport in the morning. I caught a bus instead and changed my expensive Concorde ticket for a tourist seat on a Tri-star. The refund would come in handy, now that I was jobless again. In the event, I had to change my new ticket yet again a few minutes later—they were paging me over the PA system. A call was waiting for me at the information desk. What was up? Nothing wrong at home, please! My heart thumped as I raced to the phone.

It was my agent, Bobby. Could I change my plans and fly straight to New York for a meeting with Paddy Chayefsky to discuss the possibility of my directing his latest screenplay, *Altered States*, for Columbia Pictures? It was going to be a big Hollywood blockbuster with a big, big budget. Other directors were also under consideration but I was a hot favourite. Wow! Three hours later I was back in the world of the stretch-limo, purring over George Washington Bridge to a penthouse suite in the Sherry Netherland Hotel on Fifth Avenue as a guest of the executive producer.

The rooms were palatial with slender gothic windows giving onto the park, walls rich in designer art, a fridge full of champagne, a canopied bed with mirrors, a Cimarosa oboe concerto playing on the hi-fi and a note from my host, who had just left for Hollywood, inviting me to make myself at home and wait on a call from Paddy. The call never came, though someone called Howard Gottfried phoned on his behalf to arrange an immediate meeting. Paddy wasn't there either, *there* being a cheap deli on Broadway where Howard—a slight figure with pebble glasses, receding chin and slit mouth—smiled and made excuses for the great man's non-appearance. Howard resembled a very pleasant lounge lizard who plied me with cheese blintzes and beer and gave me the third degree. When I had satisfied his curiosity, he said that although Paddy had seen *Tommy* and was familiar with the fantastic side of my work, he wondered if I could direct actors who didn't have to sing and dance. I referred Howard to *Savage Messiah*, which was as low on fantasy and high on acting as anything I'd ever done. He promised to show a copy to Paddy and give me his verdict within twenty-four hours.

"But what's this *Altered States* all about?" I asked as he picked up the tab.

"It's a sorta satire on a bunch of Harvard scientists who get into sensory deprivation and deep quantum physics," he said, looking shifty. "It's right up your alley. You'll love it. Bye, speak to you tomorrow."

In the meantime the gothic penthouse proved to be a very pleasurable waiting room, though as I relaxed on the executive producer's king-size bed that evening, sipping his vintage champagne and listening to his canned music, I wondered, gazing into the mirror above me, how many other Hollywood hopefuls had found themselves in my position. Apart from being unbankable, I was bankrupt of any ideas on the subject of sensory deprivation. So why was he bothering to seduce me when there was plenty of local talent around?

"There must be something very special about you," I murmured to myself, falling into a dizzy slumber.

The following evening Bobby called to say I'd got the job. Although it came as no surprise, I jumped for joy all the same and was still jumping a few minutes later when Denny rang to congratulate me. I asked him how he'd got wind of the news so quickly.

"Bad news travels fast," he replied.

"Bad news? What do you mean? I'm an easy winner for the prize job of the year and you call that bad news?"

"If you think you were number one choice, I have to disillusion you," he said.

"Let me guess," I said. "They asked Spielberg or Kubrick first, but they were busy on their own projects. There's nothing wrong in coming third in that company. *I'm* not proud."

"I hear they also tried Sydney Pollack, Robert Wise, Orson Welles, Martin Scorsese, Fred Zinnemann, Woody Allen and Ingmar Bergman," he said. I could hear my voice faltering.

"Well, being in the top ten is nothing to be ashamed of, either."

"Dream on," he said. "I'm told they weren't the only ones to pass on the project. There was also Brian de Palma, Bertolucci, John Boorman, Andrei Tarkovsky, Irwin Kirshner, Francis Coppola, Roman Polanski, Dick Lester, Michael Winner, Sidney Lumet, Dick Donner, George Lucas, Nic Roeg, John Schlesinger, François Truffaut, Franco Zeffirelli, Bryan Forbes . . ."

"Stop! You're having me on."

"Am I?"

"OK, go on then. I know you're dying to tell me. How far down the list did I come?"

"Try your lucky number," he said.

"Twenty-seven!" I said disbelievingly.

He laughed. "Seems you got lucky at last," he said and hung up.

Bastard! I went to call him back and then checked myself. He'd been bitchy ever since he discovered that Shirley and I had split up. I dropped the receiver back in its cradle. I wouldn't give him the satisfaction. Even if he'd exaggerated, or even lied through his teeth, it was disturbing news all the same. If it really was the big, prestigious movie Bobby had cracked it up to be, why had everyone turned it down? What did they know that I didn't know? I was tempted to call Bobby and ask him, but having just got the twenty-seventh most wanted film director in the world a job he was unlikely to spill the beans. I was soon to find out for myself.

Once under contract to Columbia my seduction was accomplished and I was moved out of the palatial suite in the Sherry Netherland to less elevated accommodation on the other side of the park, not far from the Broadway office of the elusive Paddy Chayefsky, whom I was at last to meet. Seated in a rickety high-backed chair next to Howard, I had ample time to take in my surroundings, which were more in keeping with those of a bookish professor in old Russia than the slick, Oscar-winning writer I knew to be the reality. As the minutes ticked by and Howard ran out of small talk I began to feel I'd been here before and suddenly remembered a Chekhov play I'd seen in London recently.

There was a rattle on the door handle and in walked Uncle Vanya himself, portly, in his mid-sixties, grey-haired, slightly stooped, mild in manner, self-effacing, simply dressed with a pince-nez on the end of his nose, absentmindedly stroking a well-trimmed goatee. After embracing me warmly, his eyes moist as he congratulated me on *Savage Messiah*, which had apparently brought tears to his eyes, he blew his nose on a large silk handkerchief and sank into the swivel chair behind his mahogany desk, shuffled through a mass of papers and eventually unearthed a dog-eared script.

"This is a modern version of the old Jekyll and Hyde story," he announced with a growl that was intended as a laugh, "updated to Harvard Medical School in the Sixties to give it added credibility, and although this is the third and final screenplay, there are still a number of things I'm not completely happy with, including most of Dr. Jessup's halluci-nations. Take this script back to your hotel and work on them." Then, as an afterthought, ". . . and I'd also appreciate your comments overall. We'll meet here at the same time tomorrow."

"How long do we have before shooting?" I asked, taking a script as heavy as a telephone directory.

"Six weeks, but don't worry," he said. "I know we haven't much time but if the worst comes to the worst we can always fix the script as we go along. I'll be hanging around the set anyway," he said, smiling benignly. "I'm known in Hollywood as the *benign influence*." This was a cue for Howard to come in.

"Say, Paddy," he said, mimicking Schnozzle Durante, "how d'you spell *benign*?"

Paddy, relishing the moment, sat back in his squeaky old chair, brought his fingertips together, fixed us with beady eyes twinkling behind his glasses and, in a fair imitation of Red Riding Hood's phoney grandmother, growled, "**W.I.C.K.E.D.**"

We all laughed—me nervously. Uncle Vanya had just turned into the big, bad wolf.

The next day my fresh thoughts on the hallucinations and suggestions for cutting scenes and tightening dialogue were met with a thunderous silence by Paddy and nervous twitching by Howard. A film script is often referred to as "the Bible," and, as everyone knows, to tamper with the Bible is sacrilegious. This was never more true than in the case of *Altered States*. Every page, every paragraph, sentence, word and comma was as sacrosanct as the script engraved by Moses on Mount Sinai. Likewise, Paddy's script was holy writ and Paddy's word was law, a law which found my new ideas for the hallucinations too close to the New Testament for comfort, even though the hero was a lapsed Methodist. It now became clear to me why the original director, Arthur Penn, had resigned and twenty-six other talented directors had supposedly turned down the project before me. It was a no-win situation.

I rang Viv to break the news that I was coming home.

"What's it all about, this *Altered States*," she asked, before I could gently drop the bombshell, "the Civil War?"

"No," I said, "but at first I thought it was about the United States, as well." And in order to delay the evil moment, I went on to put her in the picture. "It's about the efforts of a Harvard scientist—who had religious visions as a child—to project himself back in time using isolation tanks and hallucinogenic drugs. Not only does he achieve this in mind, but also in body—reverting first to a primitive man and then to a purely molecular state and finally to one of chaos. It's all sci-fi stuff based on the experiments and out-of-body experiences of Huxley, Lily and Castaneda."

"And they got you in to supply the trips," said Viv. "Aren't Chayefsky's good enough? He must have dropped acid in the Sixties, surely?"

Judging from the "trips" in the script, I suspected not and said so to Viv. Most of them were unimaginative and unfilmable. How does one visualise a sinister black shape travelling through eternal darkness at a billion light-years a second? The team of special effects people, doctors and scientists who'd been working with Arthur Penn on the project for the past six months didn't know, and neither did I, though I was willing to try and find more relevant alternatives. In so doing I was learning the hard way what everyone else in the business knew already: that Paddy could never readily accept any idea that was not his own. But even the most powerful writer ever to hit Hollywood was beginning to realise that unless he got a move on Columbia would stop pouring money into a black hole that had already swallowed up a million dollars.

"I was Paddy's last chance," I said to Viv, finally getting to the point of what had become an unnecessarily expensive call. "He's blown it— I'm coming home."

An icy wind blew down the line from Borrowdale, followed by some cold reasoning. This was a chance to pull myself back to acceptability, the only chance I'd been offered. It was also a chance for me to realise on the screen, for the first time, my wildest flights of fancy, unrestrained by considerations of budget. Viv also pointed out that until I made a film in America I'd never be accepted into the Hollywood community. In vain I pointed out that I'd never been dictated to before or made a film just for the money.

"Then you're lucky to have got away with it for so long," she said, "and don't worry, you'll turn it into a Ken Russell film yet!"

This pulled me up short. I was expecting sympathy, not orders. "But I can't work with this man, he's a complete egomaniac," I stammered.

"Then you should get on just fine," she said.

"He's chosen all the actors himself."

"And probably made a better job of it than you did on *Valentino*."

" . . . and he can't bear to have a scene cut even though the film would be better without it."

"You should hear how you go on when anyone cuts one of your scenes," she laughed.

"He says my hallucinations have a Catholic bias."

"So what else is new?"

"The working lunches are killing me and it's not the work, it's the eternal Sanka and turkey sandwiches."

"Do you good for a change," said Viv to the sound of baby Molly howling in the background.

"I take enough of his shit all day. I don't need it at mealtimes as well," I said.

"Shit today means caviar tomorrow," said Viv, "and baby's hungry. Bye." Click! I suppose she does mean Molly, I thought to myself as I slowly replaced the receiver.

Reluctantly I flew to Hollywood, rented a Ford Thunderbird, a Mexican housemaid and Shelley Winters' place on Coldwater Canyon, complete with kidney-shaped swimming pool. I was also furnished with an office on the Burbank lot but no parking space for the Thunderbird till a memo on my desk informed me that this was being taken care of. It read: "Paint out Arthur Penn, paint in Ken Russell." I was now ready to get the show on the road and had only four weeks to do it, having wasted a fortnight with Paddy in New York arguing over the script.

We had argued in his office and out of it, mostly out, and I began to suspect, from the shifty behaviour of people I met on the stairs, that Paddy shared his office with either a shyster lawyer or a shady doctor. The props and decor would have fitted either party, or even a private eye, come to think of it. Strange behaviour for a millionaire, perhaps, but then millionaires don't usually live on a diet of pressed turkey sandwiches and Sanka. We discussed the script in diverse places from cheerless delis on Broadway to the primate house at the Bronx Zoo where I once saw Paddy, who had rather long arms and a pronounced stoop, give a pretty fair imitation of a chimpanzee on becoming agitated over a remark I made concerning his dialogue. When Columbia called me to Hollywood to start pre-production I thought I might shake him off for a while but the monkey on my back was always there and wouldn't let go. And wherever Paddy went his shadow, Howard, went too, questioning my suggestions, vetoing my decisions.

I was refused the cameraman of my choice and the assistant of my choice.

"What need do you have of an assistant, Kenny, when you have me to assist you?" said Paddy benignly.

That's what I was afraid of. Paddy didn't know a matte shot from a doormat. But he did unwittingly give me an ally in the person of a British production designer, Richard McDonald, who was hired simply because he promised to utilise the sets that had already been built by the previous designer (who had resigned, I heard tell, when Paddy walked onto the set with a chainsaw and hacked off the bits he didn't approve of). Paddy was an autocrat, feared and revered in Hollywood. He could write words, win Oscars. His films made money, he was a commercial intellectual, he was a revolutionary, he attacked institutions: Network, The Hospital. He glorified the common man: Marty. He was outspoken. He made speeches attacking Vanessa Redgrave's anti-Zionism. He was a simple man who loved simple things: a turkey sandwich and a cup of Sanka was all he asked of a meal (or ever gave). He resembled an overweight Trotsky, dressed as Chairman Mao, talked democracy and practised fascism. He also had two false names, Paddy and Chayefsky, and didn't trust me out of his sight. And if at last he was beginning to accept my input on the hallucinations, it was only because he was bereft of any visions of his own.

With only three weeks to go we commenced rehearsals in an empty

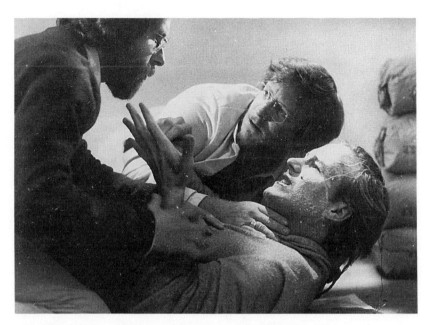

Bob Balaban (left), Charles Haid (center), and William Hurt
in a scene from *Altered States*.

storeroom on the Burbank lot. The dialogue was loaded with scientific
mumbo-jumbo which the actors spat at each other across a long table
watched over by Paddy and myself at either end. Paddy wanted everyone
word-perfect and we sat there day after day until they were, and then he
asked them to overlap their dialogue so that what had been barely comprehensible before degenerated into incomprehensible babble reminiscent
of the Bronx Zoo, rendered all the more comic by the utmost seriousness
of all concerned.

"Perfect for me," said Paddy, kissing his script the way Bernstein kisses
the score of Beethoven's Ninth. "Over to you, Kenny." All eyes stared
expectantly at me, waiting for some revelatory output.

"You can't improve on perfection, Paddy," I said. "Why don't we
rehearse the scene where Jessup fucks Emily on the kitchen floor? I'd
appreciate your input on the grunts." There was a shocked silence which
Paddy broke with a growl worthy of the big, bad wolf.

"I'm only concerned with dialogue just now, Kenny," he said. "In
matters of barking dogs, grunting ape-men and moaning lovers you
have carte blanche. But while we're on the subject of words, would it

bother you if Charlie said 'Come inside' instead of 'Come in'? It kinda scans better." Everyone watched expectantly for a showdown. I failed them.

"No, Paddy," I said, "not at all. It's fine by me."

Averting their eyes, the actors all picked up their biros and dutifully made the amendment.

The next day we were allowed to perambulate. The actors had learned their lines parrot-fashion and now it was my turn to play Dr. Coppelius, make a few magic passes and turn these puppets into human beings. But moving actors around imaginary science labs, caves and kitchens has never been my forte—for without the real environment, the real props and the real clothes which all go to mould an actor's performance it's a complete waste of time. In fact I'd never worked that way in my life, but Paddy was calling the shots and I was expected to play ball. Apparently he always rehearsed with his cast and director as if they were putting on a stage play—for an audience of one.

Intermission came at one o'clock when he took me to one side and gave me notes on individual performances and how he wanted them changed. Contrary to public belief, I am a mild-mannered man, so I listened attentively, thanked him courteously and told him evenly that although I appreciated his input during rehearsals, when it came to shooting I would brook no interference from him. He smiled beguilingly, promised not to talk to the actors, and reiterated that he would only stick around on the set to help with script amendments—and act as a benign influence. We shook on it and went to lunch with Richard McDonald, who began to show me that it was possible to maintain one's independence in Hollywood without bucking the system—a thing my one-time friend, poor David Puttnam, never learned.

Richard *did* use all the sets as promised, but he used them as timber— had them all demolished and rebuilt as a carpenter's shop on one of the sound stages we were using. He also flouted Paddy's parsimonious dictatorship in culinary matters by countermanding a universal order for turkey sandwiches and Sanka and choosing a sirloin steak and a bottle of Châteauneuf du Pape '75. Paddy, who had requested this working lunch (working lunches instil a sense of urgency and purpose), was quite put out and quite unable to discuss the burning question of the moment— whether the banana used by Dr. Jessup in a lecture on male aggression should be green or yellow. And it wasn't as if Paddy was paying the bill. All working lunches came out of the budget. So did his palatial bungalow at the Beverly Hills Hotel, the new hi-fi system and the princely living allowance that went with it. To Paddy hot food and a glass of wine when you are supposed to be working (in your own free time) was an indulgence and a sin. He wasn't bright enough to see that these are the things that nourish the mind, lubricate the soul and generate the creative juices.

But at least I was free of him at the weekend even if my time was not always my own. If it wasn't spent relaxing around the pool with Viv and Molly, it was spent researching my subject around the pool with Viv and Molly. On one occasion, in the interests of veracity, some anonymous well-wisher on the production team slipped a little something into the glove compartment of my Thunderbird: a transparent packet with a rainbow logo containing dehydrated mushrooms; similar, I presumed, to those taken by Dr. Jessup on his drug trips. I half expected a label saying "Eat Me." I was tempted to sample one anyway but even Alice didn't take acid at 80 m.p.h. so I waited till after Sunday brunch. Then, while Molly took her siesta beneath the sheltering palms, watched over by Lily, our Mexican maid, Viv and I sampled our first (and last) hallucinogenic mushroom.

Nibbling and giggling, we waited impatiently for something to happen—either for us to grow large or small or to jump in the pool and start a caucus-race. Actually something far more sinister occurred. The extensive garden, which until now had seemed akin to a tropical paradise, began to assume a disturbing malevolence. The plants and trees which had reacted passively to the ministrations of our Japanese gardeners, who did little more than hoover up dead leaves, took on a positively threatening air, more animalistic than botanic. The waving palm leaves were savage claws ready to tear our flesh. Wherever we looked there was no escape. Around the pool, down the slopes from Charlton Heston's garden and up the hill from a starlet's pad, the carnivorous jungle was on the march, stirred on by a stiff breeze from Malibu. We were surrounded by cruel, green talons, the bared fangs of vicious razor-sharp leaves and snaking tendrils lashing at our bare bodies. Seeming to sense the danger, Lily snatched Molly from the cradle and hurried indoors, leaving us to dive into the pool for safety—only to be immediately threatened by a revolting, undulating blue monster we'd always taken for a lilo. Gasping with fear, we scrambled out a milli-second before its rubbery, blubbery, mouth could goose us to death. And while the blue-nosed leviathan bumped against the side of the pool endeavouring to wriggle out and devour us, the vegetation advanced upon us, millimetre by millimetre, growing ever more frenzied. We gripped each other's hands, closed our eyes and waited for the end. It came at dusk as the drug wore off, the wind dropped and the sunlight ceased to glitter on the leaves.

We helped each other inside, locked the doors, took a stiff drink, switched on the alarm system and went to bed.

The next day I had an even bigger shock: Columbia Pictures, finally tired of Paddy's shenanigans, dropped the project, allowing their good neighbours, Warner Brothers, to pick up the pieces—reluctantly, I feel.

Ted Ashley, the president of Warners, who had cut *The Devils* to pieces because of an apparent fear of pubic hair, had said on more than one occasion how much he'd like Paddy to do a film for the company. Now he had a chance to put his money where his mouth was. He read the script, and agreed to take over the project on the proviso that I would be replaced. By this time pre-production was in full flood; sets were being constructed, models made, costumes designed, bit parts cast and special effects planned in minutest detail. I'm sure that Paddy would have been happy to let me go if Howard, always the realist, hadn't convinced him that to introduce a new director at this stage with only two weeks to go would have spelt disaster. And when this was pointed out to Ashley, he bowed to the inevitable and permitted me to stay on. That made me happy because I was warming to the project. The script was still way overlength but I was getting my way with the hallucinations and Howard, now that the film was becoming a reality, was starting to back me up.

Meanwhile, I continued to research my subject whenever I had a free moment. From magic mushrooms I turned to sensory deprivation—in a house full of bad vibes near MacArthur Park. It was almost dark when I arrived by Thunderbird at the isolated bungalow which, according to the information on an anonymous office memo, was the address where I could expect a trip in an isolation tank. The door was opened by an Incredible Hulk who said, "Love your movies, Mr. Twilight Zone. Come inside and say hello to Maw." The inside smelt of dogshit and when I met Maw I thought I'd met the Yeti. But as my eyes adjusted to the fading daylight and the creature rose to her feet I realised she'd been sitting on a settee draped in salukis. They bounded after her down a dark corridor and, encouraged by a nod from the Hulk, I followed. In a small back room we assembled around a plinth supporting a sinister black casket that would not have been out of place in a Dracula movie, and neither would my strange companions, come to that.

With something of an effort, Maw lifted the heavy lid. This was a coffin with a difference—it was one-third full of a greyish milky fluid glowing very uninvitingly in the dying daylight filtering through a single murky window. The Incredible Hulk folded his arms and filled the doorway, the dogs sat in the corner looking at Maw who was looking at me.

"Strip off now," said Maw without ceremony. I hardly knew which way to turn. To face Maw would have been immodest, to turn my back, ungentlemanly, so I compromised by doing something of a striptease. When I was down to my socks she looked me up and down and said to the Hulk, "Humph! Reckon we'll need another sackful." The Hulk grunted and, as Maw turned on a stopcock, dragged a sack of salt from a corner and emptied it into the tank. When the level of the solution had risen a couple of inches Maw turned off the supply and said, "You can hop in now." I removed my socks and was contemplating how best to hop in without doing myself an injury when the Hulk scooped me up and deposited me inside. As the goo slopped around my navel I sat there in my waterlogged coffin, wondering what on earth was going to happen next. Maw started to explain:

"The saline solution in which you are about to float will be maintained at blood temperature throughout your incarceration. You will hear nothing, you will see nothing. You could almost be back in your mother's womb—without the encumbrance of an umbilical cord. Deprived of every sensory stimulus, you will be free to float through the subconscious regions of the mind into limitless peace.

"When you step out of the tank in an hour's time you will leave behind you all the cares and worries of the world, as countless others have done before you. Now lie down, relax and we'll shut you in." Not the words I would have chosen myself to allay the fears of a claustrophobic who had been scared of the dark all his life—but then they weren't to know that, I thought, as I stretched out in my coffin.

Clang! The daylight died and my spirits along with it. I was entombed in a blackness that not even Paddy could have dreamed of. And as for floating free of my senses, I was as firmly grounded as a beached whale. Maw had obviously underestimated my bulk. There simply wasn't enough liquid in the tank to launch me into the infinite. Instead of escaping my senses, I became prey to them.

The experience was agonising. There were several abrasions on my body caused by my mad scramble out of the pool as a result of the mushroom trip and they really stung. Talk about rubbing salt into a wound. Instead of becoming carefree I fell victim to every anxiety, every neurosis, every evil thought left behind by all those nutters who'd peed in the dark before me, as I was peeing now.

My fear escalated. What if the lid jammed, what if they locked me in? What if I suffocated? What if she turned on the stopcock and drowned me? Christ! This was worse than the premature burial of Edgar Allan Poe. I hammered on the lid. I pushed. Nothing happened. I hammered again, hammered and pushed. Finally I heard the dogs barking. Suddenly the lid was flung back and two concerned faces looked down at me in a blaze of light. Then the Hulk was lifting me out and Maw was wrapping me in a bathrobe and the dogs were jumping up and licking my face and I was laughing and trembling, laughing and trembling at the same time.

Sitting on the settee half an hour later with a drink in my hand, freshly showered, back in the security of my clothes, I began to wonder, as had Maw and the Hulk, what all the fuss was about, though they did chide themselves for not checking out my claustrophobia. And they were really sorry I'd missed a trip to Nirvana, though slightly sceptical when I told them I could get an out-of-body experience, if I so chose, every time I played the right kind of music.

All the same, isolation tanks caught on in LA and for a short time after the film was released enjoyed something of a vogue. There was even a showroom on Beverly Boulevard. But it was doomed from the start as LA is nothing if not a social town, and floating in the dark on your own is about as unfashionable as sleeping alone. The hot tub took over. You might not have an out-of-body experience but peeing in a tub in a group is so much more meaningful than peeing alone.

On to the first day of shooting, in an Italian restaurant on Santa Monica Boulevard, with our hero, Dr. Jessup, enjoying a farewell dinner with his friends on the eve of an expedition to Mexico in search of the hallucinogenic mushrooms. It was to be a festive occasion and you don't go to an Italian restaurant to feast on cold turkey and Sanka, even if the restaurant is in Hollywood. So the wine and pasta flowed, along with the conversation, and gave the actors a chance to leaven all that heavy sci-fi chitchat!

The set-up was at the back of the restaurant, looking towards the street, and there was nowhere for the benign influence to hide other than behind a stack of Chianti flasks on the bar near the entrance, so he didn't have much idea of what was going on, apart from what he could hear on a headset plugged into the soundman's recorder. Although this was a highly unorthodox procedure (writers are not usually allowed anywhere near the set), it didn't worry me because we were all being terribly faithful to every word and comma of the script. And even when I saw Paddy talking to our heroine, Blair Brown, behind the chuck wagon at lunchtime, I thought nothing of it.

It was only when I was having a happy-hour drink with Blair after the shoot that I learned Paddy had been hanging around the lavatories all afternoon and secretly cross-examining the actors at every opportunity as to how I was directing the scene, and giving them contrary advice. Obviously such a state of affairs, apart from being extremely unethical, could only lead to confusion and disaster. I arrived *chez* Winters all hot and bothered and told Viv my troubles and that I was going to do something about it. Acting on her advice, I jumped into the pool to cool off. By the time I climbed out the Hollywood stars were glittering malevolently. Hearing voices, I put on a bathrobe and joined Viv and my agent Bobby, who were plotting in the living room. Silence! Then a united assault. I must do nothing hasty, nothing to jeopardise our position, nothing to rock the boat. I counter-attacked by pointing out that no film could have two directors and that Paddy had broken his word and come between me and the actors. We argued until we were hoarse. Then as Viv went to fix some drinks and Bobby slipped off to the loo I crept to the telephone and dialled Paddy's bungalow at the Beverly Hills Hotel. Luckily I got straight through and asked him point blank what the hell he thought he was up to in breaking his word and usurping my authority. In turn he demanded to know what the hell I thought I was up to in making the actors play a perfectly normal scene "drunk" and shooting the scene in very long takes. Why couldn't I shoot scenes like other directors in a long shot, medium shot and close-up, for chrissakes?

"So that you can't re-edit them after I've gone," I shouted.

"And don't think I fucking won't," he screamed back.

And that's when Viv arrived with a tray of drinks, and, quickly assessing the gravity of the situation, unhesitatingly poured a jug of Pimms No. 1 over my head, with ice and lemon. At least it was an improvement on beer, but this time it did not reduce me to silence.

"Why don't you . . ." I shouted as Bobby returned to join Viv in trying to wrestle the receiver from my grasp. ". . . Why don't you take your turkey sandwiches and your script and your Sanka and stuff it up your ass and get on the next fucking plane back to New York and let me get on with the fucking film."

Having said my say, I relinquished the phone, leaving Viv and Bobby hanging on. A click at the other end made Bobby leave go as if he'd received a shock. He had! That trip to the loo had probably cost him his ten per cent. Viv alone held on and, ever practical, started dialling British Airways to check on flights back to England. Drying off the Pimms with Shelley's tablecloth, I, too, thought I'd burned my boats—but I was wrong.

In the event Paddy went, we stayed; not because Warners were on our side, but because they were in too deep financially to act otherwise. Yet although I'd won that round, Paddy still had artistic control. All the rushes were flown to New York for his approval and we were forbidden to change a single word of dialogue, no matter how trivial, without his permission. So I shot the script just as it was—typos and all. But I shot it in such a way that the excess dialogue could be junked later if I should get lucky, and my luck was improving all the time—even with my "trips" . . .

My final experience came at the hands of a Hollywood born-again Christian who was brought in to help me conjure up Dr. Jessup's religious visions with the aid of a little dope. As a one-time addict, I knew I was playing with fire and fire can be very attractive as long as you don't get burned. And who knows, if I did see visions that topped those I'd experienced when listening to Gustav Holst's *Hymns from the Rig Veda*, then it would be worth the risk.

We met behind the secluded gates of Bel Air in a luxury home which had been put at our disposal for the night by an anonymous donor. The façade was pure Tara and I wouldn't have been surprised if a black man-servant had answered my knock. I was not prepared for a Lana Turner lookalike in horn-rimmed glasses.

"Good evening," I said, "I believe you're expecting me." She looked at me in alarm and made to close the door. "I'm Ken Russell," I added hastily.

"Oh," she said, smiling with relief. "Please come in." She closed the door behind me and bolted it. We shook hands and sized each other up. She certainly wasn't my idea of a born-again Christian and I obviously wasn't her idea of a film director. I'd expected someone in a caftan and sandals and had dressed accordingly. I should have known it was possible to be a BAC and still be dressed by Frederick's of Hollywood.

"Shall we go upstairs?" she said, leading the way up a gracious staircase.

"Where are we going?" I asked, unable to keep my eyes off her svelte naked body visible through a black chiffon negligée.

"We're going to bed," she said nonchalantly, tip-tapping across the landing and down a Regency-style corridor in her cute black mules. They looked vaguely familiar, those mules, and I began to wonder if this was some elaborate joke dreamed up by Denny. So far I'd managed to avoid him; perhaps this was going to turn into a humiliating spectacle at my expense. I wouldn't put it past him. I could almost see the headlines: "BRITISH FILM DIRECTOR CAUGHT IN DRUG SWOOP ON HIGH CLASS BROTHEL." I could also see her cute little ass beckoning me on.

"You'll probably get an erection," she said, fuelling my suspicions. "Don't let it worry you. It's a perfectly normal reaction brought about by the chemical properties of the drug."

This was my chance. "I'm not sure I should be going through with this," I blurted out. "I had a drug problem once. I'd hate to get hooked again."

"Don't worry," she said, opening a door to a room that seemed designed as an observatory, "it wouldn't harm a baby. In fact it was developed to provide something between a local and a general anaesthetic for use with children undergoing minor surgery. Would you undress, please!" She smiled reassuringly, kicked off her mules, slipped out of her negligée and placed her horn-rimmed glasses on a bedside table. If this was one of Denny's jokes it was far more elaborate than usual. I nonchalantly kicked off my sandals, slipped out of my caftan and removed my Popeye underpants.

"I'm a pediatrician," she said, "and what got to me was the beatific expression on the faces of the kiddies while they were under sedation. Wherever they were, they were having a ball, and most of them didn't want to come back. Naturally I wondered why and gave myself a shot to find out. So did a lot of old spoilsports, with the result that the stuff was withdrawn from the market, but not before I syphoned off a big supply. Get in." By now she was lying naked on a large circular bed where the telescope should have been, and patting the space beside her with one hand whilst offering up a hypodermic with the other. I slid in beside her and received my jab. She jabbed herself and covered us with a silvery sheet of lightest silk.

"Now lie on your back and relax," she said. "And no monkey business. This is strictly in the interests of science." So it was for real after all. I'm ashamed to say I felt a twinge of disappointment.

"You are going on a spiritual journey," I heard her say as from a distance. "All journeys into the unknown are best taken with an experienced guide. You are safe in my hands..." Her fingers touched mine reassuringly and for a moment I thought of all those happy little boys who had gone before me with their stiff little willies pointing to Nirvana. By now I was feeling pleasantly woozy.

There was music, real or imaginary, I can't say, and then we were floating up towards the dome which gradually dissolved into a myriad flying molecules and reformed into layer upon layer of moving patterns vaguely reminiscent of Chinese Chippendale. As our journey continued through the night sky and layer upon angled layer of these elegant shapes, I had the sensation of passing through a new dimension into a hot and trackless desert where a writhing cloud of dust snaked over the sand dunes from horizon to horizon. And as we got closer I was able to see through the rising dust the form of a great serpent with no head and no tail—it was endless. And as we got closer still, I was able to see through the skin to its skeleton, moving slowly, rhythmically forward. And as we got even closer, I was able to see that each of its countless vertebrae was the naked soul of every man, woman and child that had ever walked the face of the earth. And as they stamped their rhythmic dance of eternal life, every face was lit up with joy and the chant that arose from their throats was an ode to joy. And I knew that this dance of the great snake which encompassed the face of the earth was going on around us, every moment of every day, and that we were rubbing shoulders with the souls of the living dead and were totally unaware of it, just as we were unaware that this great collective soul was protecting us, sustaining us and blessing us until the moment of our death, when we would become part of it ourselves. It was a revelation. I was in ecstasy and I wanted it to last forever but already the cloud of dust stirred up by the stamping feet was getting thicker, obscuring my vision, and filling me with a great sense of loss.

Then a voice, close to my ear, was saying, "You are coming down." I obviously was in more ways than one. A moment later the whirling particles solidified into bricks and mortar and I was awake in bed with my guide.

"Would you like to go back there again?" she asked drowsily, refilling the hypodermic. My instinct was to say, "Yes, yes, yes. I want to go back there," as all those children had wanted to go back to somewhere over the rainbow. It was all so wonderful—too wonderful! If I went there again I might never want to come back here. I might not be *able* to come back here.

My guide, needle poised, was still awaiting my answer. I shook my head. I think she got the message. Anyway, she smiled and said, "Wanna monkey around a while before I shoot up again?"

Strange talk for a pediatrician, I thought to myself. I mumbled that it was getting late and got up to dress.

"Was it good for you?" she said, sticking the needle in her arm.

"Too good," I said, and added out of politeness, "How was it for you?"

"Positively beatific. It always is, when I see the man," she said, her eyes closing. I tiptoed out of the room, somewhat reassured, for I was beginning to wonder if she really was a born-again Christian. Either way, it had been a valuable experience so far as the film was concerned, but as I drove the Thunderbird back to Coldwater Canyon I swore that in future I'd lay off all stimulants more exotic than the twelve-tone scale.

My Hollywood nights were generally less exotic and more often than not were spent conducting therapy classes for cast and crew, usually at the dinner table. Undoubtedly my most regular patient was Bill Hurt, who must have spent more time with me during the filming of *Altered States* than with his girl friend. In fact, I remember him shouting to me across Santa Monica Boulevard at the top of his voice one warm autumn evening, "I love you." And his girl friend was at his side at the time, holding his overcoat. I think if his bed had been a little bit bigger I'd have been invited to join them. Inevitably, as new father figures arise, these relationships turn out to be as ephemeral as shadows on a screen. Once the film was finished I never heard from Bill again, but neither did his girl friend, so I don't feel too bad about it.

Discussing a sex scene with Blair Brown and William Hurt
during the making of *Altered States*.

The trouble with Bill is he can't stop talking. In the end his eternal
nattering, usually about himself, became so unbearable that Viv and I
would only take him out to dinner if he remained silent throughout the
meal. If he spoke he paid the bill. He never got further than the fish
course before having to get out his cheque book. As some people are
compulsive eaters, Bill is a compulsive talker. When I heard that he was
living with a deaf lady I came to believe in the old adage that marriages
are made in heaven. But even that didn't work out—he probably insisted
she wore her hearing aid to bed.

Meanwhile the eminence benign stayed in his cell in New York, hating
me, hating the rushes, hating everything and even insisting on a re-shoot
when, because of weather conditions in the wilds of Mexico and the
absence of a public telephone, I had to change a few lines of dialogue
without his say-so in order to prevent the characters talking nonsense.
Well, there was no way even Warners, who were beholden to Paddy's
every whim, were going to remount another costly expedition south of
the border, but they did agree to a re-shoot on the Fantasy Island set on

the back lot at Burbank—which is more akin to Santa's grotto than the wilds of Mexico. Then, just as we were all geared up to shoot this bit of egomaniacal nonsense, there came an amazing announcement from the front office.

"Owing to Mr. Chayefsky's withdrawal from the production, the reshoot is cancelled." But why, oh why, at this eleventh hour? I wondered. Rumours were rife. Paddy was ill, Paddy was humiliated, Paddy was mad, Paddy was paralysed with anger, Paddy had suffered a nervous breakdown, Paddy liked the film so much he was ill with envy, Paddy hated the film so much he couldn't bear to think about it, Paddy was schizophrenic. Whatever the reason, there would be no more interference from him, or so I thought.

A few days later the final wrap was called and with the exception of the editors and a small special-effects unit everybody split—including Molly and Viv, who said she had urgent work to do back home in Borrowdale. She didn't say what and I didn't press her, though I guessed it was yet another script. After the failure of *Mothers* and *Every Little Breeze*, written at the poolside, Viv was rather touchy on the subject of writing. The fact that my name was linked with her first effort probably didn't help matters, while her second attempt, based on the high life in Hollywood, was probably too savage for the natives to stomach. Regretfully I kissed mother and child goodbye at LAX and braced myself for the monumental task of perfecting the special effects which was to occupy me on and off for the best part of a year. And so my days were mostly spent in talking to boffins at optical houses, supervising "small shoots," devising and recording terrifying sounds, arguing with lab technicians and, between times, editing down hours of dreary dialogue. All this was essential but very humdrum stuff, far from the glamourised lifestyle the general public usually associates with a Hollywood director. But that's the way it is: ninety per cent organisation, ten per cent direction!

Away from the studios I became a recluse, happy with my books and my music and a swim in the pool. Once I went a-rambling in the pleasant wooded area adjoining Shelley's property but was warned off by a mean-looking guy with a shotgun. After that I did my best to keep out of trouble, though I did have a couple of brushes with the police— once for jay-walking in Westwood and once for driving too slowly in the fast lane. Both times I was let off with a caution after the cops heard my accent. They think us Brits are barmy, out there, with our bangers and mash and croquet and cream teas. And yet they don't really know us at all. Mention the word "English" and you'll get a muffin. That's our greatest contribution to the American way of life—the English muffin. England is an eccentric little place best known for its Beefeaters,

Royal Family, beef tea and Gilbert and Sullivan. And whenever I saw rare flashes of England, through the TV looking glass, that's how it appeared to me—a dusty Victorian operetta with everyone got up as their favourite character from *HMS Pinafore* and *Alice in Wonderland*, endlessly parading around in circles and squabbling at some Mad Hatter's tea party.

Closer to Hollywood there was a party that made *me* mad. It was thrown by an executive producer connected with *Altered States* who wanted some reflected glory. The film was finished and the word was going around that Warners had a hit on their hands. Naturally I was not invited, but all the Hollywood top brass were apparently blown away by the screening which followed the bean feast. Bobby got me two offers for work on the strength of it.

But would the public be equally enthusiastic? Warners organised a public preview to find out. Their choice of venue was bizarre. For a movie obviously geared to college kids, they chose a suburban shopping precinct in San Diego. The audience consisted mainly of overweight women in slacks with beehive hairdos—and they loathed it. Warners began resharpening the long knives they had used to butcher *The Devils*. But this time it was the hallucinations, not the pubic hair, that were due for the chop. This was senseless—the only thing left would be dialogue only comprehensible to Harvard professors, and that's a pretty small audience when it comes to selling tickets. Then I remembered that Paddy had friends in high places and that infanticide was not unknown in Hollywood. All sorts of weird ideas went through my head including driving the Thunderbird through Ted Ashley's office window, until I remembered it was on the second floor.

In the event, I was spared any such kamikaze notions by the intervention of Howard Gottfried who, ever since Paddy's exodus, had grown into a staunch supporter. Somehow he managed to organise one more preview—in Westwood, on the doorstep of UCLA. The audience of students went through the roof and the thing they enjoyed most about the movie was the hallucinations. Warners had no alternative but to release it without cuts. Many of the kids went back time and again for the hallucinations alone—sitting in the foyer between trips, getting high, while a lookout was bribed to stay in the auditorium enduring the dialogue until it was time to poke his head around the door and shout "next hallucination!"—when everyone would belt inside to be tripped out by the 70-mm images and six-track stereo sound. Paddy got to hear of this and was less than pleased. He saw the film and disliked it, insisting his name be removed from the credits—which then read, "Written for the screen by Sidney Aarons, from the novel *Altered States* by Paddy

Chayefsky." Sidney Aarons was his real name, of course. Poor Paddy, schizoid to the last.

Sailing past 42nd Street on my way back to England on the QE2 with the setting sun romancing the towers of Manhattan, I looked towards Broadway and tried to pick out Paddy's office—in vain. But I could imagine him there, sitting alone in the dusk and the dust, rocking in that creaky chair, ticking his life away, consumed by hate, eaten up with envy. In less than a year he was dead.

12

Albatross on High

The Atlantic crossing was as tedious as a journey on British Rail and far less eventful. The food was similar, too, as was the speed. This time none of my films was programmed to be shown on board so no one asked me to speak—and I spoke to no one but the stewards. My only companion was an albatross—a big brown and white bugger that must have weighed close on a hundredweight. It reminded me of the last time I saw Skiddaw, wings outstretched, hovering over Keswick. Somehow the spirit of Skiddaw seemed to be accompanying me home—a pagan guardian angel, perhaps.

I also recalled the last film I made under its shadow. It featured Samuel Coleridge quoting chunks of his autobiographical poem *The Rime of the Ancient Mariner* as he rowed an erratic course around Derwentwater, tripping out on chloral, a drug available in every chemist shop throughout the land during the last century. No wonder there was never a revolution in England. When the poor could get as high as a kite for a penny piece, what need of revolution?

Another drug of days gone by which is no longer fashionable, though still readily available, is snuff. One usually associates the taking of snuff with foppish dandies in Restoration comedies, and it was while dancing such a role in a ballet based on Alexander Pope's *The Rape of the Lock* that in the interests of characterisation I took my first pinch—and sneezed my head off, causing general merriment to cast and audience alike. The ballet master, who was something of an authority on the subject, advised me to throw away the shilling tin of "Wilson's" I had picked up at the local tobacconist's and go along to a bow-windowed establishment in the Haymarket where I would find something more refined.

According to the white-coated assistant behind the counter, Fribourg & Treyer had been purveyors of snuff to the crowned heads of Europe for more than two centuries and were world-renowned for the high quality of their product. Between us was a glass specimen case displaying, in a score of small compartments, a variety of the choicest blends. He lifted the lid and invited me to sample them. Seeing my bewilderment, he suggested I take a pinch of the dryest and a pinch of the most moist.

"High Dry Toast" resembled the sands of the Sahara, had a fragrance of sandalwood and cinnamon and the kick of a camel. "Prince's Special," according to my informant, was a favourite with the Prince Regent, who used the copious navel of a favourite concubine as a receptacle for the mixture. That variety had the look of Beluga caviar, the aroma of a Sultan's harem and sensations to match.

Impressed, I paid my five shillings and took a tin of each—and handsome tins they were too, cylindrical in shape and covered in copperplate lettering with medals of excellence and seals of royal approval. In the early days I was able to make two small tins last a month or so, but as my intake increased I looked around for a cheaper blend and discovered Dr. Rumney's Mentholyptus. It came in mottled brown tins a couple of inches square bearing a portrait of the good doctor himself, whom I eventually came to loathe as much as his addictive mixture of eucalyptus and tobacco. It's the tobacco, of course, which does the damage. No matter how much they douse it in scents and spices, that happy dust you are sniffing into your lungs is ground tobacco and it goes straight to the bloodstream—inducing a rush of instant high. Eventually neither your blood nor your body can forgo it without screaming.

Naturally I tried to give it up, tried not to take a snort at less than ten-minute intervals, tried not praying for the second hand to go faster than a funeral, tried not waking up several times in the night to grope about in the dark for that little tin of heaven on the bedside table, tried not to run to the nearest tobacconist's when the very last particle had been carefully tapped out of the last corner of the empty tin onto the back of my hand and sniffed into my clogged-up lungs. Once I even tried scattering the remains of a tin into a coal bunker minutes before closing time—when all of those awful tins would be unobtainable—only to grovel on my hands and knees a few minutes later to sniff up a disgusting mixture of coal dust and snuff, coughing and retching, eyes watering and face covered in dirt and vomit and foul grey mucus.

There came a time when I could no longer function without it, couldn't stop shaking, couldn't bear the agony of deprivation, couldn't think beyond the next snort and the heavenly rush and the unbelievably wonderful moment when the fiery demons tormenting every nerve in your body are exorcised and you are free, free, free—for five glorious minutes!

It was at the height of my addiction that I first bumped into my saviour outside the bathroom in a run-down boarding house off the Bayswater Road. We'd both grabbed the door handle together and struggled for possession. My adversary, who I subsequently came to know as Morton Lyndhurst, was of indeterminate age. He was also short and frail with a lantern jaw, wispy beard and thick horn-rimmed glasses, and he was definitely coming off worst in the struggle until suddenly he produced a crucifix from beneath his pyjamas and held it up before him with all the bravura of a Hollywood priest confronting Dracula. I was so startled that I stepped back. A second later he was inside the bathroom and bolting the door in my face. This was my first intimation of the power of Rome! Until that fresh autumn morning in my twenty-eighth year the closest I'd come to religion was the veneration of the stars in *Picturegoer* during compulsory prayers in the College Chapel at Pangbourne.

Lyndhurst brought me to my knees again. It was a time of transition. I was scraping a living as a freelance photographer during the week and shooting my first amateur movie with the proceeds at the weekend. And the cast for the film—a slice of low-life fantasy called *Peepshow*—was drawn mainly from the tenants of the boarding house, including Morton Lyndhurst, who I learned from the housekeeper was a civil servant who enjoyed amateur theatricals in his spare time. He ended up playing the lead in the film and converting me to Catholicism. According to Lyndhurst, most films had a religious message, science-fiction films most of all. He gave me a completely new slant on religion, awakening in me the wish to become a Catholic space cadet. And when he thought I was ready, Lyndhurst sent me to a group of space sisters for briefing.

In a windowless cell in an anonymous building behind high brick walls near Portobello Road, a teenage space sister in a simple black and white uniform tuned me in to Alpha and Omega. Behind her on the wall was an example of early sci-fi art showing a winged astronaut in a golden space helmet zapping a kneeling figure. The picture was captioned: "St. Francis receiving the stigmata." Another amazing picture, worthy of that soft time-traveller, Salvador Dali, depicted the astro-saviour parting his chest to reveal his sacred heart jetting through space. There was also a print of the virgin space mother hovering above St. Peter's in Rome, surrounded by seven heart-shaped UFOs of shining silver. My space sister made the sign and took me through the basics. It seems that when the Great Spaceman in the Sky created man he was no more successful than Baron Frankenstein. Homo sapiens, unlike every other creature on the planet, was prone to malfunction. His circuits were continually blowing and tripping into the "abort" and "destruct" modes. Now we all know what happened to Frankenstein when he attempted to restrain the monster he had created—it went bananas and destroyed its maker. But the scientific know-how of the Great Spaceman was aeons in advance of poor Frankenstein, for not only was he able to reconstitute himself when his creatures went berserk but also to give them the chance to work out their salvation and perfect themselves—with the bonus of an extra-terrestrial life potential when their working parts became subject to mechanical failure and had to be scrapped.

And as my space sister swept me along on this wonderful journey she manipulated an instrument of baffling simplicity and extraordinary power. Constructed of wooden beads and wire and operated by coded telepathy, it sent messages through the infinite direct to the Great Spaceman in the Sky. These awesome communication systems, I learned to my surprise, were readily available to all, and on the day of my induction to the launching pad at the Victoria Space Station, I was presented with one by my space sister who fuelled it with a few drops of a highly volatile liquid, known as "Holy Water"—the extra-terrestrial properties of which have so far defied scientific analysis. On to the Big Moment as a space captain talked me through the ritual of Countdown. I gripped the rosary, as it was called, closed my eyes, took a deep breath, made the sign and mumbled the code. "Lift off" was followed by a pleasant feeling of weightlessness. My cosmic journey had begun.

Across the road from the space station at Victoria is a galactic repository, and as I was about to board the No. 31 bus to take me home I saw in the window a replica of the virgin space mother. Barely three feet in height, the plaster and paint reproduction personified for me the perfect woman, the Venus of Botticelli. She cost twenty guineas—money I could ill afford. Nevertheless I got out my chequebook, took her as she was and carried her onto the top deck of the bus, shaking like a leaf. It was ten minutes since I'd had a pinch of snuff and already my palms were sticky, my forehead was damp and my blood cells were tearing themselves to pieces. Burning a hole in my pocket was a tin of Dr. Rumney's. No, I thought, I won't give in, and I didn't, until we reached Knightsbridge ten minutes later. Then, with one arm locked around the Space Mother perched on the scat alongside me, I pulled out the tin with my free hand. I had trouble opening it. I couldn't get my nails under the lid. I had no nails, they were bitten down to the quick. I tore at the lid and cut my forefinger. Damn! I put it in my mouth, sucked it and searched my pockets for a coin to prize the tin open. No luck! Only a couple of ten-shilling notes. Nothing for it but to hang on till the conductor arrived to collect my fare and give me change.

I hung on, hung on to the virgin space mother, hung on for an eternity, hung on till such time as I could get the bloody tin open. By the time I reached the Bayswater Road a lifetime later the lid was still firmly closed. The conductor never came upstairs and kept his back turned when I shouted at him on the lower deck before stepping off the bus. Ten minutes later the snuff tin was on my marble chimneypiece still unopened. The virgin space mother stood beside it. I went out to buy something. No, it wasn't another tin of snuff. When I went to bed that night the snuff tin still remained unopened but the virgin space mother was wearing a crown of flowers.

A short time later there was more cause for celebration—my marriage to Shirley.

But that was all many years ago, years before the flowers withered and the virgin space mother became neglected and dusty, years before she was consigned to the damp cellar while Shirley and I redecorated, years before she was forgotten and left behind in the dark when we moved house, years before the five children, years before I began to suspect I'd given up one drug for another, years before *The Devils* and the divorce.

The Devils was about the self-destruction of a citadel from within. Loudon, a provincial walled-city in seventeenth-century France, was a thorn in the side of Louis XIII. So long as the inhabitants could shelter behind their solid city walls and the crossbows of the local militia, they posed a threat to Louis' totalitarian ambitions. Already the ramparts of many such towns had been torn down on one pretext or another. Loudon was one of the few remaining bastions of independence in the country. Cardinal Richelieu, the real power behind the throne, sent in his secret agents to find a way of undermining the town surreptitiously. In an enclosed order of Ursuline nuns they found Sister Jeanne of the Angels, who claimed to be possessed by the devil in the form of one Father Urbain Grandier. In fact, it was her way of getting back at the handsome priest for his refusal to become father confessor to the convent when the old incumbent up and died. And so the scene was set for a rigged trial complete with naked nuns running amok while the Inquisition tortured the unfortunate priest, whose only crime was a weakness for a pretty face. And while Grandier's parishioners watched him burn at the stake, their city walls were razed to the ground.

It was a harrowing story, graphically told, and left its mark on many of those involved. So did the music I used to create the atmosphere of religious hysteria it was necessary to whip up every day. And to that end

Vanessa Redgrave and Oliver Reed in *The Devils*.

I had four powerful loudspeakers placed around the set blasting out the grand finale of Prokofiev's cacophonous opera *The Fiery Angel*, in which an entire convent of nuns possessed of the devil get the screaming hab-dabs. Played at full volume through every take this music of religious dementia possessed most of those who heard it in a similar manner.

With some poor sods, this state continued even after the music was turned off. Small wonder that Shirley was driven off the sound stage to seek peace in the arms of one not caught up in torture, violence and death. Nor is it surprising that both our faith and our marriage began to crumble. It was altogether a disturbing experience, and so, indeed, was the film itself. It was meant to be.

Was it worth it? To me, yes. *The Devils* was a political statement worth making. Although the events took place over four hundred years ago, corruption and mass brainwashing by Church and State and commerce are still with us, as is the insatiable craving for sex and violence by

A crowd scene from *The Devils*.

the general public. The film itself was universally condemned as sacrilegious by the irreligious, was a disaster in America where Warners got out the scissors and circumcised twelve minutes off it, and an all-time hit in Italy where the Doge of Venice was burnt in effigy when he tried to ban it. Ironically, one of the greatest champions of *The Devils* is the Reverend Gene D. Phillips of the Society of Jesus. He teaches film at Loyola University and was so impressed that he immediately included it in the curriculum.

For all that, *The Devils* was the last nail in the coffin of my Catholic faith, a faith that had sustained me for more than ten years and given my life purpose and direction. But my picture of God was hazing over: too much incense, too much stained glass, too much sci-fi in the sky. It was time to come down to earth. My Catholic missal was falling apart. I needed a new prayer book.

I found it in Wordsworth's *The Prelude* and started devotions anew in *his* church, where the nave was Borrowdale, the transept was Catbells and Grange Fell, the altar (where a memorial stands to the local men killed in the Great War) was Castle Crag, and the roof was Clouds of Glory. The font, of course, was Derwentwater, where we left our other lakeland poet, Samuel Coleridge, stoned out of his mind and rowing around in circles, quoting verses from his autobiographical epic *The Rime of the Ancient Mariner*. I wonder if he turned to his god, Skiddaw, and prayed to be free from *his* addiction! If so, his prayers were answered in the rather surprising form of a sympathetic vicar and his wife, who took Coleridge into their own home at Muswell Hill in North London and effected a long and painstaking cure. I wonder if he ever longed to cast off the chains of respectability and escape to his old life in Cumberland with his drugs and his dream lover, "Asra"? Probably not, when he recalled his wife's cruel tongue, which lashed him into seeking refuge in his boat. But she was a persistent creature and, in the poet's chloral-crazed mind, followed him like a bird of ill-omen, compelling him to take his crossbow and shoot the albatross. In the poem, his shipmates hang the dead bird around the mariner's neck as punishment for killing something innately good, which is exactly how Coleridge felt when his friends accused him of killing his wife's love.

Quite a few of us suffer from the Albatross Syndrome, and as the QE2 neared Southampton my thoughts turned to Dad, who was now something of an ancient mariner himself and had tattoos to prove it. Had he shot the albatross too? He'd complained of a bad back for years—the dead love of Mum hanging around *his* neck perhaps. But even in the days when there was still a flutter of feeling between them, Mum had always been a reluctant bird of passage on the mariner's Sunday voyages up and down Southampton Water.

I remember the first trip well. It was some time in the late Thirties when the big liners on which Dad and Uncle Jack had served briefly were being broken up for scrap and their contents auctioned off. Now it may have been the *Mauri* or it might have been the *Levi* (as the *Mauretania* and the *Leviathan* were affectionately called by us Sotonians), I can't say for sure, but I do know that the Russell brothers bought a lifeboat each from one ship or the other for a hundred pounds a piece. They were exceptionally seaworthy craft and very well made—the thirty-foot hull was of double-skinned teak—but of course there was no superstructure and they were basically only raw material suitable for conversion into customised motor-boats and cabin-cruisers. So it was a proud day for Dad when he stood in the wheelhouse in the stern and took the helm of *Louanhen* (Louise and Henry were my parents' second names) and led the Russell fleet from their moorings on the Itchen, down river on a fishing trip, with all the wives and kids along for the ride.

Sunday outings had always been popular with the Russell family as far back as I could remember. Before boats it was bungalows and before bungalows it was cars and before cars it was motorbikes and sidecars—but that's only hearsay. The cars I *do* remember, bouncing along bumper to bumper through the ancient New Forest throughout the seasons.

So that first boat trip started off one glorious morning in summer as a new adventure. What fun to forsake the hot asphalt and foul exhaust of the Sunday traffic for the fresh breeze of the rolling main. We all climbed aboard with our suntan lotion, portable radio, costumes, sailor's caps, baps, sunglasses and Tizer. We were a motley crew, dressed more for the Riviera than the River Itchen. There was Mum and Dad and Ray, my five-year-old brother, and Moo, Jack and June. For the first hour or so all was happiness as familiar landmarks, seen from an unfamiliar angle, were spotted and identified. The gasworks, "The Plaza," the Civic Centre and Camper Nicholson's Shipyard (where in those times of unemployment Jack was lucky to be working as a painter and Grandad Smith, with his bad feet, was luckier still to be hanging on to a job as nightwatchman).

Down the winding river we chug-chugged, waving to the passengers on the floating bridge and on to Dockhead where the big liners berth and the Itchen meets the Test and broadens out into Southampton Water. And that's where the fleet split up to the four quarters. Fewer landmarks now as the town drops astern and we head south.

"Netley 'ospital," suddenly shouts Mum, pointing at a stately Victorian edifice dominating the coastline off the port bow.

"That's where our Dad had to go for his trench feet. Our Mum had to cut through his skin with a pair of scissors to get his socks off when he got home from the front," confided Moo for the hundredth time.

"Never got a chance to get 'is boots off for the last six months of the war," said Mum for the hundred and first.

"And that's Calshot Point, our destination," said Dad, changing course for a spit of land dominated by a large aircraft hangar off our starboard bow.

"Excellent fishing grounds, according to the captain of the *Queen Mary*," he continued, dragging in our most illustrious neighbour.

"'E should know. That's where 'e used to dump all the sewage when 'e was on the barges, according to Mrs. Mann," retorted Mum, dragging in our less illustrious neighbour.

I could see a row brewing, so could Aunt Moo.

"Come on, Eth," she said, creating a diversion. "Get up on the cabin roof with Jack and the kids and I'll take a nice snap." So as Dad pulled down his cap and pulled on his pipe, we all did as we were told and sat crosslegged with our lifebelts around our necks.

"Watch the birdie . . . Smile please," said Moo, squinting through the tiny eyepiece of her box Brownie. We tried our best, but the sun was in our eyes and seemingly getting brighter all the time and louder and windier until it was a blinding roaring whirlwind. Everyone threw themselves flat on the deck as a giant Empire Flying Boat nearly gave us a haircut before touching down gracefully in a plume of spray a few yards off our stern. It was only then that I noticed we were cruising down the centre of an avenue of orange-coloured buoys marking a maritime landing strip.

"I wondered why there wasn't much about," muttered Dad, swiftly changing course to the busy fairway. Soon we were weaving between craft of every description—from a floating tea-chest up to its gunnels in fishermen to a streamlined gin palace with Jean Harlow types in satin beach-pyjamas leaning over the rails clutching cocktails in red talons. Yachts of all classes, people of all classes, floating saloon bars in the shape of paddlesteamers packed from stem to stern with day trippers bound for Cowes, nursing mild and bitters and gin and bitter lemon—for the breeze was freshening and the sea was getting choppy. Nevertheless, we pressed on into the wind and dropped anchor as planned at Calshot Point where Southampton Water, confronted by the Isle of Wight, splits into the Spithead and the Solent. It was getting too chilly to sunbathe so we weren't sorry when Dad said it was time to catch our lunch.

Few of us had fished before. I'd caught minnows in a jam jar with lumps of bread, but this was my first attempt with rod and line. Accordingly, I stuck a bit of milkloaf on the end of my hook. But when Dad saw the others about to do the same he scoffed and slapped a big wooden box of seaweed down in front of us.

"This is the bait we use down here," he said with authority.

"Fish aren't vegetarians," said Mum dismissively. "Who told you that one—the captain of the *Queen Mary*?"

For answer Dad plunged his hand into the box and withdrew a Medusa's head. Mum shrieked and my hair stood on end as I recoiled in horror. This was worse than the Loch Ness Monster film. The others also fell back, mouths agape, except for Jack.

"King Ragworm," he said ominously. Now I saw the apparition for what it was. Through Dad's fist were writhing the most repulsive things I've ever seen—thick-ribbed worms a foot long with hundreds of flailing legs protruding from slimy, convulsing bodies of green and black and purple—colours of putrescence. Dad opened his hand and they all slurped back into the seaweed, except for one the colour of a syphilitic prick, which wrapped itself around his thumb and rolled back its foreskin to reveal a black parrot's beak which gave Dad a severe nip before disappearing into its repulsive flesh again. Dad pulled the beast into two, four and eight, each break resulting in a spurt of sewerish liquid which sprayed everywhere. The stench made us gag.

"Here, bait your hooks with this," said Dad, offering a handful of writhing offal all round. Nausea swept over us in waves as the sea, responding to a south-wester blowing up from the Needles, rose up in sympathy. We must have looked a sorry sight sitting in the stern dangling our rods over the side, frightening away the fish with the drowning king rags on the end of our hooks.

With the boat bobbing about like a cork, the women and children staggered below, green to the gills.

"I think she's a bit light on ballast, Harry," said Jack as the boat started imitating a porpoise standing on its tail. "I think we'd better sling our hook."

Dad sucked on his pipe, considering, and unfortunately spat into the wind. Jack and I busied ourselves with our lines. Then I heard the engine start and Dad shouting above the roar, "Well, if you don't mind taking the wheel, Jack, I'll trawl my line on the way back." What a relief it was to be on the move again, even if we were rolling like the drunken sailor. And it was even more of a relief when I hauled in my line to find the worm had slipped away.

It began to rain and although we had an awning the rain blew in from the stern and soaked us. I was trying to summon up courage to ask permission to go below when Dad suddenly had a bite, a big one too, judging from the struggle he was having to haul it in.

"Get the net," he shouted to me. "Jack, get the gaff." Acting on the captain's orders, we sprang into action. A moment later there were three asses pointing into the sky as we leaned over the stern to grapple with the monster. When its ugly snout broke the surface we struck. Jack's gaff hooked into my net, pulling me against Dad's legs and knocking him off balance. As he slipped to the deck something bright and shining flew through the air and landed in his lap, barking its head off.

"Conga!" shouted Dad. I thought he'd gone mad. The only conga I knew was a dance. For a moment I contemplated grabbing Uncle Jack around the waist and kicking my legs, for I was an obedient child.

"Watch her teeth, Harry," shouted Jack, lunging at it with his gaff.

"Watch that gaff, Jack," shouted Dad as it took off his cap. Then it dawned on me. Not "conga," "conger"! This yard of gleaming muscle was a conger eel with a body as thick as a man's arm and the teeth of a mongoose, snap-snap-snapping around Dad's crotch. Then as Dad lurched to his feet and collided with Jack the eel leapt free, only to disappear inside the engine housing, which was half open for reasons of ventilation. Sump oil sprayed everywhere as the men wrestled to extract it. If the eel had been difficult to hold before, it was impossible now. In the mêlée I had the impression of three men arm-wrestling, one of them disembodied.

The sound of an almighty fart fit to split the universe snapped me out of it. Simultaneously we all looked up and froze—a black and white city the size of New York was bearing down on us. It was the biggest ship I'd ever seen. For what seemed a century we watched in a state of paralysis. A second fart blew us into action. We all made a grab for the wheel. Naturally I lost out and watched from the scuppers as Jack pulled one way and Dad pulled the other. We sailed straight on.

"Ease her to starboard," shouted Dad. "Green to green, red to red, perfect safety straight ahead."

"No, no, he should give way to us, Harry. Steam always gives way to sail."

"But the sail's still in the locker," shouted Dad, at which moment Jack loosed his grip and we began to change course.

We missed her by inches, only to nearly capsize with the force of the bow wave. As the Great Wall of China swept past us, close enough to spit at, two awesome words filled my field of vision. QUEEN MARY. I looked at Dad. His face was ashen. He was thinking of our illustrious neighbour and wondering if he was the tiny uniformed figure on the bridge observing us through binoculars. Oh, the humiliation if he should recognise us. Dad turned his back in shame and caught my eye. I tried to give him a reassuring smile. Whatever happened, the secret of his appalling seamanship was safe with me. Mum would never hear of it from my lips. Dad must have got the message, for his anguish seemed to melt away as he relinquished the wheel to Jack and retrieved his drowned eel from the engine sump. What a day!

Directly we got home, Mum put Ray to bed and turned in herself, leaving me to watch Dad skin the brute and fry it in chunks for our supper. It stuck in my gullet and made my eyes water, but I never said it tasted of sump oil and I never said the words, "Thank God for my good dinner *please may I get down*," with more feeling. And for once Dad let me get down without leaving a clean plate. As I did so I said a silent prayer for the captain of the *Queen Mary*, in gratitude.

From then on I looked forward to Sundays with dread. Moo, Jack and June suddenly became devout churchgoers, but Mum and I, and even little Raymond, were pressganged into a weekly rendezvous with King Rag and of course we had to plunge into that nightmare forest of seaweed and bait our own hooks. I don't remember if I ever caught a fish. I only remember those bloody worms, to which I gradually became inured. Not so Mum, who only came along because the alternative was to stay at home and look at the four walls, for she had no friends and no interests other than the picture houses, which were closed on Sunday afternoons.

The boat was a turning-point in our lives. Both Mum and I infinitely preferred our car trips, or weekends in our bungalow at Highcliffe, but they had become a rarity. Now our Sundays were spent tearing king ragworms apart and drowning them.

"Cheer up, Ken. It'll be better when the winter comes," confided Mum. "He'll lay her up then till the spring." Winter was a long time coming, but the dank November morning that *Louanhen* was hauled up the slipway in the family boatyard at Bitterne Park was a happy one. Our joy was shortlived. Worms gave way to something equally repellent—the paintbrush. To give her credit, Mum mutinied after only one session, preferring to stay at home with only the four walls and Ray for company. I had no option but to follow the captain's orders and join him in painting the hull—almost three hundred square yards of it. And after that we painted the superstructure.

"And remember, no holidays, Ken," said Dad. Holidays to him were the tiny cracks and pits in the wood where the paint did not penetrate unless it was worked well in with the brush. But it was also no holidays in the usual sense. Every Sunday we drove to the yard, painted all morning, ate our bloater-paste sandwiches, drank our thermos of tea, painted all afternoon and drove back home to bed.

I remember one return journey when, drowsy with fatigue, I suddenly heard the loud hissing of snakes behind me on the back seat and cried out in alarm.

Dad spun round, as cool as a cucumber, to deal with the situation.

"What a brave father," I thought, burying my head in my hands for protection. Instantly the hissing stopped, but to my horror Dad gave no sign of stopping the car.

"Stop, stop, let me out!" I cried, imagining cobras slithering under the seat to bite my ankles. I pulled my feet up onto the seat and started yelling and rattling the door handle.

"What *is* the matter with you?" said Dad with a disparaging laugh. "All this fuss over a couple of battery leads." Trying to control my trembling, I snuck a look over my shoulder. It was indeed a battery—a large twenty-four-volt one. I remembered he was taking it home to recharge it.

"The leads were touching. It was shorting out. Fancy being afraid of that." Then, quietly, almost to himself, he said, "I never thought I'd have a coward for a son." My world fell apart. I was devastated. I attempted to explain my behaviour but the words wouldn't come and it was only after several moments of wretched silence that I managed to blurt out, "I thought they were snakes." Dad seemed unconvinced and said nothing. "And snakes can kill," I said in little more than a whisper a minute later.

Dad considered my explanation and after an agonising age said, "I see." I doubt that he did. Ever a practical man, he must have seen my story as a childish attempt to hide my fear of a harmless phenomenon. To him the idea of a couple of deadly snakes hissing away on the back seat of his car was beyond his comprehension, whereas to me it was always a possibility, one I hope to realise one day in a film.

At home I choked down my baked beans on toast and for once did not prolong the business of going to bed.

"You're off early," said Mum. "Don't forget to wash those ears. You could grow carrots in them."

I was close to tears and only nodded as I went upstairs. After doing as I was told I went into the bedroom, collected my overcoat and crept downstairs. Through a crack in the living-room door I could see Mum with Ray on her lap listening to *The Ovaltinies* on Radio Luxemburg. It would have been safer to go out by the front door, I wouldn't have to pass them, but I'd never used the front door in my life. It was reserved for very exalted personages such as our family physician, Dr. Chambers, and Grandfather and Grandmother Russell. Lesser mortals, such as Granny and Grandad Smith, had to use the back door, along with the tradesmen. Tail between my legs, I did the same, preferring discovery to the breaking of a taboo. Luckily, I escaped detection. Closing the back door quietly behind me, I crept in the darkness past the garden shed where Dad was silhouetted in the window by the glow of a paraffin lamp, engrossed in filing a piece of metal.

The street was deserted as usual and rather eerie. Unperturbed, I crossed over and hugged the shadows till I came to a narrow alley between a derelict house and a piece of waste ground. I'd never ventured down it at night and hesitated a moment before plunging into the darkness, but only for a moment. I was so wretched I didn't really care what happened to me. So I ran down the narrow path, heedless of the spooky trees and wild brambles, knowing that I would soon be under the care and protection of St. Denys, who I knew not as a saint but as a railway station. It was a second home. For as far back as I could remember, it was the place I liked being most, more than the pictures, more than my conker tree, which at the age of ten I was already outgrowing. But it wasn't the Victorian station itself, set on a lonely embankment, that really mattered. It was the covered lattice bridge which crossed the gleaming tracks. Two of these curved away on a branch line to Portsmouth and held little interest for me. It was the main line to London, shooting away as straight as an arrow to Waterloo, that held the real excitement; the excitement of anticipation and fulfilment hinted at in the wonderful song "Something's Coming" by Sondheim and Bernstein I mentioned earlier. What that something could have been to a boy of ten, I know not.

Perhaps it was a yearning for the unknowable, the inexpressible. It would be easiest to say it was a yearning for love. Love for me at the time was a big black and white close-up of two film stars, slobbering all over each other, nibbling each other's ears and kissing, which I found even more insufferable than birdsong on the cinema organ. It never occurred to me that people actually kissed like that in real life. Kissing was a habit. Kissing was something you endured from your aunts and uncles, who stank of tobacco, scent and gin when they kissed you goodbye. And when your parents kissed you it was usually as a prelude to being put to bed. Kissing was also a kind of medicine. If there was no ointment around for a grazed knee, Mummy always kissed it better. Kissing was a duty. "Well, aren't you going to kiss me?" Mum demanded every time Dad entered or left the house. The most she ever got in my presence was a peck on the cheek. There wasn't much love in our home, not of the demonstrative variety, at least, not even a hug. But if my parents weren't kind to each other, they were certainly kind to us kids, even if they were a little thoughtless at times (as, for instance, when Mum said once in passing that if her little girl who was born three years before me had lived she wouldn't have had me).

A wail sounded in the distance. The signal clanked from red to green. I waited in the moonlight. The silver rails began to sing. A distant white cloud raced towards me, eating up the night. The bridge began to shake, the very air was vibrating. I gripped the latticework and pushed my face to the gap. It was coming, coming fast, it was nearly upon me. I was dead over the track but never more alive. My blood felt as if it were racing the train, the last few yards took on the space of a delirious eternity. And then it hit me with the force of a great warm wave breaking painlessly on my face. And even as it engulfed me, I whirled to the other side to witness its collapse. And away on the undertow went all my troubles and cares, away in that joyous white cloud dissolving into the stars.

The bridge is still there today, remarkably unchanged. Soon I was to pass beneath it in a train drawn by a diesel with an exhaust pipe instead of a funnel, on my way back to the Lakes, but first I had a call to make.

Having steamed up Southampton Water on the *QE2* without running into Dad—he had a small yacht now called *In Nuce* ("in a nutshell") I disembarked and took a cab to Fareham to see Mum.

Physically, she was about the same, gaunt and pale, but a spark of recognition shone in her eyes when she saw me. I kissed her on the cheek.

" 'Ello, Ken," she said quietly. " 'Ave you brought the divorce papers?" Taken unawares, I could only shake my head and smile. Then I remembered the Hershey bar in my pocket.

"Er, no. But I brought you this," I said, producing it with a conjurer's flourish.

She wasn't impressed. "I'd rather 'ave a solicitor," she said.

"Sorry, Mum," I said, reverting to a standard childhood reply and turning away from the glare of her pale blue eyes.

"I should have divorced 'im years ago," she said, shaking her head.

"You need grounds for divorce, Mum," I said, foolishly leading her on.

"I've got grounds," she said firmly. "Withdrawal of conjugal rights."

This was awful; she was nearly eighty. I hoped she wasn't going into details.

"It was 'is snoring," she continued. " 'E snored like a pig. I stood it for years until it got unbearable. I 'ad to wake 'im up or go barmy. 'You're snoring fit to wake the dead,' I said. 'E said nothing, just got up and went to sleep in the spare room. The next night 'e did the same and the night after that for the rest of our marriage and never once did 'e come to see me, never once in all those years."

I could feel myself blushing as I tried to work out just how many years that was. Mum had never spoken this way to me in her entire life. What could I say?

"So next time you come," she said, her voice growing weaker, "don't forget to bring a solicitor."

A minute later she was asleep. I was about to leave when a nurse came in.

"She seems a lot better," I said hopefully. The nurse tried to hide her surprise.

"They have their good days and their bad days," she said with a nursey smile. I wondered if Mum's brief recovery was due to shock treatment, but doubted if the nurse would tell me. Instead I said, "Does she get many visitors?"

"Once in a blue moon," she said, starting to make up an empty bed. I glanced around me at the half-dozen elderly patients. They looked sedated and were sleeping as Mum was now sleeping. But they had one thing in common that she did not—signs of family care: fruit, flowers on the bedside table and, most telling of all, photographs of loved ones pinned to their lockers. Mum had nothing. I remembered a spare black and white passport photo in my wallet. It wasn't much but I propped it up against the Hershey bar on the bedside table. I gave the nurse money to buy Mum some sweets and went back through the double-locked doors to the car.

"Bassett Avenue now?" asked the driver.

"No, I've changed my mind." How could I face Dad after that? "Take me to Southampton Central, please."

With a bit of luck I might reach Euston in time to catch the midnight sleeper to Carlisle. I was aching to see Molly and Viv again and the mysterious project Viv had been working on—apparently a surprise for me. As we whizzed through St. Denys under my bridge I felt a thrill of anticipation.

13 Don't Cry for Me, Sherry Lansing

I arrived home at 8 A.M. as the sun was climbing over Shepherd's Crag and about to fall into our garden. In years gone by that would have excited little comment, but for the rarity of the event itself. The sun's rays would have slipped through the leaves of the Portuguese laurel, touched a couple of yews, skimmed over the cess pit and picked their way across a small wilderness of weeds and boulders. We were always going to do something about it—now Viv had.

There was a lawn, a riot of

flowers, old roses and scented shrubs, all flourishing luxuriantly together, and through the windows of the small Victorian conservatory, which had been nothing but a mausoleum for a barren vine, I could see lilies, geraniums, plumbago and jasmine shimmering against a sea of green. And all this from someone who once boasted she couldn't tell a dandelion from a buttercup.

I rushed indoors to shower the gardener with kisses and congratulations. But Viv's greatest achievement, according to her, lay on the other side of the dry-stone wall which separated our garden from a disused neighbouring field. She led me across to peer over at the spot where she had dumped a small mountain of stones and boulders that had waited a thousand million years for her to shovel. She said they were easier to grow than the flowers and as soon as she'd dug up one lot another crop would be ready for harvesting after the next shower. The stones and soil were loath to be parted, and she had sore fingers and an aching back to prove it. They haunted her dreams, those stones, rising to the surface of her mind like schools of turtles swimming up from the depths of some primeval sea, to be caught barehanded and wrested from the security of their native darkness. Sometimes she dreamed the boulders were malevolent eggs absorbing the fertiliser meant for the plants—germinating, swelling, ready to break surface and reveal their armoured shells at the first hint of rain.

As I've said before, the locals don't take kindly to off-comers in Borrowdale, a characteristic they inherit from the land itself. And in starting to conquer the land, Viv was beginning to make a dent in their defences, to the extent of Farmer Weir asking her advice on his kitchen garden. In the evening as we sat in wicker chairs in the conservatory beneath lemon blossom, sipping Sancerre after a game of croquet on our new lawn, we talked over plans for a future which looked far less rosy than the garden.

On its general release in America *Altered States* had not done well. I think it was due to an uninspired marketing campaign, but Warners would probably disagree. Contrary to general opinion, the director has little say in how his film should be presented to the public. The publicity departments pay lip service to his input and generally go ahead with something in direct opposition to his suggestions. It's the safest way of justifying their existence. And if the film's a flop it's always the director's fault. I could certainly see I was at fault in turning down those two offers that came along during the fortnight that *Altered States* was the talk of Hollywood. And I turned them down because I didn't want to be typecast as a sci-fi movie-maker.

"Rather that than be pigeonholed as unbankable," said Viv, ever practical.

"What am I going to do?"

"For starters you could take Molly for a walk," she said. My God! The idea hit me with the force of a thunderbolt as it struck me that in all my years of parenthood I'd never taken *one* of my kids for a walk— and how old was the eldest, twenty-seven? I emptied my glass, plucked Molly from her babywalker down among the potted geraniums and made for the door.

"I didn't mean this very minute," said Viv, chuckling at my impetuosity.

"I've got a lot of time to make up for," I said, crossing the lawn to the front gate. I was only half-joking. Across the road and into Farmer Weir's field I carried Molly, and over to the old swimming hole, where in summers gone by my other kids had climbed the overhanging beech tree and dived into the depths of the Derwent, only lightly polluted by the effluent of twenty-three guest houses up the valley. Anyway, they survived and I guessed Molly would too, once she learned to swim. A baby Viv with streaky blond hair and open, freckled face looked up at me, smiling, but she didn't speak—she didn't know me. I'd never got to know any of my kids very well.

The first three seemed to arrive all at once. At least I remember a photograph of them all in red and white checked pinafores, sitting up in a Rolls-Royce of a pram, as alike as three smiling buddhas. Xavier Francis (named after a couple of saints), James Paul (named after a couple of popes), and Alexander Huw (named after a couple of great men, Alexander the Great and Huw Wheldon—the latter signifying that we were coming down to earth). There was only a year or less between them and as they were born progressively larger, they soon evened out. That was in the early days when Shirley was raising a family in our damp Regency house in Upper Norwood and I was working for the BBC. And you don't have to be a Sherlock Holmes to deduce from the names of the next two that we had either discovered the rhythm method or our religious fervour had declined—or both. They were Victoria and Toby, named after a queen and a dog respectively. And that is how they saw their place in the hierarchy.

Whenever there was a chance to go anywhere we went as a group and the kids played as a group with little or no interference from us adults, who were working all hours anyway. Our housekeeper, May, was mother and father to them and even took them on long summer holidays to the beach hut we had acquired at Calshot on the Solent. The only time I remember playing with them was during filming, which started at a very early age and was treated as a game. Victoria in short Greek tunic and long blond hair played Isadora Duncan's daughter at eighteen months, exhibiting the playfulness and charm she also showed as a Latvian peasant in *Billion Dollar Brain*, Tchaikovsky's niece in *The Music Lovers* and Sally Simpson in *Tommy*. And here in this cautionary tale our twelve-year-old star really shone. She played the part of a vicar's daughter who rejected her father in favour of Tommy, the rock messiah. Disobeying her parents, she tarts herself up and dashes off to one of Tommy's rock prayer meetings, gets kicked in the face by a bouncer and is carried away above the heads of oblivious fans, marked for life. However, Sally's a spirited girl and bounces right back to marry a teenage rock star from California, with the Rev. Simpson tying the knot. The last scene in the number shows them a year later at a rock concert with the husband driving the fans wild as Sally, in a fabulous fur coat, rocks a pram with one hand and admires the "rocks" on the other.

The tale had prophetic overtones. Victoria *did* marry a rock star, in spirit anyway, and she *was* scarred. From what transpired, it became clear that she had been under a terrible strain during the filming, scared of failure and desperate to please Dad. I had no inkling of this. All I saw was an apparently happy child who did everything I asked of her brilliantly. Nevertheless, her hidden anxiety manifested itself in a disturbing way—she started losing her hair. She managed to hide this calamity from us until I went in to wake her up one morning and found golden locks on her pillow and in her hand. Fortunately we managed to finish her sequences before she went completely bald. Not long after this she was knocked down by a car in busy Notting Hill Gate. Apparently she wanted to find out if there was a God. "If there is He will save me," she thought to herself—and, closing her eyes, stepped off the pavement to cross the four-lane highway. Victoria is still with us and is sound in mind and body, so we may draw our own conclusions.

I hugged Molly close, vowing never to be responsible, even unwittingly, for any scars on *her*, mental or otherwise, for the other children had suffered too, one way or another, especially at the time of the divorce. Oh, for a second chance, a chance to make amends. We don't often get one, but I was lucky. I wasn't going to screw it up again. On all fours, I started playing hide and seek with Molly among Farmer Weir's sheep. I don't know who was most surprised, Molly or the sheep.

I got to go on a solitary walk with another of my kids earlier than expected. For even as I crouched between the sheep with my ass irreverently pointing at Skiddaw, there was someone sitting in a cottage on the other side of the mountain who still had a little faith in me and was about to pick up the phone to prove it. I'm talking of the novelist Melvyn Bragg. Actually, novel-writing is only one of his talents. He is also scriptwriter, journalist, film-maker and editor and presenter of *The South Bank*

Show, the only consistently good arts programme on British TV since the days when we worked together on *Monitor*.

Hearing I was back in the country, he wanted to know if I would care to do something for the show. Having been almost drowned in words on my last film, I was in need of resuscitation, so I chose to revivify myself with music—and pictures. Consequently, I took Gustav Holst's orchestral suite *The Planets* as my theme. It was ideal programme material: fifty minutes of colourful music made up of seven miniature tone poems, each representing a planet and its particular characteristic—Mars, war; Venus, peace; Mercury, motion; Jupiter, jollity; Uranus, magic; Saturn, old age; Neptune, mysticism. The combination of pictures and music has always been my favourite form of expression—surmounting all language barriers. Getting the music was easy. Getting the pictures was less so, but I had a brilliant researcher in London called Helen Bennitt who ransacked the film archives for visual material connected with the above subjects and shipped it up to me. Now I needed an editor to help me fit the pictures to the music, and who better than my eldest boy, Xavier, who was making a name for himself as an editor specialising in musical subjects. So we hired a moviola and made our film in the cottage to the bleating of sheep and the pitter-patter of little feet as Molly kept an eye on our progress.

It was all trial and error, but eventually from a jigsaw of old newsreels and documentary footage we built up a musical picture of man's fears, hopes, joys, sorrows, failures, achievements and aspirations, all expressed without a single word of dialogue.

It was a good feeling, actually working again with one of my children and going out for walks and talks, man to man, and not in a party of seven. Not that there's anything wrong with that, and that's what we did when the other kids, having spent Christmas with their mother, came to spend a few days with us. By now everyone had come to terms with the status quo and we all had a great time celebrating the New Year. There wasn't much to celebrate on the work front, once *The Planets* was completed, though my new agent, Peter Rawley of ICM, was brewing up a couple of development deals which might also involve Viv, who, now that she had Molly and the garden to look after, was settling down to her new life better than I'd dared hope.

Apart from winning her fight with the boulders of Borrowdale, she was winning new friends, one of whom was a professional hypnotherapist who said she could help Viv give up smoking whenever she was ready. Viv hates being pressured, so took her time and, ever the cynic, drove to her appointment on the fatal day chainsmoking two cigarettes at once. After that she never smoked again. A fresh breeze seemed to blow through the house, making everything more relaxed and easy, including our collaboration on the scripts which resulted from the development deals, even if they never came to fruition. The reasons for this were many and various: with *Cleopatra* there was a switch of personnel at Home Box Office and the new boys were not interested in what the old boys had commissioned— so far as our particular project was concerned, anyway. One script, one rewrite, six months' work.

With *Maria Callas* the reason was less obvious and we got pretty far with that one before it was "clappers on end," as the saying goes. In fact, I travelled all over Italy with a production team finding locations—yachts and palazzos in Venice, villas and opera houses in Rome and Milan. We even started casting and had Sophia Loren eager to star in the name role. Eager, that is, once one or two script changes had been taken care of. Viv and I were flown out to her ranch in California to discuss them. Her ageing husband, Carlo Ponti, met us at the door and gave us the grand tour. We saw acres of parched earth and scraggy trees and the biggest private swimming pool we'd ever set eyes on—actually two pools linked by a manmade waterfall. It was very Roman and would not have been out of place at Cinecittà on a film set of Caesar's Palace. It wouldn't have been out of place in Caesar's Palace, Las Vegas, either.

After the tour, Carlo, a little wizened old man with a perpetual smile the size of a slice of watermelon, took us into the ranch-house to meet Sophia, who towered above him with a smile which even outdid Carlo's. We smiled back, Carlo disappeared, Sophia sat on one settee and we sat opposite her on another, sipping coffee from dainty cups. After she'd said how much she liked the script and we'd said how much we liked her collection of coffee pots we eventually got down to the nitty-gritty. She went through her points one by one and they all added up to the same concern—our portrayal of the relationship between Maria Callas and her Italian husband, Meneghini, a much older man. She didn't care for the scene where we showed him snoring in a nightcap and bedsocks, or the familiar way in which Maria spoke to him. In a sequence where the press are laying siege to the couple in a hotel room after one of the famous Callas walkouts, Meneghini asks Maria what he should tell them. "Tell them you can't get it up," she says playfully, giving him a silly answer to a silly question. According to Sophia, Callas would never have said such a thing to her husband, even if she was just kidding. It was unthinkable! And in no way would she be convinced otherwise. Further discussion was cut short by Sophia glancing at her watch and running off to put on the pasta for Ponti's lunch.

"Too close to home for comfort," said Viv, as we flew back to England on the jumbo.

"Bang goes another year's hard labour," I said, "just because a woman's afraid of saying to a man, 'You can't get it up.'"

"That's something they obviously don't joke about in Italy. Anyway, let's see if *you* can," said Viv, grabbing me by the hand and pulling me into the loo. By the time we'd managed it there was quite a queue outside the door—but that was in the days before they introduced those courtesy tables. Now, when Viv heads for the loo on a jumbo clutching a male hand it's our baby son and she's off to change his nappy.

But that was way in the future, a future which didn't seem too cheerful even after a bottle of champagne to celebrate our becoming members of the "Five Mile High Club." Then I remembered an unfinished script gathering dust on a shelf in the cottage. As soon as we arrived home I got it down and while Viv attacked the garden, I applied the finishing touches. *The Beethoven Secret* was a detective story based on a love letter to an anonymous woman found in a secret drawer in Beethoven's desk the day after his death. Find the woman and you find the man. We found everything but the money. It's easy getting two thirds of the cash, it's always the final third that's the problem. And by the time you eventually get your hands on that, the first third has vanished—invested in another project by an itchy hustler. We got close, very close. Jodie Foster and Glenda Jackson as two of the mystery women and Anthony Hopkins as Beethoven were cast and costumed. We were only days away from shooting when the money dropped through, along with our high hopes. Bang went another year. It was bloody depressing. I was beginning to think I'd made my last movie.

Film festivals were beginning to show retrospectives of my work. I attended one as guest of honour and heard a young woman remark to her neighbour, "Oh, I thought he was dead." May as well be, I said to myself. I was becoming desperate and once again thought of getting out my old Rolleicord and putting up a placard in the front garden advertising portrait photography.

And then *Evita* came along. Three months went into writing the script, a month scouting Europe for locations and nine months on and off organising screen tests. There were three producers involved: Robert Stigwood (an Australian pop impresario for whom I'd made *Tommy*), Andrew Lloyd-Webber, and Tim Rice, composer and librettist. Favourite for the title role, so far as my trio of producers was concerned, was Elaine Paige, who created it on the stage. And although there is no doubt that across the footlights her performance brought tears to the eyes, the eye of the camera proved to be made of sterner stuff. And as I watched her screen test it was clear to me that the camera did not love her. My thumbs-down was an unpopular decision with the producers, who saw only what they wanted to see, but the search went on.

Andrew suggested a girl in *Sophisticated Ladies* which was playing on Broadway at the time. So I flew to New York to test her along with a few other hopefuls. They were each poured into the famous Evita gold lamé costume and forced into the famous blond wig. And by the time they were made up it was impossible to tell t'other from which—even their own boyfriends wouldn't have known the difference. They were all Evita lookalikes and soundalikes—Evita clones!

Then we tested a girl who'd sung with Meatloaf. She had a thrilling voice which soared to the heights of "Don't Cry For Me, Argentina" with such emotional impact that many of those who saw the results on the screen were moved to tears. Not so Tim Rice, who remained dry-eyed throughout. And while the hunt for the star continued we were also testing for other roles, including that of a waif ditched by Peron in favour of Evita. She has only one number, "Another Suitcase, Another Hall," but it's a regular show-stopper. We tested several young girls, any one of whom could have played the part. It was a toss of the coin so far as I was concerned, but Andrew fancied one girl in particular, to the extent of asking me quietly, well out of earshot of Tim Rice, if I thought she might be suitable for the role of Evita herself. "Not a hope in hell," I said dismissively. Andrew fell silent, keeping his thoughts to himself. The ingénue's name, I seem to remember, was Sarah Brightman.

The tests continued, and one thing on which we all agreed was that David Essex was perfect as Ché Guevara. But Evita herself was still a big question mark; so was Elaine Paige. Tim Rice believed that our cameraman had done her less than justice and ordered another test. So we hired an equally prestigious name and tried again.

As expert make-up and hair artistes lavished their skills on Miss Paige, the top cameraman and his team of electricians laboured with the lamps, perfecting the lighting. The wardrobe people pampered Miss Paige into her costume, and after two hours of toil we were ready. She crossed the studio floor with her retinue and stood before our most flattering lens. The camera rolled and Miss Paige sang along to the playback, entreating the people of Argentina not to cry for her. When Evita herself appeared on the balcony of the Palacio Rosado waving to the adoring masses, they wept with joy. On seeing the rushes, I felt Miss Paige would have been more at home on the balcony of Buckingham Palace with the Royal Family waving to a crowd of dry-eyed tourists—and that was not the image we were seeking at all—or was it? Personally, I felt we needed someone more earthy and said so. After all, Evita was something of a whore.

Barbra Streisand's name came up. She was in London setting up her film *Yentl*, so I was invited to dinner at her hotel to discuss the matter. After being refused entry into the restaurant for being improperly dressed, we settled for dinner in her room. Being American, she didn't order wine, so I asked if I could have a glass of Chablis to help wash down my fish. She generously ordered half a bottle, most of which she drank herself as, for the next hour and a half, we discussed *Yentl*, which she was about to direct and star in. We talked mostly about lighting cameramen and I gave her a list of names I felt would bring out the best of her features without underlighting her co-star, as was the case in one of her recent films when she looked great but Ryan O'Neal looked as if he was standing in for Sammy Davis, Jr. This was all very well, but when she got around to discussing specific scenes in *Yentl* with reference to crane shots, zooms and tracking I felt I was more than singing for my supper.

"What about *Evita*?" I asked, forcing down a glass of water. I can't repeat her exact reply, but I don't think the idea of a Jewish Princess playing a Catholic whore exactly appealed to her. I'm not sure that working under me did, either. Disappointing!

But, following a similar train of thought, I suggested Liza Minnelli to my producers. Andrew, who was getting as desperate as I was, embraced the idea. Rice and Stigwood were less enthusiastic but could hardly say no, though their patience was also running out. Nearly a year had gone by since the search for Evita had been undertaken. This was to be the last test, Stigwood announced, and it was to be done immediately! In vain I pleaded for a little more time—a few days' grace for Liza to rehearse a couple of the songs and have a costume- and wig-fitting. Absolutely not, Stigwood decreed. Poor Liza. She even had to hold the make-up girl's baby as they tried to force on a tatty blond wig two sizes too small. She had the same trouble with the dress and there was no wardrobe lady to give her a hand, either. So Liza sang in her jeans and tee-shirt, and when she didn't know the words she improvised, soaring above obstacles that would have floored most aspirants to produce a performance so char-ismatic, so charged, so inspired, that she totally transcended the senti-mentality and superficial glamour of the stagy, two-dimensional character and turned her into a vibrant woman of flesh and blood who had clawed her way out of the slums and slept her way to the top to possess the very soul of a nation. For the first time in my experience the character took on a life that was deeper than the make-up and lacquered wig. Liza was giving out with a million volts. Here was a woman who could start a revolution and sway a nation—if she'd marched out of the doors and down Whitehall to overthrow the Government there wasn't a person there who wouldn't have followed her. Waves of electricity, waves of power, swept through the studio, waves of sound, waves of sex. And when she reached her climax with an orgasmic "I'm coming," so was everyone else in the place, man, woman and dog. At the eleventh hour, it seemed we had found our Evita.

I phoned Stigwood with the good news and was promptly summoned to his private island along with the screen test. I flew off to somewhere in the tropics, I forget where exactly. I was in a euphoric haze and the only name connected with the entire trip that sticks in my mind is Minnelli.

I landed at a sweltering hot airport with palm trees, where a speedboat was waiting at the end of the runway to transport me to Stigwood's pirate island. The sun beat down unmercifully; I wished I'd brought a hat. We sped away across the bay towards an empty horizon. There was a fresh wind blowing and as we hit the open sea I fell flat on my face. For those unfamiliar with the experience, let me tell you how it feels to traverse choppy waters in a power boat travelling at 70 mph. It feels exactly like motoring along a highway up for repair in a car with square wheels made of concrete. I picked myself up and tried to sit. Sitting on a pneumatic drill is easier and gives more pleasure, I promise. I hauled myself to my feet with difficulty, grabbed onto a rail and hung on for dear life. I glanced at the bronzed young helmsman, staring straight ahead through dark glasses, steady as a rock. I opened my mouth to ask him "how much longer?" and had the words rammed down my throat by the wind. Silly idea, anyway; the twin engines screamed all other sounds into submission. My eyes filled with tears. I could no longer see properly. I shut them and endured stoically, until a lifetime later when the boat suddenly went into reverse. I was on all fours again and stayed there for a moment, giving thanks for a safe voyage. Then the bronzed young man helped me ashore, where I pitched forward yet again as if I'd just stepped onto a stationary escalator. Servants led me to a guest bungalow where I was told to take my ease until Mr. Stigwood was ready to see me. I've never been more grateful for a bath and a lie-down.

An hour later, feeling much refreshed and only trembling slightly, I was led past a luxurious swimming pool, only yards from the sea, and across neat lawns to what might once have been the residence of a colonial governor in the eighteenth century. Slender columns, delicate wrought-iron balconies—I almost expected Judy Garland to throw open the shutters and break into "Mack the Black." Indeed, I was standing on Captain Black Morgan's pirate island (as a sun-tanned Stigwood, oozing Aussie charm, explained later as we climbed to the lookout point—a green hillock on the little island's most westerly tip). When I'd been ushered into his presence, Stigwood, who'd been watching world news on TV, seemed keener to show off his island than to see my screen tests. The tour itself didn't take long, and once we had taken in the view from the hillock— the scene of a recent wild party involving some of the greatest names in pop—it was time to indulge in a pastime which might well have rivalled what I came to believe was Stigwood's prime occupation—watching world news.

Cautioning me to remain quite still as we lurked behind a yucca, he directed my attention to a peppering of what appeared to be rabbit holes but were actually the homes of giant spider crabs. We watched and watched and watched for crabs, when we should have been watching Liza Minnelli. But my priorities were not Stigwood's, I came to realise, as he began to explain, with a touch of pride, that, unlike most crabs, his spiders were not promiscuous but practised strict monogamy. And, unlike some of the pop stars cavorting over their heads recently, they must have read the Fifth Commandment, I thought to myself. Aloud I said, as we gazed at the deserted hillock, "I guess they're all at home fucking their brains out." Stigwood affected not to hear but eventually even he became bored and we returned to the house, passing a TV dish the size of a radio telescope on the way. Much to Stigwood's delight, we arrived just in time to see the latest news bulletin, which was a repeat of the news bulletin we had seen an hour before. I discovered, as a simple dinner was served, that the news channel was available twenty-four hours a day and that Stigwood was an addict. He could barely tear himself away from it, over coffee, to see a video cassette of the test which had been burning a hole in my pocket all day long.

Reduced to a frosted screen and a tiny loudspeaker, Liza was still dynamite. Stigwood looked and listened and smiled like a Cheshire cat. But whether it was a smile of delight or derision, I couldn't say. All the other Evita tests were on the tape as well and he said he'd make his final decision after playing through them later in the day. He was very optimistic about the project and said a deal was in place with Fox, who were keen to get started. But then he'd said the same thing six months earlier about Paramount. That deal had fallen through when I told them confidentially that I couldn't guarantee the delivery of a successful film if Elaine Paige played Evita. It was as if Stigwood had sold them a package including Elaine Paige, with the tests as a mere formality. I had surprised everyone with my unpopular action and it must have been quite a blow to Stigwood, who was used to having his own way. However, he bade me an affable farewell and said we'd talk tomorrow. I gritted my teeth in anticipation of the return journey in the ball-breaking motor-boat.

Imagine my surprise when I was ushered to a waiting taxi. The island, I discovered, was attached to the mainland by a bridge, making the sea journey totally unnecessary. As I was driven in comfort towards the airport I wondered why I had been subjected to the Stigwood water-torture. Perhaps it had been part of a softening-up process. That, plus jet lag, plus the crab-watching and the nightmare repetition of the news (delivered in terms of extreme urgency even though it was always the same news) had reduced me to a state of silent passivity. And I'd promised myself earlier that I would not leave him without a final decision—a decision I was still confident would be in favour of Liza.

A message was waiting for me at Heathrow. I opened the folded paper bearing my name scribbled in pencil. The message consisted of two words: "Elaine Paige." I immediately phoned my agent, who brushed aside my protestations. Sherry Lansing herself, President of Twentieth Century–Fox, together with her Head of Production, was on her way to London to finalise details. I couldn't believe it. I'd been set up. I'd been humoured. It was always going to be Elaine Paige. My dreams of coming up with an alternative Evita were just dreams.

At last I woke up, phoned Richard McDonald and his wife, Ruth, who were to design the film, and invited them for drinks at my hotel. We discussed our predicament. We all agreed that *Evita* was a great subject and that we had a lot going for us. We had a good script, a very commercial score, exciting locations and, with one exception, a great cast. They also pointed out that my last feature film had been a flop and that I needed a hit to get back into circulation, and if I wasn't happy with Elaine Paige it didn't really matter because the audience would be swept along by the sheer power of the production.

I said I'd sleep on it and with the help of a bottle of Beaujolais managed to do so, but only for about an hour. I woke up at twenty to two. I could just catch my agent at the office. Nursing a headache, I called ICM in Hollywood and broke the bad news. Nobody enjoys losing ten per cent of something they've worked hard to procure, but my agent put a brave face on it and promised to tell Stigwood. A few minutes later the phone rang. Guessing it was Stigwood himself, I let it ring. I wasn't prepared to be talked into accepting Elaine Paige at this time of night or any time of night or day, come to that. I'd had it! After my payment on the script I'd not received a penny for over six months' work, only promises, and I'd had enough. All the same, I felt a little guilty next morning when a message was pushed under the door asking me to attend on Sherry Lansing & Co. at Claridge's for lunch. Having come over from Hollywood especially to see me, I felt I owed her an explanation. Come noontime I went along to face her.

The room seemed to erupt as I entered and executives poured all over me. I'd expected a wake, this was more of a wedding, and if I was the groom, the gushing bride was Sherry, the most beautiful movie mogul the world has ever known and the most brainy. Everyone was very happy that we were getting into bed together, as the saying goes in Hollywood. It began to dawn on me that something was up. They were getting out a magnum of champagne—Tinseltown's favourite—Perrier with the lilies on the bottle. It was time to speak now or for ever hold my peace.

"But I'm not going through with it . . ." I said.

Silence! Stunned incomprehension! Silly faces! Gaping mouths!

". . . Haven't you been told?" A sillier question was never asked. Obviously neither my agent nor Stigwood himself had broken the news, hoping that I'd change my mind, I guessed. In as few words as possible I told them that I could not make the picture with Elaine Paige and guarantee its success.

To my amazement Sherry's first reaction was to put the champagne back in the fridge.

"What are you doing?" I said, raising my voice at the sight of my lunchtime tipple being locked away.

"We've nothing to celebrate now, have we?" she said, icily.

"I'll say we've got something to celebrate," I said with unaccustomed vehemence. "I've just saved you fifteen million dollars. Isn't that something to celebrate?" I meant it! I had! But at that moment no one saw it that way. I heard subsequently that *Evita* was one of the favourite musicals of the boss of the company and that it was being made to please him with nobody really caring who was in it, but whether that was true or not I can't say. I do know that I was looked upon by everyone as the villain of the piece. Since then, at regular intervals, a number of big names have been linked with the title role, including Meryl Streep and Madonna, but so far the film remains unmade. Maybe it's because fascist dictators just aren't box-office anymore—either in South America or anywhere else.

Back to Claridge's, with me being, metaphorically, thrown out on my ear. Not only was I unbankable again—worse, I was untrustworthy. Worse still, I was unlovable! I'd really burned my bridges now. There was nothing left for me but to go home and help Viv with the garden—which was now turning into one of those incredible cottage gardens full of hollyhocks, lilies, wistaria, sweet williams and festoons of honeysuckle and rambling roses you only see on the best Christmas calendars. However, my offer to help was met with a certain diffidence on Viv's part. She was happy I wasn't directing *Evita* just as long as I didn't attempt to direct *her* in the garden. Soon I was relegated to weeding around the cess pit. After a week or so of pottering about I grew bored and my rests (between bouts of back-breaking drudgery) taken in the shady conservatory with a cool glass of

Chablis became longer and more frequent. Whereas I used to get under Viv's feet in the house, I was now under her feet in the garden and in the conservatory—from which I was eventually fumigated along with the red spider mite. The hills had lost their attraction too—I'd climbed everything in sight and quite a lot out. Why go through the exertion of doing it all again? What was the point? It wasn't worth the effort. Neither was the time and love I'd lavished on all those still-born efforts over the past few years.

My mind went back to that other time of forced unemployment after *Clouds of Glory* when I'd forsaken the warmth of the cottage fire and gone for long walks in the snow, always leaving Viv with those immortal words, "I'm going out now. I may be some little time." Unlike Captain Oates, I'd always returned in time for my dinner. Nevertheless, that scene had a certain poignancy that was unattainable when enacted at the height of summer. I thought of Melvyn Bragg sitting on the other side of Skiddaw with the power to commission me for more TV work and turned to the mountain to pray. Next day I had a phone call. Mum had died of pneumonia. Poor old Mum, she was better off out of it.

I packed a bag and set off for Southampton. The mourners met at the house. Moo and June were there, looking tearful, and so were a few of the kids in their Sunday best. Dad looked chipper as he pottered about making Nescafé in his raincoat, pipe and trilby. We talked about everything but Mum—the weather, when we'd last seen each other and how well we were looking, all things considered. Nobody sat, we all stood about awkwardly, sipping our insipid coffee. A discreet tap on the door announced the funeral cortège. We were a car short; most of us had to get in the hearse along with Mum. The kids squeezed in front, with me, June, Moo and Dad sitting side-saddle around the coffin. "Anyone fancy a game of cards?" I felt like saying. We all grabbed the handles as the hearse took a sharp corner—we were running late. The driver turned on the windscreen wipers.

"Is that rain, Harry?" asked Moo, peering through the sheet glass. Dad removed the pipe from his mouth and said, "Just spitting, I believe, Muriel." I hasten to add the pipe was not lit. Then Jim said, "Are we going the right way, Uncle?"

"Well, *I* would have gone down St. Mary's Road, turned left at the Six Dials and gone over Cobden Bridge," said Dad.

"Then why's he going through Bittern Park?" asked June.

"Maybe they charge the same as taxis," said Xavier, "so much per mile."

"Then he's taking you for a ride, Harry," said Moo.

Dad glanced inadvertently up front to see if there *was* a meter. Naturally there wasn't and we were soon on course again so there was no further cause for concern. Up Lancers Hill we went towards West End. It was quite steep. We were almost in each other's laps.

"Oh, look," shouted Moo, pointing through the window, "there's a sight you don't see very often these days." We all looked out. An elderly man was standing on the pavement, paying his respects to the dead. He was holding his hat and his head was bowed. Slowly, everyone in the hearse looked from the bareheaded man to Dad sitting there in his trilby— and burst into manic laughter.

"Oh, I do beg pardon," said Dad, removing the offending article. "I put it on because it looked a bit doubtful."

"Cast not a clout till May be out," said Moo, trying to put him at ease. Mum would have had a good laugh at this, I thought to myself as we arrived at St. Mary's Extra, for which she'd developed a soft spot since her parents had been buried there some years back. I don't think she'd have enjoyed the service, though, which was held in a small brick chapel as cold as charity. The Smiths and the Russells sat against either wall facing each other over the coffin, which stood on trestles between them. The Montagues and the Capulets at the tomb of Juliet came to mind. Half those in attendance were there for Dad's sake rather than Mum's. The Russells were doing their duty. The vicar read the prayers he was paid to read, the coffin was carried out, and the two sides of the family were left glowering at each other. This was dreadful. No one had said a word about Mum, "Not a word of thanks," as she herself would have put it. No thanks from me for all the afternoon tea dances and days at the flicks, not to mention my upbringing. No kind sisterly word from Moo for Mum's charity—not that she'd have wanted it. No word from Xavier for all the cruises she took him on and no thanks from Dad for all those bacon-and-egg breakfasts, cooked lunches, high teas and Ovaltine and digestive biscuit suppers for all those "three-six-fives of the year." Not one of us had spoken up. We had just sat there with tight lips, holding our peace.

Outside, after another formalised prayer from the vicar, Mum went down the hole and everyone went to look at the wreaths (and mentally attach price tags to the name tags). Then, as Dad had made no arrangements for a wake, everyone mumbled goodbye and drove off in different directions. Out of duty, I felt, Dad suggested that the immediate family should go for a snack. As most of us had come from London and beyond and had long journeys ahead of us, it seemed a good idea, so off we went to a café in town which one of the departing mourners had recommended. At least we'll be able to reminisce, I thought, and drink Mum's health. Our order of beer and hamburgers arrived simultaneously with the heavy rock. But for that, we'd have left at once. Conversation was limited to phrases such as "Pass the ketchup, please," bellowed to your nearest neighbour. Maybe it was all for the best. It would have been difficult to have said anything that wouldn't have offended Dad. The only communication I had from him was a note passed along the table. It read "Shall we go 50/50, Ken?" I looked up, met his eyes and nodded.

It wasn't until I was on the train to London with the kids in a compartment almost to ourselves and plenty of canned lager that it was possible to pay full tribute to the Ethel we all knew. With imitations, anecdotes, jokes and cherished sayings flying around his ears, the city gent sitting in the corner must have conjured up a picture of a very extraordinary woman indeed. He was right.

14 A Year at the Opera

Springtime with bluebells in Borrowdale" could well be a lyric from a Mel Brooks movie, but that is how the story continues. After a hard winter with no money coming in, we were down to our last case of Moët et Chandon (non-vintage), a bottle of which we'd taken into the meadow opposite the cottage, along with Molly and the Pentax. As we gambolled knee-deep in flowers, clicking the camera, everything in the viewfinder was blue and gold—flowers, sky, eyes, hair, champagne! Pity there was no one else to share it with. But there wasn't a tourist in sight. Everyone was at work, poor sods—even Postman Pat, who was about to join us in the line of duty. Spotting us in the meadow, he redirected his steps from the cottage gate and, waving a telegram in the air, came across to deliver it. Click! Click! Got him too!

Thank you, yes, it probably *was* important! We gave him a paper cup full of happy bubbles. Yes, it *was* cause for celebration! "WORK IN ITALY. THE RAKE'S PROGRESS." We all drank his health.

In the evening when the euphoria had mellowed out I rang my agent in Hollywood for more details about the movie.

"What movie?" he said. "We're talking opera." My heart sank. I hated opera, *The Rake's Progress* most of all. I'd yawned through early Verdi, dozed through Donizetti and snored through Wagner's *Ring*, but it was finally Stravinsky's *Rake* that had got me swearing I'd "never enter an opera house again, even if you paid me." Naturally I didn't tell my agent that. I stalled. In the distance Molly was crying. Viv, who was standing nearby and shared my feelings on opera, simply gave me a meaningful look and said, "Baby's thirsty," and walked off. She knew we were running low on Moët too. Well, I guess I'll have to eat my own words, I thought to myself, but at least I'll be able to afford something decent to wash them down with. So I swallowed my pride, accepted their offer, and quickly hung up before I had second thoughts.

The next thing I did was to rummage through a shelf of records devoted entirely to Stravinsky, including a bargain box of *The Rake's Progress*, which had remained sealed since the day I'd bought it over twenty years before. I could never resist a bargain. To my complete surprise and utter delight, I loved it. So did the dog. At least he didn't run out of the house when I put on the record, as was usually the case. He was a brindle Staffordshire bull terrier pup we'd picked out of a litter of six in Bradford. They were all lovely and cuddly. Making a choice had not been easy, so we took the one with the biggest smile—he was humping his mother at the time. For reasons which soon became evident to any visitor, we named him Fartacus. Not only was Fartacus faddy about food, he was faddy about music as well. The music of the Second Viennese School was definitely out—out of the house, fast. Szymanowski sent him into a trance, he danced to *Die Dreigroschenoper* and laid flat on the floor with his hands over his ears for Shostakovich, a habit he picked up from Viv and Molly. But everyone loved *The Rake*. It had witty lyrics, good tunes and was a faithful mirror held up to the original paintings of Hogarth, which had inspired the opera in the first place—none of which had been evident in the production I'd walked out on years ago.

I was wary of falling into the same trap—of trying to create faithful

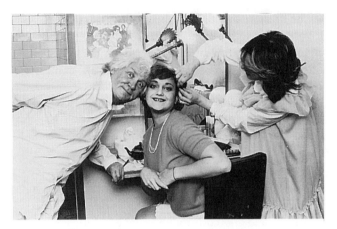

Ken Russell with Cecilia Gasdia in her dressing room on the opening night of his first opera: *The Rake's Progress* in Florence.

reproductions of the original paintings. I'd seen it work with dancers in Gavin Gordon's ballet of the same name, but I could not see it working with opera singers, few of whom are nimble on their feet. Auden himself, as one of the librettists, gave me a clue, via an old programme note in which he stated that both he and the composer considered their simple tale of moral decay to be a timeless one. Accordingly, my designer, Derek Jarman, and I updated it to Thatcher's Britain. The Italians were delighted with the idea, so we locked up the cottage, lent Fartacus to a friend and set off for Florence. And if we imagined the world of opera would be similar to the film world, we were about to be disillusioned.

To start with, there was the language barrier. Even though our opera was in English, the majority of the cast were unfamiliar with the language. Our Rake was Swedish, his wife Greek, the heroine Italian and her father Chilean. Most of them didn't savvy the English and spoke only the pidgin variety. The poor Devil, from deepest Bulgaria, didn't know a word. And when they all sang together for the finale in Bedlam—it was! But the Italian audience was perfectly happy—only a handful understood English anyhow. After all, it's the singing that counts and we had some very fine vocalists, though I was far from happy with them at the commencement of rehearsals. For a start, very few of them actually knew their words, but that didn't worry anyone very much because there were a couple of chaps sitting by the piano who bellowed out the singers' lines a beat before they were due to sing them—even more bedlam! Interpretation was another problem I had to contend with, one which seemed to increase with the popularity of the opera and the number of times the particular individual concerned had sung it. I was pretty lucky with *The Rake*—the piece is rarely staged and even those who had sung it before were young and relatively flexible when it came to accepting any sort of revolutionary concept. This was really brought home to me when I was subsequently asked to stage a new production of *Madame Butterfly* at the Spoleto Festival.

This story of a Japanese geisha double-crossed by a lieutenant in the US Navy is usually set at the turn of the century in something resembling a pretty Japanese tea house with plenty of lanterns, lotus blossoms and lovely kimonos. I set *my* version in a brothel in downtown Nagasaki in the Thirties and ended it with the atomic bomb. I also had my heroine smoke opium from time to time—it made much more sense of her romantic daydreams, and Puccini had written it into the stage directions anyway, though most directors choose to ignore his instructions. I also wanted to hot up the night of passion between the randy Lieutenant Pinkerton and his lovely Butterfly. Fortunately, I had a willing ally in Barry MacCauley, playing the lieutenant, who suggested he carry Butterfly into the bedroom and sink to the floor with her on top of him while singing the duet—a vocal marathon if ever there was one. It invariably brought the house down. My Butterflys were not always so accommodating. One oriental diva never got to sing a note. When she came to her first rehearsal and I demonstrated what I wanted her to do, she shook her head and simpered, "Me no lie alongy top side Prinkerton. Me fry home, Kolea, chop, chop!"

And though no singer walked out on *The Rake*, all of the stage hands threatened to—simply because Derek Jarman had used a "Solidarity" banner as a bit of stage dressing. The hard-line commies in the theatre, who were very anti Lech Walesa, saw this as reactionary propaganda and threatened to go on strike. Another bone of contention was the sex doll. Because these things are unknown in Italy, thanks to the ready availability of the human variety, we had gone to the expense of having one smuggled in from England, only to be told by the Intendant that he would bring down the curtain if the offending object appeared on stage. Come the dress rehearsal, there were plenty of things which gave *me* offence because they *failed* to appear on stage. Half the costumes for the chorus hadn't arrived and the half that had made me wish they hadn't. They were supposed to be air hostesses and stewards, that motley crew, and the only things that fitted were the women's forage caps. The scenery was also a mess, crudely painted and creased, the make-up was garish, wigs resembled birds' nests, cues were missed and at times the noise backstage rivalled the noise in the pit. By the end of the run-through, around midnight, Derek and I were suicidal—despite the general air of satisfaction. What else could you expect of a people who see the Marx Brothers' *Night at the Opera* as a documentary?

We all had the next day off, so to prevent me going mad with frustration Viv took me along with Molly on a grand tour of the gardens of Florence, which, not being in the official guide book, were all but deserted. They acted better than a tranquilliser—until the following evening, when it was back to "heart in the mouth" time as I rushed around backstage giving everyone my notes, which they promptly forgot, and echoing everyone's "*In bocca del lupo*," which is the Italian equivalent of the French "*Merde*" and the British "Break a leg."

Moments later, I collapsed breathlessly between Viv and Molly in the front row of the balcony, surrounded by the buzzing first-night audience, and waited nervously for Riccardo Chailly, the conductor, to appear in the spotlight, which had a tendency to wander. Zap! Bullseye! Applause!

"Well, they got that right," said Viv, smiling at my obvious concern. "Where's Derek?"

I glanced at his empty seat. "Backstage destroying the Solidarity banner, sewing knickers on the sex doll and standing by for emergencies."

Viv squeezed my hand reassuringly, the lights dimmed, the orchestra played, the curtains parted. Molly craned forward all agog, the fake diamonds in her tiara sparkling in the footlights' glow. Shit! The TV set wasn't working. Suddenly the words "captive audience" had a new meaning for me. I held my breath. The tenor kicked it. It worked. The audience laughed. I breathed again but remained tense as the catalogue of catastrophes continued. But when the chorus of air hostesses came on minus their forage caps but with enormous bouffant hairdos of their own creation (each one designed to outdo the others) I gave up. Viv, seeing my despair, whispered in my ear, "If you're going to be fucked you may as well sit back and enjoy it."

"Shit," I replied. "This is rape." Even so, I tried to take her advice—why not? Everyone else seemed to be enjoying it.

But for me the show resolutely failed to take off—until the moment when young Cecilia Gasdia sang the final repeat of "I'll Go to Him" and her last note—a top E—sailed effortlessly above the orchestra, taking the entire audience with it, yes, straight through the sound barrier. We *were* lifted out of ourselves, transported. We knew her fear, her excitement, her love, her joy. We *were* her! We all knew purity and innocence again. That note signalled hope, it was a prayer and its affirmation. It was also great art. Whenever I hear the carefully modulated tones of an Olivier, or a Gielgud or a Scofield, they all pale into insignificance when I recall that one note. I've heard other voices in other theatres that have been nearly as good, but none of them has obliterated the memory of that one sublime note.

At the Staatsoper in Vienna Pavarotti was good, standing centrestage with three spotlights on him while poor Tosca circled around his vast bulk singing her head off in complete darkness. Yes, he was very good, especially during the aria which culminates in his death at the hands of a firing squad. The applause went on for minutes on end and might still be going on even now if the star had not risen from the dead to sing his farewell to life, only to be shot dead and crash to the stage for a second time. Again the applause was deafening, yet again there was resurrection and yet another farewell, another fusillade of shots and another death. It makes nonsense of the drama, but who cares, it's the voice that counts.

I was once at an intimate supper party with Cecilia when someone put on a record of Puccini's *Turandot*—the great aria in which the Princess of Peking sings a series of pure notes which gradually ascend the scale. Well, Cecilia swallowed the last of her pasta, took a gulp of Barolo, jumped up, and sang along with the disc, completely obliterating the other singer. It's a notoriously difficult aria and an incredibly sensual one. I tell you, it was indecent. It was as if she was having sex with everyone in the room. In this respect she even topped Liza's raunchy performance in the studio, transforming a carnal experience into a spiritual one. It occurred to me that angels may communicate in a similar way—angels of both sexes— for I've experienced a similar sensation in the dressing room of the great Russian bass, Paata Burchuladze, when I was turned on by a series of vibrations that were definitely not of this world, yet set the testicles tingling. You can't imagine how the women present were reacting! If angels really do give out in the same way, then heaven may not be as dull as it's made out to be.

Now, just in case you are all rushing out to snap up a bunch of record albums, let me save you the money. It doesn't work through electricity, amps, microphones or loudspeakers. It only works in the *flesh*. You've got to be there and even then there's no guarantee it's going to happen, even if the singer is hitting the right notes and hitting them good. It's in the lap of the gods—literally!

After working in Italy for a while the word "operatic" took on a new meaning for me. Some Anglo-Saxons of a puritanical bent have accused me of being "operatic." I say "accused" because they use the term in a derogatory sense, presumably because they are unmusical. In Italy opera is very much a part of everyday life and opera singers are discussed with as much fervour as soccer stars. The fans are equally vociferous in both sports and hooliganism is not limited to the soccer stadium alone. I've seen rival fans fighting over the merits of rival singers during a performance until the law had to intervene. The miscreants were not ejected for causing a breach of the peace but merely separated by a policeman who handcuffed them to their seats and sat between them for the rest of the opera.

Fighting can also break out on the operatic terraces if someone shouts "Foul! Kill the director!" Productions as well as singers can raise passions in Italy. Then it's the traditionalists versus the progressives. Remember, most of the audience have seen evergreens such as *Butterfly* a hundred times or more and there are those who love it the way it was at its première eighty years ago and there are those who crave a new interpretation. I cater for the latter so naturally there is going to be controversy, and that's the way the opera managers want it, especially if they can't afford an all-star cast. Who wants to play to half-empty houses?

Having caused a scandal in Vienna, fist-fights in Spoleto and riots in Macerata, the local authorities were taking no chances when the Grand Opera of Genoa invited me over to stage a production of Boito's *Mefistofele*. On the first night there were two bus-loads of riot police outside the theatre, armed to the teeth. Trouble started on day one, though, with the conductor walking out after refusing to rehearse Faust and Helen singing their love duet over a bowl of pasta. The whole production had a very Italian flavour, with Marguerite's prison cell transformed into a modern Italian kitchen. When the curtain went up on our deranged heroine vacantly ironing and watching TV whilst yearning for a different kind of life, the audience got the message, macho men and enslaved housewives alike. And when Marguerite's mother was found cut up in cling film in the refrigerator and her drowned baby seen going round and round in the washing machine, it was time for tear gas. I was lucky to leave the theatre uninjured, but needed a police motorcycle escort to take me to the reception afterwards. From then on until the heat was off I was accompanied everywhere in public by two plainclothes men from Rome. Well, it certainly put Genoa on the map—up until that time it didn't really rate on the operatic scene—and there were speeches in public acknowledging the fact, a medal was even struck in my honour and the tenor, usually given to eating directors, presented me with a painting and, more important, became my personal pasta chef. Record shops gave me records, people bought me drinks in cafés and in the streets passers-by either stopped me for my autograph or spat on me. I was never invited back. I had served my purpose in Genoa, which had ceased to exist when its opera house was bombed in the war and was now back on the operatic map, despite the fact that the present house is in a renovated strip club.

So much for opera! It came as a shot in the arm when I was most in need of it. More than that, it was a blood transfusion—red blood—the colour of Chianti Classico. The pay wasn't up to much but in Italy living in a garret on bread and garlic sausage with a few olives and a bottle of vino followed by a little singing is a great way to enjoy a summer holiday. Of course, it's too hot to work in the afternoons if you happen to be staging an opera in the open air, as was the case with *La Bohème* at Macerata. Then, as Cecilia Gasdia's velvet tones fell on the balmy evening air, the locals used to drift in to the arena to enjoy a smoke and drink in Puccini's intoxicating melodies. God, the Italians have got it made! Small wonder they have no sense of urgency when the lunch break lasts seven hours. Enjoyable as it is, this tradition of two thousand years' standing can present problems when you have only three weeks to stage an opera, particularly when it calls for unusual props or special effects.

We needed artificial snow in Macerata for *La Bohème* and according to the administration it was always on the way. Daily reports were conflicting: the lorry was leaving Milan, the lorry had broken down, the lorry had reached Assisi, the driver had been taken ill, and through the intervention of St. Francis had miraculously recovered, the snow would arrive tomorrow. And though there is no tomorrow in Italy, you live in hope. In actuality there probably was no snow on the way and never had been. Maybe they couldn't afford it, maybe there was none to be had—the Italians never like to disappoint, never like to say no. It's an endearing frailty which is never problematic—once you have learned to take precautions. Accordingly, on the afternoon of the première I went to town and bought up every can of Christmas tree frosting I could find. Then, during the interval, I went up on stage—which, being situated in an open arena was curtainless and in full view of the public—and sprayed everything in sight for twenty minutes. This caused laughter and won applause. Some of the audience probably guessed what had happened, others thought it was an integral part of the production. Either way, it didn't really matter. They were relishing the moment—one of their happiest characteristics. I also found the Italians by and large an honourable people, ready to surmount difficulties and keep promises. For instance, the vast interior of Mephisto's space ship, which was powered by live nuns dropped one by one into a roaring furnace, presented no problems to the technical staff, but the rocket unit of the small model flying around heaven *did*. I was told not to worry and that a special-effects team was working on it night and day and the spectacular rocket propulsion unit I'd asked for would be ready and working in no time. And although there were the usual daily reports, it wasn't until the opening night that I saw the fruition of their efforts as the rocket ship circled uncertainly around the stage on wires with one pathetic old sparkler fizzling from its tail which died with a splutter even as I watched. Pathetic, but it got a laugh. Italian audiences are the most generous in the world—and the most critical. I wonder if I will be able to say the same of our British audiences when I come to stage my first opera in England.

There's another first I've yet to chalk up—the filming of a classical opera. Actually, the two mediums couldn't be more different. With a movie you rarely rehearse the piece straight through. You rehearse each fragment, usually out of context, until it's as perfect as you can make it, then you commit it to film, gradually building up a collection of scenes which you are always reshuffling until you have the completed movie—then you fix the soundtrack. With an opera you start off with the soundtrack, as it were, and gradually fit your pictures to it—generally taking it from the top and working through to the final curtain. The great advantage of this method is that the singers can grow into their roles, which you have time to adapt to their individual capabilities. The big snag about opera is that, come the first night, the director can only sit in the front row of the balcony—and pray. Come to think of it, you have to pray at a film première as well. For although your music is canned and your characters are only flickering shadows, there is still one person who can screw the whole thing up—the projectionist.

I've had films out of focus and out of rack, films with dialogue coming out of the surround system and ambient sound coming out of the main speakers behind the screen and, worst of all, I've had wow and flutter. That's why when people ask me the most important thing a film director has to know, I invariably reply, "The way to the projection box." Knowing the projy's name helps too because he can make or mar your film. For the première of *Billion Dollar Brain* I knew neither. But when the sound failed on Reel Two and the slow handclapping began, I went a-lookin'. As usual there was no entrance to the box from the auditorium so I asked an usherette. She thought I was being fresh and referred me to the Manager. His office, when I found it unassisted, was empty. Probably in the pub, I thought, and sought out the commissionaire. Miraculously, he knew the way—out of the theatre, turn left, down the alleyway to the fire escape, up onto the roof, along a catwalk to something the size of a brick shithouse, then knock three times and ask for Bert. I left the foyer with boos and catcalls sounding in my ears and eventually found Bert engrossed in a copy of *Playboy*.

"Thought it was a bit quiet for a Bond film," he said indifferently, getting up to switch on the sound of No. 2 projector. What did he care? He knew it was a Harry Saltzman film and to him that name was synonymous with Bond. The fact that the audience had missed five minutes of important plot was of no concern to him. Still, it is just about the worst-paid job in the business, so what can we expect? I know it's heretical for a film director to even think it but I'll be glad when the last cinema has been turned into a bingo parlour and films are seen under optimum conditions in the home.

Back to that hybrid, the "opera" movie, which I'd love to have a crack at one of these days. So far I've only managed to capture a single "aria" on film, but in the process I also got an insight into the Cannes Film Festival which, despite thirty years in the business, I'd never felt obliged to visit, prize or no prize. Since Viv was in the mood, though, and everything was buckshee, I decided to break with tradition and go along for a few days on the Riviera.

We met at Heathrow on a sunny morning in May: a group of British directors bound for the Cannes Film Festival with the film *Aria*, to which they had each contributed one of the ten sequences which went to make up the complete feature. Ushered towards the crowded check-in by Linda Gamble of Virgin Vision (one of our backers), I was more than a little nervous at the prospect of a sudden confrontation with more film directors than I'd met in a lifetime. I searched the throng for the colleagues I'd never met. Not one figure shone with sartorial elegance—in fact everyone looked a little shabby. I'd heard that most of them were taking their wives along and searched for clues in that direction, but was equally baffled. They looked like a group of mums queuing at a supermarket checkout. The exception was Viv, who at thirty-four looked like Mariel Hemingway, but shorter. Unfortunately, the luggage yielded no secrets either, there was not a single Louis Vuitton piece among the lot—just a collection of battered old things, colourful, individual and desperately unfashionable, a true reflection of our status in the British film industry, I thought. Most of us had been ignored in British Film Year—from which you may deduce that Sir Richard Attenborough was not a member of our party. In fact, most of the British film establishment would probably equate us with our producer's greatest hit, *Scum*.

I'm talking of producer Don Boyd, who has a vision and passion for film that the so-called "saviours" of the British cinema sorely lack. Who else in this country would gather together ten maverick directors, give them a budget of £50,000 each and say, "Go film your favourite operatic aria"?

When Don handed me the RCA music catalogue and told me to take my pick I expected an embarrassment of riches, but the classical section was disappointingly small and by the time nine other directors had got there before me most of the goodies had gone. Top of my shortlist was "One Fine Day" from Puccini's *Madame Butterfly*, which I had produced on three continents with the help of a young friend who had recently met her death in a car crash. On brooding over the enigma of her short life, however, another Puccini opera came to mind: *Turandot*—a tale of love and death in Old Peking. So I chose the aria *"Nessun Dorma"* ("None Shall Sleep") which concerns the identity of a mysterious stranger. Is he life or is he death? That became the theme of my nine-minute scenario, which I eventually shot in a primitive studio on the Thames at Battersea.

Clutching my boarding card, I wondered what my peers would make of it and how I'd react to their segments, for as yet not one of us had seen the finished picture. A tap on the shoulder made me jump. Oh! Derek Jarman, a familiar face at last. He introduced me to the glamorous star of his segment, whose name I immediately forgot. I have a terrible memory for names. Amnesia hit me as everyone introduced themselves at once. Flying over the South Downs a few minutes later, I beckoned surreptitiously to Linda as she talked to one of the directors a few seats in front of me, whose name I was desperately trying to recall. She came to my rescue.

"That's Charles Sturridge," she whispered, and went on to list his credits. Out of the corner of my eye I saw another director trying to get Linda's attention.

"Is that Bill Bryden?" I whispered.

"No, that's Franc Roddam," she whispered. "He made *Quadrophenia*." I felt a pang of jealousy. I'd wanted to make *Quadrophenia* myself, but The Who eventually chose a documentary man. I hadn't cared for his interpretation of *Quadrophenia* and had a strong suspicion that I wouldn't care for his interpretation of Wagner's *Tristan und Isolde* either. Linda went over to him. I felt my ears burning.

By the time we'd touched down and assembled in the baggage hall we'd committed names and credits to memory and felt it safe to get acquainted. The wives did likewise. And as one champagne interview followed another so we became progressively more chummy. There were interviews by swimming pools among the topless and in hotel bars among the legless. We posed for the cameras, we danced arm in arm for television on the terrace of the Negresco in a downpour—with a rendition of "Singing in the Rain" that would have put Gene Kelly to shame. This appeared on the national news and was extremely good publicity for the film—and that's why we were there, in case you're wondering. We worked a lot, drank a lot and laughed a lot. But we laughed most of all at the Royal British Film Dinner where the band played selections from *Local Hero* and *Chariots of Fire* in honour of St. David Puttnam, who had flown in specially from Hollywood to tell us that British film technicians were the best in the world and that he'd just hired a Polish director for his next movie. We all prayed the film would flop. It did!

Finally comes the big night with prizes at the Grand Palais and the presentation of the Palme d'Or for the best film of the Festival. We are sure it will go to *Aria,* which has the great accolade of closing the Festival. I dress in my tropical whites and join the British fleet of limos to glide majestically down the Boulevard Anglais. Cheering crowds throng the streets paying us homage. Our chests swell with pride. The Grand Palais, floodlit and fabulous, comes into sight through the languid palms and we purr to a halt. There are twenty limos of honoured guests ahead of us and we must patiently await our turn. Mobs of hysterical fans press against the windows of our limo. They've mistaken Viv for Mariel Hemingway— because she's seated and wearing shades, I guess. With painful slowness the limo inches towards the red carpet covering the impressive flight of six hundred steps leading to the entrance of the Grand Palais. There is a fanfare of trumpets from the National Guard. I open the door and prepare to step out. A gendarme slams it in my face. Behind me all the other directors are having doors slammed in their faces. We are told to drive on as the Mayor of Cannes and his wife step into the spotlight and waddle up the red carpet and the band plays "Stairway to Paradise." We drive round in a circle and once more come to a halt exactly where we were five minutes previously. The same fans shout and hammer on the windows but with less enthusiasm now that Viv has removed her dark glasses. They are less sure now that I am the escort of Mariel Hemingway. It's hot. We are beginning to perspire. Once more the British fleet makes a break for the red carpet, but someone who looks like a Zulu warrior is being escorted up the grand staircase and once more we are hustled back into our limos and moved on. We approach the fans for the third time and stop for the third time. Viv gets out of the car to stretch her legs. Now they are certain she is not Mariel Hemingway and there is ribaldry and catcalls. We decide to make a dash for it. We get no fanfare and no spotlight. The spotlight is following Catherine Deneuve, disguised as a Christmas cracker, up the carpeted staircase. So are the media.

Everyone seems to have forgotten we are the honoured guests. The foyer is packed with gatecrashers. We fight our way towards the auditorium. The doors slam in our faces. Derek Jarman is not wearing a tie. Consternation! We are in danger of being thrown down the six hundred stairs and they're rolling up the red carpet. An usher kindly sells Derek a clip-on bow for 250 francs and we are grudgingly admitted.

On the stage Yves Montand is announcing a special prize for Jane Russell. The band plays something suspiciously like "I've Got a Lovely

Bunch of Coconuts." Jane appears and then disappears in a cloud of dry ice that engulfs the stage and half the auditorium. When it clears we see a bimbo starlet in a mini skirt standing in the spotlight with her back to us. She is facing the Zulu warrior who is about to receive an award. The bimbo hands over the prize with a low bow. Rapturous applause. She seems not to be wearing any knickers. Her ass vanishes in a cloud of pink smoke. As it dissipates we see that Yves Montand's face has taken its place. He is presenting the Palme d'Or for the best film to . . . surprise, surprise, a Frenchman. We have won nothing. Still, we're all excited, the first public screening of *Aria* is about to commence.

However, by the time the stage has been cleared of celebrities thirty minutes have passed and the hall is half-empty. But finally the lights dim and the magic of *Aria* casts its spell. After a few tense moments I gradually sit back and have a good wallow. I like it. I like it all. Pictures and music wash over me inducing a warm glow. And much to my delight I really enjoy friendly Franc Roddam's treatment of Wagner. As the end credits begin to roll the crowd that slipped out ninety minutes earlier slips back in again. I presume they are French for they cheer Jean-Luc Godard's name when it appears and boo the British. And as soon as the lights go up they all belt out again—fast! I wonder why, until I see them in the dining room, first in line for the free drinks. We are last as usual and subjected to much pushing and shoving, and the bouncers are beginning to throw their weight around.

Viv and I are admitted because she is standing on her toes and is mistaken for Mariel Hemingway. But Derek Jarman is not so lucky. The bouncers take a dislike to his cheap bow-tie and rough him up. Eventually we get to our table. Derek arrives some time later, thoroughly ruffled and upset.

The meal is a bit of a downer. Even the ebullient Don Boyd is a little low and sinks even lower when he is presented with a dinner bill for £25,000. He learns that the accolade of being the producer of the last film in the Festival also carries the privilege of footing the bill for the entire audience of starving Frenchmen.

Next day we all flew back to London, so heavy with hangovers that it seemed the airbus would never get airborne. But somehow the pilot got it to Heathrow and everyone exchanged fond farewells and promised to meet one evening for dinner—soon! We've never set eyes on each other since. It's not that we are insincere, it's just the way the film world works. One director went to shoot a western in Arizona, another went to film a classic up the Amazon—I went to Camden Town to meet the seventy-year-old star of my next movie, who'd never stepped before the camera in her entire life. Her name was Ursula Vaughan Williams and she was the widow of one of our greatest composers, Ralph Vaughan Williams. I'd long been a fan of his and had seen him at a distance a few times during my days as a concert-goer. Back in the Fifties I'd watched him conduct his *London Symphony* in a double bill at the Royal Albert Hall with dear old Richard Strauss. I'd also seen VW sleeping through a rehearsal of Walton's Cello Concerto on the day of its première with Piatigorsky and applauded him along with thousands of others at the London première of his *Sinfonia Antarctica*. And now here I was with his wife in the kitchen of the house they had shared together, eating a cheese omelette, sipping Moselle and discussing my ideas for a film on the man and his music, courtesy of the man on the other side of the mountain, Melvyn Bragg, who alone in England was still showing faith in me and providing the wherewithal to produce a film on the sort of subject I loved best.

Like Elgar, and to a lesser extent Delius, Ralph Vaughan Williams epitomises in his work the very heart and soul of England and her people. Every bar of his music proclaims it and nowhere more deeply than in the symphonies. So I set off on my voyage of discovery around the Grand Old Man of English music by embarking, along with Ursula, on a symphonic journey—naturally taking Viv and Molly and a small film unit along with me.

Our first port of call was Tintagel, legendary home of King Arthur, on the wild coast of Cornwall, where mighty Atlantic breakers dashing against massive bastions of rock filled the air with spray and the music of Ralph Vaughan Williams' first symphonic evocation. Every Englishman worth his salt has connections with the sea and VW was no exception—his *Sea Symphony* for chorus and orchestra is as true blue as Wedgwood pottery, which is quite apposite when one remembers that Josiah Wedgwood was one of Ralph's forebears. Although he was born in the country, not far from Elgar's Malvern Hills, Ralph spent much of his life in the metropolis and considered himself a Londoner, so it's not surprising that the composer's next symphony should be called the *London*. The work opens with the chimes of Big Ben played softly on the harp, as if those familiar tones were coming to us through the mists of sleep at dawn. But soon the hustle and bustle of the rush hour intrudes and that's what accompanied Ursula and me as we drove past the mighty clock tower on the start of a symphonic tour which was to take in the autumnal melancholy of Bloomsbury Square and a lively "Cockney Knees-up" on the Embankment. And for the finale we embark on a journey down the Thames, past the *Discovery*, renowned for polar exploration, past St.

Paul's, past the Tower and Tower Bridge, swept along on a glorious flow of melody until in a ghostly diminuendo London passes, the river passes, England passes.

The third symphony, the *Pastoral*, evokes a procession of cumulus clouds passing majestically overhead on a bright summer's day. But it only needs a modicum of imagination for those clouds of glory to turn into clouds of sorrow. For this symphony, which enshrines the English countryside like no other, was written between battles while Ralph was serving as a field-hospital orderly on the Western Front during the Great War. As one might expect, it is music of nostalgia for landscapes untorn and unblooded. It is also a moving threnody for those who never lived to see their homeland again.

We shot our sombre moments on the ravaged earth of Bovington Camp, home of that great British invention the tank, and with a little ingenuity managed to capture the lighter moments as well. One of the movements of the *Pastoral* is a lively country dance which demanded a bit of visual merrymaking. Significantly the date was October the 19th and that in itself was inspiration enough. Up drove a tank with the location manager sitting on the gun turret hugging a case of wine and announcing on his loud-hailer, "*Le Beaujolais Nouveau est arrivé.*" And because our programme also involved the crew, we filmed ourselves drinking the new wine in paper cups as we danced on tanks of the 1914–18 vintage—me, the unit, Ursula, Viv and Molly. Life imitating art again and vice versa. In fact the programme was very much a family affair, with me telling Molly the story of Uncle Ralph's life and music with the help of Ursula, a photo album and live performances and recordings of his music, con-ducted, in the case of the Fourth Symphony, by the grand old man himself. In the circumstances it was very appropriate, for, according to Ursula, this music of courage, wit, power, mystery and a touch of temper, was a self-portrait. And as we played the old 78s in her sitting room a rather startling picture of the man emerged, quite at variance with the conventional one of the kindly old country gentleman. This is typical of the British temperament, where mild manners often hide deep passions. But when they are unleashed, as in the Fourth Symphony, the effect can be shattering.

The Fifth Symphony reflects the mystical side of the British and is in the nature of a musical pilgrimage through the world of John Bunyan to the Delectable Mountains. We couldn't afford the journey to that partic-ular location so made do with the hills around Lulworth Cove, which are very nearly as delectable.

The Sixth owes something to Shakespeare and although the know-alls thought the uneasy tranquillity of the finale was a desolate impression of

England after the bomb, Ralph, according to Ursula, took his inspiration from Shakespeare's *The Tempest*: "We are such stuff as dreams are made on and our little life is rounded with a sleep." And there is little doubt that Ralph, along with his beloved Shakespeare, saw Prospero's Magic Island as our own.

We do live on a magic island, without doubt, but so far as British films are concerned there is precious little evidence of this. By and large, contemporary film-makers seem to revel in squalor, glorify ignorance and extol violence. There is another kind of life outside of this which many people in this country would like to celebrate, if only they were given the opportunity and not made to feel guilty about it. It is nothing to do with religion; it is to do with the spirit of the land in which we live, that elusive quality touched on by the music of VW and his contemporaries such as Arnold Bax, Frank Bridge and John Ireland: music expressing the majesty of nature, forgotten rituals, pagan goddesses and ancient heroes. All these scores are unashamedly romantic and shamefully neglected; and desperately outmoded according to the new barbarians whose mission is to trample our heritage underfoot. Still, I agree that ours is not an age of heroes, though in his Seventh Symphony VW remembers some very gallant gentlemen who battled against tremendous odds to reach the South Pole and failed. The epilogue of the *Sinfonia Antarctica* is introduced by a quotation from Captain Scott's diary, which brings me a little solace from time to time: "I do not regret this journey; we took risks. We knew we took them, things have come out against us, therefore we have no cause for complaint."

The Eighth is tintinnabulous. Did Ralph write it for Ursula as a wedding present? I don't know and she's not saying. And so we come to Number Nine: not an Ode to Joy like Beethoven or a Hymn to Death like Mahler but something fresh, intangible and by any standards a remarkable work for a man in his eighties. Ralph was steeped in England's heritage, he loved the Tudor poets, the music of Byrd and Tallis, the lark in the clear air and Worcester Cathedral. He loved folksong—the music of the people—and conducting amateur choirs in village halls, the indomitable spirit of the British people and their ruggedness, which is very much a characteristic of this Ninth Symphony. He also loved the humble rice pudding, and who is to say that's not in there too? Certainly Stonehenge is and that's where our journey ended.

Apart from symbolising the pagan note in Ralph's music, the stones are the focal point of Salisbury Plain, which inspired the symphony in the first place. It was one of Ralph's favourite stamping grounds and the first folk song he ever collected was called "Salisbury Plain." It also had associations with Thomas Hardy and *Tess of the D'Urbervilles*, another of Ralph's favourites. And, as I say, it was here in this place of mystery and romance that we ended our journey; though, as Ursula said in her summing up: "The end of a journey is often the beginning of a new exploration."

Ralph died, aged eighty-six, on the morning the Ninth was to be recorded by Adrian Boult and the London Philharmonic. He had planned to be in attendance, but the recording went ahead just the same. It is a very heartfelt performance. Although Vaughan Williams and Elgar shared much in common, including a high regard for each other's music, they were quite different in other respects. Unlike Elgar, Vaughan Williams was a socialist, turned down a knighthood, refused to become Master of the Queen's Music and hated the Establishment. Strange when you think that Elgar came from a poor working-class background while Vaughan Williams was born with a silver spoon in his mouth. A good job too or we might have been deprived of something precious, that has become part of the fabric of my life.

While we were filming in Dorset I took the opportunity of popping over to Southampton to visit Dad at the weekend. I hadn't seen him since the funeral and felt it was time to call a truce; after all, he was eighty years old and living alone. He'd moved from his detached house to a ground-floor flat in an apartment block near the common. I knocked on the door of No. 8, loud and long. It was early evening. He should have been in, according to Aunt Moo, and I was wondering if anything could have happened to him when a neighbour came along the hall with a bag of shopping. She quickly put me in the picture. He'd collapsed in his bath and lain there unconscious for thirty-six hours. On coming to, his feeble calls for help had been heard by a passer-by who had broken in and virtually saved his life. He was now in Southampton General Hospital recuperating. I dashed over there and was met by a sorry sight. Dad was propped up in bed asleep, his big white eyelids sunken into deep mauve pits. His nose was red and his wiry, silver hair was spread out in a fan around his head, giving him the appearance of a dying clown. He was in short-sleeved pyjamas, open to reveal a puny, white chest. Then for the first time in forty years I noticed a sailor's tattoo on one of his frail little arms. A shudder ran through me. The tattoo, crudely executed, was of a heart superimposed with the word ETHEL. That night I dreamt he was in his coffin, scratching that tattoo till the blood ran.

I rarely have dreams of death, but when I do they are usually very gothic affairs lit by flickering candles and steeped in ritual. Generally I am the victim, moving slowly in chains through the shadows towards the scaffold and the inevitable moment of execution, either by axe or noose. It is always night and I always escape through an exploding maelstrom of fire. The land of my dreams is fraught with anxiety. My house is a desolate shell. Rain falls through shattered tiles, the roof is a gaping hole, floors have collapsed, plaster crumbles. I stand in the hallway on a pile of damp rubble sprouting bramble and thistle, surrounded by a group of wet, silent faces. Are they workmen gathered around to help resurrect the dying property or plainclothes men looking for a corpse that may be hidden under the rotting floorboards? Can the house be saved? Will the corpse be found, if indeed there is a corpse? Something is coming through the doorway behind me; it is a naked woman riding on the back of a giant crab . . . That's enough! Other people's dreams are so boring.

15
Sing Brothers and Sing Sisters

Dreams of love, dreams of riches, dreams of power, dreams of happiness, dreams of salvation—you can see them on American TV twenty-four hours a day, in the soaps and in the commercials. And, as we all know, this commercial warfare of the mind is on the way to becoming global, but so far the exploitation of the Christian faith by unscrupulous hucksters masquerading as religious zealots has been confined to the United States. Why these gangsters for God aren't rounded up by the FBI and put away with the dope-pushers is one of the great paradoxes of the American way of life. Recently some of the most popular evangelists on TV were exposed for the scum they are, but at the time I was asked to direct my first truly original American screenplay their mask of sanctity was yet to be torn away.

Yes, my agent had at last landed me a job—a real job, not a development deal but a definite offer to make *Crimes of Passion*. It was a package deal. The writer, Barry Sandler, was handled by the same agency. Barry was something of a maverick, though not as far out of the Hollywood mainstream as myself. He was, however, equally disillusioned. Having written an adult screenplay for Fox about a married couple who turn into a *ménage à trois* when the husband comes out of the closet with his boyfriend, Barry had the painful experience of seeing his creation castrated for being too ballsy. He hoped for better things from New World, who didn't have such a high moral profile to uphold. So did I. They were known for their cheap exploitation movies and, because no one else seemed to want us, they got us cheap too—with Kathleen Turner into the bargain. She was doubly cheap because she had to play two parts: a high-class executive by day and a low-class hooker by night. The screenplay dealt with identities, split personalities and the masks those in the rat race for the American Dream feel compelled to wear if they're out to win. Sometimes the mask becomes more real than the face underneath, especially if it's a public face. And then we're in trouble.

When I first met Kathleen Turner she was more secretary than star, mild-mannered, self-effacing to the point of hiding behind dim glasses and wearing clothes that were drabber than drab. I began to wonder if Barry's enthusiasm for her was ill-founded, but then he dragged me along to see *The Man With Two Brains*, in which she outsmarted Steve Martin, and I was reassured. So with the female lead in the bag we went on to cast the rest of the picture and were just about to go into pre-production at the Zoetrope Studios in Hollywood when I heard rumblings from New World that Kathleen wanted out. That's when the nightly calls to New York started, with me on my knees and Kathleen playing hard to get. I begged, pleaded, cajoled, flattered, in fact forced myself to start "doin' what comes natcherly" to the Hollywood set but sticks in the craw of every British man born, be he lout or lord. At her end Kathleen was cool, indifferent and vague, though she eventually admitted that some of her friends felt the part of China Blue was degrading and would be injurious to her career. I didn't get it. Why this sudden change of heart when a short time ago she'd have killed for the part? What on earth had happened to make her change her mind?

Romancing the Stone was what had happened. Its heroine was the antithesis of the slut, China Blue—a true-blue American who became darling of the blue-rinse brigade when Kathleen undertook a trans-America publicity tour. It seems that Kathleen began to identify with the retiring blue-stocking of the movie, who turns into a heroine straight out of one of her own best-selling adventure novels. She had also been "discovered" by the media, who boosted her to the skies as the All-American girl, more beautiful than Bacall, more lovable than Marilyn, more committed than Fonda and more pure than Snow White. When I understood that, I understood why the poor girl didn't want to play a thirty-dollar-a-night hooker. But play her she did! Perhaps she had qualms of conscience, perhaps she was afraid of a lawsuit from New World, who knows? Certainly my long distance ass-licking didn't achieve it, of that I'm sure—I'm too bad an actor. Nor did our nightly chats on the phone prepare me for the shock I received when she arrived for her wardrobe fittings. Despite all the hype, I still pictured her as a demure little secretary. Imagine my surprise when in walked a living Xerox of Princess Grace of Monaco. I bowed and kissed her hand. But the regal façade and icy aloofness disappeared once Kathleen got down to the acting, though one had to be discreet when discussing such things as oral sex and sperm on the lips and the best way to swallow a mouthful. After sampling two flavours in the seclusion of my trailer, Kathleen settled for lemon yogurt rather than plain. But when it came to swallowing, we needed something with more body to give the requisite tears-to-the-eyes effect, and neither mussels nor oysters appealed to her. In fact, she drew the line at swallowing anything at all, though she was quite happy to lick away a mixture of yogurt and gooey lipstick from her mouth for as many takes as necessary. She also came up with some interesting positions when it came to sexual acts photographed in silhouette against the bedroom wall, and in all things professional she was near faultless. It was her imperious off-screen manner that was the problem and her overbearing condescension even extended to the occasion when she walked into my rest room at lunchtime and declared, "I need a shower." I didn't know whether to beat it or scrub her back!

Her boyfriend, I believe, was also partly responsible for her change of personality. I soon sussed out that he was the "friends" who had been less than enthusiastic about the prospect of his future wife dolled up in chains and black leather doing kinky things to a policeman with a night-stick in Hollywood while he was at home in New York dealing in real estate. But even a princess has to let her hair down occasionally.

Fortunately, her famous co-star didn't need to act the Hollywood Royal, because he's a real prince of a man. No need to give a run-down on Tony Perkins, who's as happy playing Shakespeare as *Psycho*. He was signed to play one of those phoney evangelists mentioned earlier—the only difference being that our reverend was a pauper, not a millionaire. He was also a homicidal maniac. Perkins turned out to be one of the most dedicated actors I've ever worked with and took his role more seriously than anyone I know, to the extent of taking it home to bed with him. Knowing that a minister of the gutter would inevitably sleep rough, Perkins kipped in his costume and even made and decorated his own props, including a small folding ladder he used as a sidewalk pulpit which he painstakingly covered in pictures of saints and angels and pornographic cut-outs from girlie mags. Over the six weeks we worked on that non-union film with its endearing crew of drop-outs, druggies, has-beens and hope-to-bes, we struck up a close friendship, discussing everything from Mahler to my forthcoming marriage.

My private life was becoming complicated and our business affairs, which Viv was handling now, were in a bit of a mess. Having two names instead of one between us was turning into an administrative nightmare. It was time to simplify matters and settle for one. All you need to start the ball rolling in LA is a licence, and you get that by going down to the Town Hall and offering evidence of cohabitation, such as a shared cheque book or driving licences with the same address. We were asked to produce neither. The Mexican clerk behind the counter took one look at six-year-old, freckle-faced, barrel-chested Molly standing between us and handed over the licence without question.

Now we needed someone to bless the union. We had to look no further than Tony Perkins, who wrote off to the Universal Life Church Inc. enclosing a ten-dollar bill with his application form and received by return a certificate proclaiming his ordination as a bona fide minister of said church, with powers to solemnise births, marriages and deaths. Actually, the diploma he received was blank. He was left to fill in his name personally. There's trust for you! But was he really qualified for such a responsibility, you might ask? Well, I'm sure the intent was there and he certainly knew Vivian and myself better than the priest who married Shirley and me knew either of us. And he was more than qualified to read the extracts from the works of Thomas Hardy and Wordsworth which made up the bulk of the ceremony. The remainder was worked out by the three of us together and contained no rash promises or dogmatic "I wills" that only saints and angels could live up to but less ambitious aspirations, mindful of human frailty, such as "I'll try."

We now needed a venue to fit the magnitude of the occasion. Someone, knowing we lived close to Scotland, suggested the "Wee Kirk in the Heather" at Forest Lawn. But parched grass, even with the best will in the world, is no substitute for real heather, and the chapel with its neon

Ken Russell's (second) Wedding Day on board the *Queen Mary*. Left to right: Kathleen Turner, Vivian, Ken, The Rev. Tony Perkins and his wife.

lights and plastic stone is about as close to Scotland as *Brigadoon*. Someone else suggested Disneyland, and although some look upon Disney as the patron saint of Hollywood, the marriage service is not one of the rides yet available in Walt's World. If and when it comes along it'll be a corker. Mount Washington was suggested by someone who knew our predilection for mountains and the open air. The snag, of course, is that there is no open air in Hollywood, only smog. My old friend Denny suggested using his shrine, but that represented the darkness of the past and I wanted to escape from that.

No, there was only one place that matched the sense of grandeur the occasion demanded—one place that epitomised style, elegance and tradition, something indomitably British, even more British than the English tea rooms on Santa Monica Boulevard, redolent of London Pride, Welsh rarebit, Irish stew and finnan haddy.

Where then, for God's sake, you may ask? Where? Where else but the nearest thing to St. Paul's Cathedral afloat—the *Queen Mary*. OK, so what if she's now an oversized hotel at Long Beach, she's still the proudest sight on the West Coast. So it was a thrilling day for us Brits when I finally shook the captain's hand and took over as much of the ship as possible to make of the occasion a double event—wedding cere- mony and end-of-picture party. What a pity Mum and Dad weren't around to see it. It had a far more nautical flavour than my last marriage (in Epping Forest) and was a far snappier production.

As Viv was made up and coiffed by two members of the film crew, I was busily writing into the ceremony—I almost wrote "script"—a place for the silver chalice, a last-minute present from Kathleen Turner. Every- one involved in the ceremony, including my assistant poised at the record turntables, was in naval uniform. She was a US WAVE and I was a lieutenant in the Wavy Navy. I blew my bosun's whistle, she saluted and spun in the chimes of Bow Bells to summon the guests, including the top brass of New World films (who were footing the bill), from the cocktail lounge to the great hall, with Xavier, dressed as a tug-boat skipper, arm in arm with Victoria as a very fetching WREN bringing up the rear. Next over the PA system came Sir William Walton's *Crown Imperial March* (written for the Coronation) which the American contingent mistook for the National Anthem and so remained at attention for its ten full minutes. Then, as I waited at the altar, upstaged by my new agent, Peter Rawley, in the uniform of Admiral of the Fleet, Bobby Littman, dressed as Edward VII, complete with bowler, escorted the bride up the aisle whilst Molly scattered rose petals before them. And as Viv drifted towards me in a sheer Thirties silver dress and sailor cap she was Ginger Rogers in *Follow the Fleet* to the life. Arriving with the bride at the altar, Bobby respectfully removed his bowler hat—to reveal a yarmulke—and brought the house down. By the time everyone had stopped rolling in the aisles we were halfway through the ceremony, which included sipping champagne from Kathleen's chalice. This won a smile and a round of applause from her and was captured for posterity by the flashing cameras of the press.

So, to words eloquently intoned by Tony Perkins, in shining white, and music by Vaughan Williams, on shining black shellac, we plighted our troth. There was no ring of bondage, no impossible oaths but a sincere desire to be united in the eyes of God. Man and wife, we kissed and danced down the aisle to Ted Heath's "Bow Bells Swinging the Broadway Melody." The event was such a hit (I had many requests for copies of the ceremony) that I am now writing a sequel—a service for my own funeral. My only regret is that I won't be able to direct it.

But I'm jumping ahead. The wedding wasn't over yet. There were charades on the bridge with great scenes from British naval films from *The Battle of the River Plate* to *In Which We Serve* with David Hemmings as Noel Coward engaging the enemy, and me as John Mills directing the firepower. Our first salvo fell on Warners at Burbank and settled an old score. The next scored a direct hit on a certain ranch and turned the swimming pools into giant bowls of *pasta in brodo*, the next had "Remember *The Boy Friend*" chalked on the shells and blew away Doug Netter's office at Metro. The next salvo hit the Polo Lounge and wiped out every crooked wheeler-dealer in Tinseltown. They were never missed. We were considering our target for the last salvo when we were piped below to receive a wedding present from the top brass of New World. If I'd known then what I know now I would have fired that last broadside bang into their office on Century Plaza East. As it was, I smiled for the cameras with Vivian and received from the hands of the president . . . a ship's clock, batteries not included. At the time we thought it was a generous gift but the fact that no one ever gives anything away in Hollywood had still not sunk in. In effect that clock cost me a million dollars, maybe more.

I'd accepted a low sum for my director's fee on my guesstimate that the film would do well in the video market, where I had a fair share of the profits. But New World read my contract one way and I read it another. So I ended up with next to nothing—till I sued them. But by the time legal costs had been deducted and my agent had taken his cut it wasn't worth the aggro. Often it's the lawyers who come off best in these disputes—they get paid, win or lose, and they're not cheap. When Guccione of *Penthouse* sued me for a million dollars plus, for allegedly breaking my contract on *Moll Flanders*, I was in the embarrassing position of not being able to afford the sort of smart mouthpiece one needs to stand up to the high-powered lawyers employed by Guccione for his frequent appearances in court.

Fortunately, chance led me to a lawyer with whom I could do a deal. A. Richard Golub is his name and he is a living example of the American Dream come true. From humble beginnings as a delivery boy in Massachusetts, Golub rose to become one of the most respected lawyers in the profession and he owes it all to a movie he saw on TV as a teenager in 1958. It was called *Party Girl* and featured Robert Taylor as a crooked lawyer. Richard believes that in America everyone has got their job because they saw it on TV.

What influenced Bob Guccione in his choice of career, I cannot imagine, for his claim to fame, apart from massive wealth, is the apparent ability to avoid the pratfalls of pornography which beset many of his colleagues, and elevate photographic studies of the primary and secondary female sex organs into an art form worthy to hang alongside the Rouaults and Picassos which grace the walls of his New York home. So perhaps it is modesty on Guccione's part which deters him from hanging a Penthouse

Pet's Pussy of the Month beside a timeless nude of Modigliani. To a casual eye they have much in common, except that one might have her legs open while the other has her legs closed and one can be bought for $4.50 and the other for $4.5 million. Millions of sales of the $4.50 variety have made this unique collection possible.

But for all his wealth Guccione is ostentatious only in the gold chains and medallions revealed by his plunging neckline. And he dresses as casually as a cowboy might dress—by Gucci. If Guccione had been an actor and I was casting a Western starring a slim, mean, middle-aged outlaw with a permanent suntan, I would be tempted to ask him to play the part. And I might even have considered him for the part of the fabulous Emperor Caligula, but that film has already been made by Guccione himself with Malcolm McDowell in the part, and very good he was too. So were Sir John Gielgud and the Penthouse Pets. And if the Academy Awards included Oscars for "Giving Good Head" then most of the Pets would have been nominated—if Guccione's word and the evidence of my own eyes are to be believed. For Guccione himself explained to me the manner in which he launched them on their new careers. Apparently they had been flown to Rome and booked into a hotel on the understanding that they were to be featured in the big orgy scene. Imagine their disappointment when, after waiting for weeks in eager anticipation, the director, Tinto Brass, went ahead and shot the scene without them. The girls' tears, allied to the fact that the orgy did not live up to expectations, incurred Guccione's displeasure. So, waiting until the director was well out of the way, Guccione and the Pets and some of the biggest studs in Rome snuck into the studio one night for an orgy of their own. (And I don't think they were using yogurt.) Guccione photographed the action himself and later cut it into the sequence as edited by the director. According to Tinto's assistant, who wrote an account of the incident, Mr. Brass was less than pleased.

Guccione related this anecdote with obvious pride during our first meeting in his hotel suite in Rome where I'd been summoned to discuss a film based on the Defoe classic, *Moll Flanders*. And why I did not wish him good day, leave the hotel, hail a taxi to the airport and put as much distance between us as possible has baffled my nearest and dearest to this very day. The reason is simple: I was out of work and we needed the money. Predictably, I lived to regret it, but at the time I was delighted when he commissioned me to write a script and mentioned future projects.

To this end he invited me on a mysterious car ride to the edge of the city. After an hour's drive we arrived at a large modern apartment block heavily shuttered and seemingly deserted. One of Guccione's henchmen, a slim, baggy-eyed man in a slouch hat (who had organised the secret orgy shoot) unlocked a heavy metal door in the basement and led us inside, locking the door behind us. The place was dark and spooky, as befits the tomb of one of the most powerful despots that ever lived— Catherine the Great. Here, in air-conditioned vaults maintained at a constant temperature, but gathering dust nevertheless, were Guccione's grandiose plans for what I estimated could be the most costly film ever.

Our footsteps echoed down dim corridors, halting now and then as the henchman opened a squeaky door and flicked a switch, floodlighting a series of storerooms that had long grown accustomed to the night. Shelves of archive and research material, books and documents and drawings were revealed and model sets of tremendous scale and horror. Nothing was normal, everything was exaggerated to the nth degree. A corpse hanging from a tree that Catherine saw as a child was magnified into a tree the size of a church with dozens of corpses hanging from its branches. Death was a recurring theme. There was an infernal plague pit dominated by a skeleton a hundred feet high pounding a giant drum to the rhythm of which countless infected couples fornicated around the perimeter of the pit, only to be pitched into the flames as they climaxed. Then there were drawings of ingenious sex machines constructed to satisfy the lust of the insatiable Tsarina and story boards of fantastic scenes including one of rampant stallions being lowered by ropes onto upturned rumps of female slaves in bondage.

Guccione's weird cellar had the feeling of the catacombs. There was putrefaction in the air and the shadow of Citizen Kane. Once a staff of more than twenty artists had worked here to plan a film which, on my estimate, could have cost Guccione at least one hundred million dollars. He had the money, I'm sure. What he didn't have was a script.

That was also his trouble with me. He claimed that he never had a script that satisfied him—which, according to his testimony in court, was one of the reasons he ended up suing me over *Moll Flanders*. It was a messy business from the moment the film was announced with a lot of ballyhoo beneath a picture of Samantha Fox dressed as a Tudor barmaid with lots of cleavage in the *News of the World*. Those in search of sex and scandal turned the page, but for those sufficiently interested to read on (including the actors' union, Equity) it was revealed that Guccione was scouring England in search of an unknown to play the lead. Unknowns who fancied themselves sufficiently endowed were encouraged to write in and send a photograph.

However, Equity were not amused by this cavalier behaviour and made it abundantly clear that there would be trouble should we choose a non-union wench, while an independent journal circulated to Equity members warned of the perils inherent in a job with Guccione. Heaven forbid, a girl might end up as a centrefold in *Penthouse*—with free holidays and sports cars and unlimited lingerie from Bloomingdale's.

As things turned out, few of the non-union hopefuls were worth considering. The snapshots they sent in along with their applications usually showed them clutching either an ugly dog or their mothers—both of whom were invariably more attractive. So it was Equity members who were definitely in a majority when it came to the shortlist.

We interviewed the contenders in the flat of our producer, Harry Allen Towers of *Brides of Fu Manchu* fame, and tested the six finalists at Dormey Court, a Tudor estate near Windsor. In the misty grounds on a damp March morning five Equity members and an unknown stripped to the buff and one by one prostrated themselves across the knees of a masked highwayman to have (imaginary) splinters pulled from their shivering rumps as they set about seducing him. The erotic comedy of the situation was captured by one girl only—the "Unknown." She was a real discovery, this teenage English Rose: not only was she a ravishing beauty with her perfect figure and flaxen hair, but she could act. She was a natural; the camera loved her—and from a purely aesthetic point of view so did Guccione. What more could you want to launch a talent like that on a career to megastardom? Nothing—except an Equity card! Despite the fact that we had interviewed dozens of their members and tested five of them, the Equity committee refused our Unknown's application—effectively blacking the film. We were advised to look again, because according to the closed-shop mentality of Equity it was inconceivable that there should be no one in their ranks suitable to play the part. Equity should have seen the ranks queueing up outside the Penthouse Club in Soho for our final audition. We had advertised for a Moll nationwide—and from the four corners of the kingdom they came: the long and the short and the tall; fat girls, thin girls; girls from England, Ireland, Scotland and Wales. The Penthouse Club became the Tower of Babble—Glaswegian, Scouse, Brummagem, Gaelic, Geordie, Mancunian, Cornish and Kentish—all sorts and colours. And all unsuitable in every respect, save one—they each waved an Equity card the way a whore waves a clean bill of health. How they came by these cards is another story. Some undoubtedly earned them the hard way in weekly rep, others had got them bumming around pubs and clubs and had papers to prove it. That's all Equity needed to satisfy their requirements—contracts; talent didn't come into it. It took me all day to interview the applicants—none of whom equalled our Unknown. We informed Equity of our endeavours and once again the Unknown applied for membership. And once again she was turned down. And how that élitist journal scoffed at the idea of an untrained young girl (who thus far in her career had only posed in the nude for a calendar) being able to act. By the same token, they would have refused Marilyn Monroe a card as well—but fortunately she was not born in the British Isles.

Meanwhile, Guccione was impatient to start shooting with the girl of his choice, Equity or no Equity, until I explained that no Equity member would work with her and neither would our technicians. Guccione didn't get it. Here he was willing to spend ten million dollars of his own money in England on sets, costumes, film stock, labs and studios and employ dozens of actors, hundreds of extras and a host of technicians, only, in effect, to be told, "Piss off, we don't need you." That decision came from Equity on high. I wonder how the rank and file who were on the dole might have voted if they'd been given the chance.

Well, if England didn't want Guccione's money, he was prepared to look around for somewhere that did—just so long as it looked like England—where most of the story took place. I suggested Ireland. And heaven knows the Republic could certainly use the cash. Towers and I arrived in Dublin, scouted the area with a fixer named Major Mike and found some spectacular locations and plenty of talented actors and technicians all eager to work. It seemed that our troubles were over—but we reckoned without the long arm of Equity. Their grip extended to the local unions, and our efforts to film in the Republic were crushed. So we drank a last glass of Guinness with Major Mike and regretfully flew away, leaving a lot of hungry Irishmen behind us.

Now what? or rather, now where? Where would we be free of this Equity witch-hunt? I sensed the film was in jeopardy—a feeling that was intensified when Guccione invited me to spend a few days at his home in New York. A TV camera recorded my arrival at the Penthouse Palace, a stone's throw from Central Park. In the marble entrance hall I was greeted by a pack of killer ridgebacks—vicious South African dogs that have been known to savage lions. I was soon to learn that they were not the only household pets around. I looked over a marble balustrade to a cunningly lit swimming pool of warm marble and blue mosaic framing a nubile "lovely," apparently floating in space. More shot marble stretched before me through a series of halls full of old masters and a number of middle-aged ones. The prowling ridgebacks began to growl. I hastened to the elevator to join a manservant waiting with my bags. Soon the killer dogs were behind bars and we were shooting up a stairwell of high art, finally coming to rest outside a room with a black door. This, I was informed, was the black room. I was ushered inside. The manservant had not exaggerated—it was the blackest room I have ever seen. Even the furnishings and fittings were black and on the black walls hung the black and white erotic art of Aubrey Beardsley. I felt right at home. Its atmosphere of Nineties decadence was redolent of the Oscar Wilde room in L'Hôtel, Paris, where I had once spent a debauched weekend with Oliver Reed.

In need of a lie-down after my long flight, I flopped out on the four-poster bed—it felt warm. It was illuminated by a galaxy of pea bulbs around a full length mirror in the canopied ceiling. Ho hum, here I was again lying alone on a voluptuous mirrored bed in New York City wondering if, come the morning, I'd be directing a major film or not.

At dinner in the marble banqueting hall Guccione introduced me to the gorgeous Penthouse Pets, who acted as if butter wouldn't melt in their mouths—except for a girl in a black mini skirt who came and sat on my lap. I think she was in search of a small part and, like the others, was auditioning for the whorehouse scene—as Guccione had made it crystal clear that he wanted his pets heavily featured in the movie. My mind raced as a dozen heaving breasts threatened to tumble out of their dresses into steaming plates of *fettucini alfredo*. Among their number I was surprised to see a familiar pair popping out of a skimpy pink frock worn by the Unknown. She confided to me afterwards that the frock was a gift from Guccione and that she was now living upstairs in Petland. We talked about the black room. She knew it intimately and had recently been photographed on the mirrored bed by Guccione himself—a shiver ran up my spine.

The next day a meeting was convened in the Georgian room (shipped intact from England) by members of the board of directors of *Penthouse*, who looked no better and no worse than any other grey-suited US corporate body it has been my misfortune to stand before. The main item on the agenda was "what to do next." We talked around in circles—Hamburg, Paris and Copenhagen were all discussed as possible production venues but with little enthusiasm. I think Guccione was in two minds about pulling the plug on the production, when a diversion occurred which lightened the atmosphere somewhat. Guccione's bodyguard arrived with a large rectangular object wrapped in brown paper. Guccione nodded, the paper was ripped off and an exquisite Toulouse-Lautrec oil painting revealed. Guccione looked at it and smirked with pride. But whether he did so because of its beauty or its bargain price of $2 million I couldn't say. Either way, the picture was stacked on the floor with its back to us along with several rows of what I guessed to be similar masterpieces—another "collectable" investment for the Penthouse Empire. This put Guccione in a good mood and he decreed that we should try Italy. Accordingly, I was shipped off to look for locations that would pass for England's green and pleasant land within fifty kilometres of Rome—where hopefully a hounded-into-exile film-maker could get on with his work, free from persecution by his fellow countrymen. There would be no restrictions there, I reasoned—some of Italy's greatest screen actors had been picked off the streets.

I started the search with the help of my assistant Vicki Wallis, who had worked as a producer in her own right and had taken the place of Towers ever since the time he had fallen out of favour with *Penthouse* and disappeared without trace during my sojourn in New York. One day he was there, the next he was gone—yet ironically enough, the project had been his idea in the first place. I'd been disappointed by Towers before over the stillborn Beethoven saga—so I pressed on with Vicki more determined than ever to prove that *Moll* could be made in Italy. Ten days later, having found all our locations by driving around in dusty circles from morning to night, we went on the town to celebrate—and who should we bump into but the Unknown with a *Penthouse* minder and the sinister baggy-eyed henchman I remembered from my last visit. But there was only time for a brief hello before she was whisked away into the darkness. A sinking feeling of déjà-vu swept over me as I recalled the Tinto Brass situation. Then I had a sudden, intuitive flash of the Unknown costumed as Moll Flanders in front of the cameras with Guccione in the director's chair—a prophecy that was destined to come to pass a few months later at Cinecittà.

The very next day a new producer arrived without warning. The fact that he was not on the shortlist of producers I'd put forward to Guccione on the departure of Towers caused me some concern, as did the fact that he was taken care of by one of the *Penthouse* lawyers. And I didn't need to see his tomahawk to know he was the acting hatchet-man. I nicknamed him Geronimo. The first thing Geronimo did was brutally dispatch Vicki, who had worked like a slave organising the entire operation from the very start.

Worse followed as Geronimo added three more scalps to his belt when my cameraman, editor and costume designer (all standing by in England) all bit the dust. This was Ten Little Indians with a vengeance, but still I pressed on—because I believed in the project and, given the chance, felt I could still make it work. Then came the Roman holidays when the city goes to the seaside for a couple of months. So I took the opportunity of returning to England to see if I could find some military uniforms which were unobtainable in Italy. While I was still looking around the costume houses Guccione summoned me to his London *Penthouse* suite. Bad news! Equity, who may have got wind of our Italian job, had announced that the International Federation of Actors had placed a world ban on the film. There was nowhere left. I suggested flying to the moon. How else could we escape these monsters? A union getting a fair deal for their members is one thing, but when it becomes dictatorial and repressive that's something else. If a person has a genuine talent it should be cherished and fostered, not strangled at birth. There's not a so-called "civilised" country on earth where this could have happened except Great Britain— thank God the writing is on the wall at last.

Over an improvised pasta supper, Guccione seemed more concerned with the script (which I discovered later he was re-writing in secret) rather than the fact that our start date was rapidly approaching and that with the exception of the Unknown we had not a single actor under contract and little prospect of getting one. In a game between grand masters it was stalemate. So long as Guccione never made a move to hire any actors then Equity could never ban them. And I was the unlucky pawn in their game.

After the meal, while Guccione listened nostalgically to Geronimo and the bodyguard reminisce about gang warfare on the streets of New York, I had a few stolen words with the Unknown. She was a mess. Her hair was dank and she was pale and unwashed. Worst of all was the running scab on her lip. I could see her dreams of stardom were turning to ashes. She wondered how long this commedia dell'arte would last and whispered that she had grown tired of endless spaghetti and longed for a plate of good old fish and chips. Before she could say more Guccione joined us, but I saw the despair in her eyes and got the message. I never saw her again. God knows what became of her. The next time I saw Guccione was in court a year after he had closed down the production and laid the blame on my shoulders. He claimed the *Moll Flanders* folly had cost him over a million dollars. He wanted his money back—from me. If I had him typecast as an outlaw, then perhaps he had me cast as the "fall guy"—on the film that never was.

Naturally, I saw myself as the aggrieved party and looked round for a good lawyer to plead my case. And that's where Richard Golub came in. Earlier I mentioned that in his youth Richard had seen a film starring Robert Taylor called *Party Girl* which inspired him to take up the law. *Jailhouse Rock* launched him on a parallel career as a pop singer. And if at forty Richard doesn't have the voice to match Elvis Presley's, he certainly has the edge on Robert Taylor when it comes to winning over a jury. Taylor used a pocket watch supposedly given to him by his dying father, as a symbol of rectitude and a promise not to waste the jury's time. Richard uses the same gimmick to mesmerise *his* audience. But that's just for starters. He also wears a different suit every day of the trial (from a selection of eighty or so from Savile Row at "two grand a time") to bewitch, bother and bewilder the jury—men and women alike. After one trial a female juror who'd had the pants charmed off her rang him for a date. I don't have to tell you which way she voted.

Cuff links are also an important item in Richard's armoury and are chosen with care—they too, it seems, have hypnotic powers, as do every one of his forty-five pairs of handmade shoes. But there was one woman in the court room who did not fall under Richard's spell—the judge. I had the feeling that she had the feeling she was being upstaged.

I donned judicial robes myself to play a small part in the music-video I was making for Richard as part-payment of his $Fee,eee! His life's ambition is to write and perform a rock 'n' roll song cycle called *Trial of the Century*. I'd seen a pop video of his first opus—an autobiographical extravaganza called "He Is My Lawyer" which featured Richard and the jury jiving on the judge's desk. "Dancing for Justice" was his Opus 2 and, appropriately enough, was to be shot mostly on location in Sing Sing! The song itself follows the exploits of a bible-punching, gospel-singing lawyer who steals into prison in a laundry van (in movies they always steal *out* of prison in a laundry van) and exhorts the convicts to:

> *Dance right through those prison gates*
> *Coz now you're gonna celebrate—*
> *Once you're on the outside*
> *You're never gonna be re-tried*

In this he's abetted by an unlikely partner:

> *Hear the warden on his guitar*
> *He's playing like a superstar*

For all that, Sing Sing was no joke. The sense of latent violence I always feel in New York (the Bronx reminds me of the Gaza Strip) is laid bare a few miles upstate on the Hudson. Killers of all colours pace their cells in the manner of (that old cliché) caged beasts, or stick their heads through the narrow feeding grills, or hold up mirrors through the bars to beam out hatred which is even more unnerving than the constant abuse they howl at the same time. The cages are in blocks three storeys high and the effect is of many small cages inside one enormous cage; it's more frightening than the Gorilla House at the Zoo, and if you don't think gorillas are dangerous, remind me to tell you someday of the white gorilla that tried to kill me in Barcelona.

Sing Sing stinks of violence enough to make you vomit, and just because the lifers have radios and TVs in their cages, don't be fooled into thinking these are human beings. If you put a radio or a TV in the cage of a Bengal tiger at the zoo you wouldn't join it to watch *Dallas,* would you? The day before we arrived, there had been a vicious killing. A referee who'd ridiculed an argumentative spectator during a game of basketball was stabbed in the throat for his impudence. What had the killer to lose? He was a murderer two times over and was never coming out anyway. But out of a thousand or so inmates there were a few trusties and these were allowed to be extras and dance out of the prison gates. But what the camera didn't show was another set of prison gates beyond the first and wardens in watch-towers armed with machine-guns. If my hair hadn't been white before I went in, it would certainly have been white when I came out. It was a great relief when I flew back to England a free man. Yes, the jury, thanks to my rock-star lawyer, found the plaintiff's charge not proven, and I was not dispossessed, as would have been the case if the verdict had gone against me. Once home in my humble cottage I realised for the first time in my life just what it means to have a roof over one's head. And it was great to be back with the family again. Be it ever so humble, there's no place like home.

"If it wasn't for you Americans," I said to Viv, lifting her in the air with difficulty, "I'd lead a very dull life indeed!"

After a few days spent counting our blessings, we travelled south to see Dad, who was being cared for in a hospital for the elderly in the New Forest. He'd been discharged from Southampton General, coped at home alone for a while, then suffered another fall which had put him back inside again. He was quite chirpy and could manage, with the help of a frame, a daily constitutional through the wards of rotting carcasses (coughing, sneezing, wheezing, farting, shitting, weeping, cursing and praying— for death, most of them). While Molly engrossed herself in an aquarium of tropical fish—the liveliest things in the ward—we chit-chatted away until we ran out of chat, when we all fell silent at once. It was time to go.

"Have you seen the grave lately?" said Dad as I got up.

"Why no, we've only just got here, but I was planning to drop by on the way home. I'm dying to see the headstone."

"I mean Marion's grave," he said. I shook my head.

Viv looked at me quizzically. A patient in a nearby bed began moaning; a bell rang. Sudden activity. The nurses pushed a screen around the bed. A hidden cry of pain was followed by whispering. Molly took Viv's hand. We kissed Dad goodbye, promised to write and crept out.

"Marion was my cousin," I said as we got in the car. "We used to take a wreath to her grave every Christmas when I lived at home but I haven't been there for years."

"Then you're about due for another visit, Christmas or not," said Viv. "Is it far?"

"Less than a mile," I said. "That must be why he mentioned it."

We swung out of the hospital car park and past a small parade of shops. I stopped and bought a few bunches of spring flowers and a packet of Mars bars, Marion's favourite chocolate bar. Biting into one as we drove up the Lyndhurst Road to the cemetery, I realised that the delicious layer of sticky toffee which in Marion's day used to comprise at least half the bar had shrunk to a sliver. But Marion's days had been expansive and generous days, as I well remember.

"How old was she when she died?" asked Viv as we approached a Victorian spire rising through the trees.

"I'm not sure," I said. "She died in 1940, I think, and was a year or so younger than me, so she must have been about twelve; strange, I can't remember exactly. Anyway, the headstone will tell us."

Skirting the church, we passed through a screen of yews to the cemetery, which was situated on a small hill, protected by a circle of oaks doubled up in mourning. Everything seemed very familiar. I walked straight up to the place where I thought the grave to be, stopped and looked about me.

"What's the matter?" said Viv.

"It *was* here, I'm sure," I said, glancing uneasily around. It had gone. I searched the immediate area—nothing but a few chipped flowerpots on uneven, overgrown mounds and some neglected graves that had lost their headstones. Perhaps one was Marion's. No, the names on the marble surrounds, cracked and discoloured though they were, could still be deciphered. Only the dates—early Forties—confirmed that I was standing in the right area. So what had happened?

"How long since you were last here?" said Viv.

"Not that long ago," I said, doing some mental arithmetic. "My God, it's nearly forty years." We both laughed. Molly, contemplating a fallen angel, wondered what was up. Between us we examined every grave in the churchyard in case she'd been moved for some reason. But there was no sign of her. It was as if she'd never been. It was a disturbing thought. Standing by a recent grave at the bottom of a hill, I looked up to the place I remembered standing all those Christmases ago. There were hundreds of graves in between. Nearly half a century rose before me, measured in tombstones. I walked back up the hill, watching graves marble-bright gradually fade, become untended, unkempt and neglected as I climbed through the intervening years. Graves that were only fifty years old looked as if they'd been there for centuries. Lettering was obscured, headstones had crumbled, lichen had eaten away names, brambles had pulled down holy crosses, solid memorials had themselves become entombed, voracious weeds had devoured entire families. But of Marion's grave there was no sign at all. Molly helped us scatter the flowers, hoping one would fall above her.

"Perhaps she's been disinterred," said Viv, offering solace.

"It's possible," I said. "Her parents eventually divorced, but we can't ask them, they're dead."

"Can we go back to the hotel now?" asked Molly hopefully.

"Soon," I said. "But first we're going to a place called Highcliffe, where there's a lovely beach to play on. Now there's no need to pull a face, it's on the way."

"Is that where you used to play with Cousin Marion?" asked Viv.

"And the rest of them," I said, defensively, "in the Thirties, during our bungalow phase."

"And I bet you're going to show us every one," said Viv.

"No, just ours."

"Maybe that's gone too," said Viv. "How many years since you were there?"

"About the same. We stopped going there after Marion died."

As we drove along the coast past Milford-on-Sea with the Isle of Wight a smudge in the background, I told Viv all I could remember about Highcliffe, which wasn't a great deal considering I'd been a frequent visitor for nearly a decade.

The village itself was no great shakes, being little more than a row of shops either side of the Bournemouth Road. The cliffs, which are not particularly high, lie a few hundred yards to the south and sweep down to a long beach which curves away to Hurst Castle to the east and Christ-church to the west. At the place of public access a creek and wooded glen, beloved of smugglers in the past, splits the cliff in two. And if you paddled across the creek to the eastern shore and climbed through haw-thorns and brambles for a few minutes you arrived on a clifftop giving onto a lush meadow. It was there in that forty-acre field on Naish's farm that the Russells and families like them rented their bungalows. There must have been fifty or so, all built in the Twenties. They had a rustic seasidy sort of look and framed three sides of the meadow, leaving a wide sea of grass sweeping towards the open clifftops and the English Channel beyond.

The bungalows were of various designs, most of them built in wood with a verandah and plenty of glass, though there were a few railway carriage conversions here and there. White was the predominant colour, with green running a close second, though creosote, warm and faded, was also in evidence. Pine trees in the back gardens provided a decorative wind-break, while the neat front lawns were ideal for croquet or badminton or simply sunbathing.

Sundays weren't called Sundays for nothing in those days. It was less than an hour's run from Southampton, so until the dreaded boat trips began to impinge Highcliffe was our weekend haven for six months of the year. I remember it raining only once in the entire decade and that was the day I was scared nearly out of my skin by a giant adder in the glen. I wondered at the time if that was the reason most of the bungalows were built a foot above the ground. More likely because of mice, I suppose.

I used to sleep in a bunk, I remember, and more often than not was awakened by the neighing of Poo, the carthorse, outside the garden gate. Hanging a large wooden diamond, red side out, on a hook by the front door at night was as reliable as setting an alarm clock. It signalled that the privy out back in the pines was in need of emptying by Dan, Dan, the lavatory man. Poo's neigh announced the arrival of his slurry wagon and that she wanted her sugar knob. So it was jump into my shorts, run into the kitchen and grab a few lumps before Dan had turned our diamond around to show the green side and gee'd up Poo and her load down the grassy track to the next stop.

Breakfasts must have been unmemorable, for the next thing I recall is sitting on the verandah with a *Rainbow* comic, waiting for Marion. Some days she came, some days she didn't, there was no telling. On the days that she didn't I'd be dragged off by Mum to go shopping in the village. Otherwise I'd look across the field of buttercups towards her bungalow on the far side. And the days when there was one extra buttercup among all the millions was the day she was coming. Slowly her golden head would rise above the wild flowers as she made her way tantalizingly slowly towards "RayKen." By the time she came through the garden gate my head would be buried in the *Rainbow* and I'd act surprised to see her. Then, when I could pretend no longer, I'd shout out, "Marion's here!" Somehow it broke the ice even if no one responded.

We'd known each other since we were toddlers, but I could never see her without my heart racing. There was an aura about her I would have been content to bask in for all of my days. As it is, I'm thankful for the few I spent with her at Highcliffe and on those family runs through the forest in convoy. Marion was pretty but not beautiful. At ten she had a boyish figure, bobbed blond hair, an oval, lightly freckled face with radiant blue eyes and a smile that I could never place until I saw it years later on Botticelli's Primavera. And she was blessed with an ease of movement and gesture that seemed almost choreographed in its perfection. Everyone loved her, adults and children alike. A complete stranger catching one of her fleeting expressions said it was as if she had heard the angels singing.

But for all that she was no goody-goody and had a subtle sense of fun. She was also quite a tomboy and when it came to "dares" had the courage of a lion. She'd always climb one branch higher up the tree than me and would wrestle closer and closer to the edge of the cliff until I called "pax." Then she'd laugh and roll on her tummy and look out to sea where the Isle of Wight loomed through the heat haze like a phantom dreadnought. And when she turned to catch my eye she would often catch my thoughts too—and know that I was thirsty, or whatever. Then we'd take the cliffside path meandering between brambles heavy with blackberries, which we'd sample in passing; and on through hanging gardens of honeysuckle which we'd rub ourselves in, pretending to be bumble bees collecting pollen; then on through glowing gorse bushes and cabbage-white butterflies and into her bungalow for a glass of iced lemonade.

Then, from a hammock on the verandah, we'd watch her parents strolling through the buttercups with carrier bags full of shopping they'd bought from Farmer Naish in his lofty barn at the entrance to the field. They were an attractive couple, Rob and Doris. People said he was a second Cary Grant. She was a plump redhead from the North Country, with dimples and what in those days was called a "knowing" smile. They always seemed as if they were sharing a private joke at the expense of Rob's elder brothers, who were more serious types. Rob wasn't above jumping up in a restaurant, on finding a fly in his soup, and singing at the top of his voice, in a fine baritone, "Ah, sweet mystery of life, at last I've found you," something the others would never have dreamed of doing, even if they'd been able.

Unceremoniously Doris would tip us out of the hammock; eleven o'clock—time for the family swim. Marion and I raced across the meadow and down the steps cut in the baked clay of the cliff to a gangway from an ocean liner conveniently placed at a more precipitous section. Then as I went patter, patter, patter down the steps she'd slide down the well-worn handrail to be first down the last gentle slope of compacted clay and onto the beach. Cheers from the other members of the family, including Mac in a pirate hat and Mum and Dad already there, with little Raymond sleeping under a Japanese sunshade. Rob and Doris, last as usual, would saunter towards us, arms around each other's waist. Those not already in their bathing costumes changed behind gaily coloured towels held up by giggling Mums and then it was a procession of knobbly knees hobbling over the pebbles to the water's edge. I was trying to swim in an old patched-up inner-tube—hopeless. It was too big for me by far, so Dad took me on his back and Rob followed suit with Marion. Both brothers were good swimmers and it was wonderful being a couple of water nymphs riding side by side on sea horses. It could have gone on forever as far as I was concerned, but the adults had our safety in mind and swam us ashore just in time to get the last couple of peaches Auntie Ethel was handing out.

She was the smartest of the women, with beach pyjamas and an expensive-looking silk scarf over her bosom. She had the biggest of the beach hats, too, though she wore too much rouge and always had a fag dangling from her lips. The rest of the women wore sailor's caps and shorts and divided skirts; it was all very colourful and quite noisy and noisier still when Beryl bit on a wasp feasting on her peach. A wasp sting on the tongue is not a pretty sight. Beryl—an Olive Oyl with freckles—screamed her head off. Everything about her face was swollen—her eyes, her mouth, and her tongue which seemed to be swelling to the size of a peach itself. Nobody knew what to do. It was horrible. She just had to put up with it as I had to years later at Pangbourne when a wasp got up my trouser leg a moment before the Commander's morning inspection.

We'd all been jumping on a wasps' nest by the parade ground so I shouldn't have been surprised.

"Have you a fever, Russell?" said the Commander, pausing to look at my flushed face and sweaty brow in his tour of the ranks.

"No, sir."

"Then put him on a charge for looking scruffy," he said to the Cadet Captain at his side.

"Aye, aye, sir," barked the CC.

Question: Why the hell didn't I tell him the bugger had just stung me on the knob, probably mistaking it for a maggot?

Answer: Because we were taught not to flinch under fire, because the thin red line must always hold, and because I feared six cuts from the Commander far more than a wasp sting.

"Atten . . . shun!" shouted the Cadet Captain.

"Ouch!" The bugger stung again.

"Left turn."

"Ouch!"

"Quick march; left, right, left, right."

"Ouch! ouch! ouch! ouch!"

"Squad halt. Dismiss."

I walked crabwise to the heads (lavatories) in slow motion so as not to disturb the invader, then once inside gently lowered my bags. There it was, trying to suck pollen. Flick! It sailed away over the urinals to seek fresh pastures. I surveyed the damage.

"Wanking off again, H.K.I.?" said Cadet Leader Ditton-Windsor, peering over the partition. Guiltily I stopped fingering my cock.

"Caught you red-handed. My God! Have you got the clap?"

"No, a wasp got in my bags and . . ."

"Report to Matron at once," he said, cracking up.

"But . . . I don't . . ." The prospect filled me with dread.

"Report to Matron, at once," he said, turning mean. "That's an order, H.K.I.!"

Orders is orders. A few minutes later I was standing at attention before Matron with my cock in her hand. It was a delicious and novel sensation, having cream massaged into my private parts, and the thrill was in no wise diminished by the fact that Matron was seventy-six years old. I wasn't to get so lucky again for years.

Poor Beryl. She must have been in agony as they half-carried her away, screaming fit to die. Even so, I was surprised when she was absent from tea parade. You had to be near death to miss that. Every so often the great matriarch Grandma Russell decreed that the family would take tea in the village; that wasn't an invitation but a command. And the only individual to be permanently excused was the head of the family himself. If you remember Charles Winninger, the fat old song-and-dance man of a dozen MGM musicals, then in Grandpa Russell you had a good stand-in. Winninger always had a twinkle in his eye and a way with the ladies, even late in life, and I suspect Grandpa, sporting a straw hat and cane, was much the same.

Grandma was as gracious as he was gregarious and wore her wheelchair with the aplomb with which Queen Alexandra used to wear her hats. It was a privilege to push all eighteen stone of her along the Royal Mile-and-a-half from door to door and this was undertaken in order of seniority. The three brothers in grey flannels and Aertex shirts came first and negotiated the field and the gravel track wending between the glen and fields of Farmer Naish's staring cattle. Then, as we turned onto the pavement of the Bournemouth Road, it was the turn of the women, dressed in chiffon and Ascot hats, with Mum bringing up the rear because she had once worked in a shop. So had Auntie Dolly, but in our family the handling of pastries was considered a superior occupation to the handling of winceyette. But Mum felt otherwise and always said, "Working in 'aberdashery beats working in a pessary any day."

When we reached the final straight the kids took it in turn two by two, Mac and Gloria, Roy and Derek, me and Marion. She was in a Kate Greenaway bonnet, I seem to remember, while I was got up as a cross between Gainsborough's Blue Boy and Little Lord Fauntleroy.

The tea itself has paled to insignificance beside the importance of the royal progress, which was a slow-mo pageant, Grandma as regal as Britannia herself, acknowledging those of her subjects who felt impelled to raise their hats or drop a curtsey, but completely impervious to the backfiring upstarts passing by the simple delights of Highcliffe for the bogus sophistication of Bournemouth—the poor man's Monte Carlo. (It didn't even have a casino.)

By the time we'd pushed her back we were ready for a second and more substantial tea. But just as the parade was about to be dismissed, signalling a return to quarters, something happened which caused us kids to break ranks and abandon Grandma to the grown-ups. First it was a drone then a coughing and then a spluttering coming from no-where and getting closer—then it hopped over a bungalow near the edge of the cliff and glided down to a bumpy landing among the buttercups. We raced over to get a closer look. It was a two-seater bi-plane, probably a Tiger Moth. We stood around and gawped. Most of us had never been that close to an aircraft before, and of course none of us had ever flown in one. The pilot and navigator with their goggles, leather helmets and jodhpurs were my comic heroes, Biggles and Co., come to life.

I, for once, was part of the adventure.

"Hello, chaps. The old kite's acting up a bit; spot of bother with the carburettor. Anybody got a tool kit?"

We stared at them open-mouthed, then Marion ran across to the uncles, who were making heavy weather with the wheelchair in the long grass. Whatever needed fixing didn't take long, and all too soon we were all running along in the slipstream as the plane taxied across the field towards the cliff-edge. Some of us screamed as it left the ground and dropped out of sight, then cheered as it climbed into view again, banked over the bungalows and, with a final wave from the pilot, vanished from sight. The buzz of excitement in the air lasted the rest of the day, past high tea and salad cream, past croquet and way past bedtime when, for once, Marion and I weren't packed off early to bed in our separate bungalows but were allowed to sit up with our parents on the verandah of RayKen by the light of a paraffin lamp in the twilight and join in a singsong around the portable gramophone:

> Sing, brothers, and sing, sisters,
> We're all leaving today
> And we'll all go riding on a rainbow
> To a new land far away . . .

The song was lively and carefree and caught the happy optimism of the day. Its upbeat tempo was irresistible and when Rob and Doris jumped up and started dancing during the instrumental I wasn't over-surprised when Mum and Dad joined in a moment later. And they didn't stop, either, when the vocal continued:

Children dancing through fields of daisies
With rosebuds in their hair.

Neither Marion nor I were into that sort of carry-on. Though it was clear, as the guttering flame of the oil lamp danced in her eyes, that the antics of the grown-ups amused her, I wasn't prepared for what happened next. Still smiling, she shifted her gaze to meet mine and did something I'd never seen her do before, something that both ravished and shocked me—she winked!

When I arrived with Viv and Molly on the scene of that memorable evening fifty years back in time, the bungalow had gone—along with a sizeable chunk of the cliff, eaten away by erosion. Water pipes stuck out of the soil, pointing to the spot in mid-air where it had once stood. And where there had been an open field there was now a field of chicken coops (of the human variety). There seemed to be hundreds of them, packed together as tight as they could get them and still leave space for the car and a couple of deckchairs.

"What do you make of that?" I said to Viv.

"A lot of people got lucky," she said.

"What do you mean?"

"Well, in your day it seems that only a privileged few got to enjoy the buttercups," she said. "Now there are fewer buttercups but a lot more people can afford to enjoy them."

"I see no buttercups," I said.

"You know what I mean," she said. "In the Thirties, while you were knee-deep in flowers, there must have been lots of kids back in Southampton who only had streets to play in."

"They had the Common," I said.

"But you had the beach and the sea."

"They had the Lido," I said. "It was only threepence to go in."

"I guess that was quite a lot of money in those days."

"Well, I can tell you, if this place had looked as it does now we'd have stayed in Southampton, too," I said. "Fancy driving thirty miles to sit in a deckchair and look at a lot of chicken coops. People will take anything these days. It's the age of the battery hen. The egg looks the same but the quality is degraded, it's downright poisonous in some cases. And it's not as if they come here for the beach; it's almost deserted. Look, they're queuing up for the cafeteria. That's new too."

"Then let's go and have a cup of tea," said Viv.

"I think you'll find it's for residents only," I said. "We're actually trespassing."

We left the field with its revving cars and ghettoblasters and started back down the glen.

"What do you think the family would make of it now?" said Viv with a grin.

"Heaven knows," I said.

"How did Marion die?" asked Viv. "I've been meaning to ask you."

"She died here," I said. Viv took Molly's hand as we scrambled down the narrow path, catching on to trees and bushes for support. "I remember it was a Sunday," I began. "We were out for a run in the car. The war had been on for more than a year and although fuel was rationed we were still able to manage an occasional outing to the Kettle Teahouse for an ersatz cream tea. The road home took us through Cadnam, a tiny hamlet on the edge of the forest, where Marion and her parents had gone to live in a modest bungalow. It was only a few miles from Southampton, where Rob still worked in the shop, but a good deal safer. I didn't see much of Marion anymore so I was glad when Dad agreed to drop in for a minute to say hello.

"As we pulled up outside the gate we were all dismayed to see Uncle Rob standing at the front door—crying. I'd never seen a grown man cry before and was dumbfounded. So was everyone else. Rob had been the personification of happiness ever since we'd known him. We couldn't take it in. We just stared at him. And he stared back with an anguish which the sight of Raymond and I only seemed to aggravate. Finally he broke away and went indoors and Dad said, 'You'd better wait here,' and followed him inside. I don't remember how long he was gone or what Mum said or whether she said anything at all, but I do remember little Ray reciting a monotonous litany over and over again: 'Netley Marsh via Cadnam, Woodlands and Brooke.' He was obsessed at the time with playing buses on his tricycle in the garden and that was his favourite route.

"Eventually Dad returned and drove off. No one dared speak. We all knew he had something terrible to tell us and were waiting for him to choose the moment when he could manage it without choking on his words.

"Finally a sort of peace manifested itself in the car and he said simply, 'Marion was killed this afternoon at Highcliffe. Apparently the military have mined the cliffs and glen in case of invasion . . . and it seems she left the public footpath and went through the barbed wire for some reason.

Rob was cleaning the car when he heard the explosion.' Mum began sobbing and Raymond said 'Poor Marion.'"

"And what did you say?" asked Viv quietly.

"I don't remember," I said. "But I suddenly noticed that it had grown dark."

16 We'll All Go Riding on a Rainbow...

My son Rupert, named after the well-dressed bear, was born in Carlisle City Hospital while I was staging *Madame Butterfly* (yet again) thousands of miles away on the other side of the world. With memories of our tractor journey to the maternity ward still fresh in my mind, even after seven years, I must admit I'd thought twice about leaving Viv alone in deepest Borrowdale in the heart of winter. But we were broke again, really broke—down to drinking Asti Spumante—and anyway we'd taken ample precautions for her safety, or so we thought. An old chum was all set to jet across from New York and local friends promised to stand by their phones during the run-up—and then the little beggar arrived two weeks early. However, there was no snow and no problem—apart from the name. I rather fancied Felix, after the famous cartoon cat that kept on walking, but Viv beat me to the Registry Office so I had to be content with second best, though now he is four he couldn't possibly be anything but a Rupert.

The second thing I did on arriving home a month later was to christen Rupert in champagne—a bottle we'd saved especially for the occasion. Apart from that, there was nothing to celebrate. No film, no opera, no development deal. I began to think of changing agents yet again when a minor miracle occurred: Elton John got in touch and asked if I'd consider directing a pop-promo for him. I suppose I should have been rather affronted, played hard to get before condescending to say "yes," but I'd never been very good at hiding my enthusiasm and there was always the chance he'd ring off and go elsewhere. Besides, I'd enjoyed working with Elton as the Pinball Wizard on *Tommy*, and putting pictures to music has always been a pleasure, like being paid to screw your favourite film star. So without hesitation I said "yes." The tape arrived by dispatch rider around midnight. We played it at once without having to put up with that awful dog, Fartacus, giving his opinion.

Fartacus was no longer with us. Gone but not forgotten. On our return from America we'd collected him from our friend, patted him on the head and dumped him back in his smelly basket under the kitchen sink. We left him as a brindle pup, we found him grown into a laughing hyena, amused by our efforts to incarcerate him. At the first opportunity he was out of the gate and off up the road. We immediately gave chase but he outran us and, scattering sheep to left and right, was over the hills and far away. A phone call from our friend four miles away in Keswick an hour later informed us that Fartacus was back in the fold he now considered home. We went to collect him and question this alienation of affection. The reason was plain to see; it was lying next to Fartacus on a rug by the fire—a handsome young male Staffordshire bull terrier by the name of Clive. During our absence, our friend had grown fond of the breed and in anticipation of missing Fartacus when we returned to reclaim him had bought a Staffordshire of his own. The result, we learned, was love at first sight. Without further ado we whipped Fartacus back home under lock and key, only letting him out on collar and lead to do the necessary.

Time heals all things, Viv and I told each other as the dog moped about the house with tears in his eyes. Before long there was a scream—from Molly, who came running downstairs in alarm.

"Fartacus has jumped out of the window," she wailed. Was it a suicide bid or the great escape? We ran to the door in time to see the sheep scattering and the dog heading for Keswick at a fast limp.

This time our friend returned the dog, full of apologies and advice—which we didn't take. The idea of taking the animal to a psychiatrist was ludicrous—even if it could lie on the couch on its back. Instead we gave it the run of the garden—on a long leash. Five minutes later there was a ferocious squealing of brakes. Molly! we thought, and ran to the front gate. There was the dog in the middle of the road, lying on his back, paws in the air, with an irate motorist standing over him shaking a fist. It really was a suicide bid this time; the dog had got through the fence, dragging his leash behind him, and lain down in the middle of the road to end it all. But the fact that it was the *middle* of the road made me suspicious. If he'd really wanted to call it quits he'd have gone to one side. Still, it was enough for us to throw in the towel. He'd won. We drove him to Keswick, booted him into the house of his poofter boyfriend and said good riddance. But at heart we felt guilty. We began to reproach ourselves, thinking we'd been too harsh on him—booting him downstairs when he spilt my wine—OK, I shouldn't have left it on the floor—and booting him out of the house when he howled at Bruckner. Well, he was gone, gone for good. At least we could listen to Elton's tape of "Nikita" in peace, or so we thought—till Rupert started letting rip.

Despite Rupert's opinion, we were excited by what we heard and in no time had knocked out a scenario about Elton falling for a Soviet lady soldier guarding the Berlin Wall. Actually I got my genders mixed up: Nikita, I realised later, was a man's name. Maybe the reason Elton contacted me in the first place was because he wanted something controversial. Perhaps he had *Women in Love* in mind and expected me to suggest nude wrestling in the snow with Arnold Schwarzenegger.

Whatever the case, he was pleased with the result and it led to more of the same from men as diverse as Dave Clark and Andrew Lloyd Webber. But to paraphrase a line from D. H. Lawrence's *The Rainbow*, "I felt like a bird blown out of its own latitude." When it came to directing pop-promos, I was a barn owl amongst young hawks. The sort of insight I brought to bear on the lyrics was uncalled for. Nobody listened to the words anyway. All they wanted was a glorification of the performer and trendy images to go with the beat. Censorship was an added hazard. In one Cliff Richard promo I showed a burning globe bouncing across a children's playground. As a metaphor for the world on fire, it was considered unsuitable for the teenyboppers by the BBC and was cut on transmission. This soporific view of life is reflected in our televised newscasts, where death always wears a shroud. If the media dared to show the mutilated face of motorway madness, for instance, there might be fewer victims.

In Elton John's "Cry to Heaven," I saw an allegory of the troubles in Northern Ireland and how the innocent are always the victims. Accordingly, I showed how a toddler (played by Rupert, who'd been walking for only a week) attracted by flashing lights, colourful machines, noise and clamour, runs onto a busy building site thinking it's all a game and wanting to join in. His black beret lying in the gutter says it all. That too was censored by the BBC. When the record companies saw what was happening they dropped me like a hot condom, so there I was, a pariah in the wilderness again—no, that's a bad metaphor. I could never say that of the Lake District. It's a veritable earthly paradise to be enjoyed with Eve and the kids. So now I had time on my hands, why not make a music video of my own, celebrating life in the Lakes? Coincidentally a BBC producer had the same idea and offered me their resources. The result was a half-hour programme called *Song of the Lakes*, which in the process of scripting inevitably became more ambitious in its aims. During the programme I rowed, walked, scrambled and climbed over my favourite bits and pieces, illustrating their musical associations with a string of classical and pop videos. "You're the Tops" was accompanied by pictures of the family, sometimes with Fartacus, sometimes without, larking about on lake and fell, which were culled from a vast collection of snapshots we had taken over the years and throughout the seasons. To Vivaldi's *Four Seasons* I showed Lakeland activities throughout the year, including rock climbing, pony trekking, harvesting, shooting the rapids, wind-surfing and hunting—on foot with honest farmers chasing the fox over crag and quarry and the Blencathra Pack in full cry so that sheep may safely graze. We also filmed Molly and her classmates from the Borrowdale School doing a country dance in the shadow of Eagle Crag.

Getting even more personal, with "Mountain Greenery," we shot a satire on life in the big outdoors with Molly and Rupert camping it up as a couple of hikers on holiday: torrential rain, collapsing tents and tons of beans. We didn't forget the religious angle, either, with Giles Swain's "Cry" filling the air with mystic voices as Viv and her friends in bare feet and caftans practised meditation at Castlerigg Stone Circle, where the ancients used to worship the sun before they found Skiddaw to be more reliable. The finale of the programme was a driver's eye view of a hairy car ride over hill and dale with the family, to Elgar's *Introduction and Allegro*, filmed as if we were travelling at one hundred and fifty miles an hour, which just about matched the thrill of the music. All good clean fun and a little pocket money besides, for being a good boy, and probably as close as I'll ever get to that impossible dream of a Lakeland film to

Mahler's *Song of the Earth*. I'd always imagined the last movement, *"Der Abschied"* ("The Farewell") taking place across the road from the cottage on the shores of Derwentwater, with the smoke from a funeral pyre drifting across the lake at dusk and rising over Skiddaw to catch the last blissful rays of the sun. That's the way I'd like to go myself, but I'm told it's against the law unless you happen to be a sikh. I'm thinking of becoming a convert.

Dad was buried as he lived (in common with ninety per cent of the population), lapsed C of E. It was a nice service, arranged by my brother, who was outside the church tapping his foot in time with the vicar when my contingent rolled up at 11:29 (the service was due to start at 11:30), having had a bit of a knees-up in the local boozer. The kids (Batch 1), who'd followed me down from London in James's car, were in the same suits they'd worn for Mum's funeral, which seemed to telescope events, while Aunt Moo mourned, as was her habit, for her dear departed Jack, pausing as I approached with two lager and limes to mutter a single word to June . . . "Marion." I pulled up short and followed their gaze . . . to Viv. I wonder . . . ?

At 11:25 we bolted our drinks and made for the door. Five minutes later, with heads bowed, we were soberly following the coffin into the church. The vicar, who apparently knew Dad, said some nice things about his interest in sailing and *Songs of Praise*—a Sunday TV programme of hymns which he used to accompany on the recorder. This was news to me, as was the fact that he was to be buried with Mum; I'd always understood his wish was to be cremated. As we walked to the grave, Ray explained that Dad had left the disposal of the remains to his discretion and that was that. At first I found the prospect of this underground reunion a touch macabre, but quickly concluded that it was probably for the best. Maybe Dad thought so too, but being too proud to admit it had left the decision open to Raymond, correctly predicting the outcome. In some respects his passing hadn't been all that different from Mum's. Having both outlived their usefulness and capacity to enjoy life, they had rotted away in State institutions with visits from relatives and friends growing ever more infrequent. And they were both robbed; Mum of her slippers and Dad of a favourite jacket and a small sum of money put aside for a few creature comforts at the hospital shop. If Mum experienced any discomfort she bore it stoically whereas Dad, being of sound mind, took it badly and fretted his life away.

Stealing that old jacket was the equivalent of stealing baby's blanket. It was his lifeline and when it was taken away he simply let go. I saw him a few days before his death when it was clear that he was sinking, with no desire to save himself. I wonder if in his last hours he fully appreciated the similarity of their predicament and regretted not replacing Mum's slippers. Anyway, they've ended up as they started out—in bed together!

Whatever happens, I don't want to be buried and if I am fortunate enough to have my funeral pyre on the shores of Derwentwater I hope Viv will not feel compelled to commit suttee, as I need her to scatter my ashes over Skiddaw. I know just what a splendid conflagration it would be because I was fortunate enough to stage a spectacular dress rehearsal—which I owe in no small measure to the vision of Virgin.

It came about when ICM's London office phoned to ask if I'd be interested in meeting Al Clark of Virgin Vision to discuss the possibility of my directing a script based on the night of horror when Mary Shelley created Frankenstein. I couldn't believe it: here was an Englishman asking me to make an English film on an English subject by an English writer for an English company in England! The age of miracles was not dead. What was up? Where had Mr. Clark been all his life? Didn't he know I was unbankable, unemployable and unlovable? It seems not. When he offered me the job I said, "Yes, yes, yes," before he found out. And in next to no time I was commissioning Farmer Weir to build a big funeral pyre on the spot I'd always had in mind, except that, contrary to my expectations, the corpse going up in smoke was that of the poet Shelley to the music of Thomas Dolby. Oh well, beggars can't be choosers. The film was called *Gothic* and was set in Switzerland in a lonely villa on the shores of Lake Leman. Not being able to afford a trip to the Alps, we settled for the Lake District and one of the worst summers on record. In a sequence that was scripted as an idyllic lakeside breakfast scene, the assistant director could barely be heard above the roaring gale as he screamed through his loud hailer for the prop men to "nail down the swiss rolls." As for the hills—they were obscured by mist. We might as well have been filming in Hyde Park on the banks of the Serpentine. It would have been a lot cheaper.

Despite the hazards, it was great to be making a feature film in England again after nearly a decade. Even so, my career could have ended then and there because *Gothic* did not do well over here at the box office—for a variety of reasons, including a monumental piece of miscasting and a hysterical pace. I'd fallen into the trap which has been the undoing of many an unsuspecting pop-video director—punchy, roller-coaster cutting, short sequences and nonstop action. All this is fine for the time it takes to play a hit single but becomes well nigh unbearable over a hundred minutes or so. But luckily for me the film was distributed in America by an up and coming company called Vestron—and they did well out of it, particularly with video sales. So well that they signed me up for a three-picture deal, which at the time of writing I have just completed. The films were *Salome's Last Dance*, a fantasy based on Oscar Wilde's play, an update of Bram Stoker's *The Lair of the White Worm* and *The Rainbow* by D. H. Lawrence.

And now my pen is poised to sign a second three-picture deal with Vestron. What occurred to bring about this miraculous change in my fortunes? Well, it's due to Vestron in general and my number one fan in the world in particular. No, not Denny, but Dan Ireland, who used to own a cinema in Seattle and is a film buff from way back, giving festivals of my films long before anyone thought I was dead. He now works for Vestron as Vice-President in Charge of Acquisitions and was instrumental in getting me involved with the company, which encourages me to write my own scripts and direct the films of my choice. In return I give them value for money. The only snag is the size of the budgets, which are so tight it hurts. They are geared to predicted box-office receipts and the number of video units the company estimates it can sell and make a healthy profit besides. Obviously they didn't expect *The Rainbow* to do big business because they gave me less money than the BBC had to make their TV version. I think they'd written it off as an art-house movie. Now it's finished they think differently: maybe they see a pot of gold at the end of *The Rainbow*, who knows?

Because we are almost up to date and this book is overdue at the publisher's and because Viv says *The Rainbow* is the best film I've ever made and because I may not have conveyed the vicissitudes of film-making sufficiently, I'd like to explain in detail how, after many frustrations, I finally came to make a British Picture I could really be proud of.

Once our relationship had been established I sent Vestron a trunk-load of old scripts for their consideration. *Dracula* and *The Rainbow* (in that order) had most appeal, but I was already making one Bram Stoker subject for them featuring a pair of fangs and didn't relish the idea of sharpening them up for a repeat performance. Fortunately, there was a problem with the rights for *Dracula* so I got a qualified go-ahead on the D. H. Lawrence script. My producer, Ronaldo Vasconcellos, budgeted the script and came up with a figure in the region of £2.5 million which, considering the scale of the production, was a real bargain.

"Too much," said Vestron, "lose half a million." That was ridiculous. Ronaldo, who had been our accountant on *Gothic* and *Salome*, had given them an extremely accurate and very economical figure. We begged and pleaded but Vestron wouldn't budge, so I cut out a costly dream sequence, lost a big crowd scene in a mining village and decided to shoot the film within the London area and not in the Lake District as originally planned, thus economising greatly on hotel expenses. I also moved two night exteriors involving a large crowd indoors, which meant I could shoot these scenes in the day, thus cutting out heavy overtime rates. And I managed this, I think, without compromising the film in any way. In fact I was able to turn my limitations to advantage—the script became tighter and the drama more personalised.

Having accomplished a major miracle in losing a fifth of our budget, we had to satisfy another major requirement of our financiers: NAMES. Vestron had always wanted Glenda Jackson to play Anna Brangwen—a devoted mother with five growing kids. Glenda herself was keen enough, but unfortunately she was appearing in a play on Broadway which was about to transfer to London. So at Vestron's request we tried for Julie Christie who, after considering our script over a long weekend, turned us down because the part was too small. (A part's as big as you make it, lady.)

Meanwhile, we were burning the midnight oil in our efforts to dredge up names for the rest of the cast. There was Uncle Henry, mine-owner and the black sheep of the family, tough, cynical and sexy. I wanted David Hemmings for the part. He'd turned in a stunning performance as Samuel Coleridge in *The Rime of the Ancient Mariner* and Vestron would have bought him, I'm sure, if they'd seen it, but the programme was virtually banned in America when it was turned down for screening on *Masterpiece Theatre*. So Vestron, not having seen David in anything since *Blow-Up*, took a look at a recent photograph and said, "Blow up is right! Forget it." That was unfortunate as I'd already offered and David had already accepted the job. Oh dear! Red faces all round.

Anton Skrebensky, the dashing young hero of the piece, was another problem. So far as Vestron were concerned, no English actor in his early twenties means a thing in America—which, after all, is where most of their money is made. Of course there was the Hollywood Brat Pack but they won't even look at a script for anything less than a million. I lost no sleep over that because few of them, in my opinion, were equipped to play an aristocratic young English officer of the Edwardian era. Despite this, Vestron put forward the name of a young American actor called Doug Savant and asked me to take a look at his performance in a film on general release. I did. He was fine as a crooked American police lieutenant but in no way could I see him as a dashing lieutenant in the Royal Engineers, so I said, "Sorry, but..." Vestron were less than pleased, but didn't twist my arm.

Then there was Winifred Inger, a bi-sexual athletics mistress. I suggested Amanda Donohoe.

"No, she's not a name," said Vestron.

"She will be when *The Lair of the White Worm* is released," I retorted. No dice! They wanted an American name. Who would you cast in that

Catherine Oxenberg (left) and Sammi Davis in *The Lair of the White Worm*.

role if you wanted a name? Kelly McGillis? Mariel Hemingway? Theresa Russell? All American and all box-office names, according to Vestron. We asked them all. They all read the script and liked it. They all said "No," the part was too small. That was the trouble. There was only one star role in the entire film and that was already filled by a little-known English girl, Sammi Davis. Everything and everyone revolved around Ursula Brangwen, our teenage heroine poised on the brink of womanhood with a passionate desire to break free of family ties and seek fulfilment outside the confines of turn-of-the-century Derbyshire. Vestron knew there was no star name, either in America or anywhere else, exactly right for the part, but having admired Sammi's performance in *The Lair* they made an exception in her case. So at least we agreed on one thing!

Now, while all these frustrating negotiations were going on during the eight-week pre-production period, I was also engaged in publicity for

Salome's Last Dance which was about to be released, and in post-production for *The Lair*; that is, editing, looping, music recording and dubbing. Fortunately Vestron were pleased with *Salome* and even more enthusiastic about *The Lair*, having recently approved my final cut. And they were particularly happy that I had gone along with the Name of their choice—Catherine Oxenberg of *Dynasty* fame. Yes, so far as video sales go, she *is* a name. Unfortunately there was no role for her in *The Rainbow* where most of the females go nude at one time or another. That Catherine would not go nude I knew from our experience on *The Lair*, when she insisted on being offered up for human sacrifice to a giant worm in her underwear. Being of royal lineage, she opted for Harrods' silk, but as we were a low-budget movie she had to be content with Marks & Spencer's cotton—and very fetching she was too.

But so far as *The Rainbow* was concerned, we still had no Name and our start date was getting closer and closer. Vestron were getting jumpy. "No name, no movie," they threatened. Things were getting serious, but not desperate—yet! The fact that we had a "star" production team must have appeased them somewhat. Three of our "key" members had contributed greatly to the success of *Women in Love* over twenty years previously and had enhanced their reputations ever since. They were Billy Williams, director of photography, Luciana Arrighi, production and costume designer, and Ian Whittaker, art director. With that nucleus I felt confident I could pull off the gamble of producing something special in spite of our budget restrictions.

Another link with the previous film was Christopher Gable, who had played one of the young lovers fated to drown on his wedding day. Now he was mature enough to play Will Brangwen, Ursula's possessive father. Vestron had reluctantly agreed to this casting only when Charles Dance and Jeremy Irons had said "No." Names! Names! Names! We had found all the locations and signed up all our crew, so there was no pushing the start date back, but with only ten days to go we had no Anna, no Winifred and no Uncle Henry, Alan Bates having turned down the part because Uncle Henry had no major scenes (I think he is in for a surprise). Meanwhile Vestron were going ape!

Then Viv had a brainwave—or was it a brainstorm?

"How about Elton John for Uncle Henry?"

"How about Benny Hill?" I replied. Then I thought again. Maybe it wasn't as crazy as it seemed. Viv had always been a big fan of Elton's and, having made his acquaintance on our pop-promos, knew he was looking for the right vehicle for his screen début as a serious actor. She reminded me of this and pointed out that it would keep Vestron happy—

for a while, at least. Well, it was a long shot but it was certainly worth a couple of phone calls.

Forty-eight hours later I was speaking to Elton in Dallas who was expecting a script to arrive at any minute. Already he'd got hold of a copy of the novel and was enthusiastic. Two days later he said "Yes" and so did Glenda, who was suddenly available following the last-minute cancellation of her play in London. So from having no names and the possibility of no movie, we had two major stars and a green light to go, go, go. Now the pressure was off I was able to have the Winifred of my choice, Amanda Donohoe. Things were hotting up. The last few days were hectic. There were auditions to find a three-year-old Ursula, production meetings, make-up tests at our base in Pinewood Studios, music recordings at St. Giles' Church, Cripplegate, and a read-through of the script by the cast, who were getting together for the first time to sort out their accents.

The day before the start of principal photography was Sunday, July 3rd—my birthday. I spent the morning working on this book in my kingsize bed, accompanied as is often the case by a lady. Quite a few can turn me on if I'm in the mood, particularly Lulu and Scheherazade. But I think Salome gets me going most of all, especially in a great performance such as that of Paul Paray and the Detroit Symphony. And while on the subject of music, I almost forgot to mention a TV special for Melvyn Bragg's *South Bank Show* that I managed to squeeze in between the features.

The programme was called *Ken Russell's ABC of British Music* and was a lighthearted look at a serious subject in which I went through the musical alphabet in a variety of costumes, introducing the best of British from the Avant Garde to *Zadok the Priest*. In K for Kitsch, for example, I donned Eastern garb and flew around on a magic carpet playing Ketelby's *In a Persian Market* on a hookah. In D for Dames I wore a US sailor suit and in a setting reminiscent of *South Pacific* sang "There is nothing like a dame . . . Janet Baker" as an intro to an aria from the great lady herself. And for Q and R I appeared on the balcony of Buckingham Palace with Her Majesty to introduce Queen and Rock 'n' Roll. Get the idea? Naturally it narked the jeremiahs who feel "serious music," as they call it, should be announced in a tone of voice usually reserved for national disasters. My point was that all music is meant to be enjoyed, so why not set the mood accordingly? That's not to say the programme was frivolous; it was a golden opportunity to extol neglected geniuses like Frank Bridge and Arnold Bax, and bulldoze a few sacred cows at the same time. Of course there was outrage from the musical establishment, but there was also dancing in the streets among the two million viewers when I showed kids bopping to Benjamin Britten in the Royal Albert Hall.

The phone went and Salome was put on pause as Viv rang in from Borrowdale to wish me many happy returns and apologise for not being with me to blow out the candles. She was busy and I was glad—for her sake. We'd written the script together years ago and now I was going into battle without her. There was nothing left for her to do but wish me luck and get on with her new career—which had nothing to do with movies. Having become an authority on Lakeland gardens, Viv had tried unsuccessfully to interest TV companies in giving her a programme showing off these remarkable creations in a new light. But she was too glamorous for the conventional image of a gardening pundit and her ideas too offbeat, so they turned her down. But someone who has jousted with the boulders of Borrowdale and come off the victor doesn't give in that easily. So she dreamed up an alternative solution—she'd photograph these "Dream Gardens of Cumbria" and find herself a publisher—just like that. Coming from someone who had trouble mastering an Instamatic it was quite a dream. It's lucky she didn't ask my advice or I'd have said forget it. But I'd have reckoned without taking into account that old American pioneering spirit and the true grit—Cumbrian grit—under her nails. She set about it in the same way she had tackled the garden—while my back was turned. She drove the length and breadth of the county photographing everything that caught her eye, from landscaped stately homes to council-house windowboxes and, unlike the general run of garden photographers, she included the people responsible; lords and ladies, lorry drivers, old age pensioners and even the handicapped. Wisely, she curbed her desire to show me the results of her efforts until she'd mastered the art, which amazingly only took a few short months. To say I was impressed with what I saw is an understatement. I was knocked sideways and, to tell the truth, a little resentful. What right had this amateur who knew nothing of the rudiments of her craft to show me a side of the place I'd known for twenty years but which I'd never SEEN? But her startling achievement was really brought home to me when she invited me to open an exhibition of her work at the Brewery Arts Centre in Kendal. Previously I'd only seen her photographs in 35-mm slide form and they had been impressive enough, but when I walked into that gallery and saw them as enlarged prints tears came to my eyes. These were no ordinary pictures—they had a unique perception. The colours were colours no one had photographed before and the people, whether they were post masters or station masters, farmers or housewives, old or young, all had that vivid, tenacious, triumphant look of a race that has fought an impossible battle and triumphed.

Some of them were as weathered as the granite fells which towered above them, glowering enviously at the bit of Eden they'd created from the stony ground. Wordsworth would have been rendered speechless and as I'm no Wordsworth I'll shut up. Not surprisingly, Viv found herself a publisher and was presently engaged in writing short essays to accompany her pictures. In one of them she thanked me for nagging her about the composition of her snapshots. Viv invariably took a camera on our walks, and we always analysed her efforts when they came back from the chemist. So it was a proud moment when I realised that after ten years my one and only pupil had finally graduated from the Ken Russell Film School.

Wishing me a happy birthday again and promising to pop down as soon as possible, Viv rang off to get the kids' lunch and meet her deadline.

I was about to release the pause button and set Salome dancing again when the toot of a car horn reminded me that the rest of the kids were coming to lunch with *me*, if caviar, cake and a magnum of champagne can be called lunch. Blowing out the sixty-one candles left me without much breath for all the "oohs" and "aahs" necessary in opening the presents, but somehow or other I survived the ordeal. Then we exchanged news and views when I learned that Haig Pit had just passed over. Shirley was heartbroken, they said, but fortunately was able to seek consolation in the arms of her paramour—who much to my surprise turned out to be one of my old assistant directors. I was happy for her. At least it was a step up from her previous conquest, even if a small one. The kids themselves were fine: Alex had given up impersonating Judy Garland in dockland pubs and similar essays into pop culture and joined the Ministry of Agriculture. Victoria was making a name for herself as a stylist on pop promos and commercials. James was doing nicely inventing and marketing video gizmos while Toby, we heard, was having hi-jinks starring in Kung Fu movies in Hong Kong. Everything in the garden was lovely. One would never have thought we were on the brink of war—until a sharp ring on the doorbell sounded the alarm. It was my Colonel-in-Chief, Ronaldo Vasconcellos, with his Staff Officers reporting for duty. The kids trooped out as they marched in. We assembled in the Ops Room for our final briefing before the Big Push.

Making a film is like fighting a war: in one you shoot the enemy, in the other you shoot the script. That's why we have a Unit Nurse among our ranks. We had fifty-one days to achieve our objective—the completion of the shooting schedule. For the last time we review our forces and go over our plan of campaign. As the general leading the attack I am assisted by five Field Officers. Several Big Guns will support my advance, including the lighting cameraman and his crew and the production designer with her team of camouflage experts. As an army marches on its stomach, we have a Catering Corps equipped to feed one hundred and fifty men, five times a day. And as war costs money there is a Pay Corps stationed at GHQ supervised by the C-in-C himself. Assisted by the General Staff he is responsible for organising the campaign so that progress on all fronts is maintained as planned; and should we suffer a setback he must devise a strategy to recapture lost ground. To this end we operate a highly efficient Transport Unit consisting of some twenty-eight vehicles, including a ten-ton generator, a make-up bus, wardrobe van, field kitchen, honey wagon (WC), mobile office, caravans, camera cars, limousines and trucks of every description for lights, props, paint, scaffolding, timber and every tool imaginable, from a Stanley knife to a spraygun. Then there are the specialist auxiliary units, including editing technicians, sound engineers, fencing instructors, animal-handlers, musicians, special-effects men, swimming instructors and sherpas. Oh, I nearly forgot our drill sergeant (choreography), propaganda (publicity) and our lone sniper (stills man). Close on a hundred troops all ready to go into action. And that does not include our entertainment troupe waiting behind the lines to be mobilised and drafted to the front with their greasepaint and false eyelashes—our Soldiers in Skirts.

The C-in-C closes his briefcase and addresses his men: "Gentlemen, synchronise your watches... it is D-Day + 0005 hours. This morning at 0830 hours we join battle with our arch enemy—TIME! God be with you!"

17 ...To a New Land Far Away

July 4: *Independence Day*—
the day the Americans threw
off their English oppressors. I
have the strangest feeling that
if it had never happened I
wouldn't be starting *The Rainbow* today. Three cheers for the
American Revolution. (I nearly
wrote "the American Inva-
sion.")

"Arrived at the location—
an old school in West London—at 0800 hrs. and by
0930 was actually behind the
camera shooting Take 1. Considering it was our first day
and the set had to be lit and

Amanda Donohoe (left) and Sammi Davis in *The Rainbow*.

dressed, it was quite an achievement. For logistical reasons we started bang in the middle of the script on Ursula's first day as replacement teacher, and considering she was thrown in at the deep end Sammi Davis did remarkably well. Billy's lighting was very moody and conveyed well the sense of impending doom. Can't get over how few lamps he's using. He's also much faster than he was twenty years ago in *Women in Love*, but then so am I—not bad for a couple of youngsters in their sixties. I think we're going to make a good team, and although I get the feeling he'd prefer to operate the camera, I must know what I'm getting on film and the only way I'll be sure of that is by looking through the viewfinder myself as I shoot the scene.

"Having completed our schedule for the day, we wrap at 6:30 and share in a Day-Glo rainbow birthday cake, courtesy of the Catering Unit, washed down with N.V. champagne. Very pleased with everyone's efforts—there's a buzz of commitment in the air which augurs well for the future. Bed at 10:30 with a cup of Ovaltine. Slept like a baby."

———

It was the last time I did, but you don't want to hear about that—at least not in forty-nine more variations on the first entry. Unless it is written with publication in mind, a diary is nothing more than an *aide-mémoire* where a word or a sentence can trigger off in the mind of the writer a whole series of vivid events that might otherwise have been forgotten. But to the rest of the world who are denied access to the author's memory it can make pretty dull reading. So I'm going to spare you the agony of a daily record of events, which needs a specialised knowledge of the problems and personalities concerned. Instead I'll streamline the next couple of months into a couple of pages.

Those of you who have seen the finished film must be wondering whatever happened to Elton John. Good question! To tell the truth, I was worried about him from the very start. One always has to worry about megastars for they have different priorities from the rest of us poor mortals, and unless these are properly addressed they can explode with the force of a super nova. Not only do their eggs have to be flown in from California, or wherever—that's understandable in Salmonella Britain today—but the baby's formula has to be flown in as well, together with the nanny's favourite mineral water, the minder's Kentucky mash whiskey and the groupies' Twinkies. And if our quarantine laws weren't so strict there would be pets and pet food as well. Now I'm not suggesting Elton would have gone to these lengths. In fact we were told that he was willing to forgo his usual luxury mobile home and slum it in your basic caravan as used by the likes of Glenda Jackson. And while Colonel Vasconcellos spent precious time in conference with Elton's lawyers, accountants and advisers, the concerns of the star himself were also made known—usually when I was directing a difficult scene, though I'm sure he was unaware of this. But his concerns were my concerns and had to be addressed right away, for as yet he hadn't even had a costume fitting and the time was fast approaching when he was due to play his first scene with Sammi Davis as young Ursula in which he stretches out his arms to her and says, "Why, it's our Lazarus! Young Billy said you were dead. Come and give your Uncle Henry a kiss."

Those lines were going through my head as I read the message the runner had just pushed under my nose in the middle of a manmade rainstorm. Before the rain washed away the ink I was able to read: "Elton wonders if he should have a voice coach and acting lessons."

"A *voice* coach! What's he been singing with all these years?" I shouted at the runner as water from the hoses poured down my neck. "The answer is 'No' and he'll get all the acting lessons he needs from me."

The next message was passed up to me on the crane while I was about to go for a complicated tracking shot. This time Elton was worried about his spectacles. Having seen something of his legendary collection, so was I.

"Tell him to wear contacts," I shouted down to the runner. Shit! The sun had gone in.

The next interruption came just as I was about to shoot Glenda bathing the baby.

"Ken, sir, please, sir," said the runner, "Elton's people say that in no circumstances will he sing. Is that agreed?"

"That's a pity," I said. "I was hoping he'd sing 'Get me to the church on time' in the wedding scene." The crew laughed dutifully, whereupon the baby yelled lustily—completely drowning Glenda's dialogue. Shit!

The next query coincided with a catastrophe! Sammi had just fallen off her bicycle, landed on her face, knocked herself out and been rushed to hospital. I was standing in the middle of a field hanging on to a mobile telephone waiting for the doctor's verdict when the runner sprinted up and looked at me in fear and trembling.

"It had better be important," I said menacingly.

"Yes, sir, it is," he said with knees knocking.

"Mr. Elton John would like to know what he should do about his hair."

"What hair?" I exploded.

The runner stuttered on. "He wants to know if he should be fitted for a wig or bring a selection of his own. He also wants . . ."

I never heard what else he wanted. I only heard fragments of a diagnosis over the crackling phone . . . "discoloration of the cheek, bruising of the eye, delayed shock . . ." I was in a state of shock myself when I rang off. Fuck the wig! What were we going to do tomorrow? Sammi was in every scene but one.

We shot it the next day, the scene in which Lieutenant Anton Skrebensky, Ursula's handsome lover, looks through her scrapbook while flirting with her young sister, Gudrun. Paul McGann was playing the soldier and it was his first day on the set, where tempers were running high. Contrary to my instructions, the make-up man had sent him on with a false moustache. A row ensued with the production designer, who had countermanded my order.

"Every young officer of his class wore a moustache in those days," she protested. "It was *de rigueur* and the shape is historically accurate."

"Then it's a pity his uniform isn't historically accurate, too," I retorted.

"He looks like a sack of potatoes. That tunic should be as tight as a condom. Kindly remove that ridiculous moustache."

Tears streaming down his face, the make-up man obeyed. This was his third attempt. He'd made one for Christopher Gable, who was playing Ursula's father, and another for the sadistic schoolmaster.

"Looks as if he's got a dead rat up his nose," was my comment on that one. What's the use of a pukka moustache if the lens picks up the net attaching it to the face? Poor Paul! Small wonder his performance seemed unrelaxed that morning.

It was a bad day and got worse when Sammi dropped in at lunchtime to show us the damage. Her face was ashen—except for her yellow cheek and black eye. I kicked myself for being beastly to the make-up man— he had suddenly become the most important member of the unit. The Colonel and I commiserated with Sammi, who characteristically made light of her troubles and apologised for the inconvenience she was causing. We kissed her better and sent her home. As usual the Colonel joined me for lunch in my caravan—there's always some new drama to digest along with the cod, Chablis and chips.

"What are we going to do now, Ken?" he asked in his fruity Brazilian accent as I filled his glass.

"There's nothing for it . . . we'll simply have to recast, that's all." I waited for him to laugh—it was meant to be a joke, a ridiculous answer to a difficult situation. But the Colonel didn't laugh, or even smile. In fact he looked more serious than ever.

"Funny you should say that," he said finally. Now he had *me* worried.

"What do you mean?" I said, taking a long draught of wine to steady my nerves.

"We've just lost Elton."

"Not another bloody air disaster?" I said.

"No, no, nothing like that," laughed the Colonel. "He wants us to release him from his contract."

"But he can't do this to us!" I blurted out. "Give him anything he wants, give him his luxury mobile home, give him a voice coach, give him acting lessons, let him wear his weird glasses and those funny boots, anything he wants."

"He wants out, Ken," the Colonel persisted. "He has emotional problems."

"Don't we all," I countered. The Colonel nodded and recharged my glass as we sat in silence considering the awful implications.

"Spotted dick or rhubarb fool?" said the runner, sticking his head around the door.

"Piss off," I said. "And don't come back . . . ever!"

He disappeared with the speed of light.

"What now?" asked the Colonel.

"You tell me. There's no one left we haven't tried."

"How about Alan Bates?" suggested the Colonel.

"I thought he turned us down."

"He did but I happen to know there's someone on the unit who is a very good friend of his and feels he could be talked into reconsidering."

"Friend? What friend? Get hold of her quick."

"It's a him." The Colonel pronounced it "heem."

"Oh, who?"

"The make-up man. He has Alan's private number."

"I don't believe it! This man is definitely the most important person on the unit. And to think I treated him like shit."

"You may have to eat it," said the Colonel.

"It's been my staple diet for years," I said, calling to mind my nights on the phone with Kathleen Turner. I don't know which was harder, chatting up the make-up man or chatting up Alan. In the event Alan said "No," though he took two valuable days to say it. Then we tried Oliver Reed, but he was still busy duelling with Cardinal Richelieu on the umpteenth remake of *The Four Musketeers*. Then we tried another recommendation of Vestron's, but he was too drunk to answer the phone.

"Looks as if I'll have to play it myself," I told the Colonel. Beneath his swarthy complexion he paled, remembering my guest appearance in *Salome's Last Dance*.

"Why don't we try David Hemmings again?" he said, in desperation.

"We've pissed him about something horrible," I said, "and why should Vestron change their mind?"

"Time is on our side," said the Colonel, "and it's time for us to get lucky."

"It's worth a phone call," I said, without much hope.

The Colonel tracked David Hemmings down to a remote holiday island in the Bahamas. Hemmings was out sailing. We bit our nails till he got back to his hotel. After a long, long pause he promised to consider it—if we upped his fee. That night we phoned Vestron. Time was running out. We'd be into Uncle Henry's scene in four days' time. Vestron hummed and hawed. They had two options: say "yes" or close down the production till we found someone else. That was unthinkable. They said "yes."

We phoned Hemmings to say that Vestron had agreed to his participation and the increased fee.

"Throw in a couple of first-class air fares and it's a deal," said David. Four days later he was coiffed and costumed and stretching out his arms to Ursula saying, "Why, it's our Lazarus. Young Billy said you were dead. Come and give your Uncle Henry a kiss." What confidence, what aplomb, what charm, what cynicism—what a sunburn! I crossed myself and thanked Skiddaw. As Dr. Pangloss put it in *Candide*: "Everything's for the best in this best of all possible worlds."

Sammi's shiner improved slowly—even under several applications of make-up it was always just visible, to my eyes at any rate. Her nose was the next problem—the poor girl was just accident-prone. That mishap occurred in a vintage open tourer when a gust of wind blew Amanda Donohoe's boater into Sammi's face, giving her "one on the hooter," as the runner put it. At the time the small cut was hardly discernible—a quick dab of iodine, a smudge of make-up and we were ready for Take 2. No one took it very seriously at the time and that was the trouble. The next day the cut on her nose was weeping, the day after it was festering, the following day it was swelling. And to think I'd had another row with the make-up man the day before for using lip gloss. Nevertheless he did everything in his power to help us—short of plastic surgery—but it all took valuable time. And from being the fastest lighting man around, Billy became the slowest, or so it seemed to me. Lighting the set took no time at all; lighting the nose took forever as he struggled valiantly to hide the growing bump in shadows. Still, we were winning. We were on schedule and the nose could only get better. But we reckoned without the ministrations of the Unit Nurse, who early one morning tried a new kind of treatment—squeezing the offending bump between her fingernails till Sammi's eyes ran and the bump grew bigger and bigger. Well, I said, there are always casualties when a unit goes into battle. I didn't realise the nurse would be the first fatality. After all, Sammi was only classified as walking wounded. We called a doctor.

Poor Sammi—the strain was beginning to tell. She began to lose weight, which was hardly surprising: up at 5:30 every morning, an hour's drive to work, an hour in hair, an hour in make-up, working some days till eight or nine at night and then an hour's drive home to get supper. No wonder she was falling asleep over her food. We moved her into a hotel near the location to cut down her travelling time. And there she generally got a good night's sleep, despite the fact that my kids were staying there—Molly and Rupert that is, with their friend, Alan Edmundson— all under the wing of a young lass from Borrowdale called Jackie.

Viv was very grateful to me for taking them off her hands so that she could get on and finish her book. But that wasn't the reason they were appearing in the film as members of the Brangwen family. We already had Ursula and Gudrun, so I volunteered to supply the rest. The alternative was a selection of kids from a London stage school with London accents which would have clashed with the northern accents of the rest of the cast. So I decided to risk our lot, who were all new to the game. My worst fear was that the ten-year-olds—Molly and Alan—would forget their lines and that the three-year-old Rupert would look at the camera— he can be a contrary little blighter at times.

The big day finally arrived and so did they, wearing their costumes— sailor suits for the boys and a smock for Molly—like ordinary, everyday clothes. They were happy and eager so I took them through the scene in which the older kids knock and knock on Ursula's bedroom door, en- treating her to come down to Sunday lunch while Rupert stands by the banister shouting "Urtler, Urtler." Lost in romantic daydreams, Ursula ignores them until Molly says, "And there's a soldier downstairs with Uncle Henry." That does it. Ursula unlocks the door and chases them all downstairs, scooping up Rupert on the way.

Well, Molly and Alan were fine: word-perfect, good accents, good acting, good everything, but nothing I could do from bribing him with chocolate mini-rolls to threatening to take away his blanket—which goes everywhere with him—would induce Rupert to say "Urtler, Urtler." Per- haps he considered it baby talk, I don't know.

"Well, if you won't say 'Urtler,' what *will* you say?" I asked him in desperation. The whole unit waited while he rested his cheek against the blanket, sucked his thumb and considered . . . finally removing the thumb to say . . . "Twinkle."

"Forget it," I said. "It doesn't matter, so long as you remember to *look at the camera.*" Brilliant child psychology, that! He never looked at the camera once, for take after take. In fact he almost went too far the other way, spinning his head through 180 degrees whenever he caught sight of the lens so that I was always shooting on the back of his head. But after a few more takes he began to ignore the camera and treat it all as a game, even improvising dialogue with Sammi, who was nearly on her knees, poor dear. He'd really taken a shine to her and got to chatting her up between takes.

"Would you like to sleep with me, Twinkle?" he said. "I've got two beds in my room." Poor Sammi was speechless, whether from surprise or exhaustion I couldn't say.

From then on the kids went from strength to strength—Molly and Alan took direction well and Rupert didn't take it at all. But the fact that none of the cast ever knew how Rupert was going to behave during a take kept them on their toes and ready to improvise at the drop of a hat—or even the tilt of a hat, come to that. Look out for the scene in the church where the family are grouped around the font discussing a piece of carving and Rupert, in his screen daddy's arms, keeps tipping Gudrun's hat over her eyes while she struggles to deliver her lines (which aren't particularly inspired at that moment, as it happens). Her giggle as she tries to adjust her hat and fight off the attentions of Rupert is a welcome diversion and gives the scene a sense of immediacy it might otherwise have lacked.

At first I thought the kids might get homesick, but they were too busy for that and saw me every day of the week, including Sunday, our one day off. Then while Alan went out with his Mum for the day, Molly and Rupert were driven up to the flat, along with Jackie. By the time they'd seen all the railway highlights from Buster Keaton's *The General*—Rupert's favourite video—I was ready to dish up the Sunday roast I'd been slaving over a hot stove with all morning. And what a relief it was not to be eating and talking shop, though there was mention of "Twinkle," who Rupert had bumped into at 2 A.M. in the car park as a result of a fire alarm which had emptied the hotel. Seeing Sammi standing there in her nightie, he wanted her to hold him in her arms whereupon he was heard to say, "I never want to grow up. I just want my willie to grow."

Next to women, our three-and-a-half-year-old Casanova loves trains, so the next stop was the Steam Museum at Didcot. The big treat there was riding up and down on the grand old "Duke of York," one of the biggest engines ever made in this country. There's only a mile of track

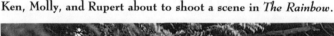

Ken, Molly, and Rupert about to shoot a scene in *The Rainbow.*

but that means you get more rides. Rupert, in his train-driver's cap, was allowed to blow his whistle and set the seventy-ton piece of gleaming Pop Art in motion—plus its three Pullman coaches in mellow brown and yellow. Then there were shunting goods trains and swivelling tank engines on turntables, and steam billowing everywhere in proud, monochromatic clouds—better than any fairground and all captured on film and video by hordes of enthusiasts in Monty Python rainwear, crouching under platforms, peering around signal boxes and standing on tiptoe on rusting cattle trucks to get the best angle—even Rupert was aiming his disposable 35-mm Kodak "Fling" at the action.

And now it's Molly's turn. Back at the hotel to the sound of a tinny cassette player she showed me her dance routine for the title role of *Scrooge*, the musical she's rehearsing for the end-of-term show at her school in Windermere. I was disappointed—she was deadpan and mechanical. And she wasn't using the top hat and cane to much effect either, so we got down to work. As usual Rupert tried to get in on the act with the result that he accidentally got whacked with the cane. Tears and Coca-Cola, Thomas the Tank Engine and bed. Then back to Molly. Half an hour later her personality was shining through and she was "selling" the number like an old pro. Liza Minnelli move over! Windermere watch out!

I kissed Molly goodnight and said goodbye. The kids were going back home tomorrow. The gamble had paid off. I'd miss them. I went home to bed feeling relaxed and carefree. Thinking of the film twenty-four hours a day, seven days a week can drive you nuts.

At dawn we renewed the attack, sometimes advancing, sometimes retreating, always consolidating our position. The troops took a tremendous hammering, some began to crack, there was insubordination—but that was quickly dealt with. And through it all we kept on shooting with only one rest day in seven. There were citations and medals for heroism—the most illustrious going to Sammi for outstanding valour on the field of battle and courage in the face of danger. Despite her wounds and battle fatigue, she continued to soldier on and was a wonderful example to the men. She braved rapids, swam rivers, survived a stampede of wild horses and ran naked to a dangerous mountain peak; she destroyed a field of lettuce singlehanded, was sexually assaulted by a soldier, chased by a miner, endured torrential rain and being screwed against a tree in the spray of a raging waterfall—which brings us back full circle to the mighty Lodore Falls where I filmed *Dante's Inferno* twenty years ago, when I first stumbled across this demi-paradise.

You can still see the tripod marks on the rocks, but instead of Oliver Reed as Rossetti about to hurl himself into the deluge of a pre-Raphaelite nightmare, we have Anton Skrebensky bonking Ursula Brangwen in the buff. The noise of the falls is deafening—you can't hear yourself speak. All thoughts of directorial subtleties are drowned out but Sammi, with the camera playing on her face, which is visible over Anton's shoulder, wants to know how to grade her orgasm. So I tell her to go for it in four stages and we turn over with someone holding the loud hailer to my lips:

"One"—she grinds away. I'm operating the camera and she's acting really turned on. "Two"—her face begins to glow. "Three"—she's beginning to smile... "Four"—ecstasy. Perfection in each of the seven takes. If only it were always that easy, I thought, especially against a tree with twenty-five people looking on.

"You've won an 'enemy,'" Viv seemed to say as I walked through the cottage door that evening.

"I've got all the enemies I need," I said, giving her a kiss.

"That waterfall's made you 'mutton,'" (Mutt and Jeff—deaf) she laughed. "I said E.M.M.Y."

"What's that then?"

"America's most prestigious TV award."

"I know that, but what does it stand for?"

"Search me," she said, "but the ABC of British Music has been voted best programme in the Performing Arts category."

"Must be my impersonation of Gene Kelly in the South Pacific number."

"You mean On the Town," she said. "More likely your impersonation of Benny Hill impersonating Chairman Mao in the 'Chinese Temple Garden' number."

"Well, let's crack open a bottle of champagne and drink to your compatriots. It's nice to know they appreciate our musicians as well as our movies."

"Oh, so suddenly we're cultured," she laughed.

After we'd finished toasting the great American public, we drank to the artists in the show who'd really won the award and given us many moments and, in some cases, many years of happiness into the bargain. "Albert Hall, the Beatles and Benjamin Britten, Noël Coward and Frederick Delius..." I said, downing a glass and holding it out for a refill. "...And Elgar, Kathleen Ferrier, Gilbert and Sullivan and Gustav Holst, Elton John and John Ireland..."

"Before you get to the end of the alphabet and run out of booze," interrupted Viv, "you'd better save a drop for *Dan* Ireland. He just rang to say it's OK by Vestron to dedicate the film to Marion."

My euphoria immediately gave way to something more subdued. I also realised just how tired I felt. Scrambling up the slippery rocks to the waterfall plus the energy expended on the actors and crew when the work had been demanding and the tension high had left me gratified but a little shaky.

Relaxing in the bath with a glass of champagne induced a pleasant mood of introspective calm. I would place the dedication after the end title so that it would read: "The Rainbow" . . . fade out . . . fade in "In Memory of Marion Russell" . . . fade to black. I was very grateful to Vestron for agreeing to my request. Marion was typical of many free spirits who never survived childhood or fulfilled their potential—all budding Ursulas full of *joie de vivre* and daring. I'm sure Marion would have forsaken the easy way and gone for the rainbow, whatever the risks. Maybe she saw one on the other side of the wire and went for it, who knows? She'd had a marked influence on my life but then, as I thought about it, so had many others—good and bad alike. There were dozens of them, hundreds, thousands, known and unknown. And in the end it seems that even your foes as well as your friends are doing you a favour.

Through the window I could see Viv photographing Molly in our magic garden. As Molly posed among the sweet williams and Mexican orange blossom, the last rays of the sun sinking behind Catbells suddenly caught her fuzzy rainbow-coloured wig and dazzled every flower in the garden. An unforgettable moment and all the more precious when I remember that Guccione might have denied it me.

Then Rupert burst in with his toys and broke my reverie. A minute later he was sharing my big slate bath and demanding to know why trains don't float. He's definitely worth a divorce—most of the time, anyway.

It's the next day and before I know it I'm going over the top with the troops for the final assault. Our objective is the old swimming hole just across the road from the cottage, but due to the light we first have to shoot up Helm Crag, towering a thousand feet above Grasmere village over twelve miles away. And this operation can only be achieved in one day by airlifting key personnel off the crag and ferrying them over the mountains to the Borrowdale valley.

By 1330 hours we have achieved our first objective and are airborne: hair-raising stuff—flying back at two hundred miles an hour, twenty feet above the ground. All my beloved lakes, hills, tarns, valleys, waterfalls that I've seen a thousand times before now experienced all anew.

Wow! What a trip! As the 'copter soars and banks over our cottage, Skiddaw is dancing. And there, running across the meadow, are Viv, Molly and Rupert, all waving, waving up at me. We've made it, made our own rainbow, and soon we'd be riding on it to a new land far away where I'd been offered another movie by our good friends at Vestron. And we're all laughing, laughing at the madness of it all. If no one will give you one—find your own rainbow. All you have to do is go for it! That was the message I read on their upturned faces as we flew towards each other.

18

And Then What...?

And that's where the story should have ended. And in some movies it would have. But life is not like a movie, especially a movie of mine, where the protagonists continue to slip on banana skins till the last reel when they usually make their final exit with a few shreds of dignity. Well, it's obvious that I still have a few reels to go before the Big Fade Out.

Post-production on *The Rainbow* went hand in hand with pre-production on my next film for Vestron, *All-*

American Murder. The script was by Barry Sandler, who wrote *Crimes of Passion.* Naturally it was a black comedy on the American Way of Life—and Death. Set against a college background, it explored the pressure which drove Tally, our Campus Queen, to murder. Seven murders to be precise, including death by incineration, electrocution, punctuation, compactation, copulation and strangulation. It was a hoot, but a hard-hitting one that exposed the corruption endemic in certain sororities and fraternities hiding behind the All-American façades that housed them.

Firstly I had to find a house for myself in Tinseltown. Unfashionable Outpost Drive at the foot of the Hollywood Hills provided the answer in the form of a hacienda-type villa where Bela Lugosi used to hang out. What more fitting place to work on a horror film, with bats in the belfry and snakes in the shrubbery? It was there, in the garden, that I conducted my casting sessions interviewing everyone from Linda Grey to Jeff Goldblum. At the same time I was crewing up and looking for locations. The University of Southern California had just about everything and the authorities were happy to accommodate us until they saw the script and figured that an impressionable student might get some ideas and be inspired to embark on a series of copycat killings—just for kicks. But the Jesuits of Marymount College had no such qualms and negotiations to shoot their campus were well in hand when Vestron pulled the plug with just three weeks to go. Apparently there was a cash-flow problem and their financiers only came up with half the money needed to keep the company going. The result was that all my friends and supporters were fired, and all new productions cancelled. The axe even fell on films that were on general release. *The Rainbow* was playing LA and NY and doing nicely when, without warning, all advertising was withdrawn. They couldn't have buried it more effectively if they'd incarcerated it at Forest Lawns six feet under. Despondently I packed my bags, said a prayer for Bela and took off.

By the time I'd recovered from jet-lag I'd gotten over my disappointment because a new and even more exciting project was beginning to materialise—the filming of this book for television with its premier all set for the day before publication in Britain.

The budget Melvyn Bragg's *South Bank Show* could afford was exactly one-thirtieth of that for *All-American Murder* so more than a little ingenuity was called for. I went about things in much the same way as mentioned on page one—by getting in a car and driving to Southampton. The scene of my childhood, 31 Belmont Road, was still there as unchanging as ever. No, that's not quite true. Even as I looked, the house seemed to shed its years and become young again. Maybe it was glad to see me. Or is that being too fanciful? Bricks absorb rain and sunlight—why not memories? Sound and pictures can be recorded on tape and film, we know, but that doesn't rule out the possibility of other mediums. Didn't someone once talk about sermons in stones? But what of the seven ages of man? How am I going to portray myself ageing from one to sixty-two? There are limits to what one can do with make-up, and if I followed Shakespeare's advice I'd need five actors to portray me. Yes, five, I hadn't quite reached the last stage yet ... sans hair, sans teeth, sans everything ... and could play the sixth age myself. But what about the others? The child mewling and puking in his nurse's arms was easy. Almost any baby would do for that one, so long as it matched my colour. Even the sex was unimportant—as I had no plans for scenes involving full-frontal nudity. The schoolboy creeping like snail unwillingly to school was also no problem. My son Rupert, aged 4½, could play that. He went pretty reluctantly to nursery school most days. I visualised him playing pirates in the garden—climbing the conker tree from branch to branch, yard-arm to yard-arm, to tie a skull and crossbones on the topmast. And without much effort I could imagine myself climbing the rigging along with him, side by side—a couple of *enfants terribles*, together. I blinked, my heart missed a beat, I gulped, blinked again and smiled. Here was the perfect answer to those who still insisted on calling me an *enfant terrible*, even if it was tongue-in-cheek. But there was more to it than that, much more. Years ago I saw a film called *The Innocent Eye*; it showed the visual impact of the world and its wonders on the fresh, unclouded vision of a child—and how quickly it can fade. The trick is in keeping it alive despite everything life does to distort it. Despite occasional bouts of blindness, I've been pretty lucky in this regard. I also wanted to disarm my audience—I make no bones about it. Pronouncements coming from an overweight, florid-faced, white haired, opinionated old man are likely to sound pompous. The same words coming from a child would have a different effect altogether; they would be the same but be perceived differently and tend to be taken at their face value, without prejudice. Now all I had to do was to convince the youngest star of *The Rainbow* to reconsider his decision.

When work on his first feature was over, Viv had asked Rupert if he'd like to make another film with Daddy. "No way," came the reply. But when he realised the new movie involved directing a musical, flying an aeroplane, driving a train and being dressed and undressed by a gorgeous blonde, he understandably changed his mind. The enterprise became a family affair with Viv playing a typical journalist asking the endlessly repetitive and vacuous questions they always ask and me playing everything from a sadistic sea captain disguised as Captain Bligh (which is how I saw the deranged skipper of the *Queen of Rataroa*), to a manic flight sergeant in the Royal Air Force shouting the obscenities on pages 76 and 77. Imagine this book transformed into a child's game played for real, almost surreal at times, and you'll have a fair idea of how the movie turned out. As in the distant past, we had a small crew—no more than a dozen—and moved fast, travelling from one end of England to another and shooting the entire story in two weeks and a day. Rupert, who was in every scene and won instant fame when the programme was aired, survived the experience better than I. And when Viv asked me if I'd ever work with *him* again, I said, "No way." What a temperament. I wonder where he gets it from? Still, I have to say it, he's a natural; his scenes portraying wonder, delight, depression and drunkenness were worthy of Oscars, the most touching moment being when his eyes mist over as he surveys the shelves holding his coveted awards, ranging from statuettes of Betty Boop and Popeye to Mickey Mouse dolls and Felix the Cat: so much more cuddly than that hard-faced Oscar.

But awards for acting *I* will never earn—excluding the Golden Turkey, of course—which made me extremely curious as to why Fred Schepisi should want me for an important role in *The Russia House* featuring Sean Connery and Michelle Pfeiffer. Wherever did he get the idea that I could act? Surely not from my brief appearance as a pornographic photographer in *Salome's Last Dance*. "Unique" would be a charitable way of describing it. But even if I am not a true thespian I do have something in common with some actors of my acquaintance and that is the problem of memorising lines. This is generally overcome by an "Idiot Board" held close to the camera and bearing the elusive words—which is fine if you have 20:20 vision or are playing a character in glasses. Neither of these options was open to me in *Salome*. In fact I am long-sighted and have a very long speech to deliver, so the words had to be spelt out in letters six feet high. The result was a gigantic banner stretching from one side of the studio to the other. As I was describing distant mountains it didn't really matter that my head ranged from side to side as if I was watching a slow motion tennis match. I wondered if there were any scenes in *The Russia House* where I'd be called upon to describe the distant steppes. If so, that technique might come in useful again. No! No need. If I got the part I'd insist on wearing my own horn-rimmed spectacles and to hell with vanity.

When the casting director finally tracked me down she breathed a sigh of relief down the phone that was almost physical. She'd been searching for me for weeks with the director, Fred Schepisi, growing more impatient every day at her lack of success. A meeting with the director was arranged and a script delivered to my door. The story was about a reluctant British spy who betrays his country rather than betray the beautiful Russian agent with whom he falls in love. I was being considered for the part of Walter, a counter-intelligence man who disappears halfway through the plot only to re-appear in the penultimate scene to ask, "What about Russell?"

What indeed? The character was vague and underwritten. And why me? Perhaps he was confusing me with Kurt Russell. I'd only seen one of Schepisi's films and found myself at odds with the subject matter, so I guessed I'd better catch up on another one before the interview. Accordingly I went along to see *Cry in the Dark*, his latest offering. In common with most of the audience, I was vaguely familiar with the story which concerned an unfortunate young mother who had her baby eaten by a dingo dog in the outback. After two reels I wished the dingo dog had eaten the young mother. My appreciation of the film was also marred by soft focus and a soundtrack turned down so low that the dialogue from the movie house next door was actually more audible. Pity it wasn't on video: not only would I have seen it properly but I'd also have given it the old fast-forward treatment into the bargain. For all that, the film was a competent piece of work and if its intention was to show the average Australian to be even more bestial than the dingo dog, then it succeeded admirably. Mr. Schepisi is a native of Oz himself, so I guess he should know.

However, I kept an open mind as I hurried to keep our appointment in a discreet hotel in Chelsea, favoured by distinguished visiting filmmakers. There I was met by Schepisi's personal assistant, a blonde bombshell in figure-hugging tights around sixteen or so. Huh, I know all about personal assistants, I thought, as I followed her through a warren of corridors to meet the man himself. We found him in a large conference room rehearsing Sean Connery and James Fox in a scene from the movie. They all said, "Hello Ken," as if they'd known me all my life. Actually we'd never met. Schepisi needed somewhere to talk. The blonde suggested her room. Schepisi nodded and led the way back along the labyrinth and got lost. Then the blonde tried and she got lost. We went back to reception and started again. They both seemed familiar with that route and, after marching up and down bewildering flights of basement stairs, finally arrived at what appeared to be a small and rather squalid love-nest— scattered underwear on an unmade bed of tangled sheets. I sensed a casual intimacy between them. "Thanks, Ash," said Schepisi. And with a familiar smile the ash-blonde left the room. We looked at each other, two strange directors not knowing what to say. Finally Schepisi blurted out, "That was Ashley, my daughter."

"Oh," I said, inwardly telling my torrid imagination to behave itself.

Well, we had one thing in common—nepotism. We sized each other up. I'd dressed for the part—I hoped he'd be impressed. He smiled. I smiled back. We smiled at each other, waiting for the other to speak. By the time he'd registered my sky-blue jacket, orange waistcoat, purple shirt, polka-dot tie, green trousers, yellow socks, Tyrolean hat and sneakers, his smile had become a little fixed. I had a sinking feeling that we did not see eye to eye on the character. That unfailing smile reminded me of something, I couldn't think what, until I remembered our stuffed fox back in the Lake District. It had a pleasant smile, that fox, and so did Schepisi, but it did nothing to put me at ease for I felt like another creature back home—our lop-eared rabbit.

"Great character, Walter . . ." said Schepisi, still smiling.

"Great," I said, smiling back and wondering what he knew that I didn't.

". . . bit of a poofter . . ."

Ken Russell with Sean Connery and his wife on location in Portugal for *The Russia House*.

Ken and James Fox as two MI6 men in *The Russia House*,
between takes.

Aah, the truth began to dawn. Like Denny, Schepisi probably saw me as a latent homosexual—could it be the way I dressed? I nodded and nearly asked him if that was the reason he was considering me for the part, but on reflecting that an honest reply might cause mutual embarrassment, merely nodded.

". . . but I think we'll play that down," he said.

I nodded again, pushing down the shocking-pink handkerchief protruding flamboyantly from my breast pocket.

"Well, would you like to come and run through a few lines with James and Sean?" he asked.

"Er, I have a train to catch," I replied.

There was a pause. I was dreading that he might ask me to read a scene with him. He was considering it, I could tell. I coughed again and looked at my watch.

"Well, fine," he said. "Thanks for dropping by."

He seemed as glad to get out of the room as I was. That's the end of that, I thought, as I caught the Circle Line train to Baker Street, but to my complete surprise I got the job next day, together with a copy of le Carré's novel, which threw a little more light on the character of Walter, but not much.

After one brief scene in London where I was merely called upon to open a bottle of wine (which, surprisingly, gave me quite a bit of trouble) I joined cast and crew on a charter flight to Portugal. Lisbon was all hills and trams and waiting, waiting, waiting. For the first time in my life I began to know what it feels like to be an actor. Unless you are the star you spend the greater part of the day in your trailer waiting to be called to the set. It was a weird experience being on the edge of things when one is accustomed to being bang in the middle. I began mixing with the other actors—all playing CIA or British Intelligence officers—and learning something of their concerns. They talked of past successes and future hopes, showed me snapshots of their loved ones, told jokes and as the rain drummed on the trailer roof, played endless games of Scrabble. What they didn't do was discuss the director—in front of me at any rate. It was quite an eye-opener watching a film director at work for the very first time. Schepisi, or Fred as we were encouraged to call him, was in some ways not dissimilar to myself when it came to handling a scene. He explained his intentions to all and sundry and gave more detailed instructions to individuals with pointers on delivery. He'd then tell us where to sit and stand and move about and then shoot it—and, unlike myself, shoot it again and again and again from here, there and everywhere, over and over and over till no one knew what they were doing or saying any more. And he could afford to—with a budget reputedly around the $25,000,000 mark.

As the days passed and I developed paella poisoning, the character of Walter began to develop too—between frequent trips to the loo. To elaborate on what I said before, he was a British counter-intelligence man, well-versed in Russian affairs, a boffin who doesn't work by the book, is brilliant but unconventional, drinks too much, won't be bullshitted, speaks his mind and is thoroughly despised by the Establishment, who do their best to destroy him. But after the Establishment have been finally discredited themselves, he bounces back in the last reel. It was a masterstroke of type-casting. But this only became obvious as the film progressed and I came to realise why Fred had chosen me in preference to Sir Richard Attenborough. This business of art imitating life gave me the confidence to step out of the confines of the script and suggest some outrageous business to Fred which he was usually happy to go along with. In spite of this, I think I'm going to end up on the cutting-room floor—because *I* was playing myself while the other actors were playing fictional characters who have no existence outside John le Carré's imagination. So thanks for the experience, Fred, I learned a lot . . . like . . . well . . . that deep down, deep, deep down inside, actors are (almost) human. In future I intend to visit them while they are languishing in their trailers and cheer them up, tell them how good they were in the rushes, tell them to be patient, that things haven't gone quite as planned and I'm sorry they were called so early and had to wait so long, and would they care to join me for lunch, etc., etc., etc. Who knows, maybe I'll end up being someone's favourite director, some day.

As things turned out I didn't have long to wait before putting my new resolution into practice.

Fittingly, the opportunity arrived with the start of the New Year when Home Box Office asked me to direct Dorothy Parker's *Dusk Before Fireworks*. It was to be part of a trilogy with the generic title *Men and Women* and the Battle of the Sexes as its theme. It all happened very fast with the cast of two as a *fait accompli*. They were Peter "*Robocop*" Weller and Molly "*Pretty in Pink*" Ringwald. And when I tell you that the ideal players would have been Noël Coward and Gertrude Lawrence, you will see that we were as far away from type-casting as it was possible to get. Not surprisingly, perhaps, I found the actor to be rather set in his ways, whereas the actress was as malleable as bubble-gum. The story, in a line, is about a dying love affair that is finally laid to rest by a series of telephone calls that always come at the great moment of reconciliation. And Molly has to spend most of the time in chic lingerie, striking poses from a Thirties

Harper's Bazaar and speaking the archaic language of a society debutante. And for someone renowned for playing simple high-school kids, she was absolutely splendid.

"Thanks," she said at the end-of-picture party, "this has been a new experience for me. Usually, directors don't tell me how to stand and walk and pose or adjust my garters just before a take. And they don't give me 'stage business' either, or suggest how I should deliver my lines."

"What *do* they say then?" I asked.

She pulled a face and shrugged. "They just say, 'Act Better!'"

Talking of directors, I'm often asked to list my personal favourites. So, in no particular order, here's my top twenty:

Robert Wiene	*The Cabinet of Dr. Caligari*
Mel Brooks	*Blazing Saddles*
Murnau	*Daybreak*
William Cameron Menzies	*Things to Come*
Powell/Pressberger	*The Red Shoes*
Truffaut	*Jules et Jim*
Frank Tuttle	*Roman Scandals*
Laurence Olivier	*Henry V*
Cocteau	*La Belle et La Bête*
Eisenstein	*Alexander Nevsky*
Jean Vigo	*L'Atalante*
Fritz Lang	*Metropolis*
Victor Fleming	*The Wizard of Oz*
Leni Riefenstahl	*Olympische Spiel 1936*
Jacques Tati	*Monsieur Hulot's Holiday*
Bondarchuk	*War and Peace*
Fellini	*I Vitelloni*
Orson Welles	*Citizen Kane*
Billy Wilder	*One, Two, Three*
Walt Disney	*Fantasia*

Most of 'em dead and buried—so what about the new boys? Sad to say, the list is depressingly small because for me most of the contemporary directors who win prizes, receive knighthoods, and are praised to the skies, are singularly untalented—though they are, if nothing else, undeniably fashionable. Bearing in mind that I can't keep up with every new movie that comes along, here's my short list:

Joel and Ethan Coen's *Raising Arizona* was a fresh comedy about babies, marred by a happy "Hollywood" ending.

Near Dark, a film on vampires by Kathryn Bigelow, was near perfect—
but once again spoilt by a cop-out in the last few minutes.

Robocop by Paul Verhoven had lots of frightening things to say about
the shape of things to come but OD-ed on kerosene.

House of Games by David Mamet was a brilliant gamble but his luck
gave out when he was caught cheating—artistically, I mean.

The Hitcher by Robert Harmen left "Hitch" at the starting post when
it came to suspense but stumbled at the last ditch of plausibility.

Clive Barker's *Hellraiser* brought a new dimension to horror but slipped
up on the banana skin of bad acting.

The Stuntman by Richard Rush, with Peter O'Toole playing God,
should have walked away with every Oscar of the year. Of course it got
none.

But for me the two most outstanding new talents are Bob Balaban,
whose *Parents* made David Lynch's *Blue Velvet* look like *Care Bears*, and
Bruce Robinson with *Withnail and I*—about two out-of-work actors in
the Sixties. Both these directors have a frighteningly perceptive vision and
the unique ability to capture a particular moment in time as well as the
heart and soul of the characters under observation. They have humour,
imagination, style and flair. I have high hopes for their future.

And as I sit in my lonely flat in London looking at the concrete walls
outside my window I wonder what the stars foretell for me. According to
a recent divination of the Tarot by a follower of Aleister Crowley, I will
shortly be making a movie on the Great Beast himself. For the uninitiated,
Crowley was accused of Devil Worship and all that went with it, including
blood sacrifices and hanky-panky on the altar. It's not for nothing that he
was known as "the wickedest man in the world." Naturally, the story is
all about sex and magic as are several other subjects under discussion.
One of them is about a beautiful Scandinavian witch with the ability to
turn herself into a "White Reindeer," who lures randy hunters to an
orgasmic death in the snow. Then there's Ruth Rendell's *The Bridesmaid*,
which continues the theme of sex and ritual murder, and finally *So Help
Me God*, a plunge into the occult with the Devil running riot in a New
York courtroom.

All four subjects were offers—I didn't seek them out. I wonder why
they came my way? All this satanic activity and it's only January 1990.
It's comforting to know that the Devil has my interests at heart, but of
course God will have the last word. While they slug it out I'm off to
Borrowdale to play trains with Rupert.

More than a year has gone by since the last line and so far none of those predictions concerning my career have come to pass. A delay in the publication of this book in America has enabled me to write an update on the topsy-turvy life of a film director in Britain today, where home-grown movies are becoming a thing of the past—unless they are cultivated expressly for TV. Lots of financiers in London admired a new script of mine called *Whore* but not one of them would put up the money for me to make it—unless I tamed the dialogue. What dialogue?

Well, I was strolling down Piccadilly on my way to work one day when a squealing of brakes and the tooting of a horn drew my attention to a London taxi pulling up by the curb. The driver, a complete stranger, leapt out of the cab and ran straight at me brandishing something resembling a night stick. Thinking I was about to be attacked I backed nervously into a doorway, wondering if this was revenge for a poor tip, when suddenly the lethal weapon unrolled itself into a script with a black cover.

It was then that I noticed the cabby was even more nervous than myself. "Excuse me, Guv, but when I recognised you I drove round the block three times before I could summon up courage to accost you." "Er, yes?" I said with sinking heart. "I've written a play, Guv, about whores—right up your street. I'd be obliged if you'd read it with a view to making it into a movie."

I thanked him for associating me with streetwalkers and took the well-thumbed script with some trepidation. Contrary to my misgivings, I was impressed. Other people had been impressed too, according to newspaper clippings he later sent me concerning its history. Moved by the tales of fare-paying prostitutes, who used his cab as a kind of mobile confessional, our author, David Hines, decided to attempt to put right popular mis-conceptions about life on the streets.

The result was a one-act, one-woman play about a prostitute called Liz who became a spokeswoman on behalf of her unfortunate sisters. She preached no moral sermon, but just laid bare, without blame or rancour, the life of a modern prostitute in a big city. Premiered at a fringe theatre at the Edinburgh Festival, the play was a shocking success. Shocking because of the language which was the authentic language of the gutter. And naturally this became an integral part of the script when I set about translating it into a screenplay. For I found the story of Liz tender, tough, raw, raunchy, humourous, humble and very touching. And to me it also seemed commercial.

And as I mentioned before, many producers in London thought so too. OK, the budget was very modest—but unfortunately the language was not. "Tone it down for TV, and you can have the money," they said. "Tame it and turn it into another Hollywood Cinderella story like *Pretty Woman.*" I replied—"Forget it!" "Right," they said, and promptly did!

But then my American Fairy Godmother Dan Ireland got to hear about it and with a wave of his magic wand and a great deal of help from my agent, Peter Rawley, got it set up with a U.S. company called Vidmark, on the condition that the nationality of the girl could be changed to American, and the London venue changed to LA.

At first this seemed rather a tall order—until Deborah Dalton came along. She was an American writer who had done extensive research on prostitution in LA for a radio feature, and on comparing notes we found that our ladies of the night shared a lot in common whether they walked the streets of London or of LA. Even the (foul) language was much the same. It was mostly just a question of accent.

Now all we had to do was find a star who wasn't afraid of a challenge. Vidmark's first choice, Elizabeth McGovern, turned us down because she had a problem with the language with its preponderance of four letter words. My first choice, Theresa Russell (no relation), had no trouble at all with the vocabulary, it was her kids that were the problem. They were due to go back to school in England in a couple of weeks' time, and who was to put them on the school bus every morning if not her? The answer was simple—the famous English film director Nick Roeg, who happened to be her husband, and between pictures.

Shooting in downtown LA in the summer was hell—with temperatures in the hundreds and bloodshed in the streets. If it hadn't been for iced champagne and our police escort we would never have come out alive. What a contrast to the film I shot before my departure from England, in the leafy glades of the New Forest early in the spring.

Many years earlier, its rolling wheat fields and silver birches had served as a backdrop for *The Music Lovers.* Now its pine trees and lakes were used to conjure up the Austrian landscape of Anton Bruckner. True, we had to sacrifice the mountains he loved to climb, but there were many compensations including an architectural oddity which easily passed muster as the sanatorium where this great composer of mammoth symphonies to the glory of God went to be cured of his Numeromania.

This is a disease that has probably afflicted most people at some time in their life, namely, the compulsion to count. To count anything, and in Bruckner's case, everything—pebbles on a beach, leaves on a tree, blades of grass in a field, clouds in the sky, etc. The cause and cure for this was the crux of this investigation into the mind of a very special kind of genius.

My next film for television was also about a very special man and was also destined for screening on TV. But whereas *The Strange Affliction of Anton Bruckner* was made for £120,000 and featured an unknown in the title role, *Prisoners of Honor* cost somewhere around $5,000,000 and starred Richard Dreyfuss—not as Dreyfus, but as Colonel Picquart, the French cavalry officer who took up the cause of the wrongly accused Captain Dreyfus and rescued him from a living hell on Devil's Island.

The "Dreyfus Affair," as the case came to be known internationally in the last decade of the last century, was a vast cover-up of a corrupt French regime which persecuted an innocent man because of his race. Classified military secrets were sold to the German military attaché in Paris. The information could only have come from an officer on the general staff. Who was the traitor? The answer was obvious—Alfred Dreyfus—the only Jewish officer in the regiment. As Jews owed no allegiance to any country, it followed that he was the culprit. But Colonel Picquart, promoted to head of counterintelligence soon after the phoney trial and ordered to tidy up the evidence, soon came to think differently. His decision to call for a retrial made him extremely unpopular with his senior officers who threatened and then framed him. All this eventually erupted into a tremendous scandal which reverberated throughout France and around the world. It was an extremely ugly business, not least in its exposure of the mass anti-Semitism rife in every stratum of French society.

This was certainly one of the aspects of the *affaire* that attracted Richard Dreyfuss to the subject, together with the fact that in many respects the story is as topical today as it was close on a century ago. And such was his belief in the project that he struggled for eight years to get it made. At the time of writing, we have just finished shooting the movie and are now in post-production. So although the Bruckner film has been aired in England to the usual mixture of great acclaim and tremendous condemnation, neither *Whore* nor *Prisoners of Honor* has been released anywhere as yet.

They make strange bedfellows, the American prostitute and the little French Jew, and in their ability or otherwise to procreate big bucks lies my future—which, as ever, remains delightfully unpredictable.

Oh, by the way, I have just seen *Russia House* and to my utter dismay my best scene has ended up on the cutting room floor! Some directors * * * ! !, know what I mean?

Index

Page numbers of photographs are listed in italics.

Borrowdale, England (Russell Cottage in),
154, 156–166, 216, 226–227, 238–
239, 242–243, 275, 286–288, 311–
312, 323
Boult, Adrian, 258
Bovington Camp (location for *Portrait of a
Composer—Ralph Vaughan Williams*),
256
"Bow Bells Swinging the Broadway Mel-
ody" (Heath), 265
Bowder Stone, 159
Boy Friend, The, ix, xii–xiii, 105, 124,
132, 138–145, *140, 143*, 165, 177;
music from, 138, 140, 142
Boyd, Don, 251, 254
Bragg, Melvyn, 229–230, 239, 255, 296
Brass, Tinto, 267, 272
Brides of Fu Man Chu, 269
Bridesmaid, The, 323
Bridge, Frank, 257, 296
Brighton Belle, The (train), xii, 177
British Broadcasting Company (BBC),
20–21, 29, 34, 64–65, 179, 228, 230,
288–289. *See also Monitor*; Wheldon,
Huw.
British Film Institute, 16
British Picture, A, x, 2, 314–316
Britten, Benjamin, 15, 297
Brooks, Mel, 322
Brown, Blair, 200, *205*
Bruckner, Anton, 154, 164, 325–326
Burchuladze, Paata, 247

Cabinet of Dr. Caligari, The, 322
Caine, Michael, 55
Callas, Maria, 231
Camden Town, 254–255
Candide, 306
Cannes Film Festival, 251–254
Canter, Peter, 26
Carmen (ballet), 84
Caron, Leslie, 84, 150
Carrier, Robert, 137, 172
Cassel, Seymour, 150
Catholicism (Roman), 10, 18, 20, 23,
125, 166, 176, 211–213
Cats, 84
Censorship, 198, 288–289, 324–325
Chamberlain, Richard: in *The Music Lov-
ers*, 57, 58, 59–60, *59*; on Russell as a
director, 60
"Champagne" (Townshend), 119
Chariots of Fire, 252
Chartoff, Bob, 132

Chayefsky, Paddy, 189–192, 194–198,
200–201, 206, 208
Christie, Julie, 293
Citizen Kane, 322
Clapton, Eric, 123
Clark, Al, 291
Clark, Dave, 288
Cleopatra, 231
Cliff Richard and the Shadows, 31, 32,
288
Clouds of Glory, x, 153–157, 239
Cocteau, Jean, 322
Codd, Jack (uncle), 10–12, 45, 217, 219–
220
Codd, June (cousin), 9–10, 45, 77, 217,
290
Codd, Muriel (Aunt Moo), 5, 9–12, 31–
32, 45, 77, 217, 290
Coen, Joel and Ethan, 322
Coleridge, Samuel, 154, 161, 210, 216,
293
Columbia Pictures, ix, 168, 189, 191,
194, 198
"Concerto to End All Concertos" (Ken-
ton), 118
Connery, Sean, 316, 317, *318*, 320
Cornforth, Fanny, 153
Crimes of Passion, ix, 80, 261–263, 314
Crowley, Aleister, 323
Crown Imperial March (Walton), 265
Cry in the Dark, A, 317
"Cry to Heaven" (John), 289

Dalton, Deborah, 325
Dalton, Millican, 159–160
Daltrey, Roger, 118, *120, 121*, 122, 155,
166
Dance, Charles, 295
Dance of the Seven Veils, The, x, 117,
155
"Dancing for Justice," 274–275
Dante's Inferno, x, 65, 87, 153, *153*, 155
David Puttnam/Sandford Lieberson pro-
duction company, 166
Davis, Sammi, 294, *294*, 301, *301*, 302–
304, 306–309
Daybreak, 322
Dead, The, 170
Debussy, Claude, 104
Debussy Film, The, x, 64, 66, 104
Defoe, Daniel, 267
Delius, Frederick, 3–4, 125, 142, 155,
255
Deneuve, Catherine, 253